The photo of hydrangea flowers above is completely unrelated, because today I'd like to talk about the mini banyan tree growing in my studio. Let's just say it's not all that "mini" anymore! When I first got it, the tree fit in the palm of my hand. Now it's over two meters high and growing taller every day. Given enough time, it'll bust right through the roof, no joke! I think our little tree friend is taunting my weight loss program by expanding its girth daily! Speaking of which, my current weight is...71 kilograms! Crud, I'm expanding too!

—Mitsutoshi Shimabukuro, 2009

Mitsutoshi Shimabukuro made his debut in **Weekly Shonen Jump** in 1996. He is best known for **Seikimatsu Leader Den Takeshi!** for which he won the 46th Shogakukan Manga Award for children's manga in 2001. His current series, **Toriko**, began serialization in Japan in 2008.

TORIKO

TORIKO VOL. 7
SHONEN JUMP Manga Edition

STORY AND ART BY **MITSUTOSHI SHIMABUKURO**

Translation/Christine Dashiell
Adaptation/Hope Donovan
Touch-Up Art & Lettering/Maui Girl
Design/Sam Elzway
Editor/Alexis Kirsch

TORIKO © 2008 by Mitsutoshi Shimabukuro
All rights reserved. First published in Japan in 2008 by SHUEISHA Inc., Tokyo.
English translation rights arranged by SHUEISHA Inc.

The rights of the author(s) of the work(s) in this publication to
be so identified have been asserted in accordance with the Copyright,
Designs and Patents Act 1988. A CIP catalogue record for this book is
available from the British Library.

Printed in Canada

Published by VIZ Media, LLC
P.O. Box 77010
San Francisco, CA 94107

10 9 8 7 6 5 4 3 2 1
First printing, December 2011

www.viz.com

PARENTAL ADVISORY
TORIKO is rated T for Teen and is recommended
for ages 13 and up. This volume contains
realistic and fantasy violence.
ratings.viz.com

THE WORLD'S
MOST POPULAR MANGA
www.shonenjump.com

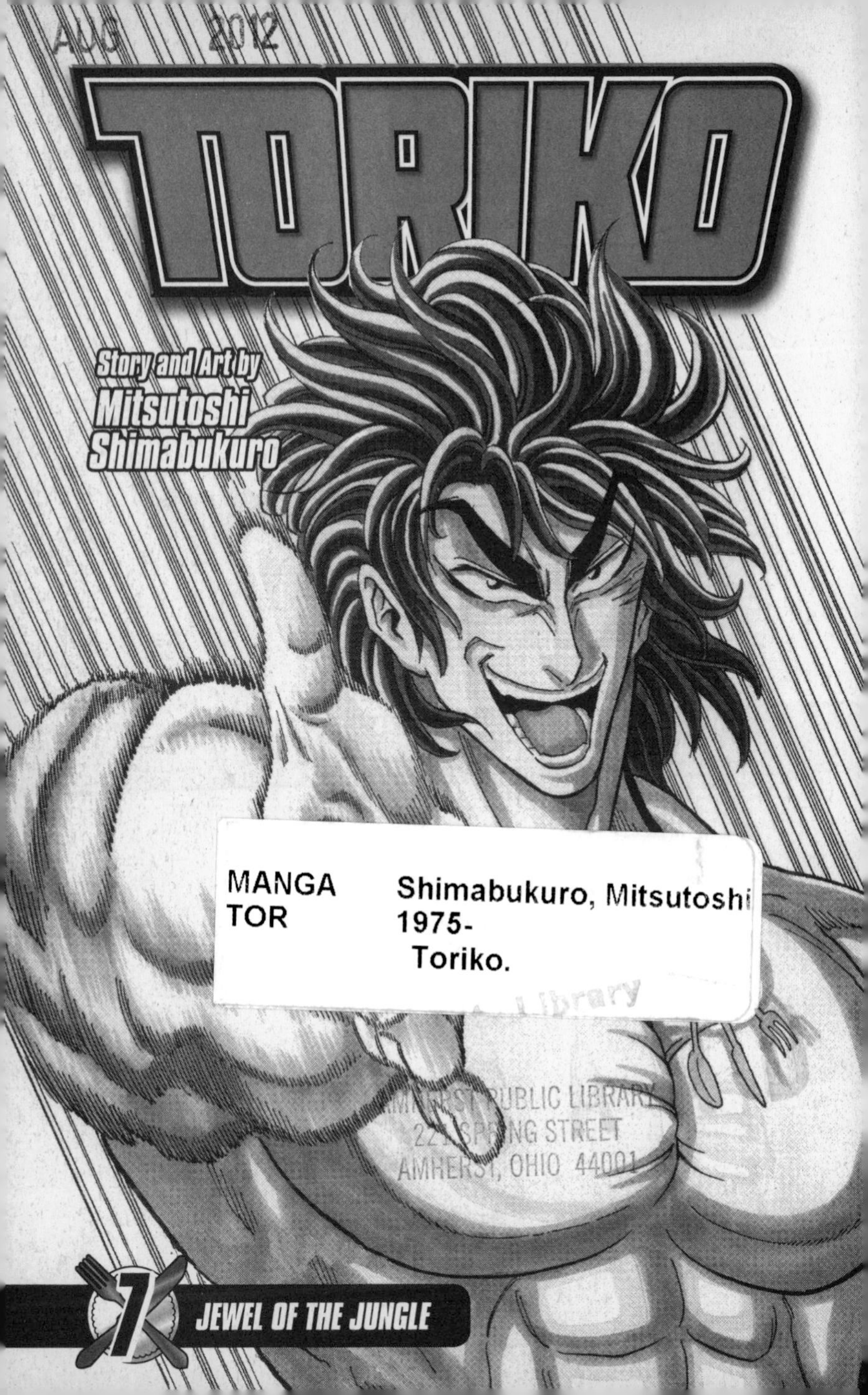
TORIKO
Story and Art by
Mitsutoshi Shimabukuro
7
JEWEL OF THE JUNGLE

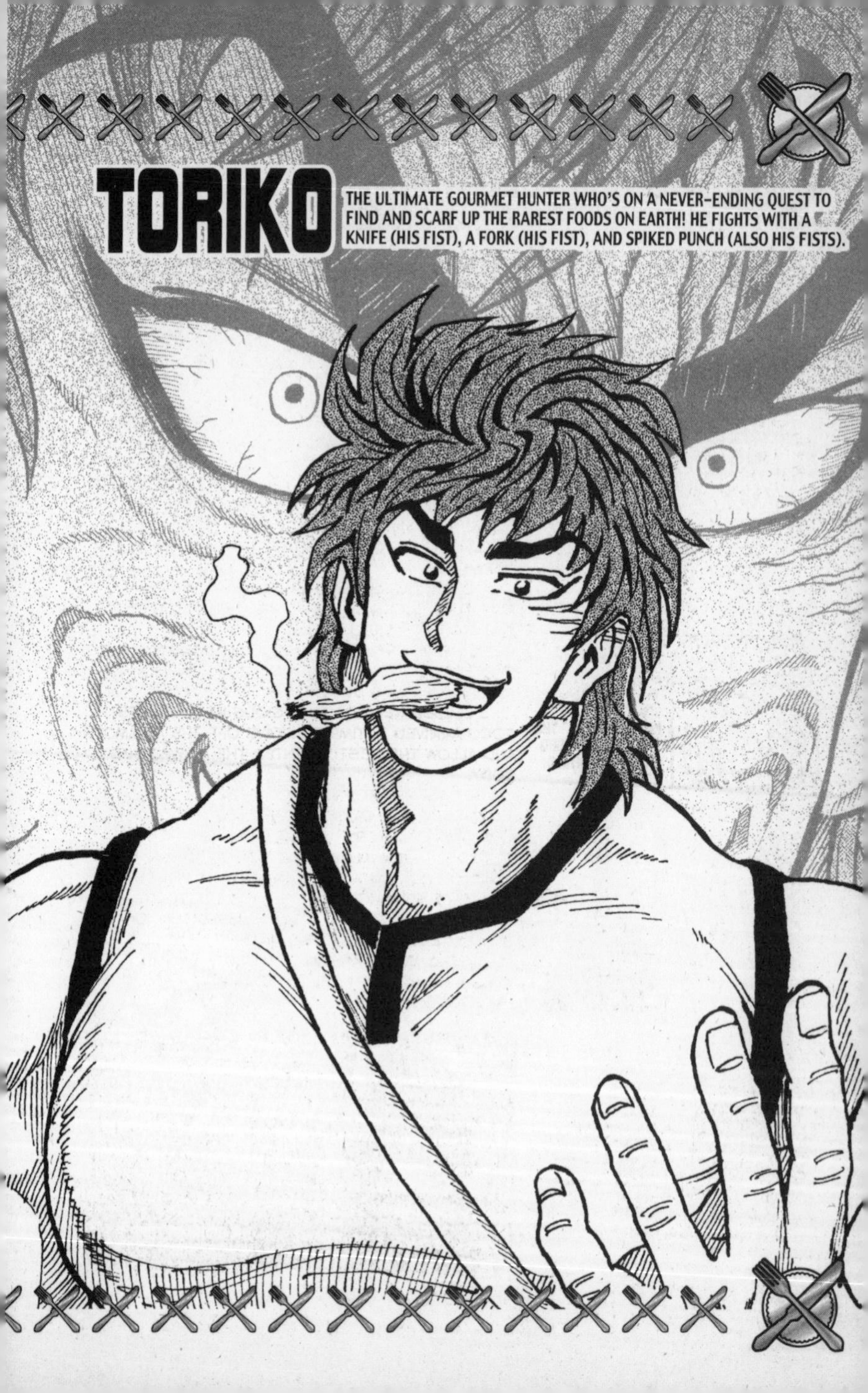
TORIKO
THE ULTIMATE GOURMET HUNTER WHO'S ON A NEVER-ENDING QUEST TO FIND AND SCARF UP THE RAREST FOODS ON EARTH! HE FIGHTS WITH A KNIFE (HIS FIST), A FORK (HIS FIST), AND SPIKED PUNCH (ALSO HIS FISTS).

WHAT'S FOR DINNER

IT'S THE AGE OF GOURMET! KOMATSU, THE HEAD CHEF AT THE HOTEL OWNED BY THE IGO (INTERNATIONAL GOURMET ORGANIZATION), BECAME FAST FRIENDS WITH THE LEGENDARY GOURMET HUNTER TORIKO WHILE GATOR HUNTING. NOW KOMATSU ACCOMPANIES TORIKO ON HIS LIFELONG QUEST TO CREATE THE PERFECT FULL-COURSE MEAL.

ONE DAY, HE AND TORIKO ENCOUNTERED A GT ROBOT, A MACHINE DISPATCHED BY THE IGO'S RIVAL ORGANIZATION, GOURMET CORP. SENSING A FOUL PLOT AFOOT, THE IGO MADE AN EMERGENCY SUMMONS OF THE FOUR KINGS--THE TOP GOURMET HUNTERS IN THE WORLD. THEY ASKED THE FOUR KINGS TO TAKE ON GOURMET CORP.'S GT ROBOTS IN AN ULTIMATE SHOWDOWN OVER THE ANCIENT REGAL MAMMOTH!

SO TORIKO, ALONG WITH SUNNY, KOMATSU, RIN AND TERRY, COMMENCED A HARROWING JOURNEY TOWARD THE REGAL HIGHLANDS OF REGAL ISLE, HOME OF THE REGAL MAMMOTH. IT SEEMED THAT THE GT ROBOTS HAD ARRIVED FIRST, LEAVING THE ADVENTURERS TO DEAL WITH A LIVID MAMMOTH AND AN ENRAGED NEST OF FEROCIOUS HEAVY CLIFFS! COCO ARRIVED IN TIME TO STAVE OFF THE MAMMOTH AND ALLOW THE REST TO ENTER THE MAMMOTH'S BODY.

BUT BEFORE TORIKO AND CO. COULD REACH THE MAMMOTH'S PRIZED JEWEL MEAT, THE GOURMET CORP.'S HEAD ROBOT DEALT SWIFT AND FATAL WOUNDS TO TORIKO AND RIN. TEETERING ON THE EDGE OF CONSCIOUSNESS, TORIKO USED HIS LAST OUNCE OF STRENGTH TO SINK HIS TEETH INTO THE JEWEL MEAT. AS THE FLESH COURSED THROUGH HIS SYSTEM, TORIKO WAS MIRACULOUSLY REBORN... AS A STRONGER MAN, ABLE TO SMASH IN THE ROBOT'S FACE WITH HIS BRAND-NEW TEN-FOLD SPIKED PUNCH!

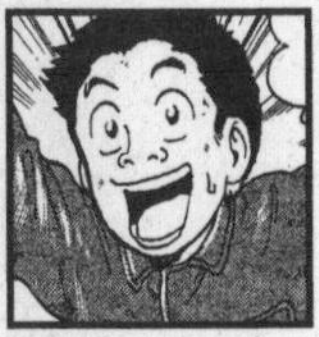

●KOMATSU
IGO HOTEL CHEF AND TORIKO'S #1 FAN

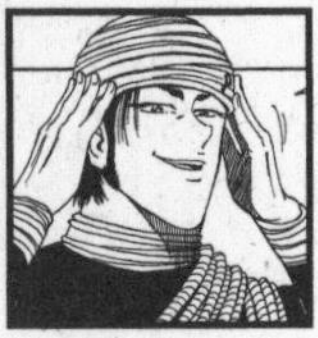

●COCO
ONE OF THE FOUR KINGS, THOUGH HE ALSO IS A FORTUNE-TELLER. SPECIAL ABILITY: POISON FLOWS IN HIS VEINS.

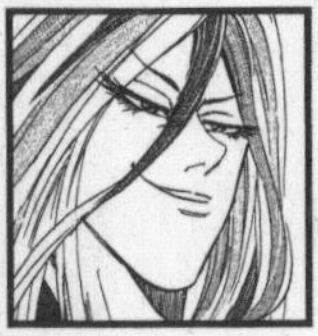

●SUNNY
ANOTHER OF THE FOUR KINGS. SENSORS IN HIS LONG HAIR ENABLE HIM TO "TASTE" THE WORLD. OBSESSED WITH ALL THAT IS BEAUTIFUL.

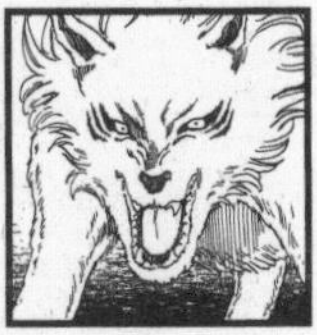

●TERRY CLOTH
OFFSPRING OF THE MOST AMAZING WOLF TO EVER EXIST.

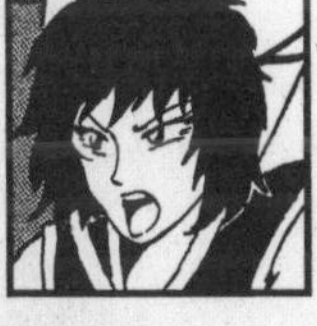

●RIN
AN IGO ANIMAL TRAINER WITH THE POWER OF SMELL AT HER DISPOSAL. SHE'S SUNNY'S LITTLE SISTER.

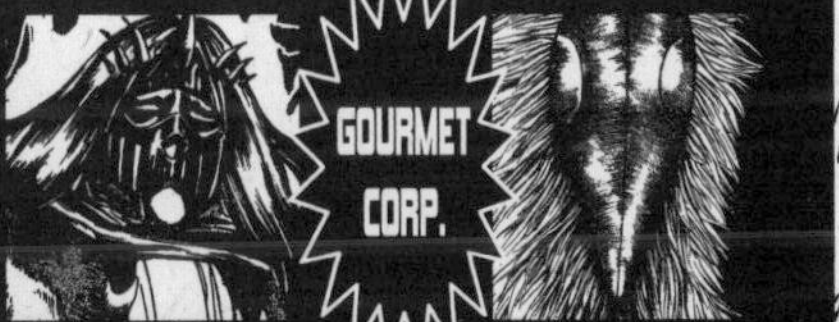
GOURMET CORP.

●STARJUN
VICE-CHEF

●GT ROBOT
THE GOURMET CORP.'S NEWEST ROBOT

Contents

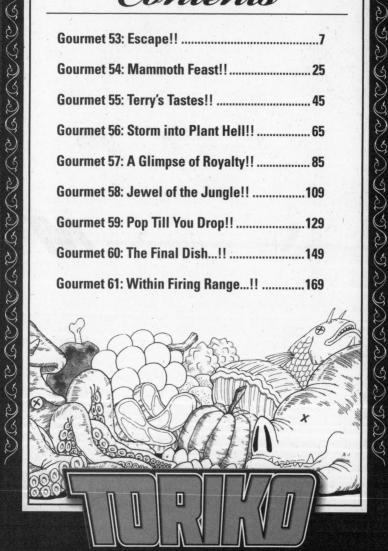

TORIKO

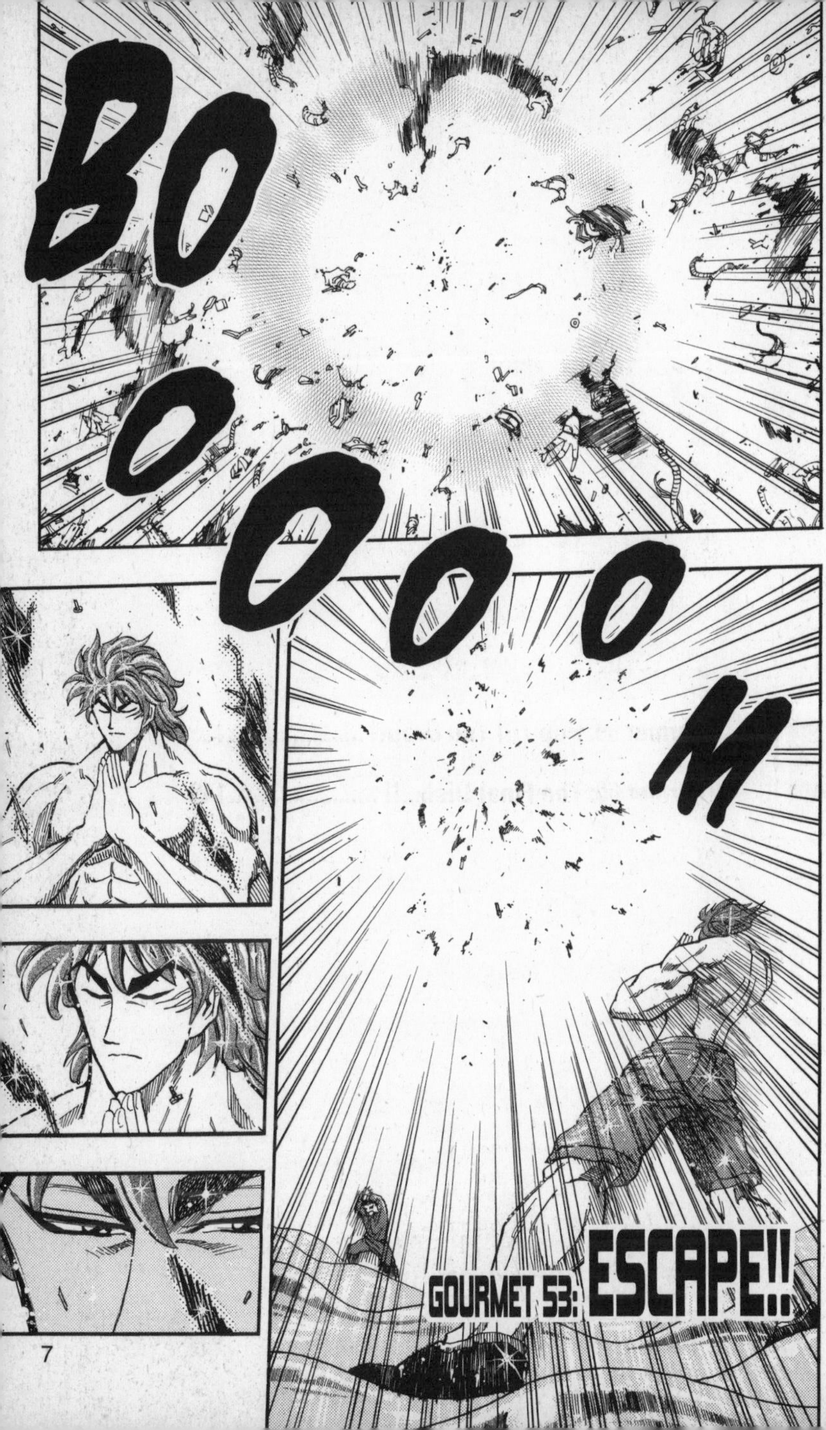
BOOOOOOM
GOURMET 53: ESCAPE!!

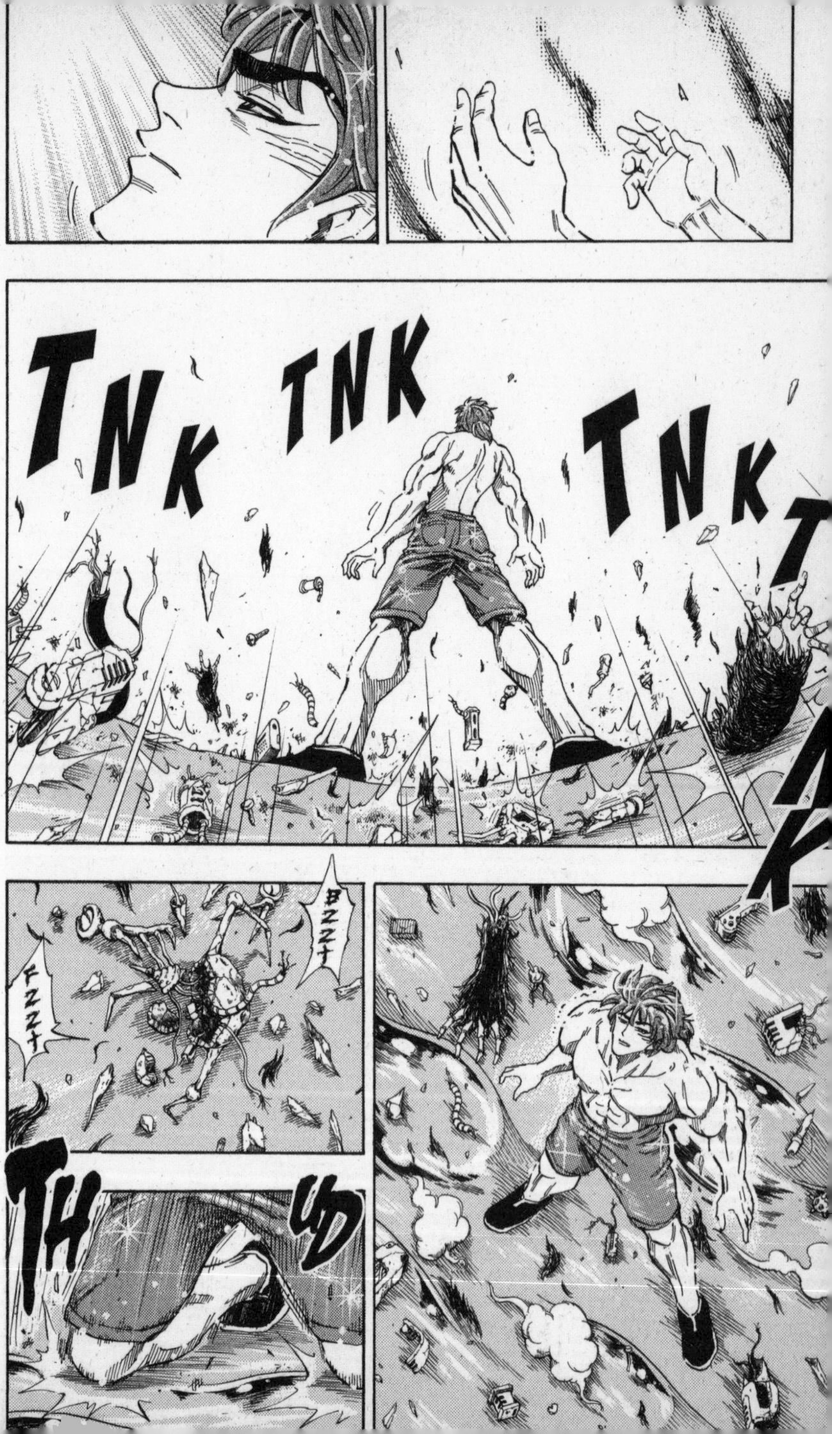
TNK
TNK
TNK
TNK
BZZZT
FZZZT
THUD

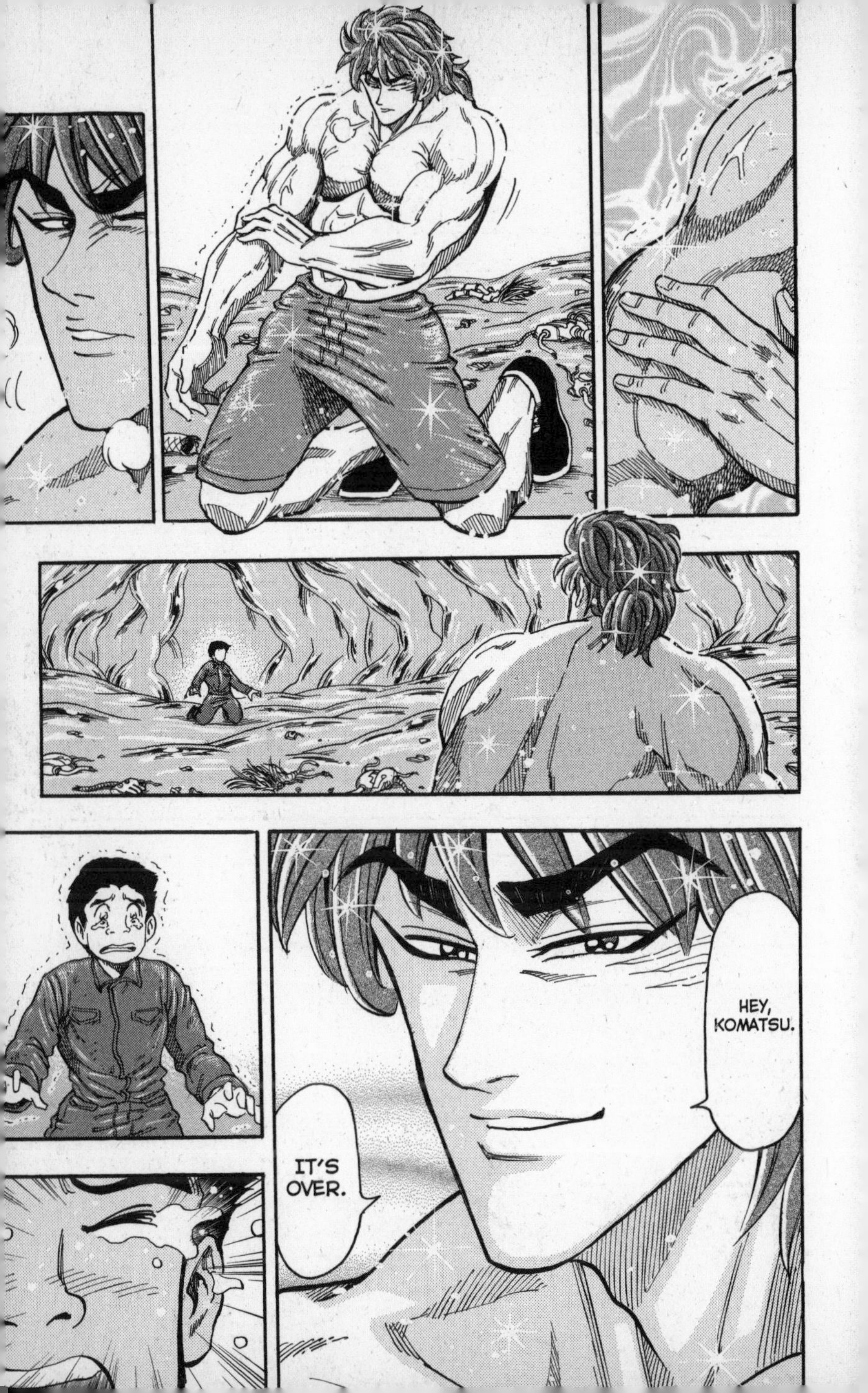
HEY, KOMATSU.
IT'S OVER.

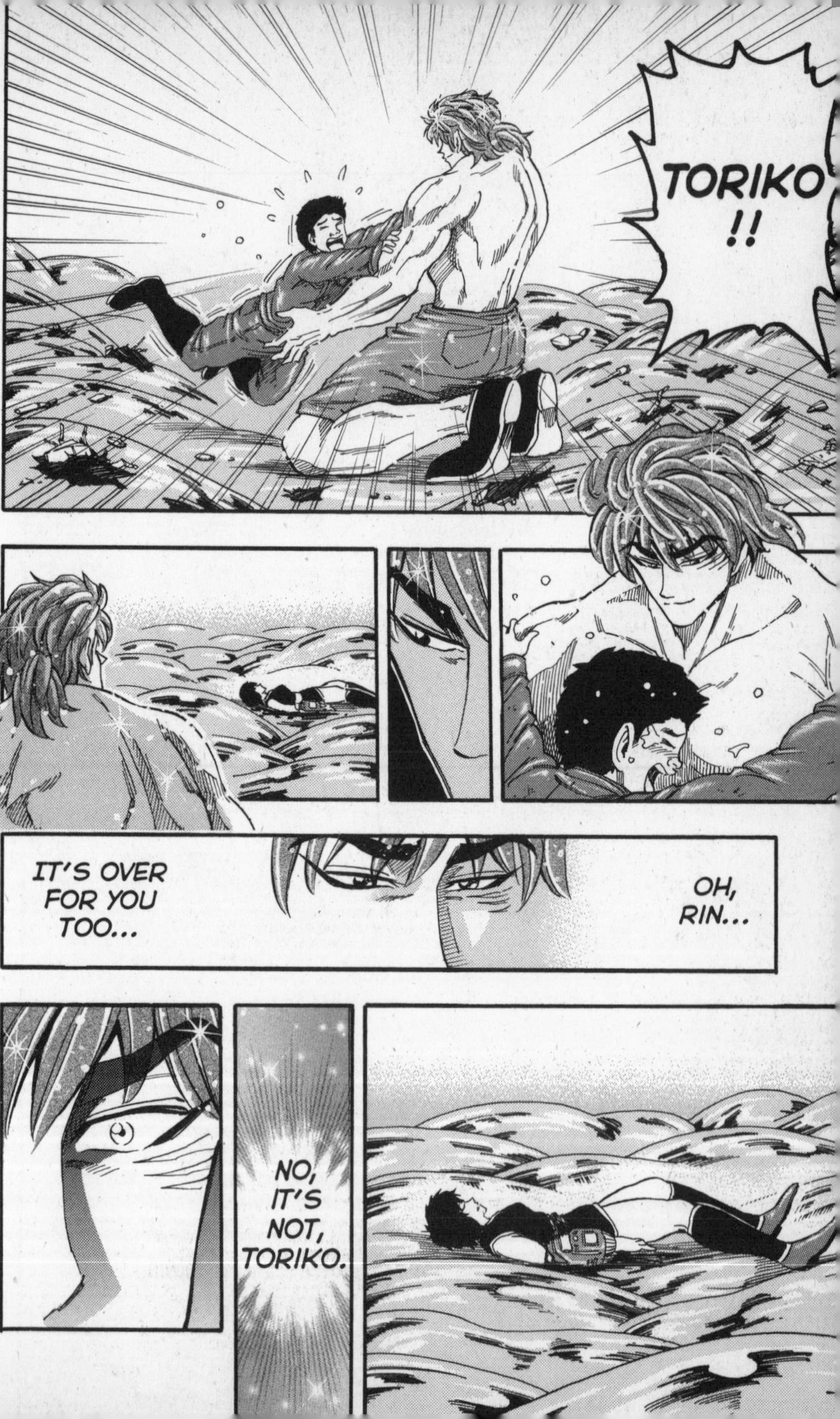
TORIKO!!
OH, RIN...
IT'S OVER FOR YOU TOO...
NO, IT'S NOT, TORIKO.

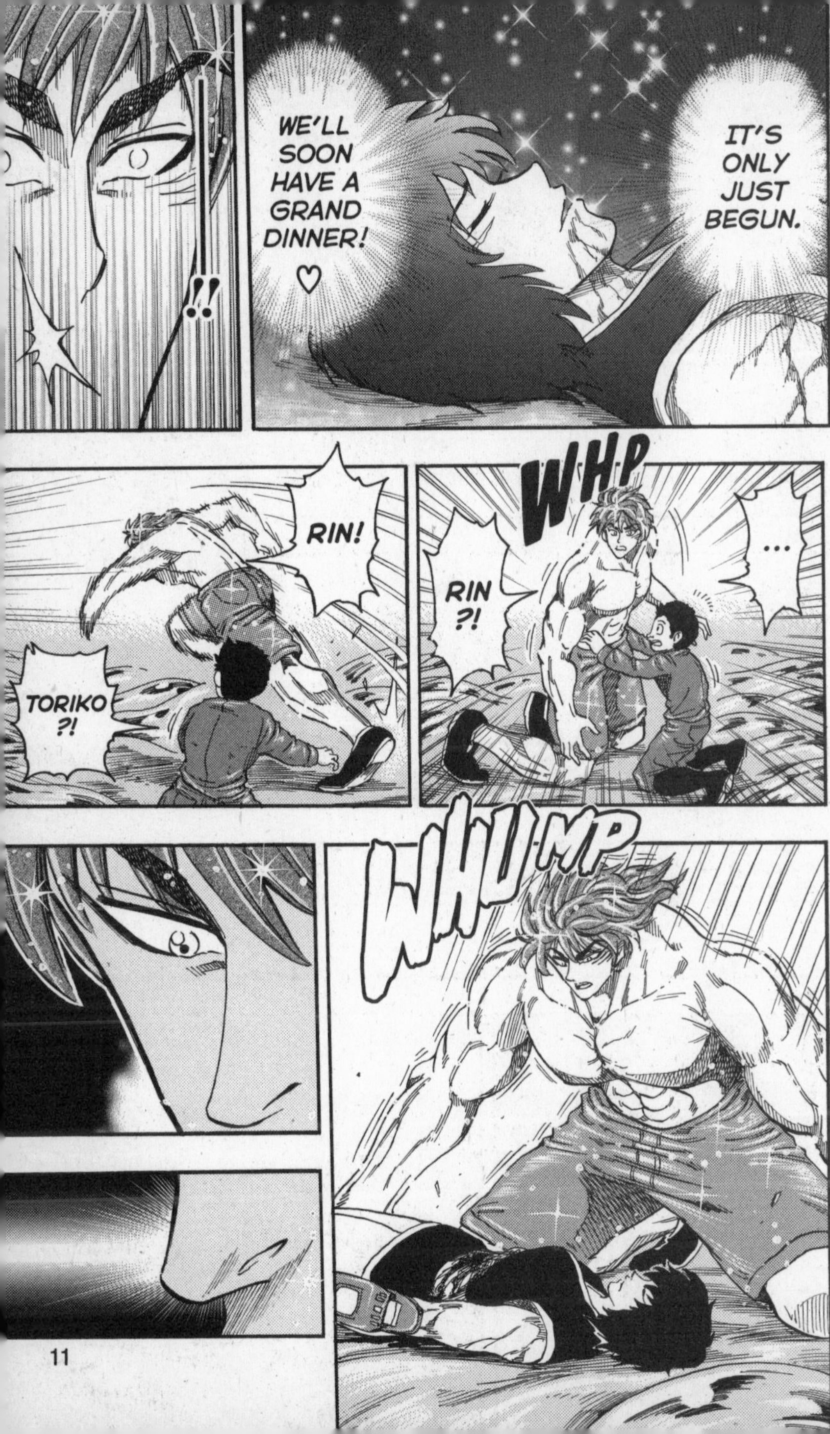
IT'S ONLY JUST BEGUN.
WE'LL SOON HAVE A GRAND DINNER! ♡
!!
WHP
...
RIN ?!
RIN!
TORIKO ?!
WHUMP

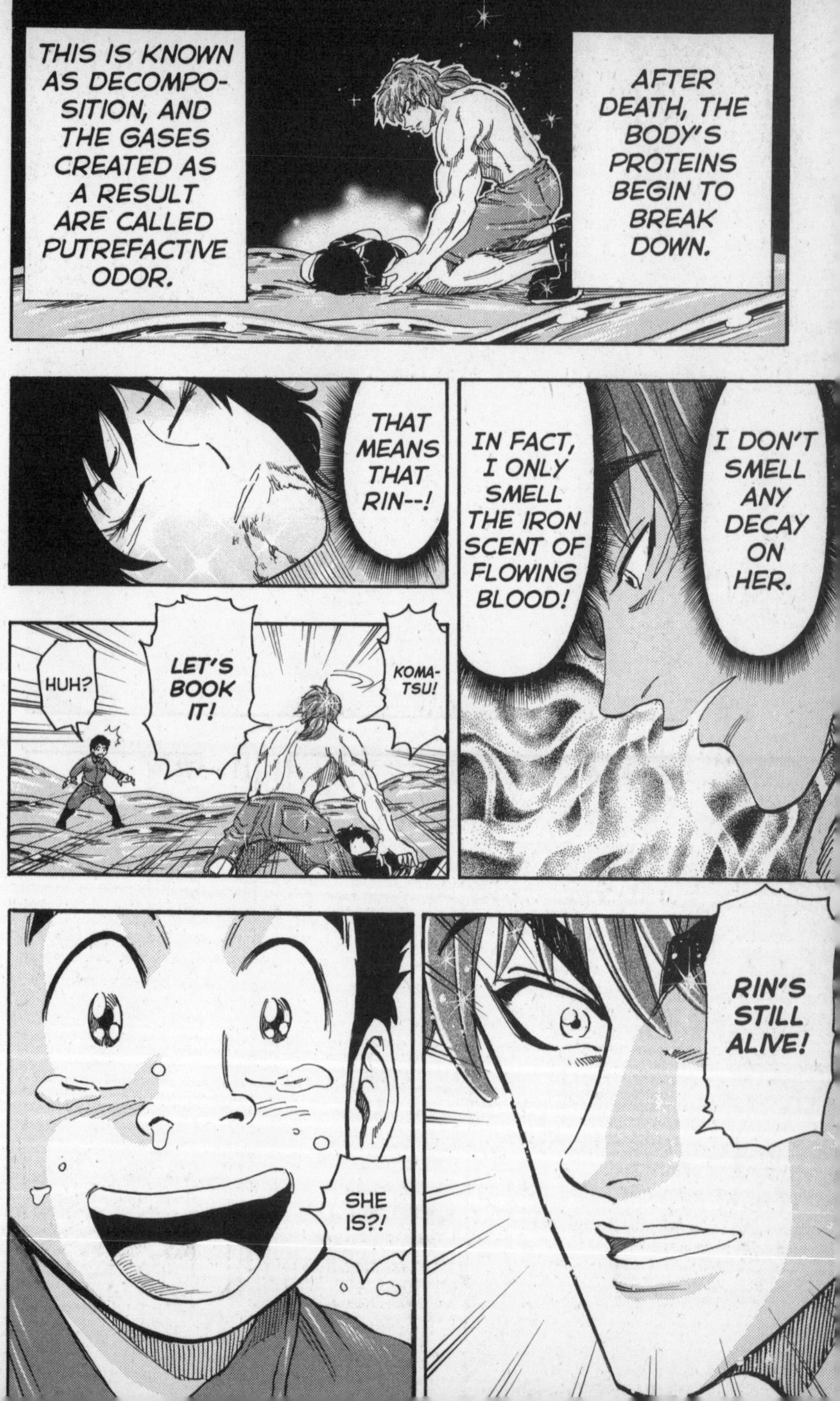
AFTER DEATH, THE BODY'S PROTEINS BEGIN TO BREAK DOWN.
THIS IS KNOWN AS DECOMPO-SITION, AND THE GASES CREATED AS A RESULT ARE CALLED PUTREFACTIVE ODOR.
I DON'T SMELL ANY DECAY ON HER.
IN FACT, I ONLY SMELL THE IRON SCENT OF FLOWING BLOOD!
THAT MEANS THAT RIN--!
KOMA-TSU!
LET'S BOOK IT!
HUH?
RIN'S STILL ALIVE!
SHE IS?!

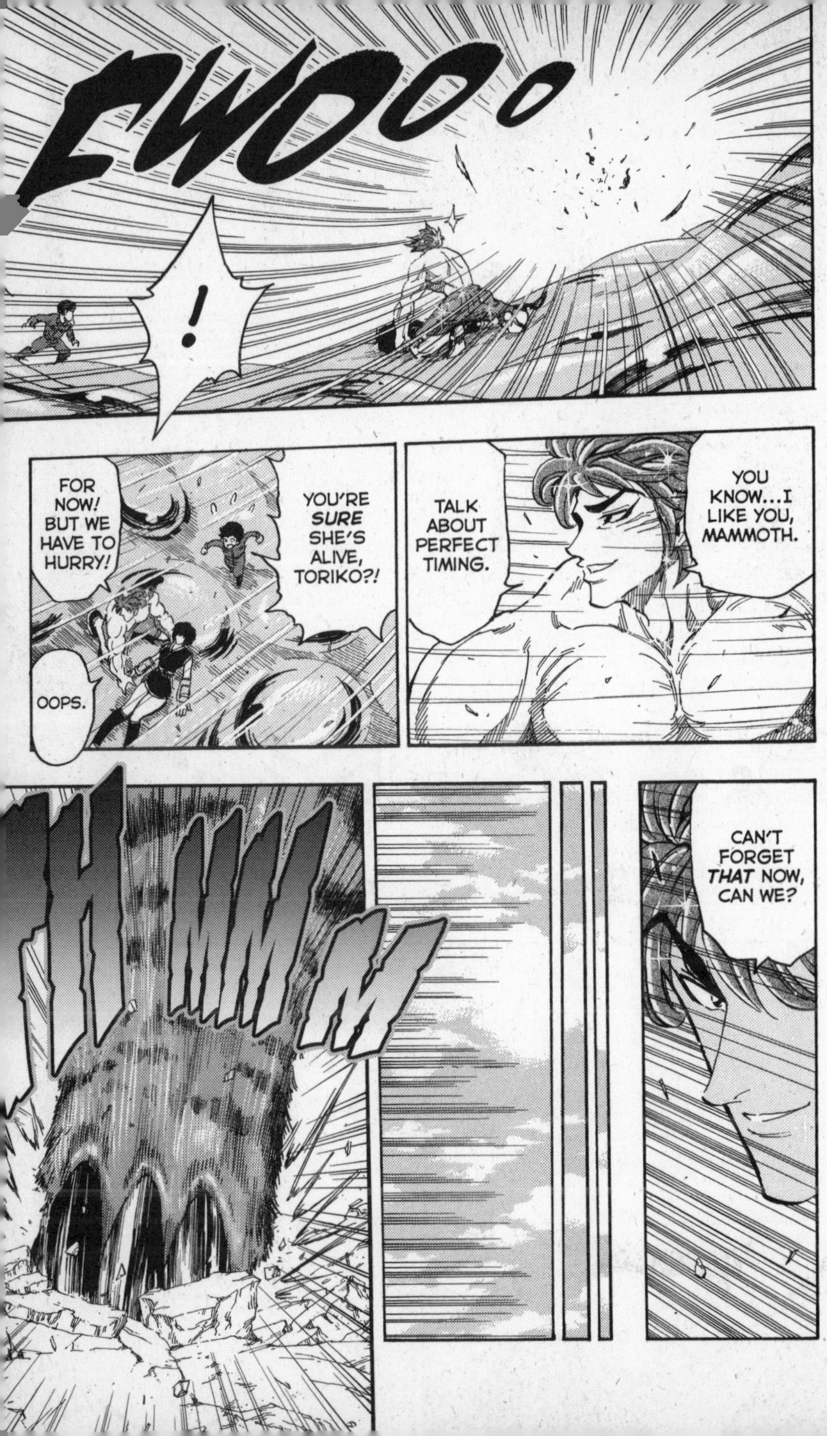
!
YOU KNOW...I LIKE YOU, MAMMOTH.
TALK ABOUT PERFECT TIMING.
YOU'RE *SURE* SHE'S ALIVE, TORIKO?!
FOR NOW! BUT WE HAVE TO HURRY!
OOPS.
CAN'T FORGET *THAT* NOW, CAN WE?

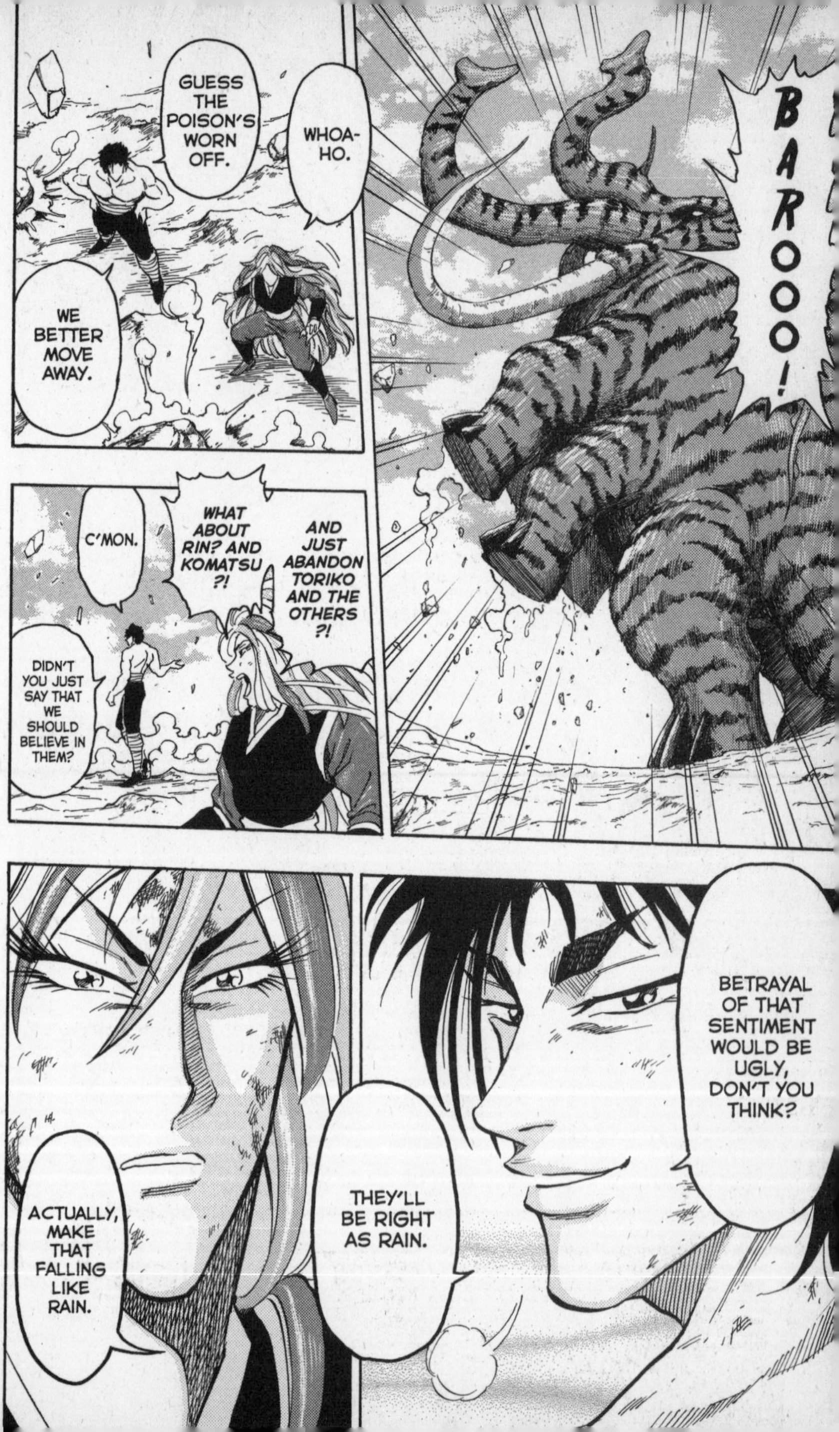
BAROOO!
WHOA-HO.
GUESS THE POISON'S WORN OFF.
WE BETTER MOVE AWAY.
C'MON.
WHAT ABOUT RIN? AND KOMATSU ?!
AND JUST ABANDON TORIKO AND THE OTHERS ?!
DIDN'T YOU JUST SAY THAT WE SHOULD BELIEVE IN THEM?
BETRAYAL OF THAT SENTIMENT WOULD BE UGLY, DON'T YOU THINK?
THEY'LL BE RIGHT AS RAIN.
ACTUALLY, MAKE THAT FALLING LIKE RAIN.

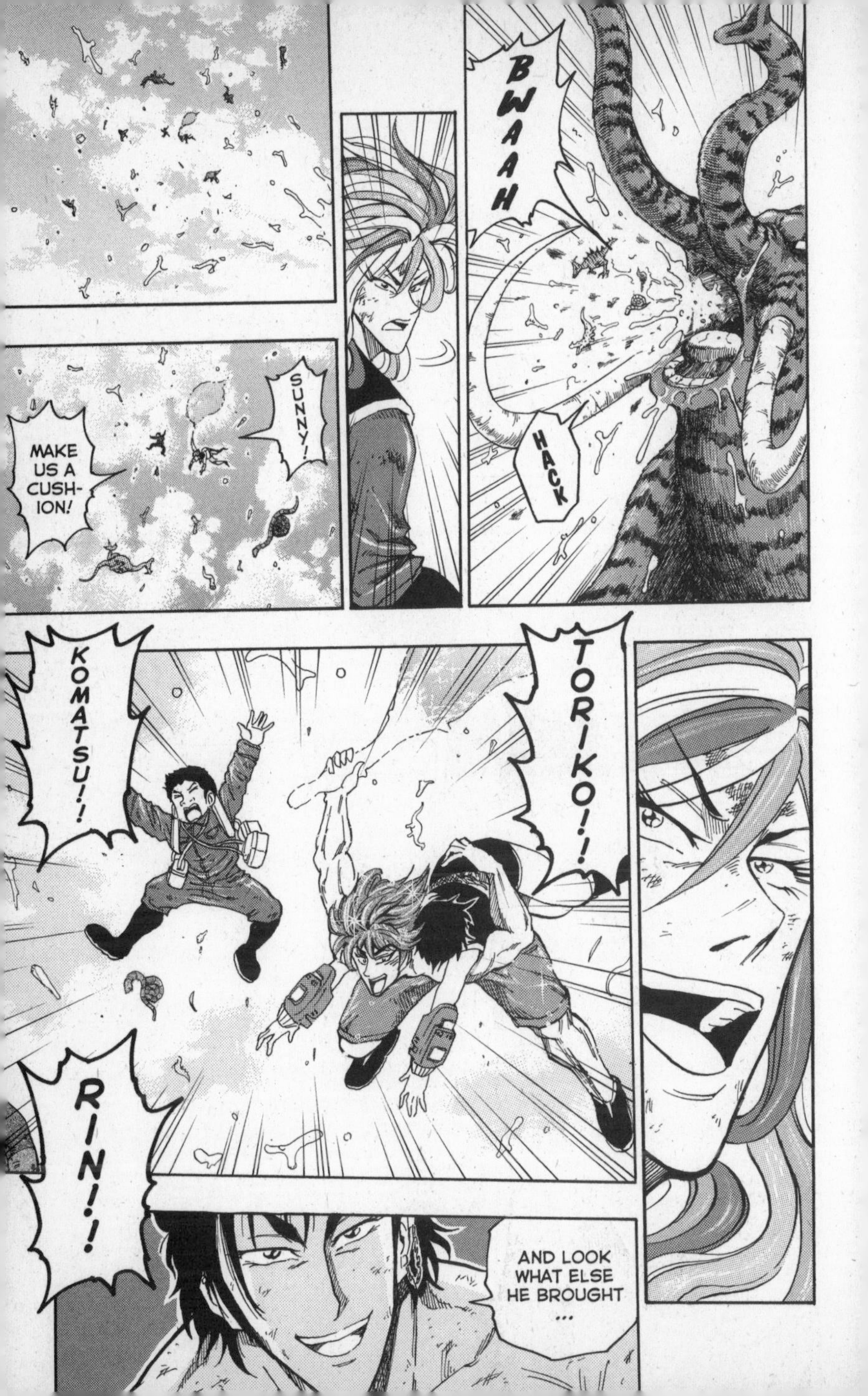
BWAAAH
HACK
SUNNY!
MAKE US A CUSHION!
TORIKO!!
KOMATSU!!
RIN!!
AND LOOK WHAT ELSE HE BROUGHT ...

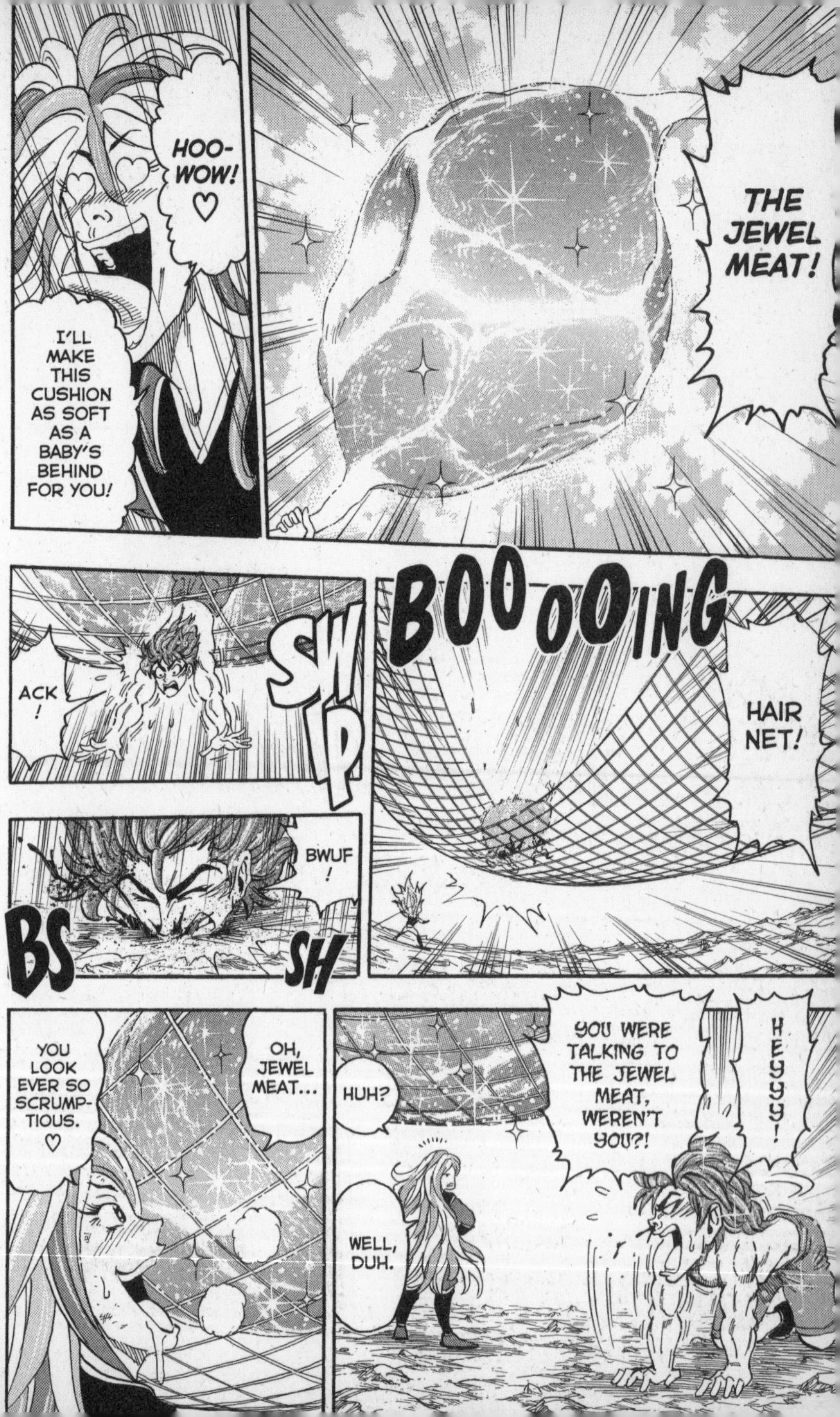
THE JEWEL MEAT!
HOO-WOW! ♡
I'LL MAKE THIS CUSHION AS SOFT AS A BABY'S BEHIND FOR YOU!
BOOOOOING
HAIR NET!
SWIP
ACK!
BWUF!
BSSH
HEYYY!
YOU WERE TALKING TO THE JEWEL MEAT, WEREN'T YOU?!
HUH?
WELL, DUH.
OH, JEWEL MEAT...
YOU LOOK EVER SO SCRUMPTIOUS. ♡

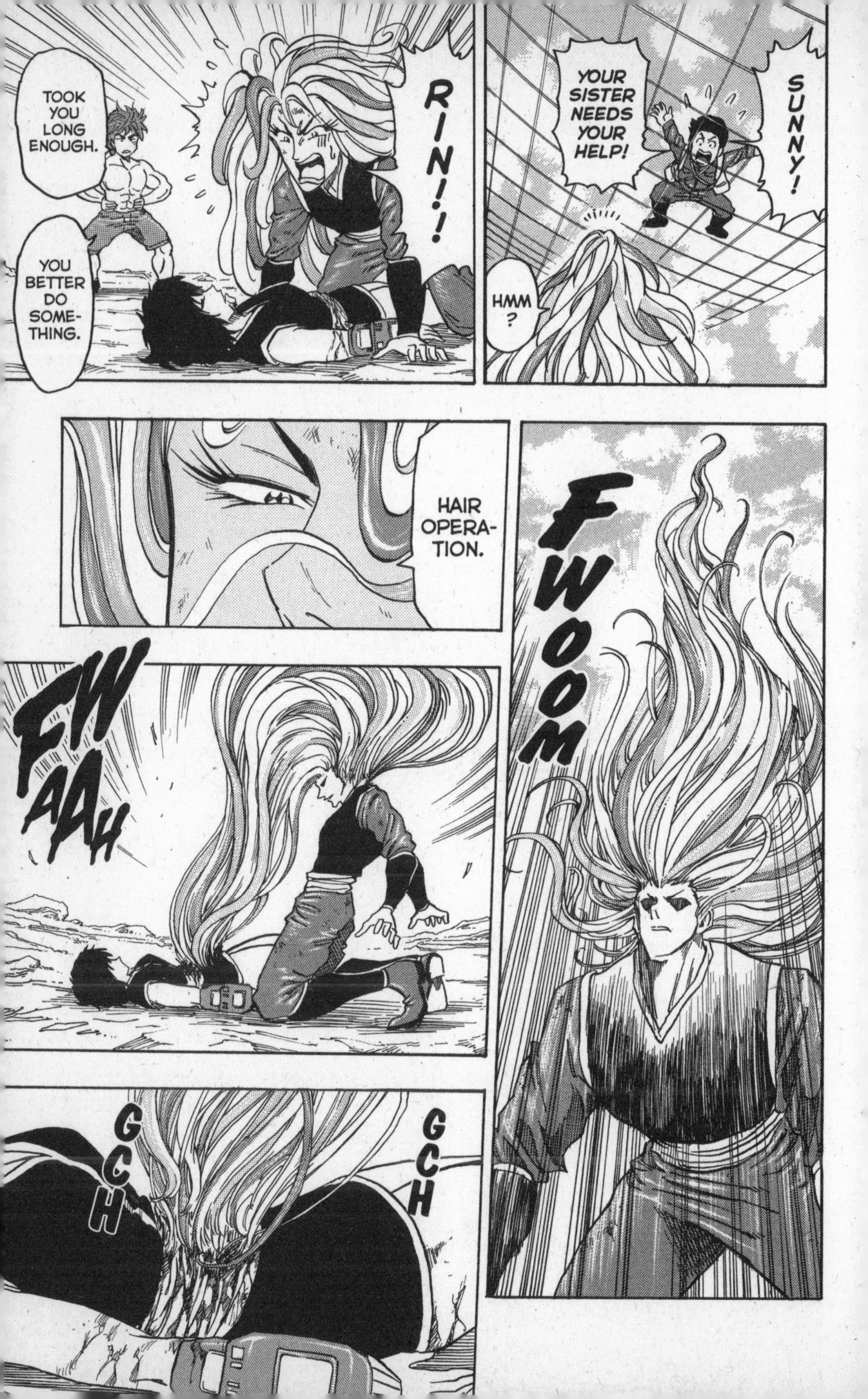
SUNNY!
YOUR SISTER NEEDS YOUR HELP!
HMM?
RIN!!!
TOOK YOU LONG ENOUGH.
YOU BETTER DO SOME-THING.
FWOOM
HAIR OPERA-TION.
FWAAH
GCH
GCH

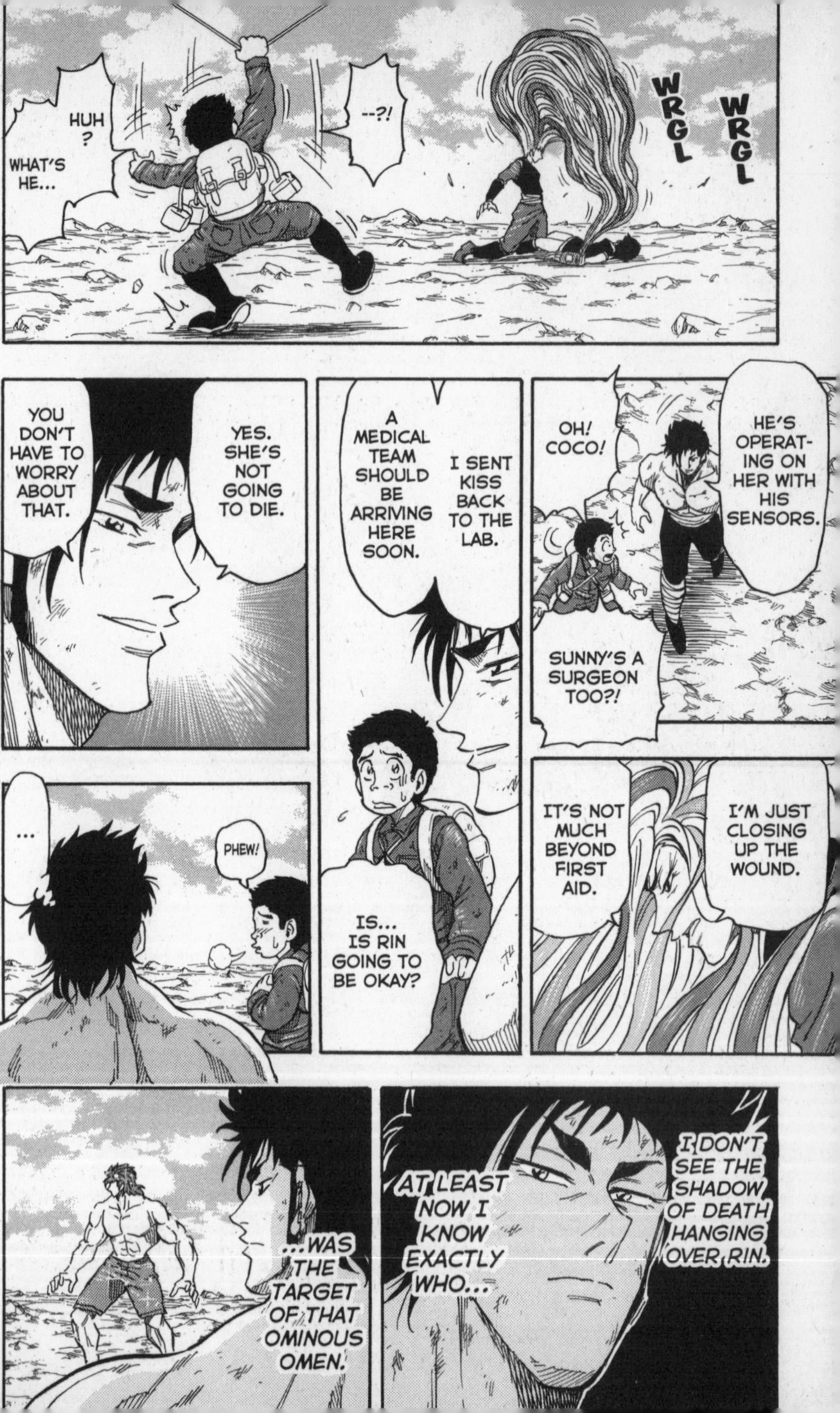
WRGL
WRGL
--?!
HUH ?
WHAT'S HE...
HE'S OPERATING ON HER WITH HIS SENSORS.
OH! COCO!
SUNNY'S A SURGEON TOO?!
I'M JUST CLOSING UP THE WOUND.
IT'S NOT MUCH BEYOND FIRST AID.
I SENT KISS BACK TO THE LAB.
A MEDICAL TEAM SHOULD BE ARRIVING HERE SOON.
IS... IS RIN GOING TO BE OKAY?
YES. SHE'S NOT GOING TO DIE.
YOU DON'T HAVE TO WORRY ABOUT THAT.
PHEW!
...
I DON'T SEE THE SHADOW OF DEATH HANGING OVER RIN.
AT LEAST NOW I KNOW EXACTLY WHO...
...WAS THE TARGET OF THAT OMINOUS OMEN.

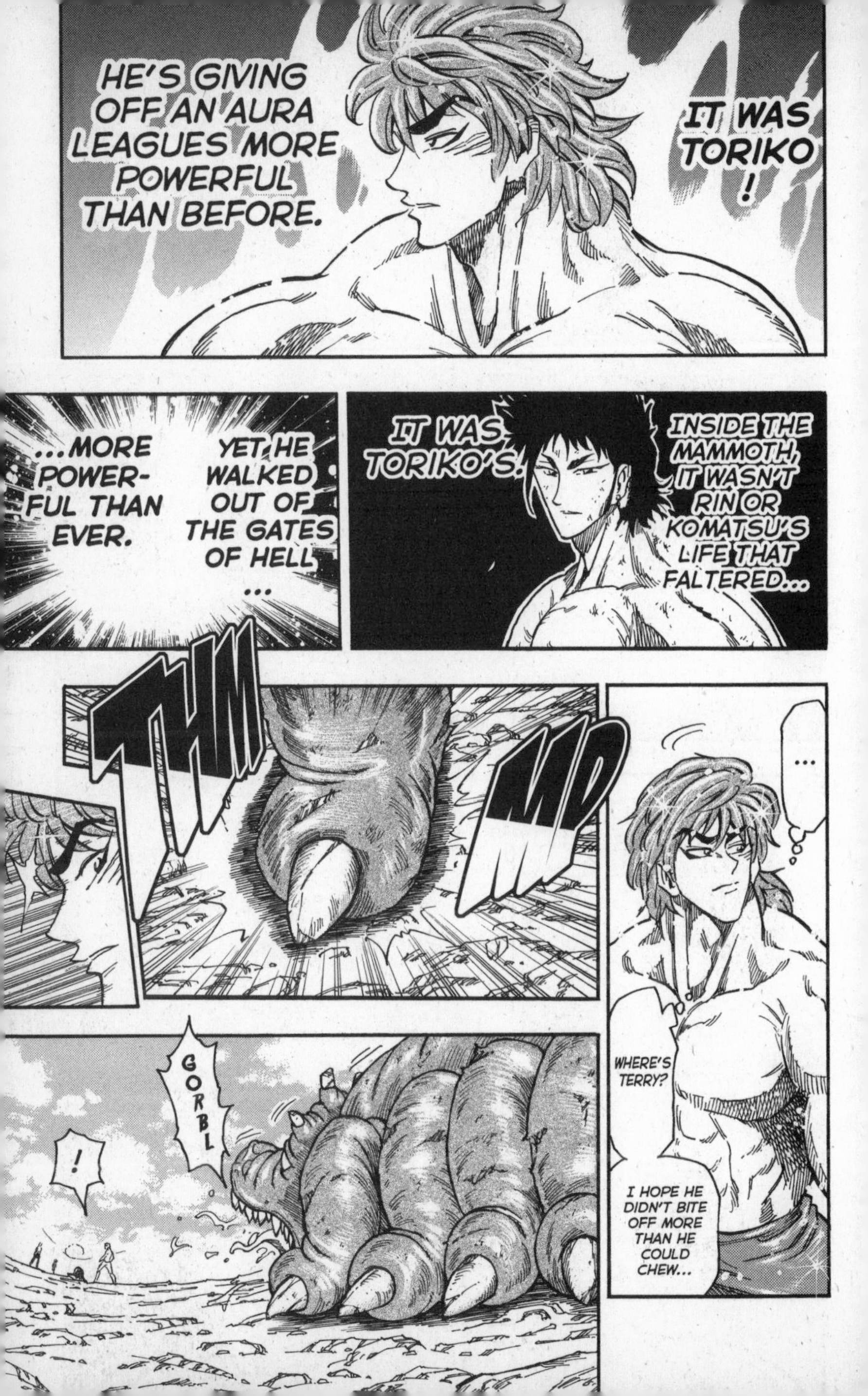

IT WAS TORIKO!
HE'S GIVING OFF AN AURA LEAGUES MORE POWERFUL THAN BEFORE.
INSIDE THE MAMMOTH, IT WASN'T RIN OR KOMATSU'S LIFE THAT FALTERED...
IT WAS TORIKO'S.
YET HE WALKED OUT OF THE GATES OF HELL...
...MORE POWER-FUL THAN EVER.
...
WHERE'S TERRY?
I HOPE HE DIDN'T BITE OFF MORE THAN HE COULD CHEW...
THUMMD
GORBL
!

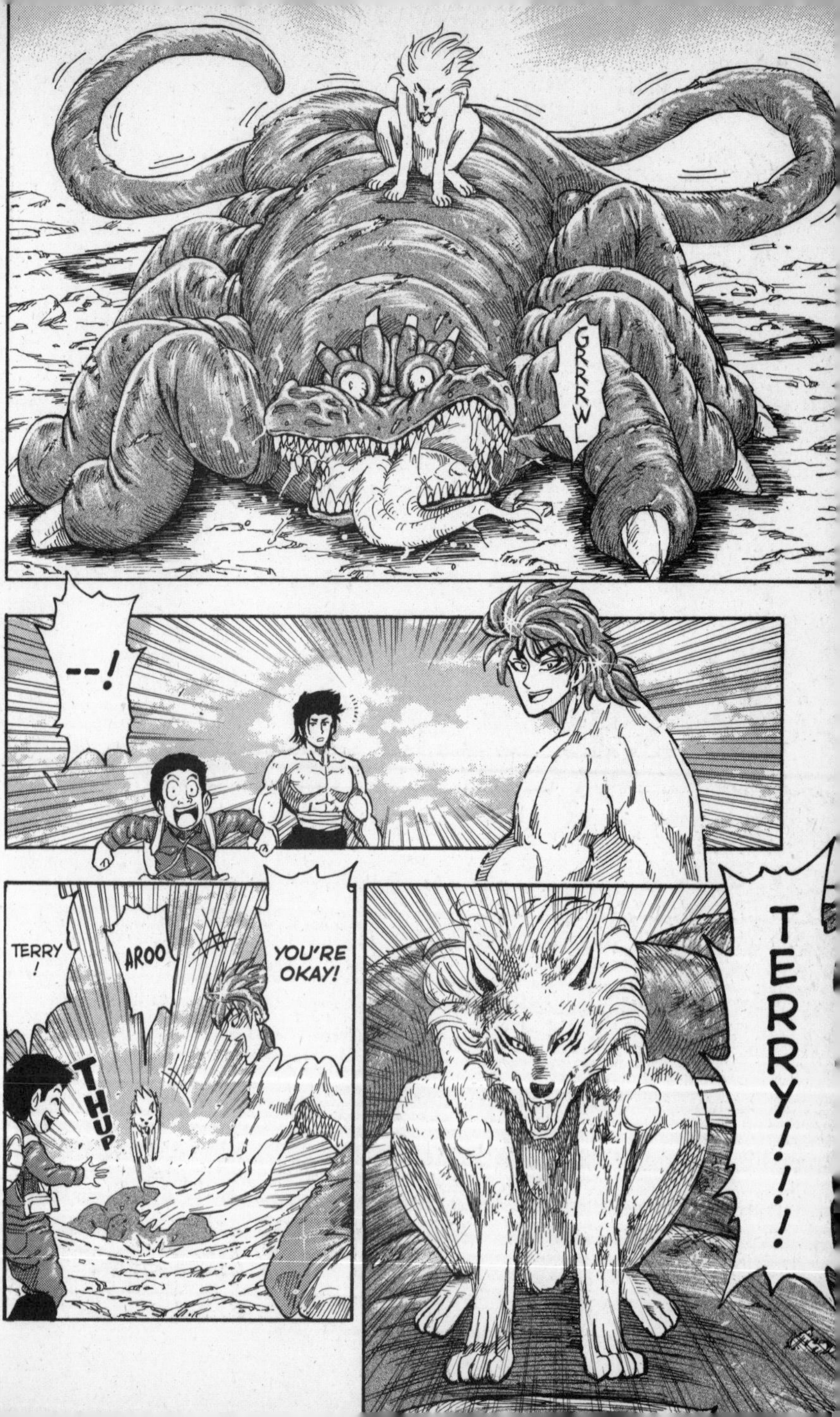
GRRRWL
--!
TERRY!!!!
YOU'RE OKAY!
AROO
TERRY!
THUP

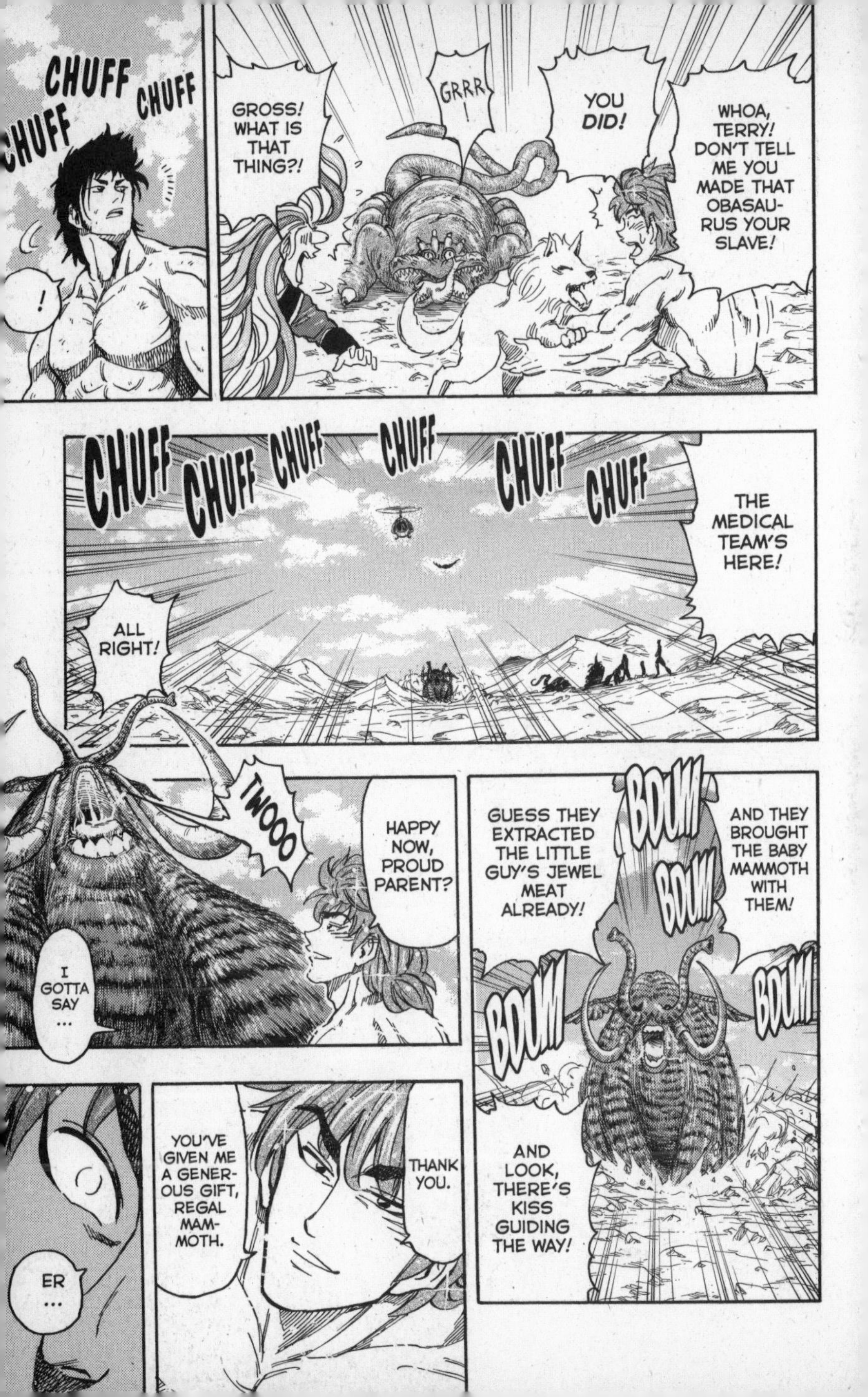
WHOA, TERRY! DON'T TELL ME YOU MADE THAT OBASAURUS YOUR SLAVE!
YOU DID!
GRRR!
GROSS! WHAT IS THAT THING?!
CHUFF CHUFF CHUFF
!
CHUFF CHUFF CHUFF CHUFF CHUFF CHUFF
THE MEDICAL TEAM'S HERE!
ALL RIGHT!
AND THEY BROUGHT THE BABY MAMMOTH WITH THEM!
BOUM
GUESS THEY EXTRACTED THE LITTLE GUY'S JEWEL MEAT ALREADY!
BOUM BOUM BOUM
AND LOOK, THERE'S KISS GUIDING THE WAY!
HAPPY NOW, PROUD PARENT?
TWOOO
I GOTTA SAY ...
THANK YOU.
YOU'VE GIVEN ME A GENEROUS GIFT, REGAL MAMMOTH.
ER ...

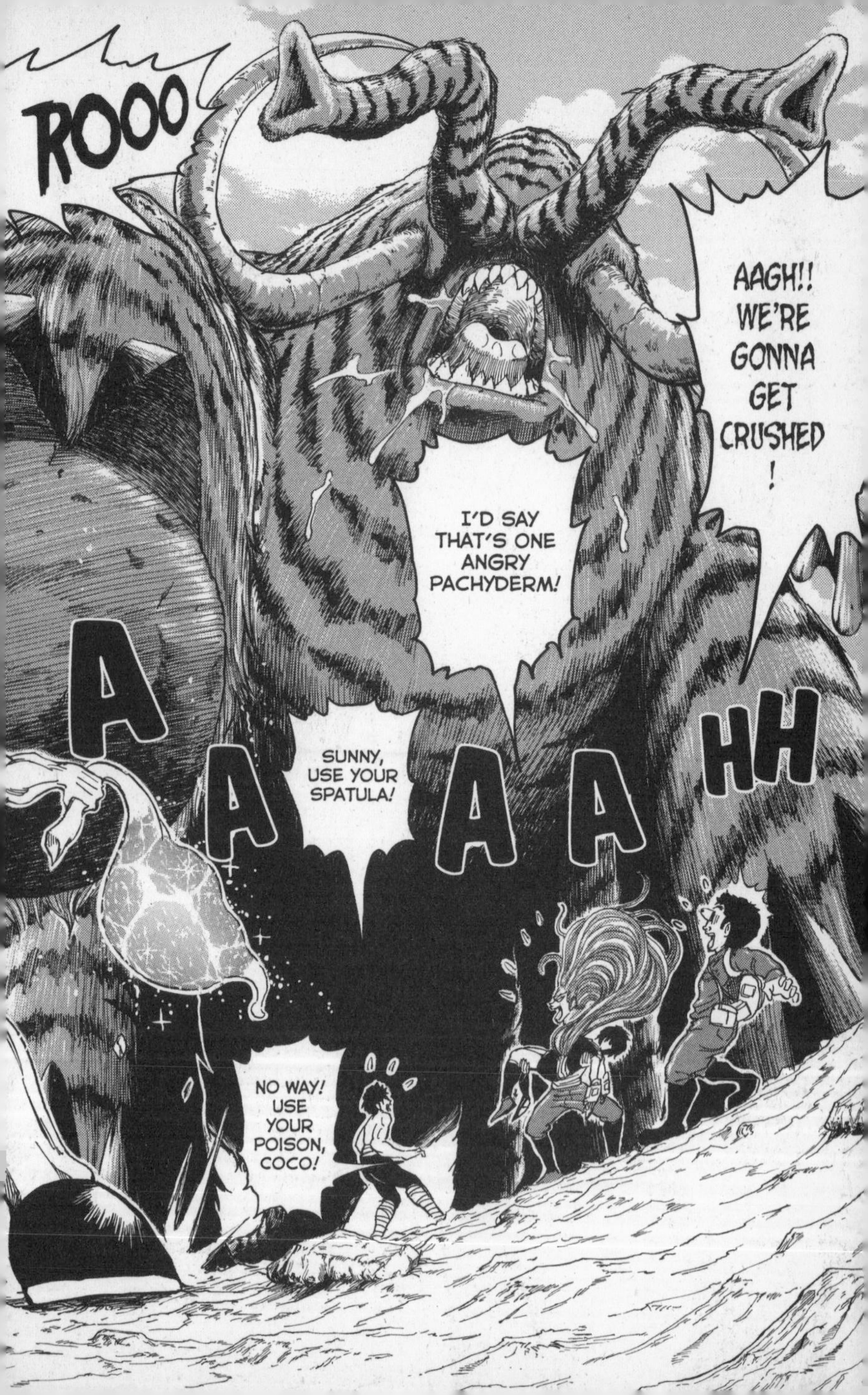
ROOO
AAGH!! WE'RE GONNA GET CRUSHED!
I'D SAY THAT'S ONE ANGRY PACHYDERM!
AAAAHH
SUNNY, USE YOUR SPATULA!
NO WAY! USE YOUR POISON, COCO!

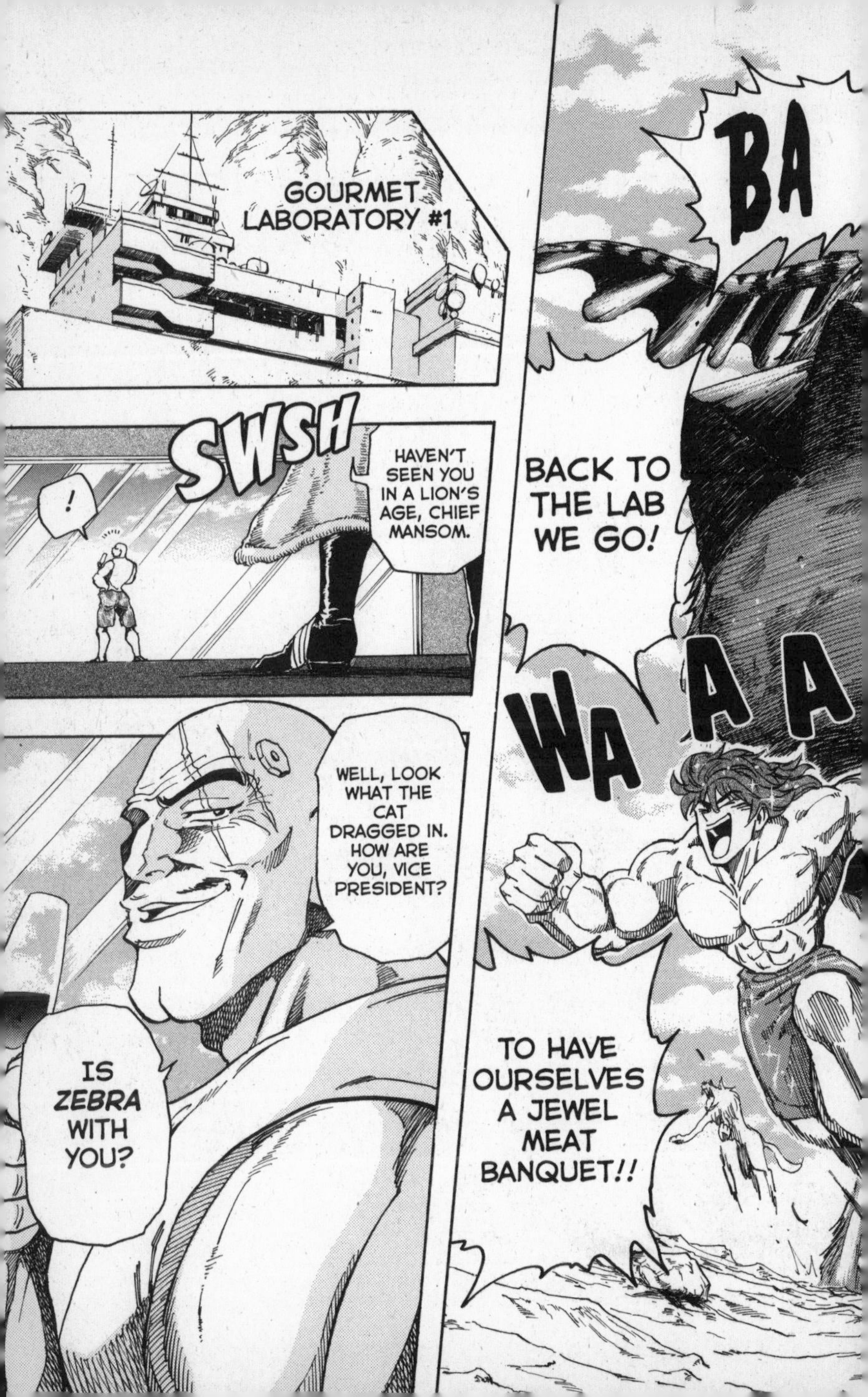
BA
BACK TO THE LAB WE GO!
WA A A
TO HAVE OURSELVES A JEWEL MEAT BANQUET!!
GOURMET LABORATORY #1
SWSH
HAVEN'T SEEN YOU IN A LION'S AGE, CHIEF MANSOM.
!
WELL, LOOK WHAT THE CAT DRAGGED IN. HOW ARE YOU, VICE PRESIDENT?
IS ZEBRA WITH YOU?

TORIKO

GOURMET CHECKLIST

Vol. 038

BACCHUS DRAGON
(WYVERN)

CAPTURE LEVEL: 37

HABITAT: BACCHUS ISLE

LENGTH: 48 METERS

HEIGHT: ---

WEIGHT: 22 TONS

PRICE: 100 G / 180,000 YEN

SCALE

THE BACCHUS DRAGON REIGNS OVER BACCHUS ISLE, A PARADISE WHERE EVERY LIVING BEING IS INFUSED WITH ALCOHOL. IN THE BACCHUS DRAGON'S CASE, ITS FLESH OOZES THE TASTE OF RICH BRANDY. BECAUSE THERE'S NOT SO MUCH AS A SCALE OF BACCHUS DRAGON THAT DOESN'T CONTAIN ALCOHOL, MINORS ARE PROHIBITED FROM CONSUMING IT. IT'S BEDTIME, KIDS; MOMMY AND DADDY ARE GOING TO HAVE ADULT TIME WITH THE DRAGON.

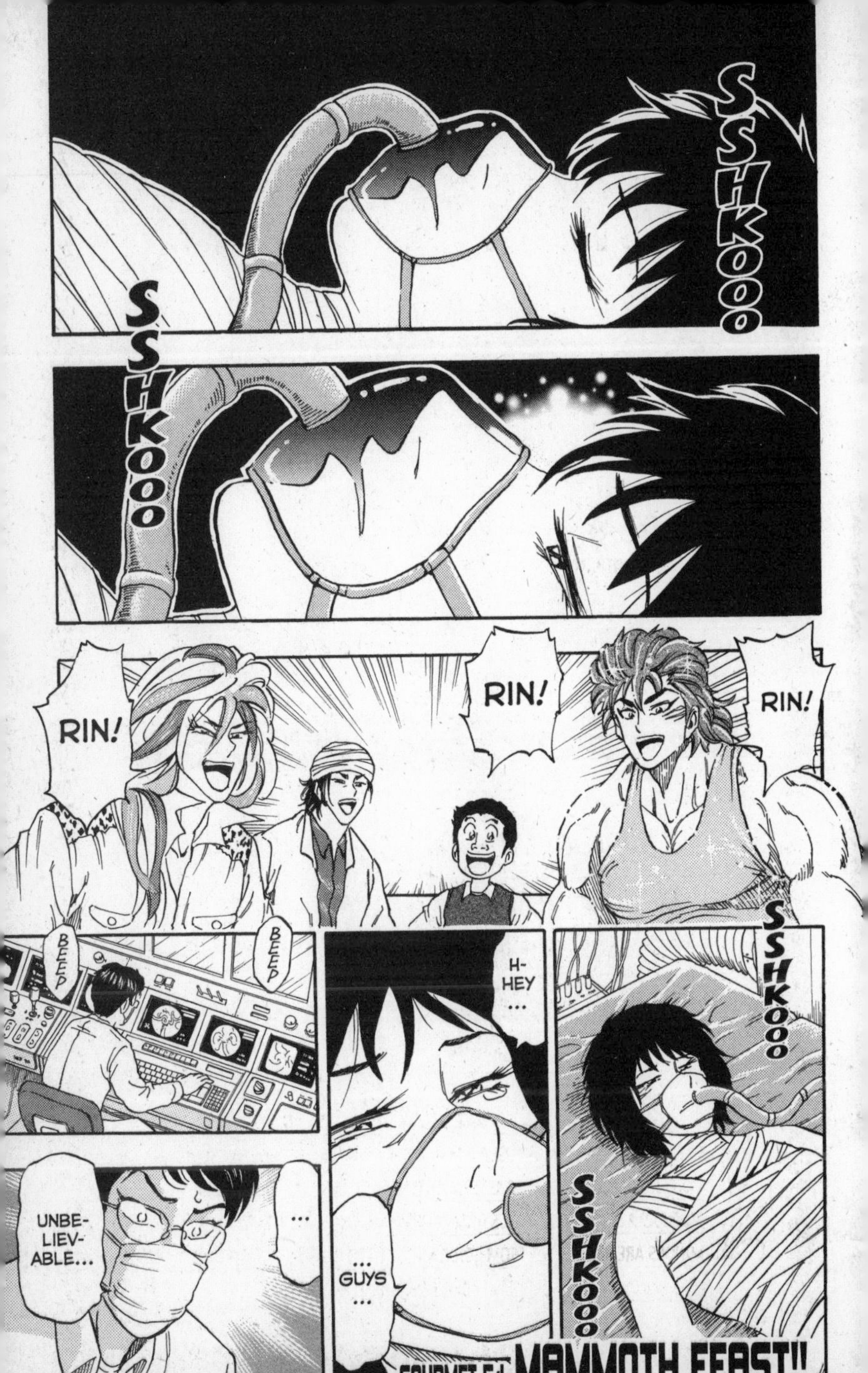
SSHKOOO
SSHKOOO
RIN!
RIN!
RIN!
SSHKOOO
SSHKOOO
H-HEY...
...GUYS...
BEEP
BEEP
...
UNBELIEVABLE...

GOURMET 54: MAMMOTH FEAST!!

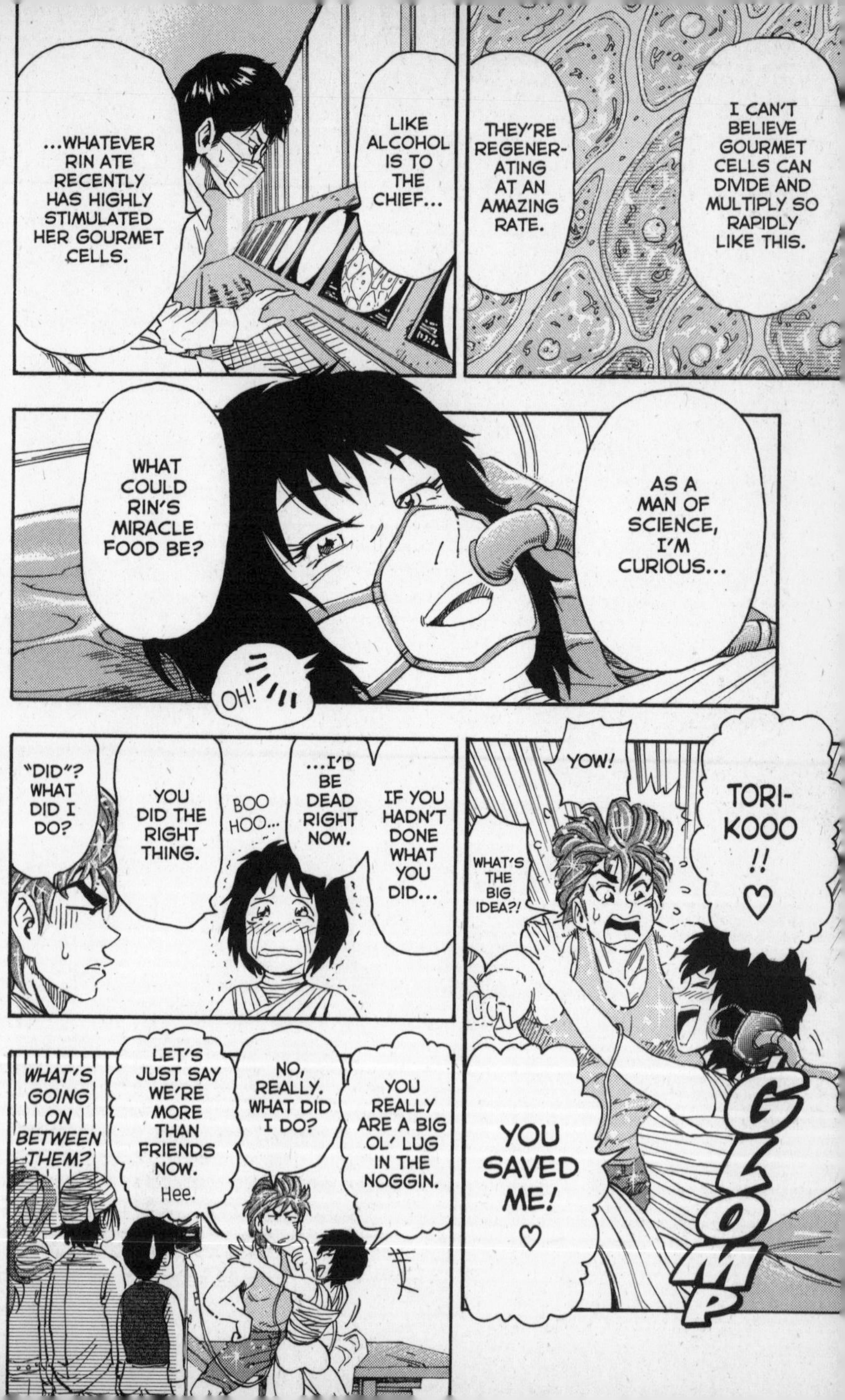
I CAN'T BELIEVE GOURMET CELLS CAN DIVIDE AND MULTIPLY SO RAPIDLY LIKE THIS.
THEY'RE REGENER-ATING AT AN AMAZING RATE.
LIKE ALCOHOL IS TO THE CHIEF...
...WHATEVER RIN ATE RECENTLY HAS HIGHLY STIMULATED HER GOURMET CELLS.
AS A MAN OF SCIENCE, I'M CURIOUS...
WHAT COULD RIN'S MIRACLE FOOD BE?
OH!
TORI-KOOO!! ♡
YOW!
WHAT'S THE BIG IDEA?!
YOU SAVED ME! ♡
GLOMP
IF YOU HADN'T DONE WHAT YOU DID...
...I'D BE DEAD RIGHT NOW.
BOO HOO...
YOU DID THE RIGHT THING.
"DID"? WHAT DID I DO?
YOU REALLY ARE A BIG OL' LUG IN THE NOGGIN.
NO, REALLY. WHAT DID I DO?
LET'S JUST SAY WE'RE MORE THAN FRIENDS NOW. Hee.
WHAT'S GOING ON BETWEEN THEM?

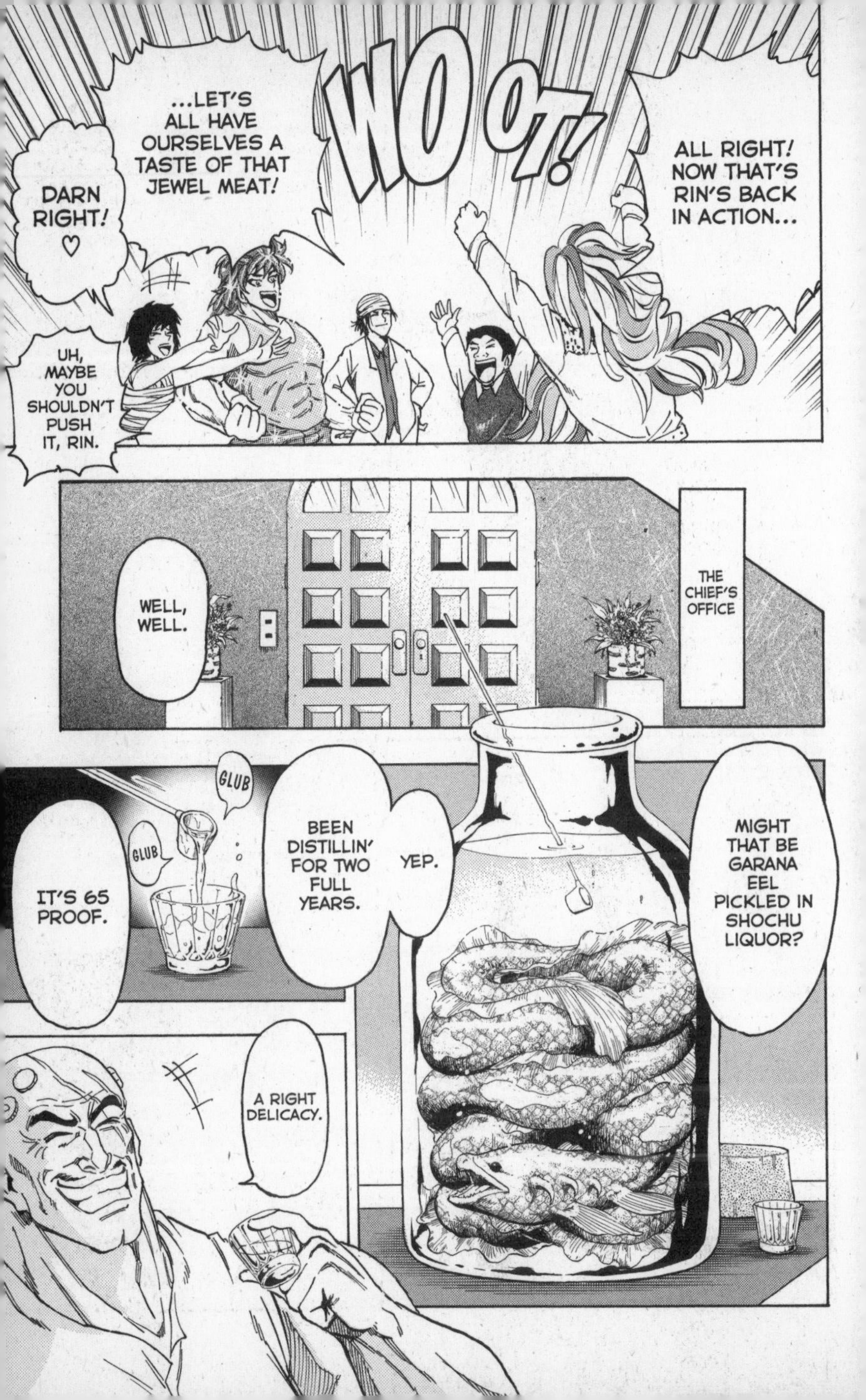
ALL RIGHT! NOW THAT'S RIN'S BACK IN ACTION...
WOOT!
...LET'S ALL HAVE OURSELVES A TASTE OF THAT JEWEL MEAT!
DARN RIGHT! ♡
UH, MAYBE YOU SHOULDN'T PUSH IT, RIN.
THE CHIEF'S OFFICE
WELL, WELL.
MIGHT THAT BE GARANA EEL PICKLED IN SHOCHU LIQUOR?
YEP.
BEEN DISTILLIN' FOR TWO FULL YEARS.
GLUB
GLUB
IT'S 65 PROOF.
A RIGHT DELICACY.

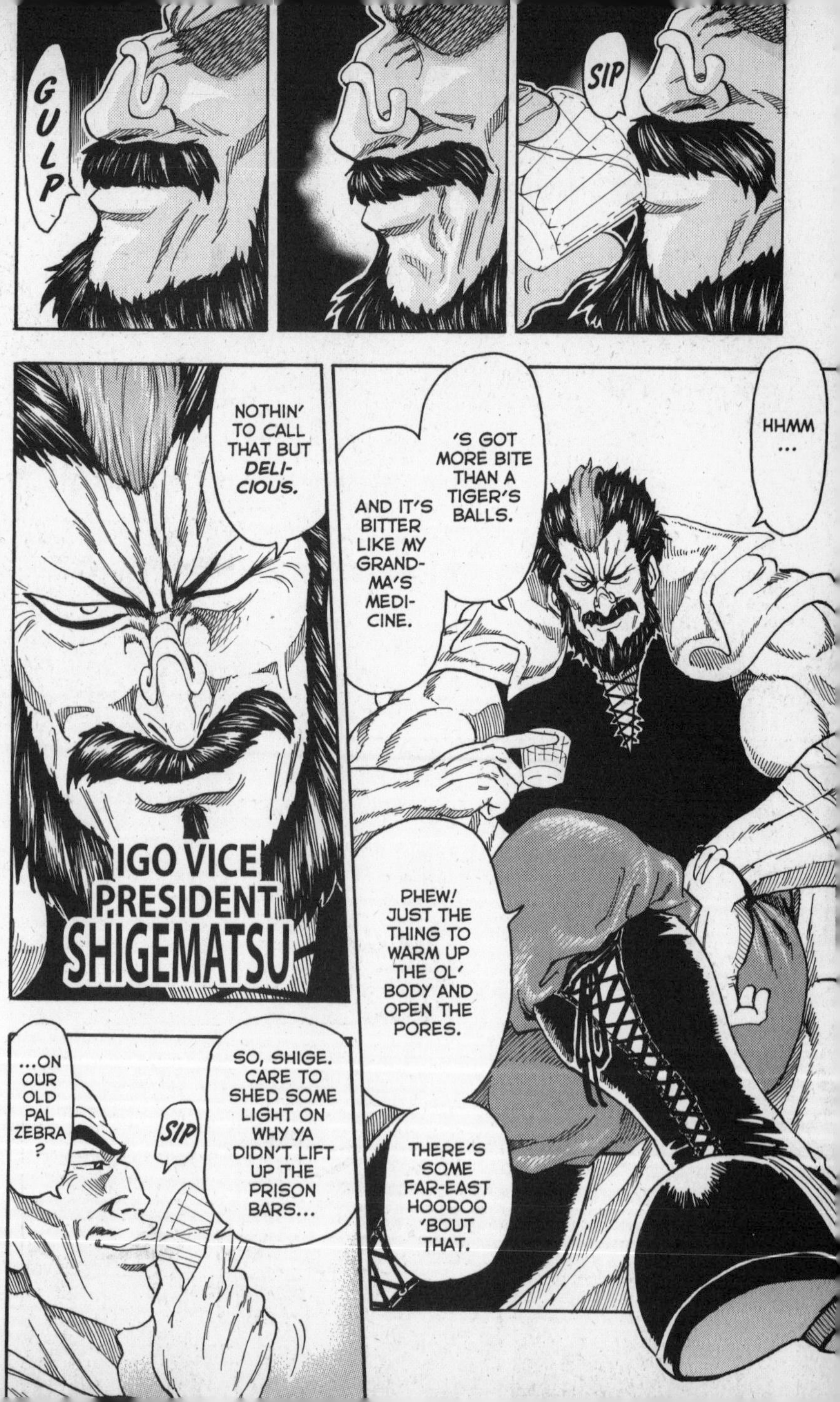
SIP
GULP
HHMM ...
'S GOT MORE BITE THAN A TIGER'S BALLS.
AND IT'S BITTER LIKE MY GRANDMA'S MEDICINE.
PHEW! JUST THE THING TO WARM UP THE OL' BODY AND OPEN THE PORES.
THERE'S SOME FAR-EAST HOODOO 'BOUT THAT.
NOTHIN' TO CALL THAT BUT *DELICIOUS.*
IGO VICE PRESIDENT SHIGEMATSU
SO, SHIGE. CARE TO SHED SOME LIGHT ON WHY YA DIDN'T LIFT UP THE PRISON BARS...
SIP
...ON OUR OLD PAL ZEBRA?

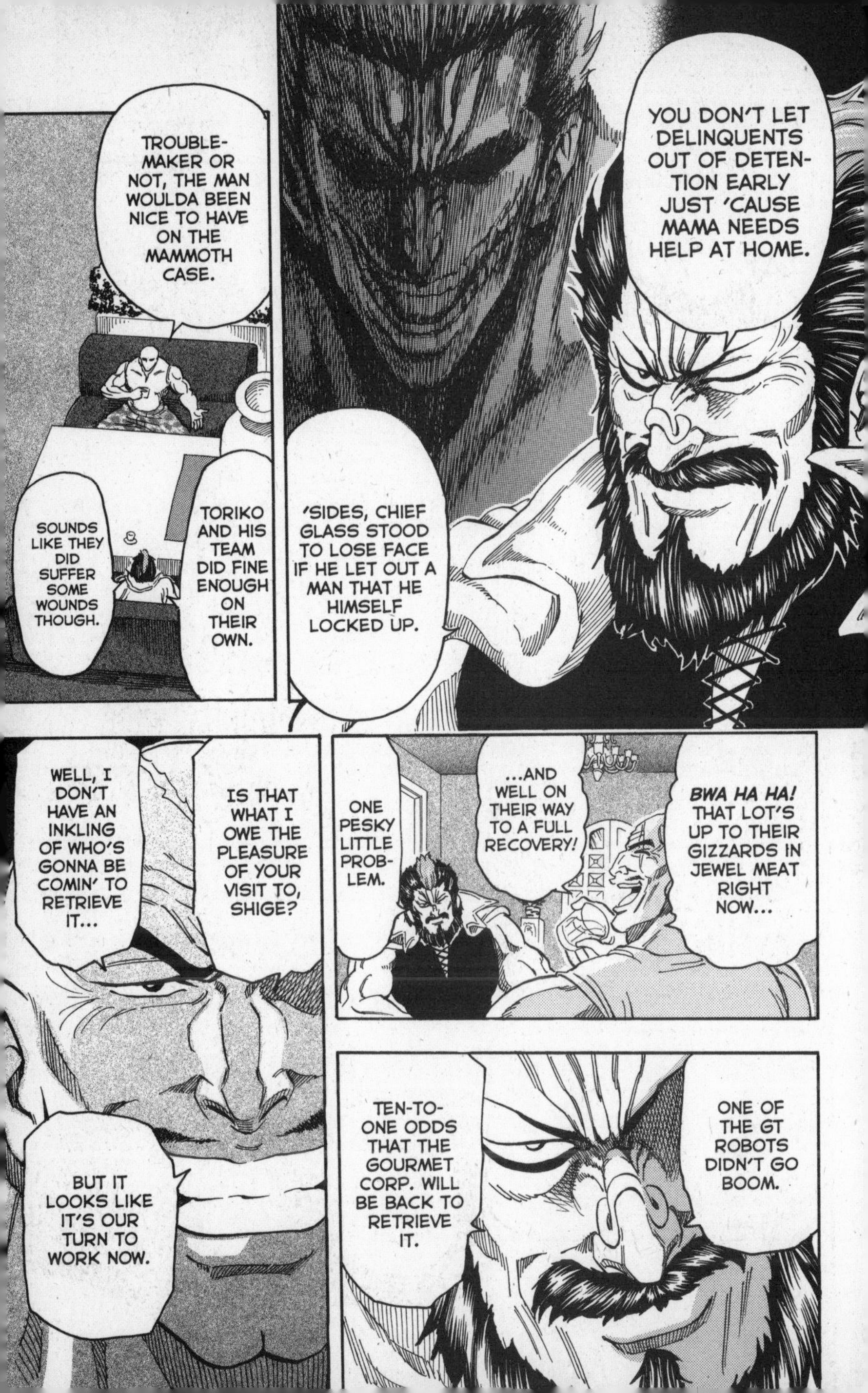
YOU DON'T LET DELINQUENTS OUT OF DETEN-TION EARLY JUST 'CAUSE MAMA NEEDS HELP AT HOME.
'SIDES, CHIEF GLASS STOOD TO LOSE FACE IF HE LET OUT A MAN THAT HE HIMSELF LOCKED UP.
TROUBLE-MAKER OR NOT, THE MAN WOULDA BEEN NICE TO HAVE ON THE MAMMOTH CASE.
TORIKO AND HIS TEAM DID FINE ENOUGH ON THEIR OWN.
SOUNDS LIKE THEY DID SUFFER SOME WOUNDS THOUGH.
BWA HA HA! THAT LOT'S UP TO THEIR GIZZARDS IN JEWEL MEAT RIGHT NOW...
...AND WELL ON THEIR WAY TO A FULL RECOVERY!
ONE PESKY LITTLE PROB-LEM.
ONE OF THE GT ROBOTS DIDN'T GO BOOM.
TEN-TO-ONE ODDS THAT THE GOURMET CORP. WILL BE BACK TO RETRIEVE IT.
IS THAT WHAT I OWE THE PLEASURE OF YOUR VISIT TO, SHIGE?
WELL, I DON'T HAVE AN INKLING OF WHO'S GONNA BE COMIN' TO RETRIEVE IT...
BUT IT LOOKS LIKE IT'S OUR TURN TO WORK NOW.

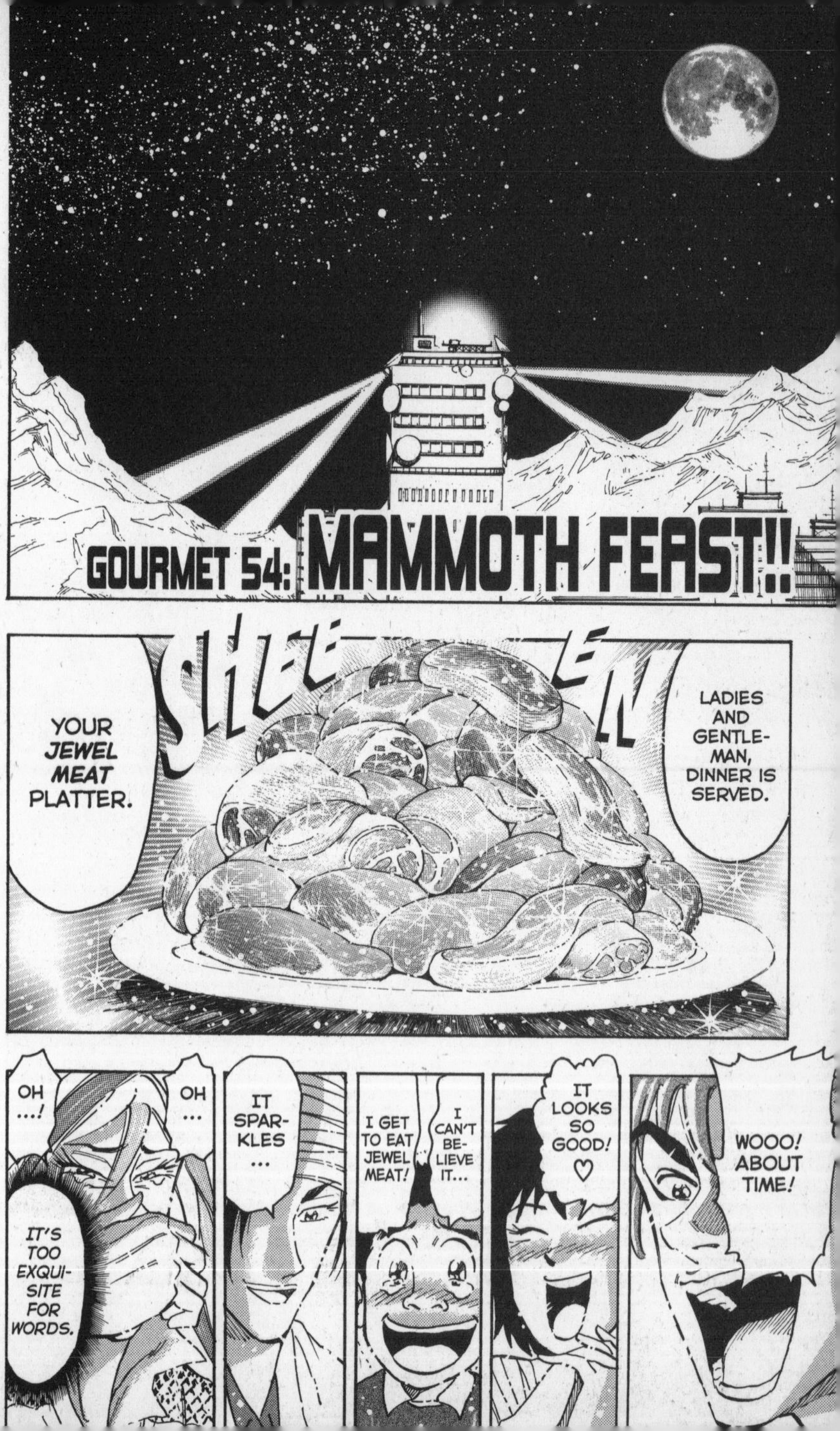
GOURMET 54: MAMMOTH FEAST!!
LADIES AND GENTLE-MAN, DINNER IS SERVED.
SHEEEN
YOUR JEWEL MEAT PLATTER.
WOOO! ABOUT TIME!
IT LOOKS SO GOOD! ♡
I CAN'T BE-LIEVE IT...
I GET TO EAT JEWEL MEAT!
IT SPAR-KLES ...
OH ...
OH ...!
IT'S TOO EXQUI-SITE FOR WORDS.

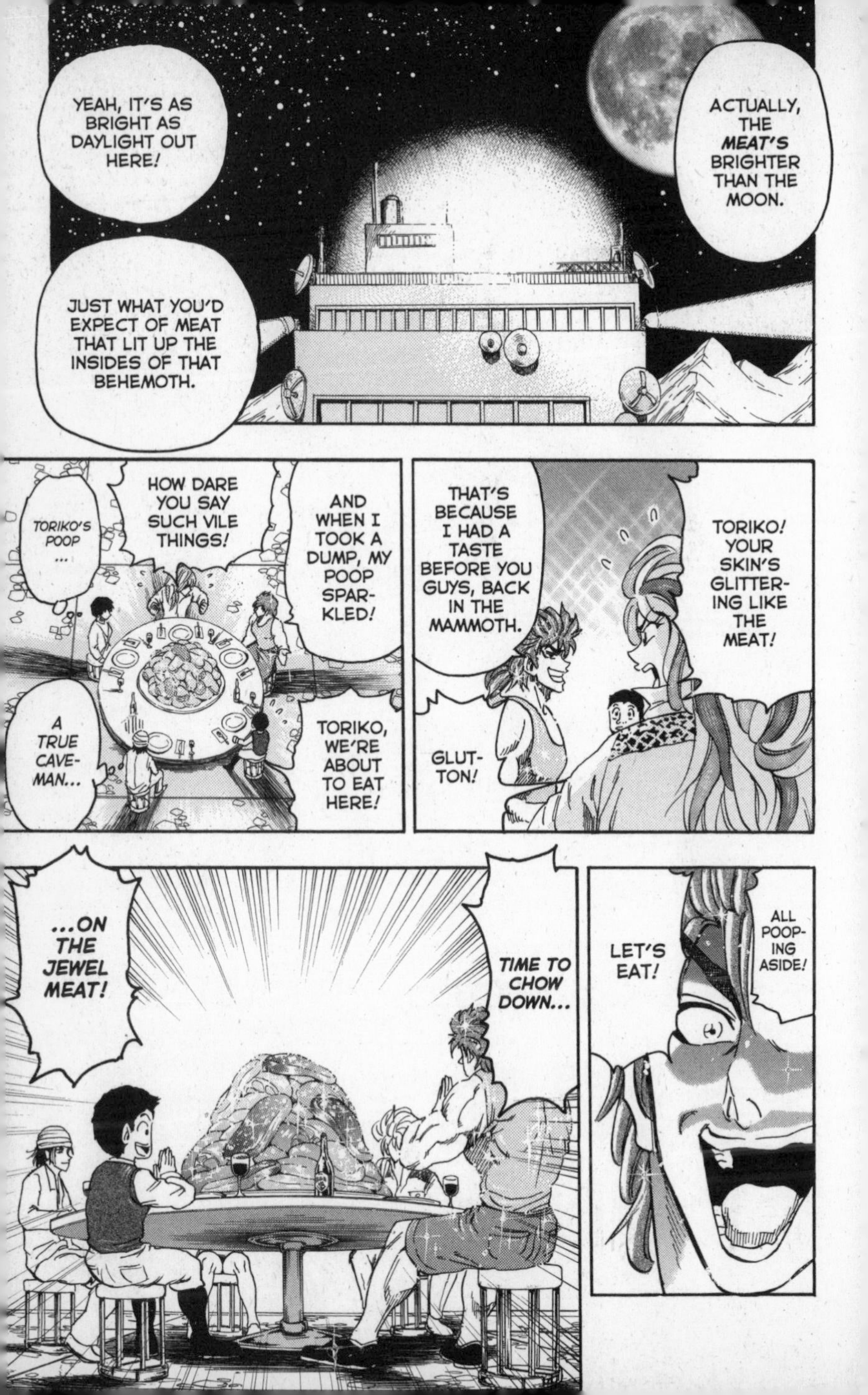
ACTUALLY, THE *MEAT'S* BRIGHTER THAN THE MOON.
YEAH, IT'S AS BRIGHT AS DAYLIGHT OUT HERE!
JUST WHAT YOU'D EXPECT OF MEAT THAT LIT UP THE INSIDES OF THAT BEHEMOTH.
TORIKO! YOUR SKIN'S GLITTERING LIKE THE MEAT!
THAT'S BECAUSE I HAD A TASTE BEFORE YOU GUYS, BACK IN THE MAMMOTH.
GLUTTON!
AND WHEN I TOOK A DUMP, MY POOP SPARKLED!
HOW DARE YOU SAY SUCH VILE THINGS!
TORIKO'S POOP...
TORIKO, WE'RE ABOUT TO EAT HERE!
A TRUE CAVEMAN...
ALL POOPING ASIDE!
LET'S EAT!
TIME TO CHOW DOWN...
...ON THE JEWEL MEAT!

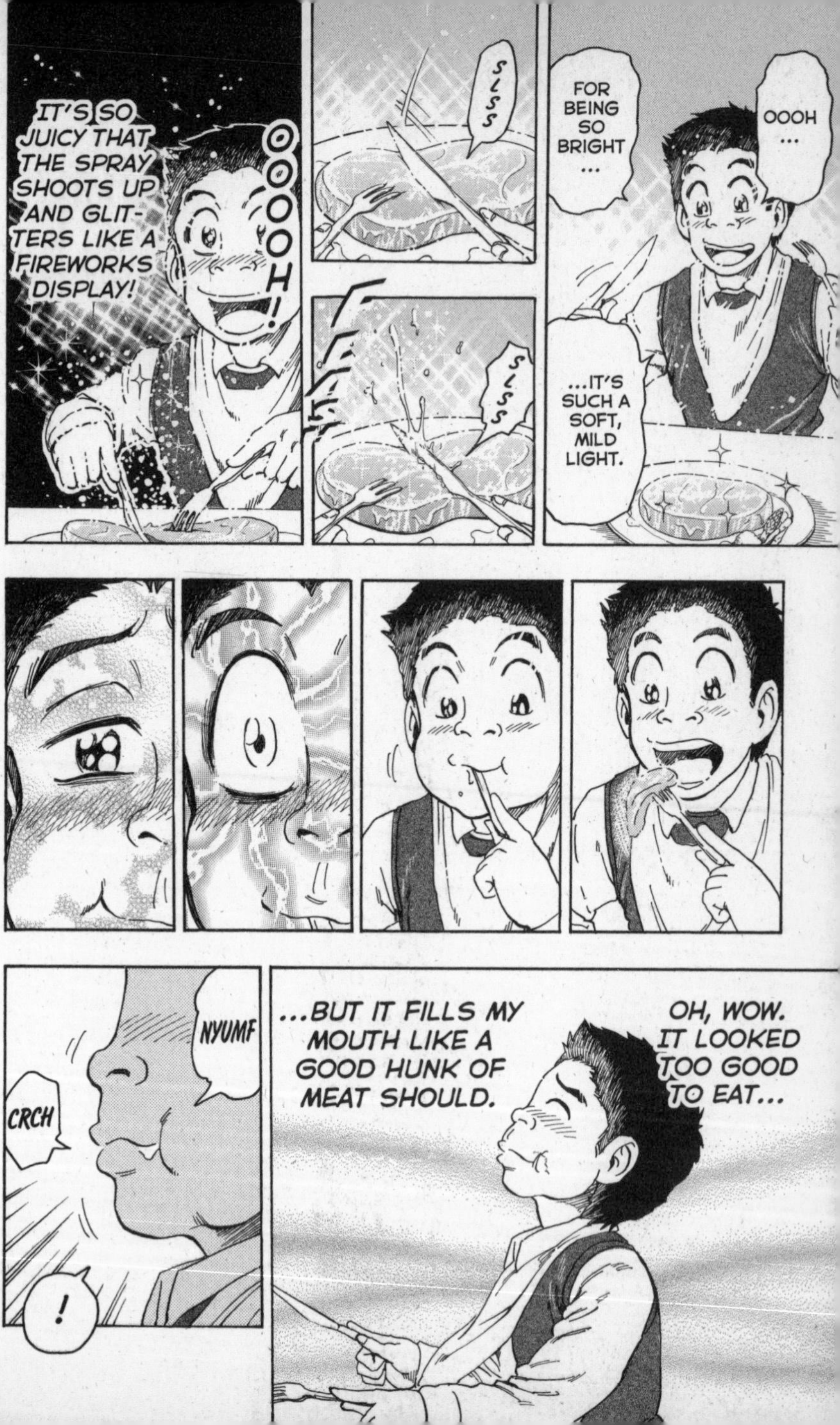
OOOH ...
FOR BEING SO BRIGHT ...
...IT'S SUCH A SOFT, MILD LIGHT.
SLSS
SLSS
OOOOH!
IT'S SO JUICY THAT THE SPRAY SHOOTS UP AND GLITTERS LIKE A FIREWORKS DISPLAY!
OH, WOW. IT LOOKED TOO GOOD TO EAT...
...BUT IT FILLS MY MOUTH LIKE A GOOD HUNK OF MEAT SHOULD.
NYUMF
CRCH
!

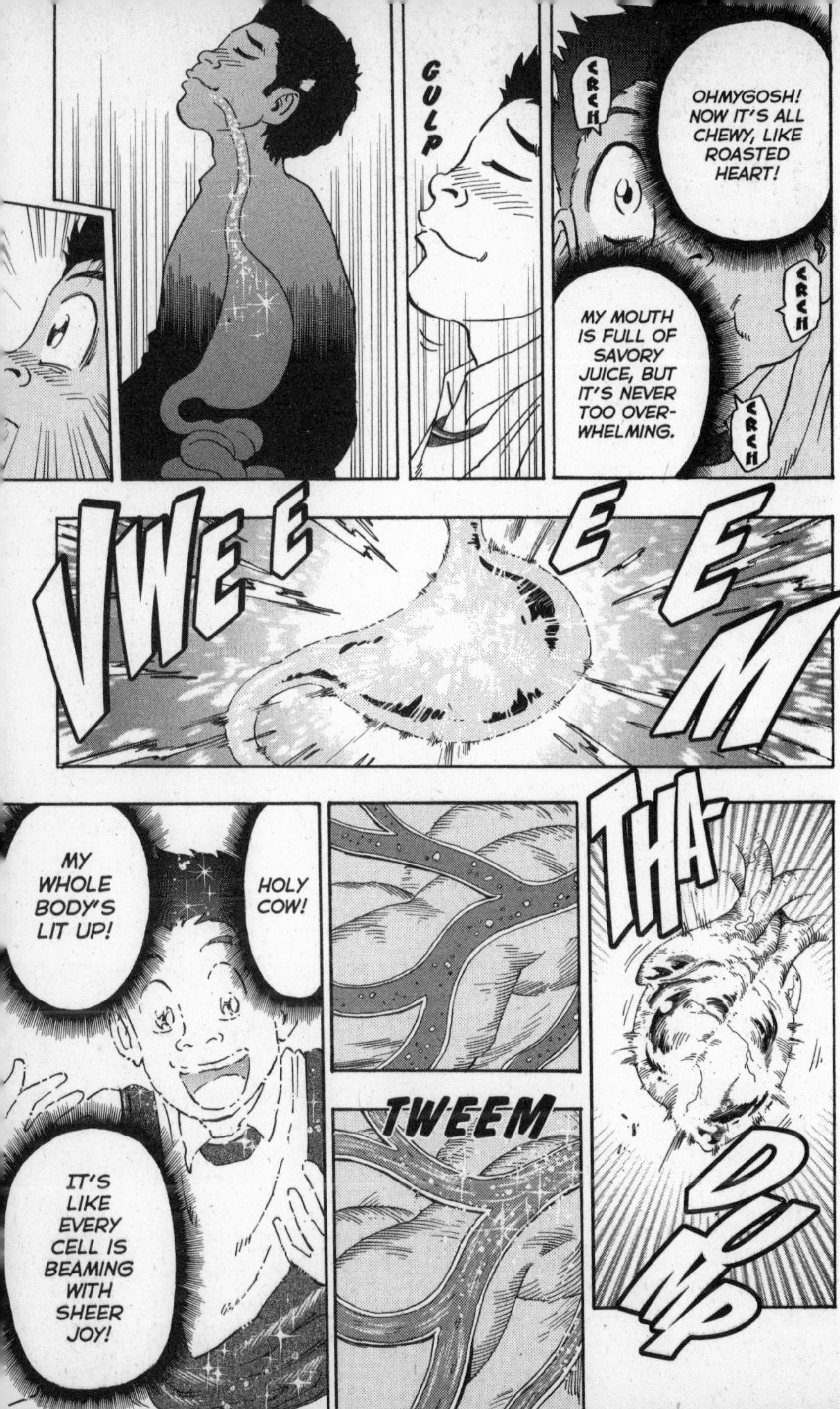
CRCH
OHMYGOSH! NOW IT'S ALL CHEWY, LIKE ROASTED HEART!
CRCH
MY MOUTH IS FULL OF SAVORY JUICE, BUT IT'S NEVER TOO OVER-WHELMING.
CRCH
GULP
VWEEEEM
THA-DUMP
TWEEM
HOLY COW!
MY WHOLE BODY'S LIT UP!
IT'S LIKE EVERY CELL IS BEAMING WITH SHEER JOY!

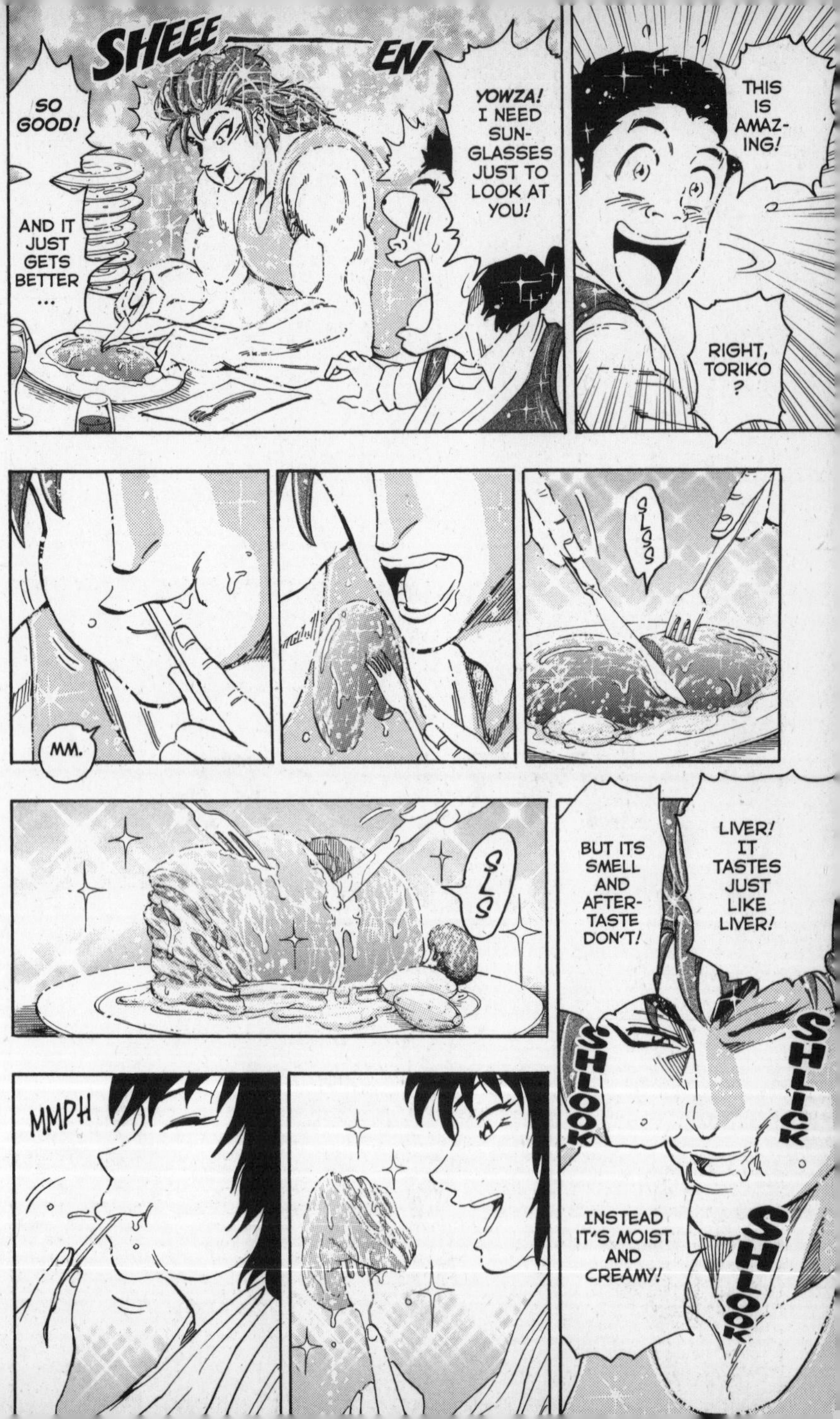
THIS IS AMAZING!
RIGHT, TORIKO?
SHEEE——EN
YOWZA! I NEED SUNGLASSES JUST TO LOOK AT YOU!
SO GOOD!
AND IT JUST GETS BETTER...
SLSS
MM.
LIVER! IT TASTES JUST LIKE LIVER!
BUT ITS SMELL AND AFTERTASTE DON'T!
SHLICK
SHLOOK
INSTEAD IT'S MOIST AND CREAMY!
SHLOOOK
SLS
MMPH

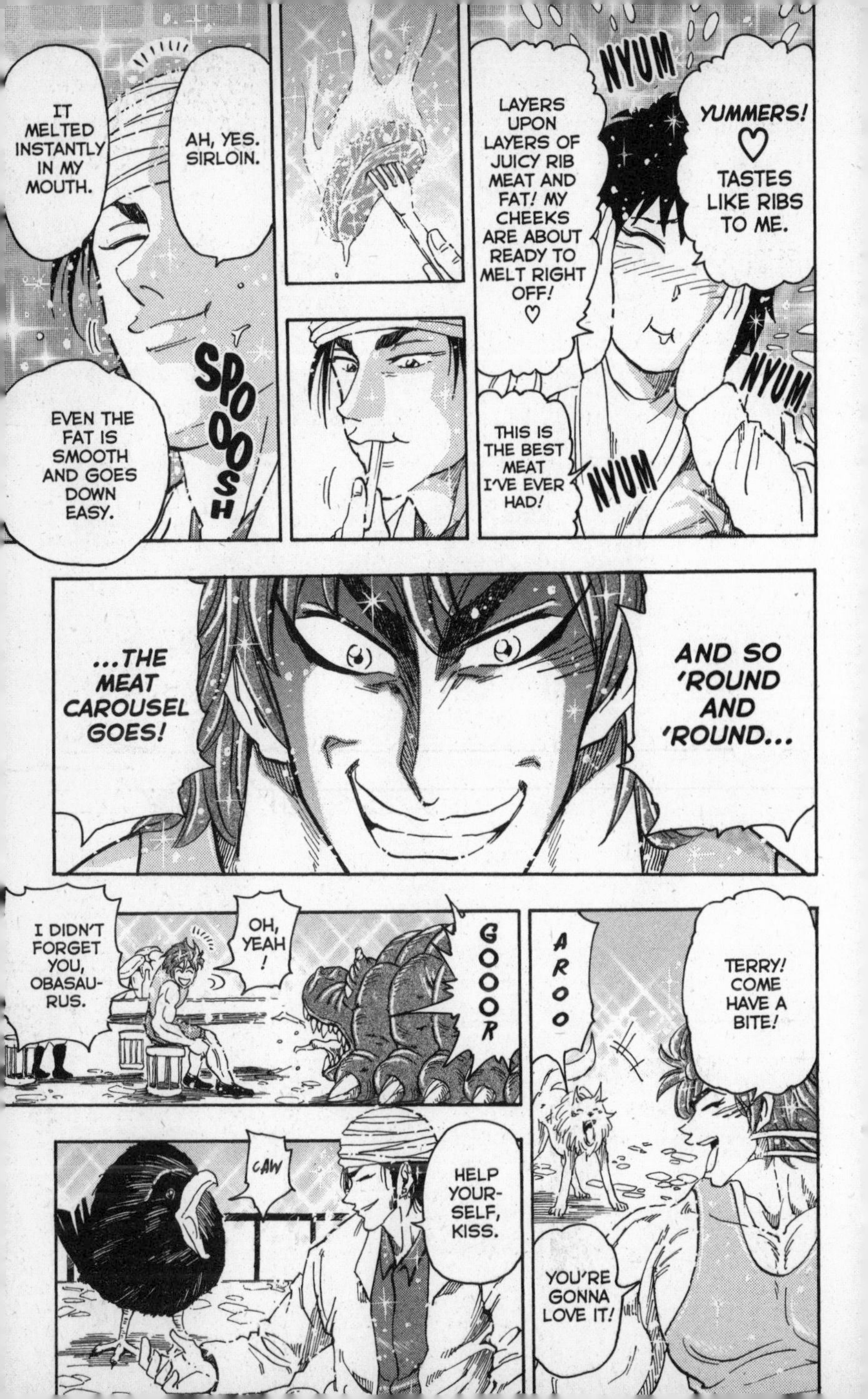
NYUM
YUMMERS! ♡ TASTES LIKE RIBS TO ME.
LAYERS UPON LAYERS OF JUICY RIB MEAT AND FAT! MY CHEEKS ARE ABOUT READY TO MELT RIGHT OFF! ♡
NYUM
THIS IS THE BEST MEAT I'VE EVER HAD!
NYUM
AH, YES. SIRLOIN.
IT MELTED INSTANTLY IN MY MOUTH.
SPOOOOSH
EVEN THE FAT IS SMOOTH AND GOES DOWN EASY.
AND SO 'ROUND AND 'ROUND...
...THE MEAT CAROUSEL GOES!
TERRY! COME HAVE A BITE!
AROO
YOU'RE GONNA LOVE IT!
GOOOOR
OH, YEAH!
I DIDN'T FORGET YOU, OBASAURUS.
HELP YOURSELF, KISS.
CAW

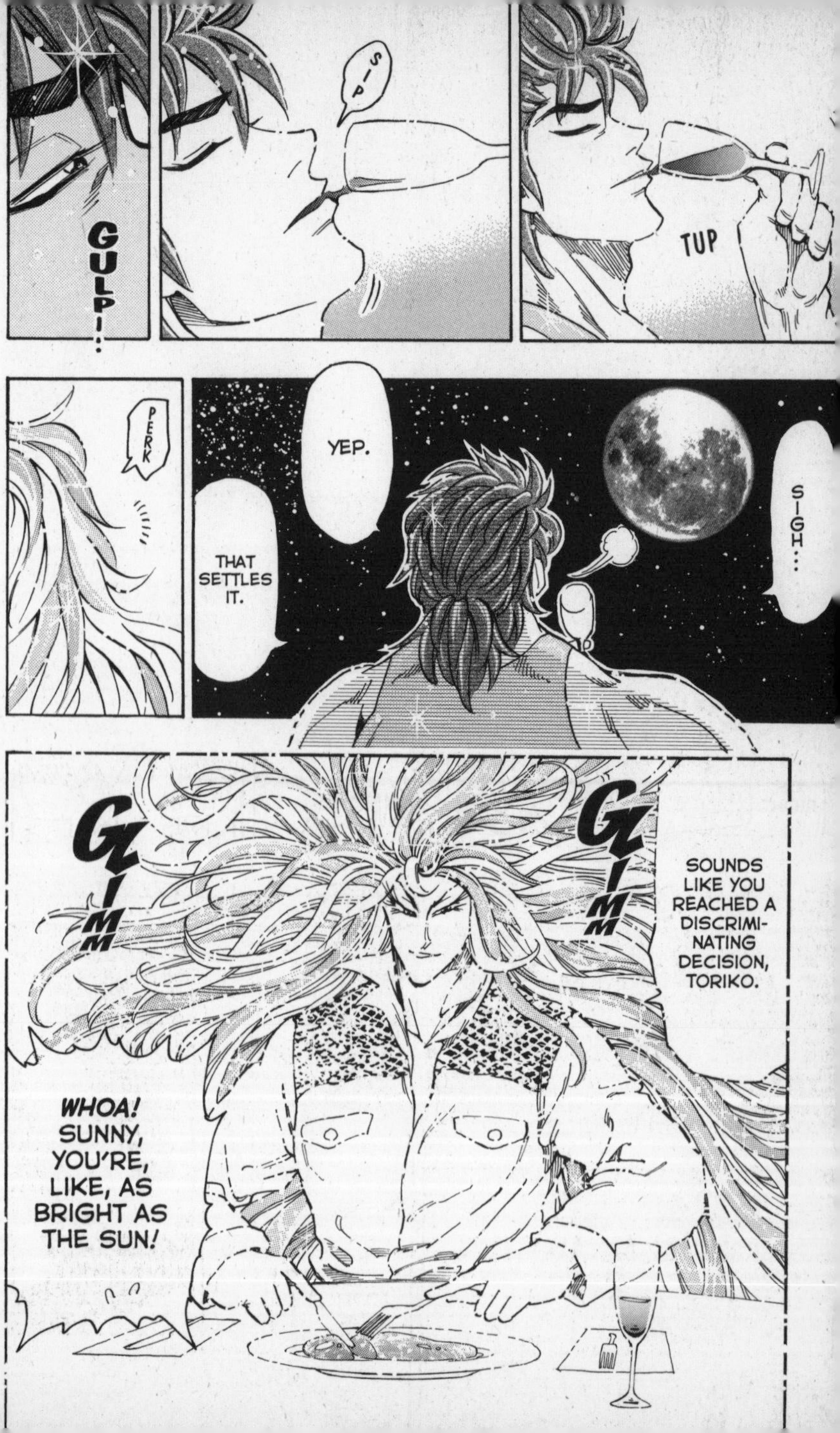

TUP
SIP
GULP!..
SIGH...
YEP.
THAT SETTLES IT.
PERK
GLIMM
SOUNDS LIKE YOU REACHED A DISCRIMI-NATING DECISION, TORIKO.
GLIMM
WHOA! SUNNY, YOU'RE, LIKE, AS BRIGHT AS THE SUN!

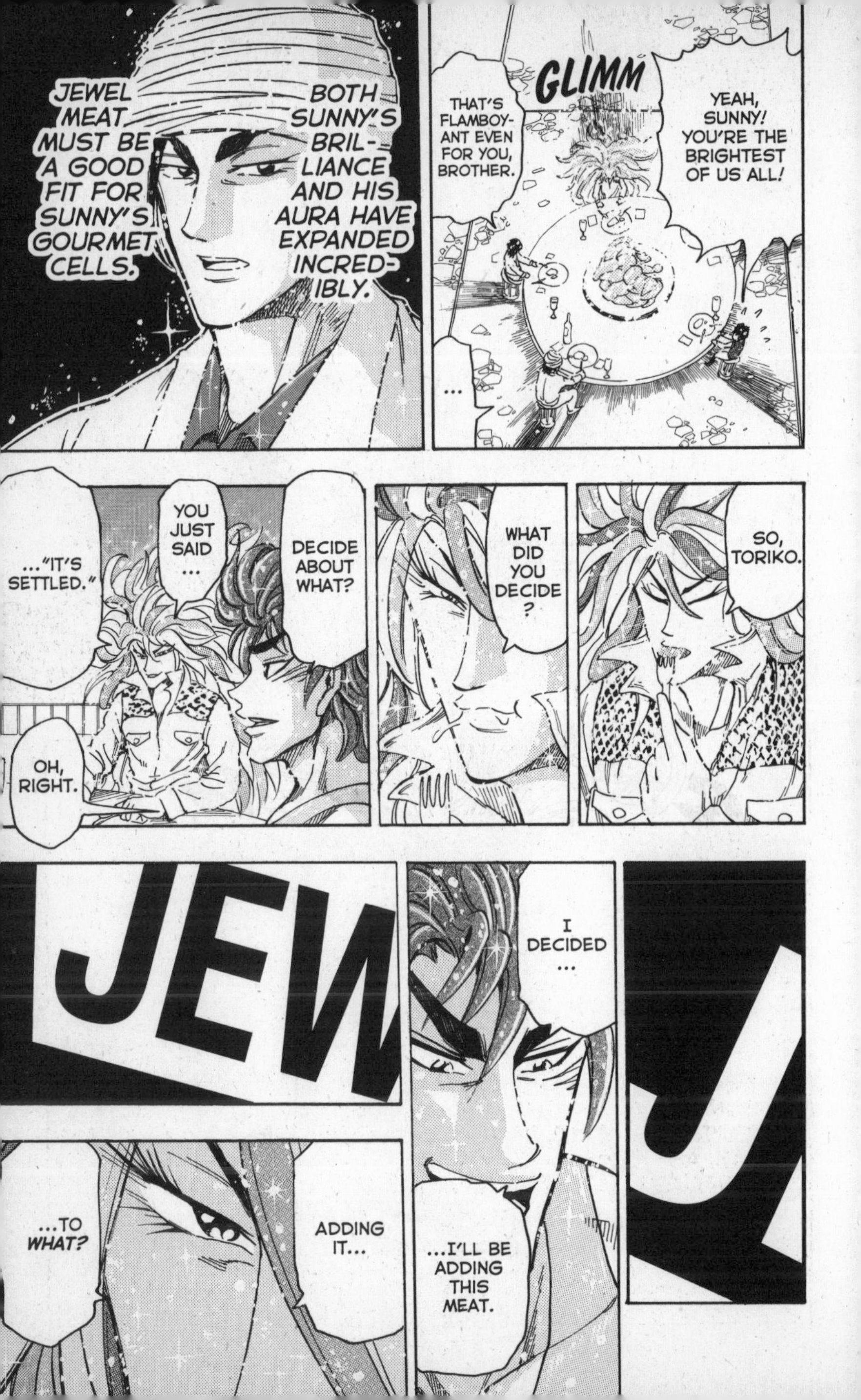
GLIMM
YEAH, SUNNY! YOU'RE THE BRIGHTEST OF US ALL!
THAT'S FLAMBOYANT EVEN FOR YOU, BROTHER.
...
BOTH SUNNY'S BRILLIANCE AND HIS AURA HAVE EXPANDED INCREDIBLY.
JEWEL MEAT MUST BE A GOOD FIT FOR SUNNY'S GOURMET CELLS.
SO, TORIKO.
WHAT DID YOU DECIDE?
DECIDE ABOUT WHAT?
YOU JUST SAID...
..."IT'S SETTLED."
OH, RIGHT.
J
I DECIDED...
...I'LL BE ADDING THIS MEAT.
JEW
ADDING IT...
...TO WHAT?

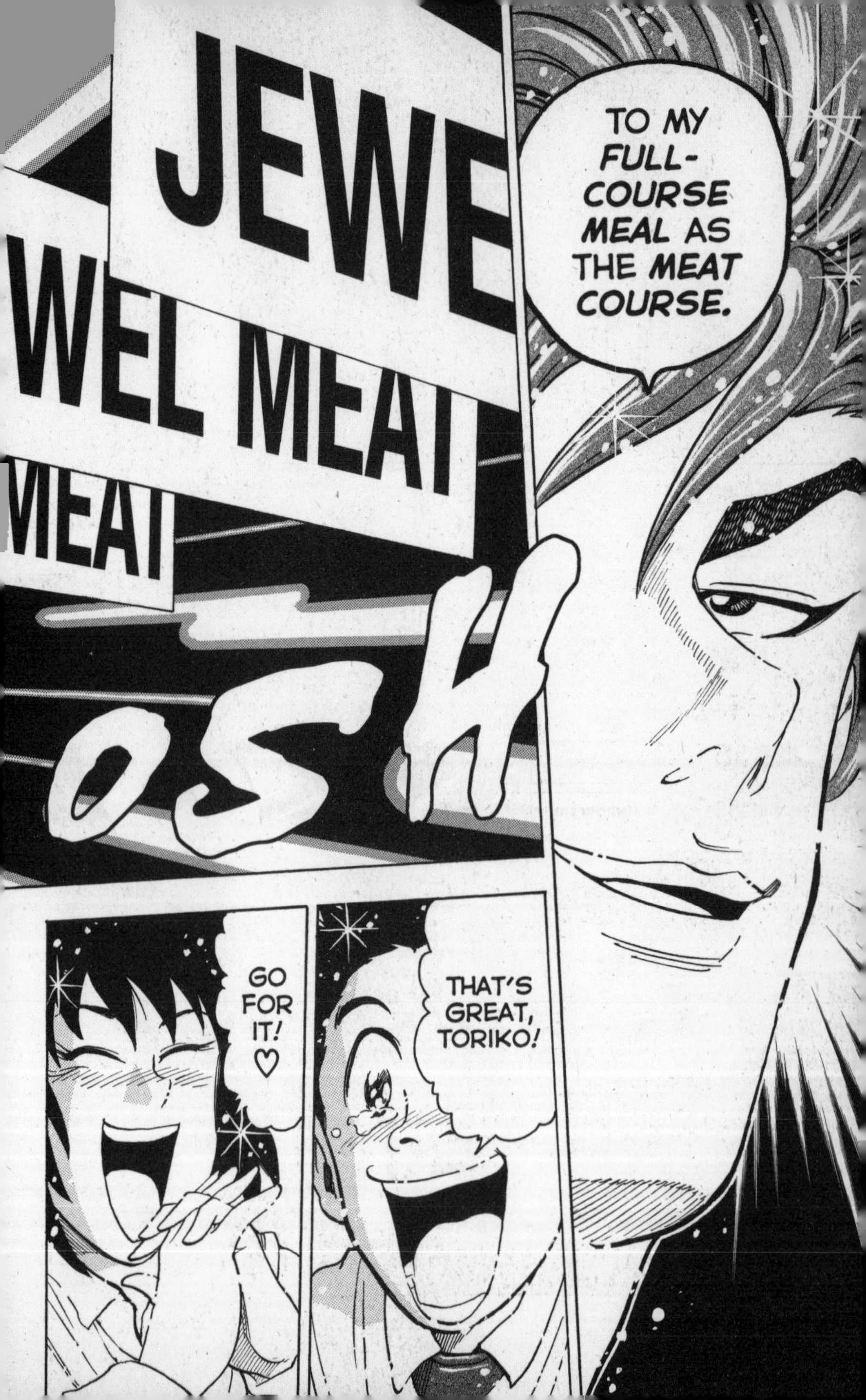
TO MY FULL-COURSE MEAL AS THE MEAT COURSE.
JEWE
WEL MEAT
MEAT
OSH
THAT'S GREAT, TORIKO!
GO FOR IT! ♡

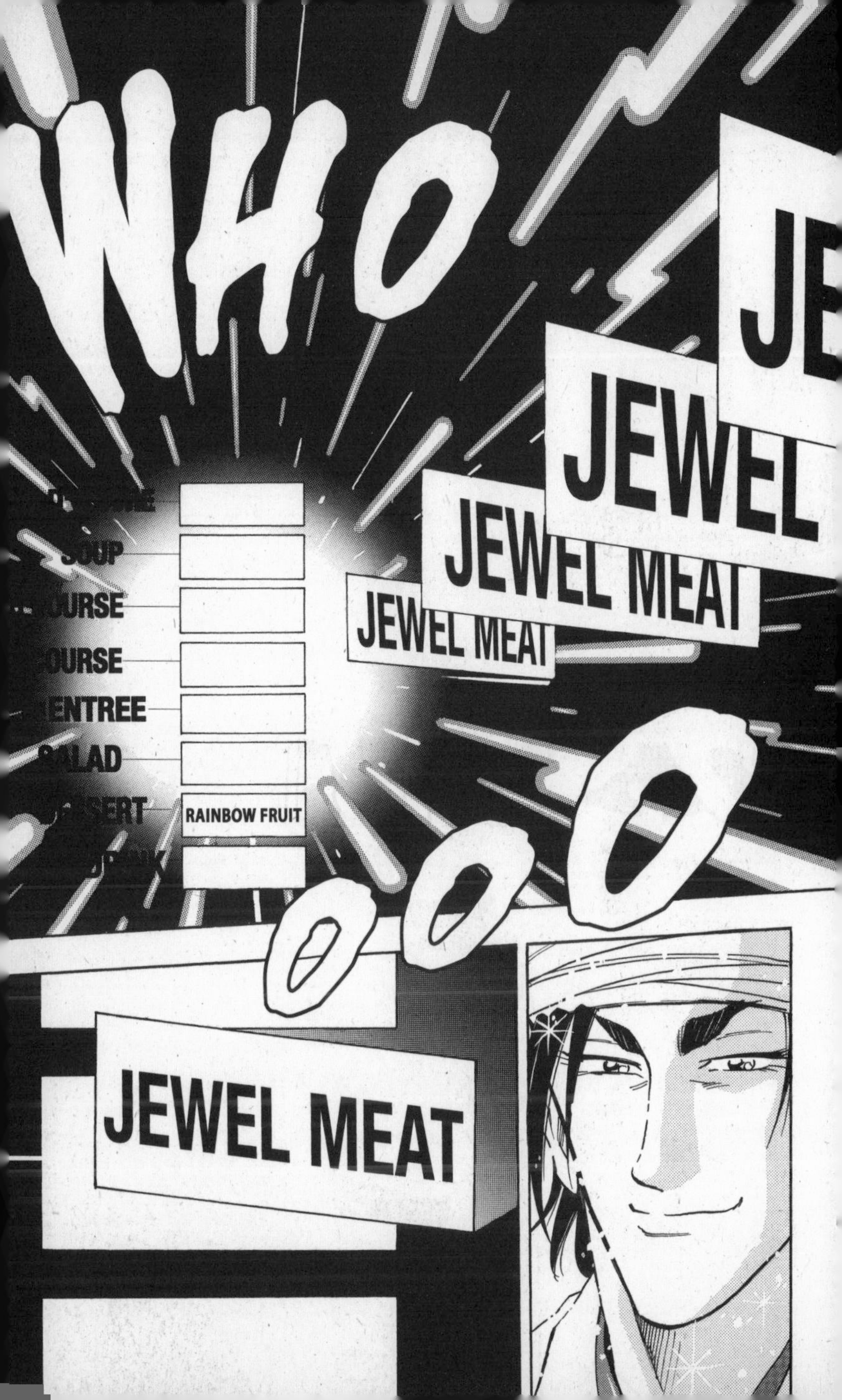
JEWEL MEAT
JEWEL MEAT
SOUP
ENTREE
RAINBOW FRUIT
WHOOOO
JEWEL MEAT

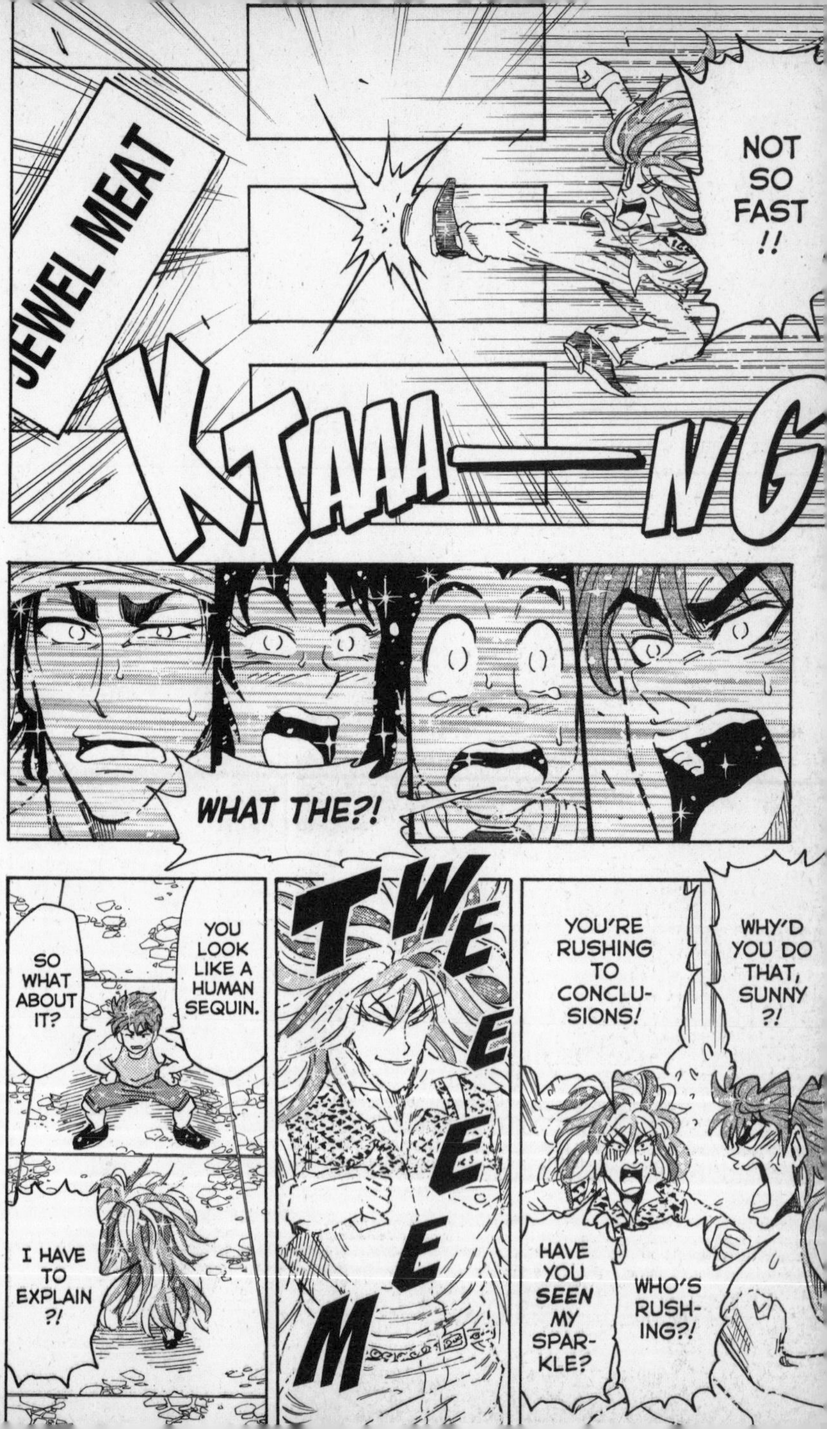
NOT SO FAST!!
JEWEL MEAT
KTAAA—NG
WHAT THE?!
WHY'D YOU DO THAT, SUNNY?!
YOU'RE RUSHING TO CONCLUSIONS!
WHO'S RUSHING?!
HAVE YOU SEEN MY SPARKLE?
TWEEEEM
YOU LOOK LIKE A HUMAN SEQUIN.
SO WHAT ABOUT IT?
I HAVE TO EXPLAIN?!

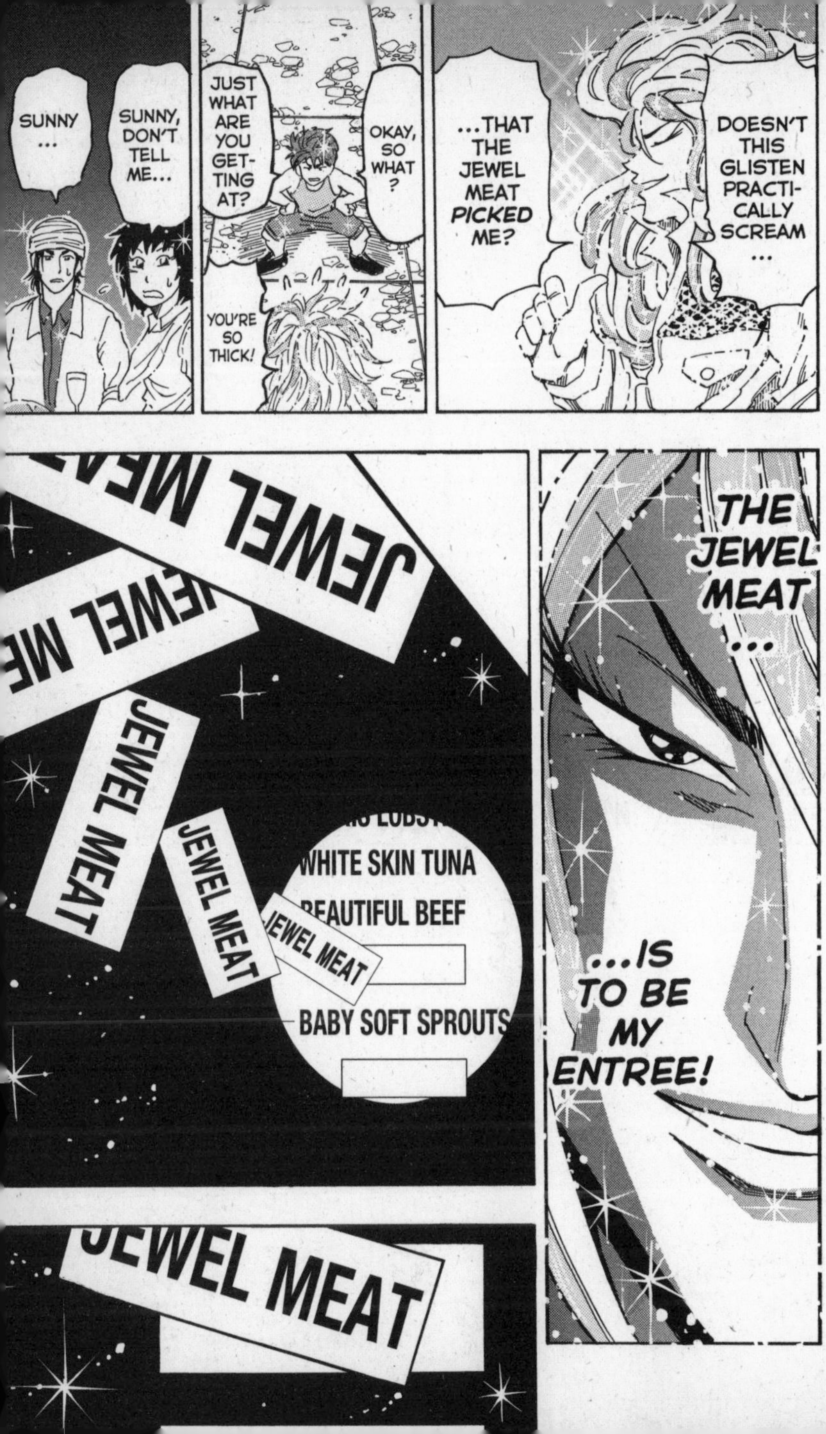
DOESN'T THIS GLISTEN PRACTICALLY SCREAM ...
...THAT THE JEWEL MEAT *PICKED* ME?
OKAY, SO WHAT?
JUST WHAT ARE YOU GETTING AT?
YOU'RE SO THICK!
SUNNY, DON'T TELL ME...
SUNNY ...
THE JEWEL MEAT ...
...IS TO BE MY ENTREE!
JEWEL MEAT
JEWEL MEAT
JEWEL MEAT
WHITE SKIN TUNA
BEAUTIFUL BEEF
JEWEL MEAT
BABY SOFT SPROUTS
JEWEL MEAT

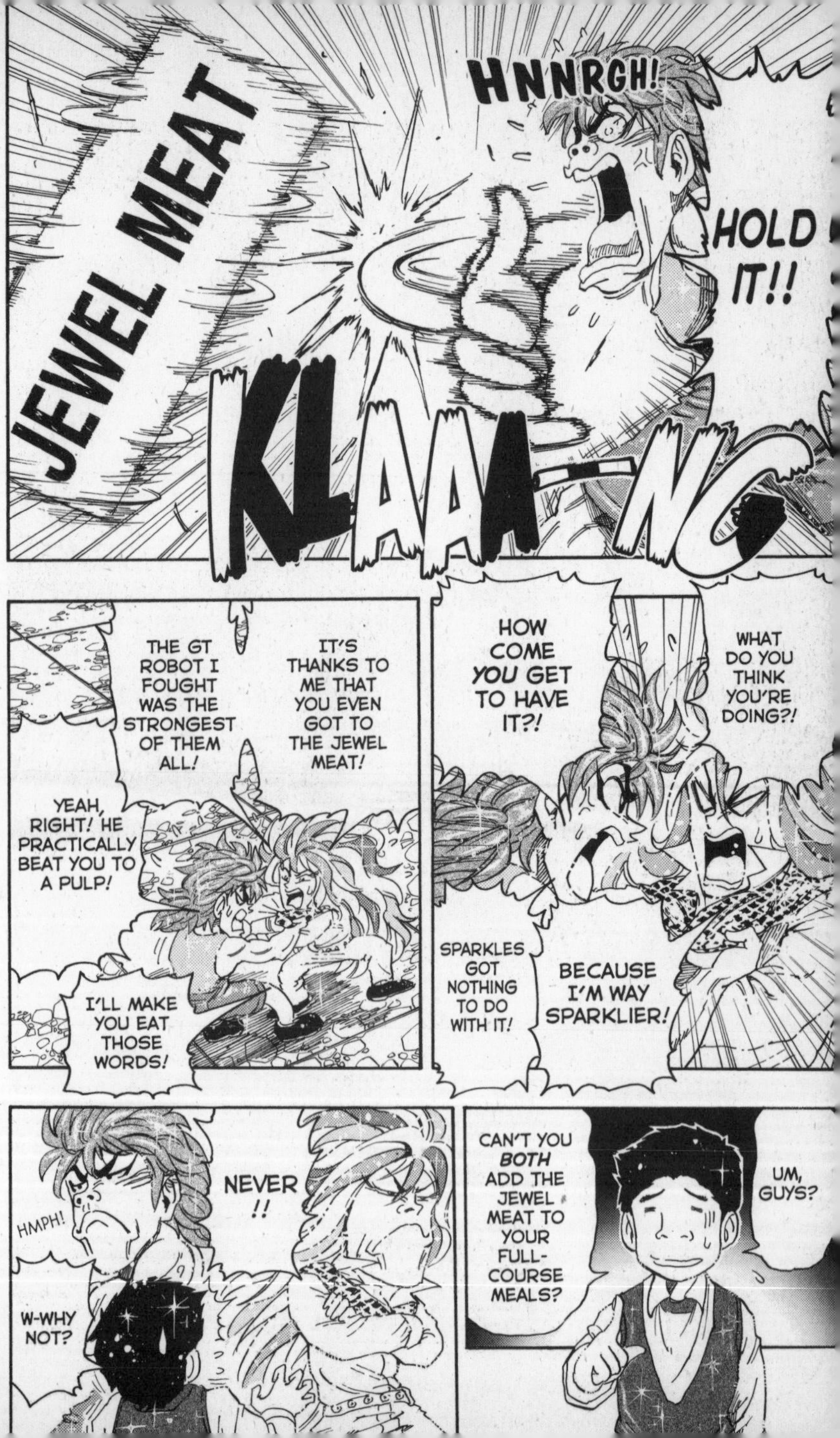
HNNRGH!
HOLD IT!!
JEWEL MEAT
KLAAA-NG
WHAT DO YOU THINK YOU'RE DOING?!
HOW COME YOU GET TO HAVE IT?!
BECAUSE I'M WAY SPARKLIER!
SPARKLES GOT NOTHING TO DO WITH IT!
IT'S THANKS TO ME THAT YOU EVEN GOT TO THE JEWEL MEAT!
THE GT ROBOT I FOUGHT WAS THE STRONGEST OF THEM ALL!
YEAH, RIGHT! HE PRACTICALLY BEAT YOU TO A PULP!
I'LL MAKE YOU EAT THOSE WORDS!
UM, GUYS?
CAN'T YOU BOTH ADD THE JEWEL MEAT TO YOUR FULL-COURSE MEALS?
NEVER!!
HMPH!
W-WHY NOT?

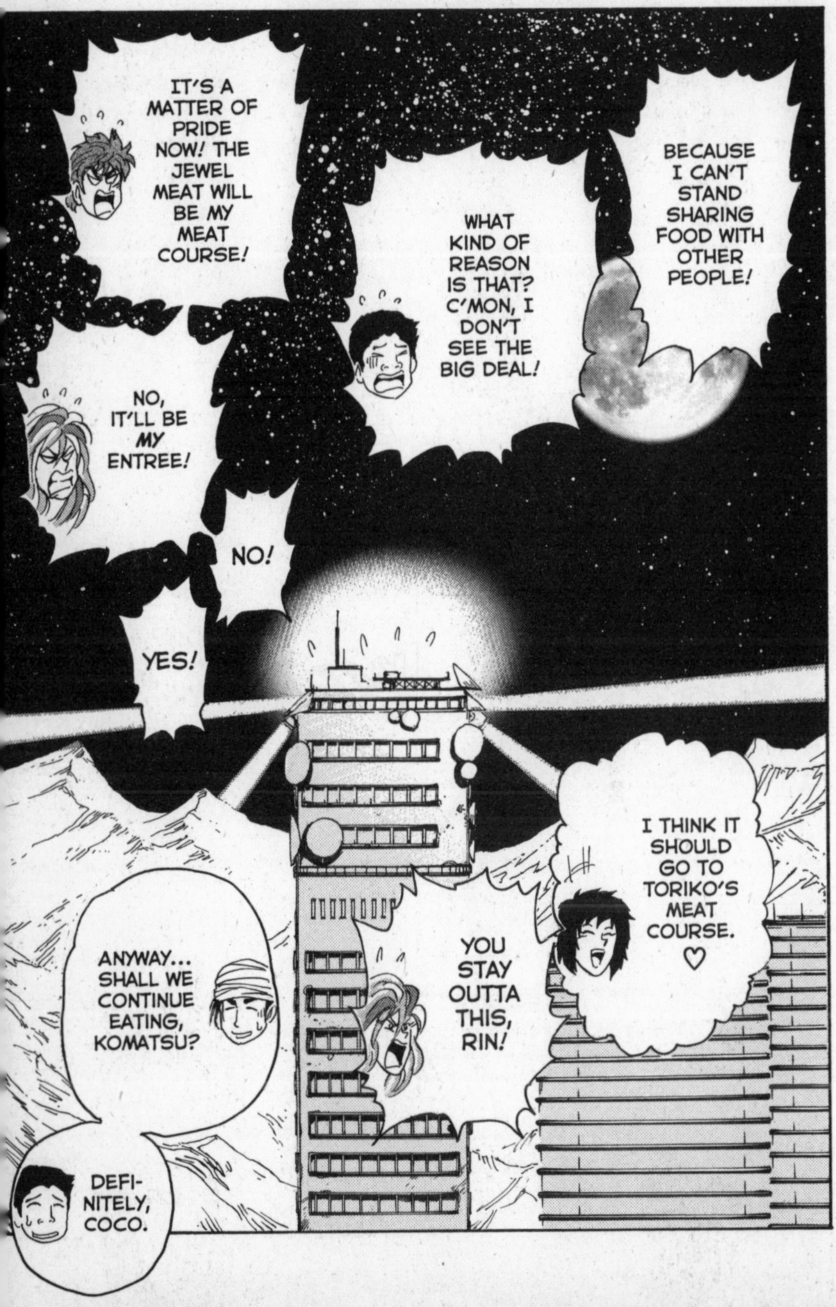
BECAUSE I CAN'T STAND SHARING FOOD WITH OTHER PEOPLE!
WHAT KIND OF REASON IS THAT? C'MON, I DON'T SEE THE BIG DEAL!
IT'S A MATTER OF PRIDE NOW! THE JEWEL MEAT WILL BE MY MEAT COURSE!
NO, IT'LL BE *MY* ENTREE!
NO!
YES!
I THINK IT SHOULD GO TO TORIKO'S MEAT COURSE. ♡
YOU STAY OUTTA THIS, RIN!
ANYWAY... SHALL WE CONTINUE EATING, KOMATSU?
DEFI-NITELY, COCO.

TORIKO

GOURMET CHECKLIST

Vol. 039

BEER LOBSTER
(CRUSTACEAN)

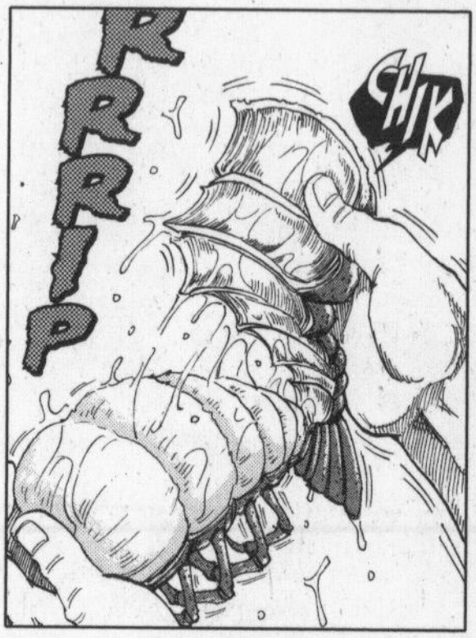
CHIK
RRRIP

CAPTURE LEVEL: LESS THAN 1

HABITAT: WARM OCEANS

LENGTH: 55 CM

HEIGHT: ---

WEIGHT: 2 KG

PRICE: 90,000 YEN EACH

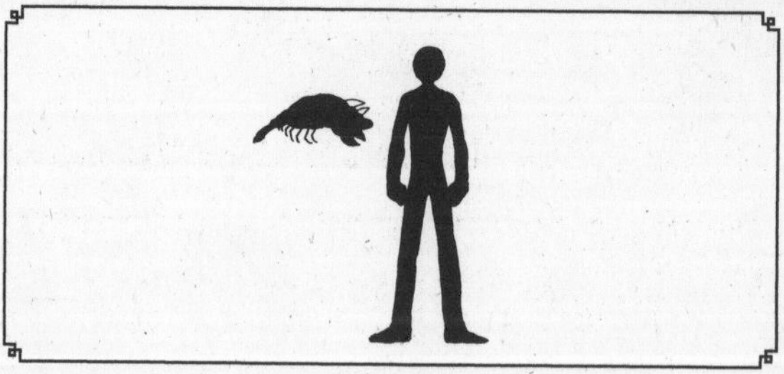

SCALE

A DECAPOD THAT LIVES IN WARM OCEAN WATERS AND IS CLOSELY RELATED TO BOTH THE SPINY LOBSTER AND JAPANESE LOBSTER. ITS SALTY FLAVOR IS WHAT GIVES THIS FOOD ITS NAME, SEEING AS HOW A SALTY SNACK ALWAYS PREPARES THE PALATE FOR A COLD BEER.

GOURMET 55: TERRY'S TASTES!!

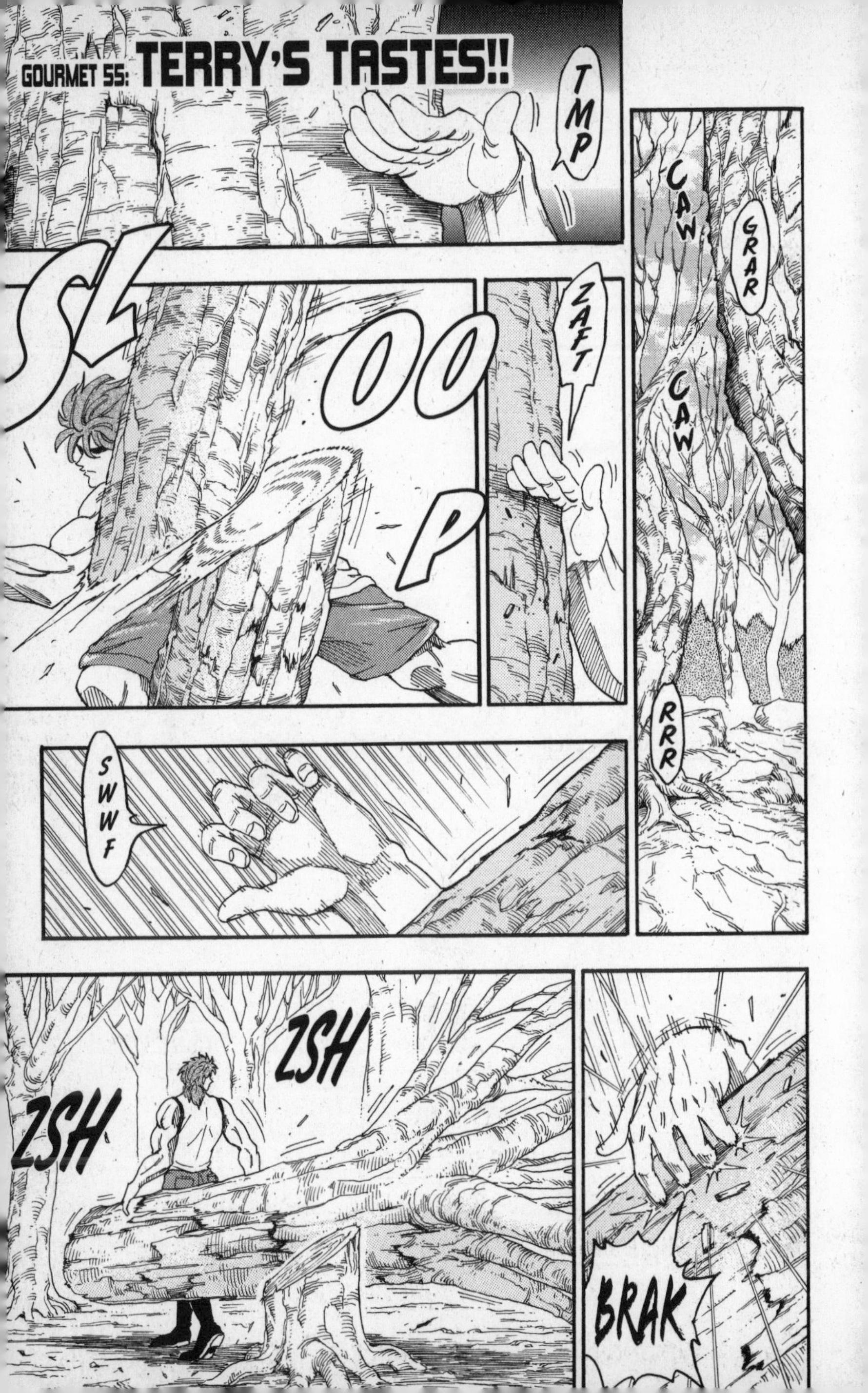
CAW
GRAR
CAW
RRR
TMP
ZAFT
SLOOP
SWWF
BRAK
ZSH
ZSH

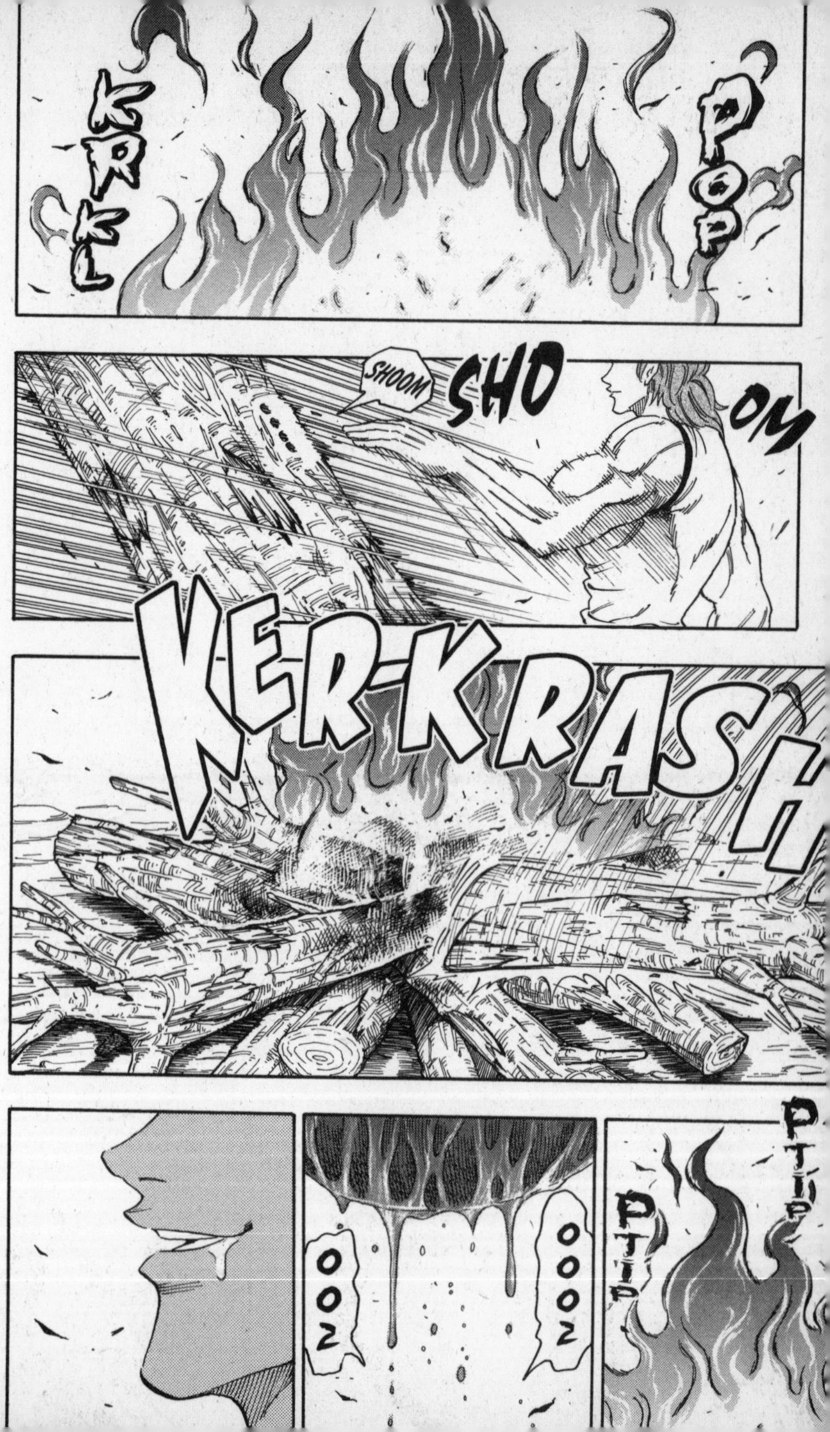
POP
KRKL
SHOOM
SHO OM
KER-KRASH
PTIP
PTIP
ZOOO
ZOO

GOURMET 55: TERRY'S TASTES!!

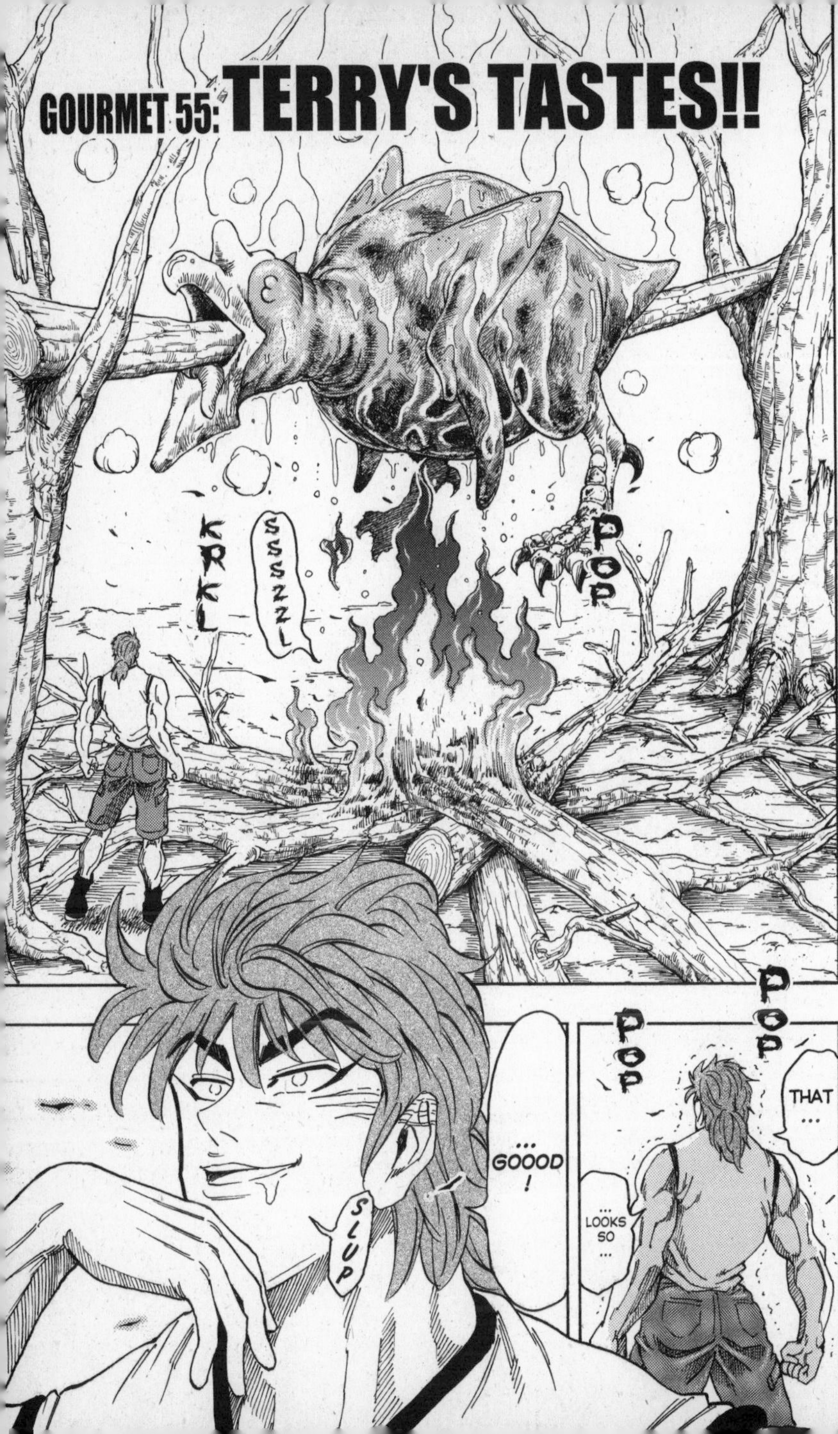
KRKL
SSSZZZL
POP POP
POP POP
POP POP
THAT ...
... LOOKS SO ...
... GOOOD!
SLUP

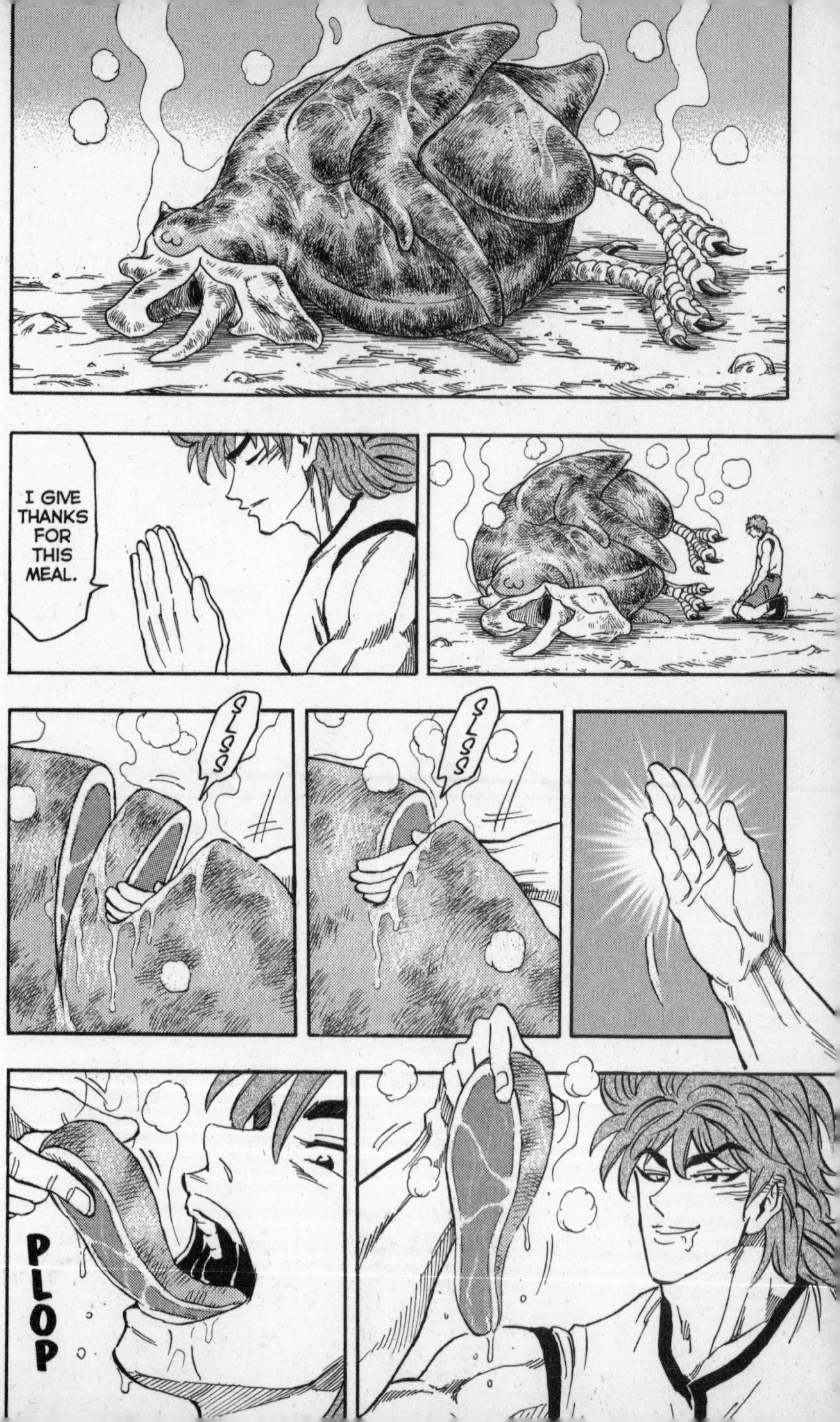
I GIVE THANKS FOR THIS MEAL.
SLSSS
SLSSS
PLOP

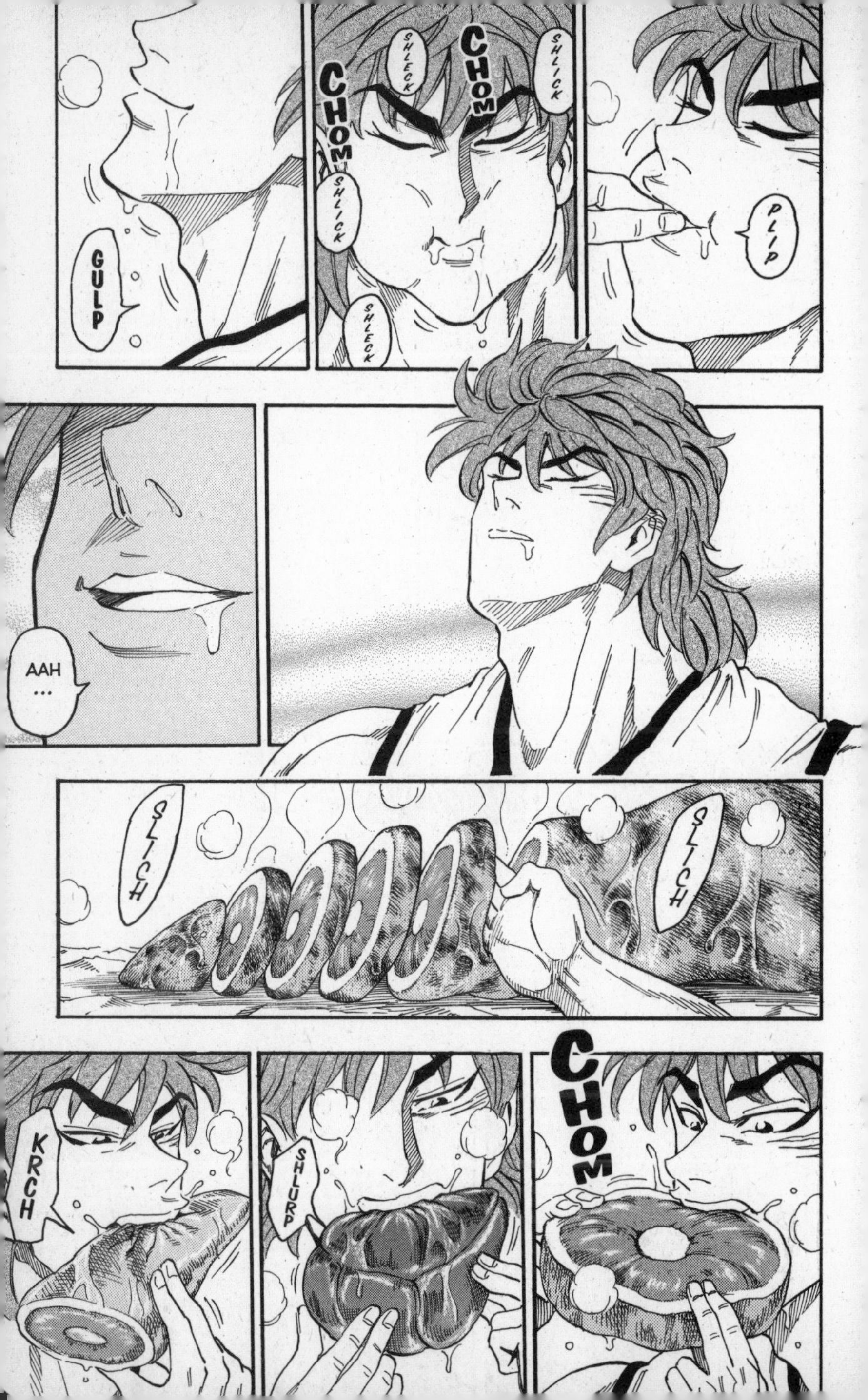
PLIP
SHLICK
CHOM
SHLICK
CHOM
SHLICK
SHLECK
GULP
AAH ...
SLICH
SLICH
CHOM
SHLURP
KRCH

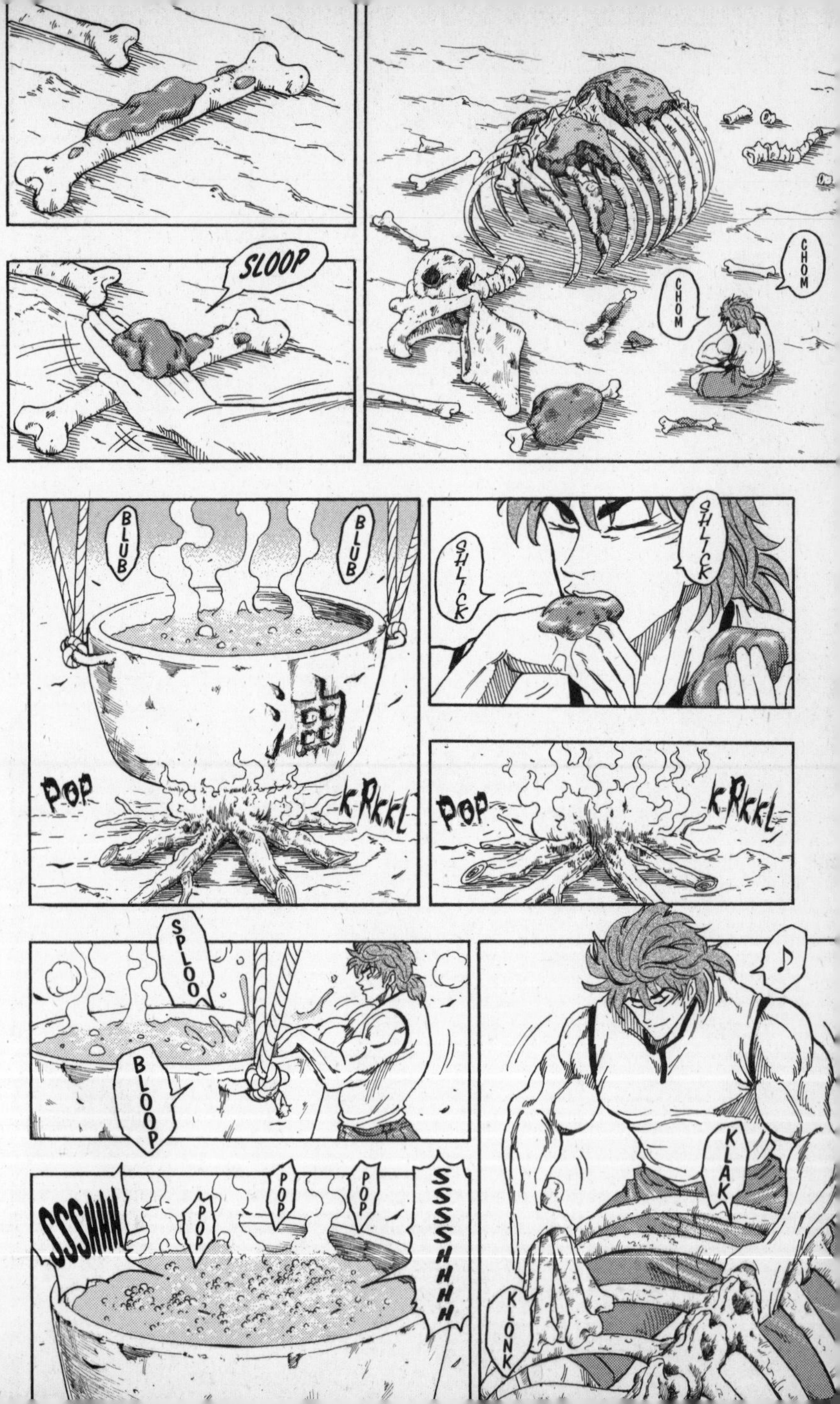
CHOM
CHOM
SLOOP
SHLICK
SHLICK
KRKKL
POP
BLUB
BLUB
KRKKL
POP
♪
KLAK
KLONK
SPLOO
BLOOOP
SSSHHHH
POP
POP
POP
SSSHHH

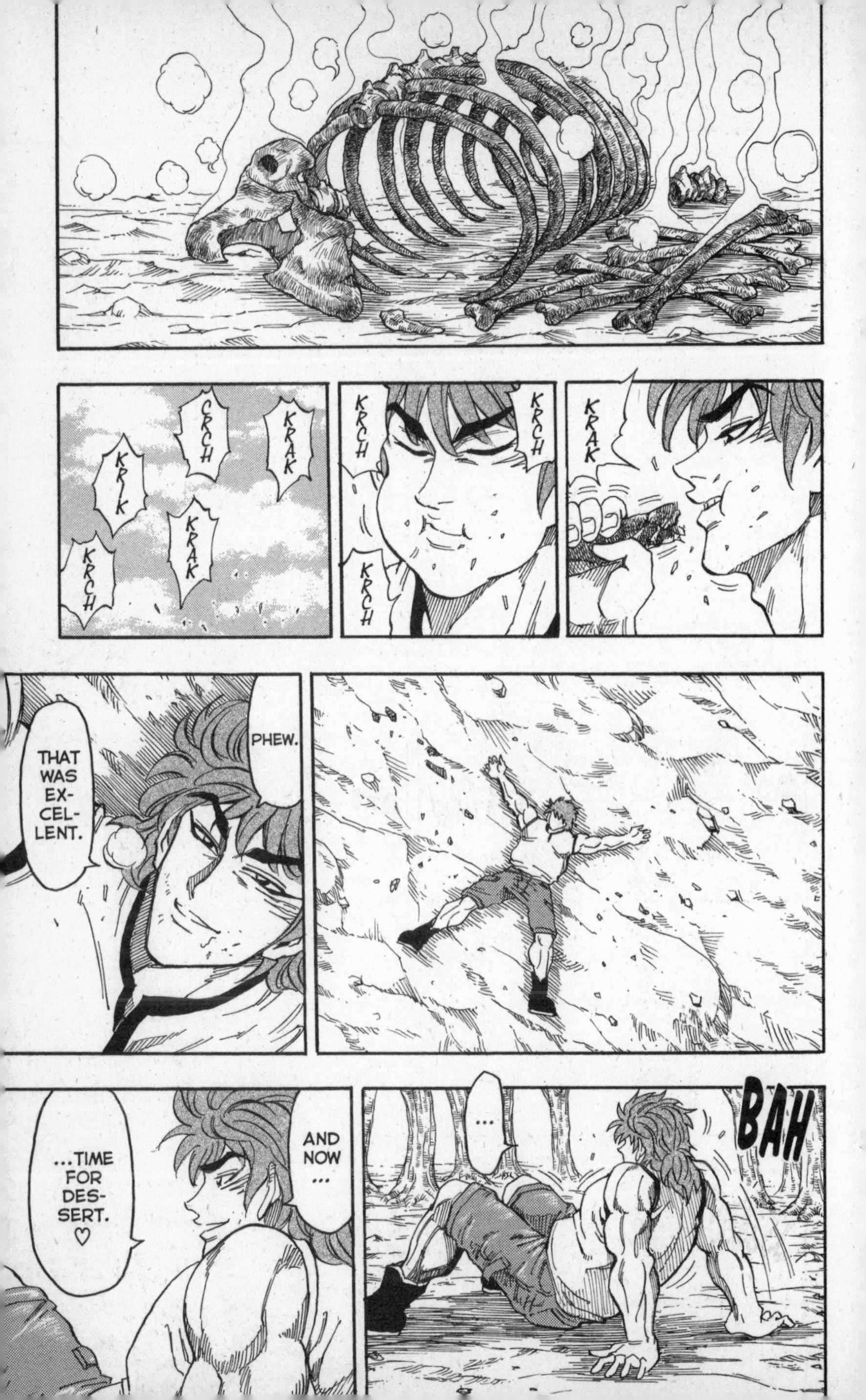

KRAK
KRCH
KRCH
KRCH
KRAK
CRCH
KRAK
KRIK
KRCH
PHEW.
THAT WAS EXCELLENT.
BAH
...
AND NOW...
...TIME FOR DESSERT. ♡

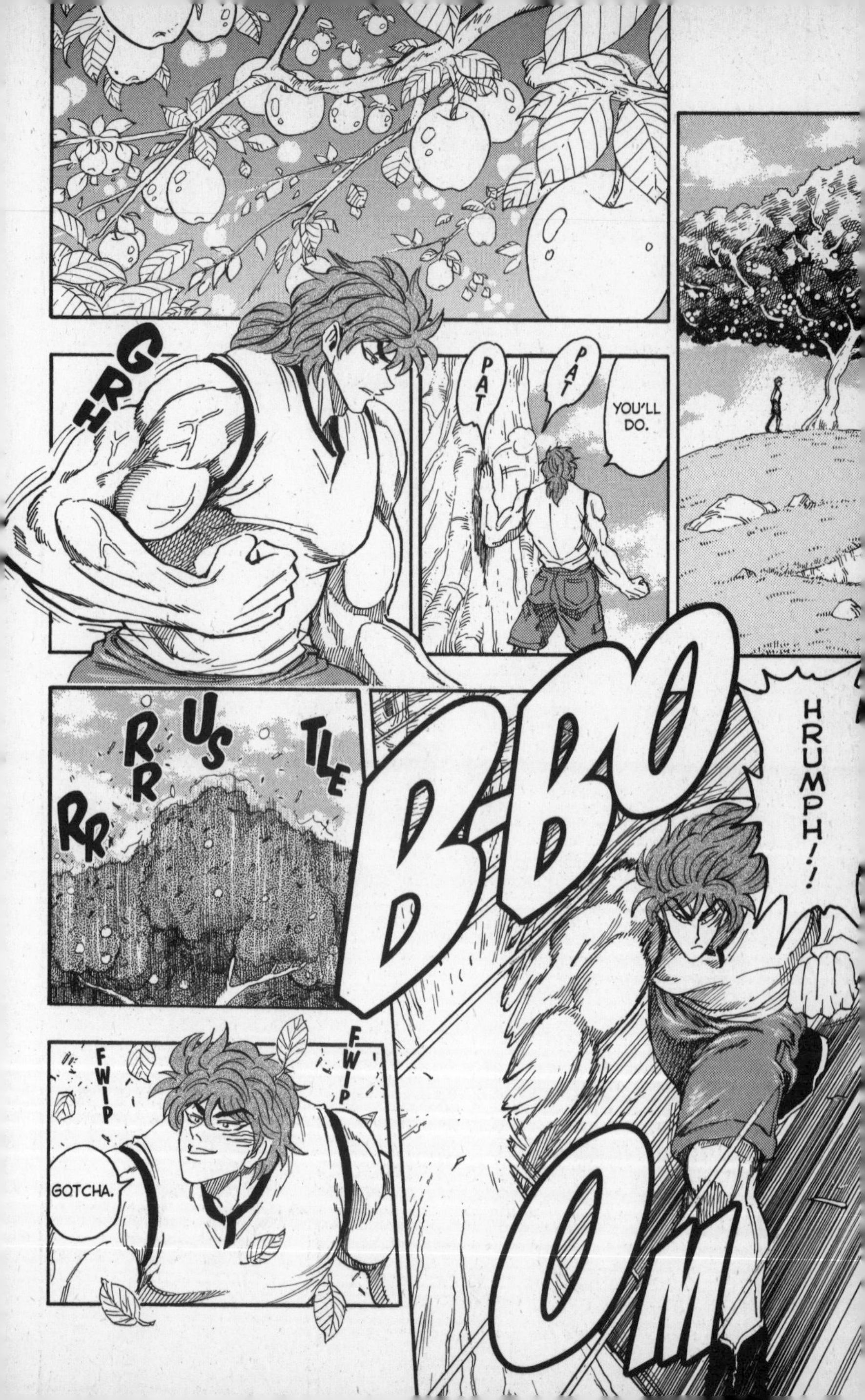
PAT
PAT
YOU'LL DO.
GRH
HRUMPH!!
B-BOOM
RRRUSTLE
FWIP
FWIP
GOTCHA.

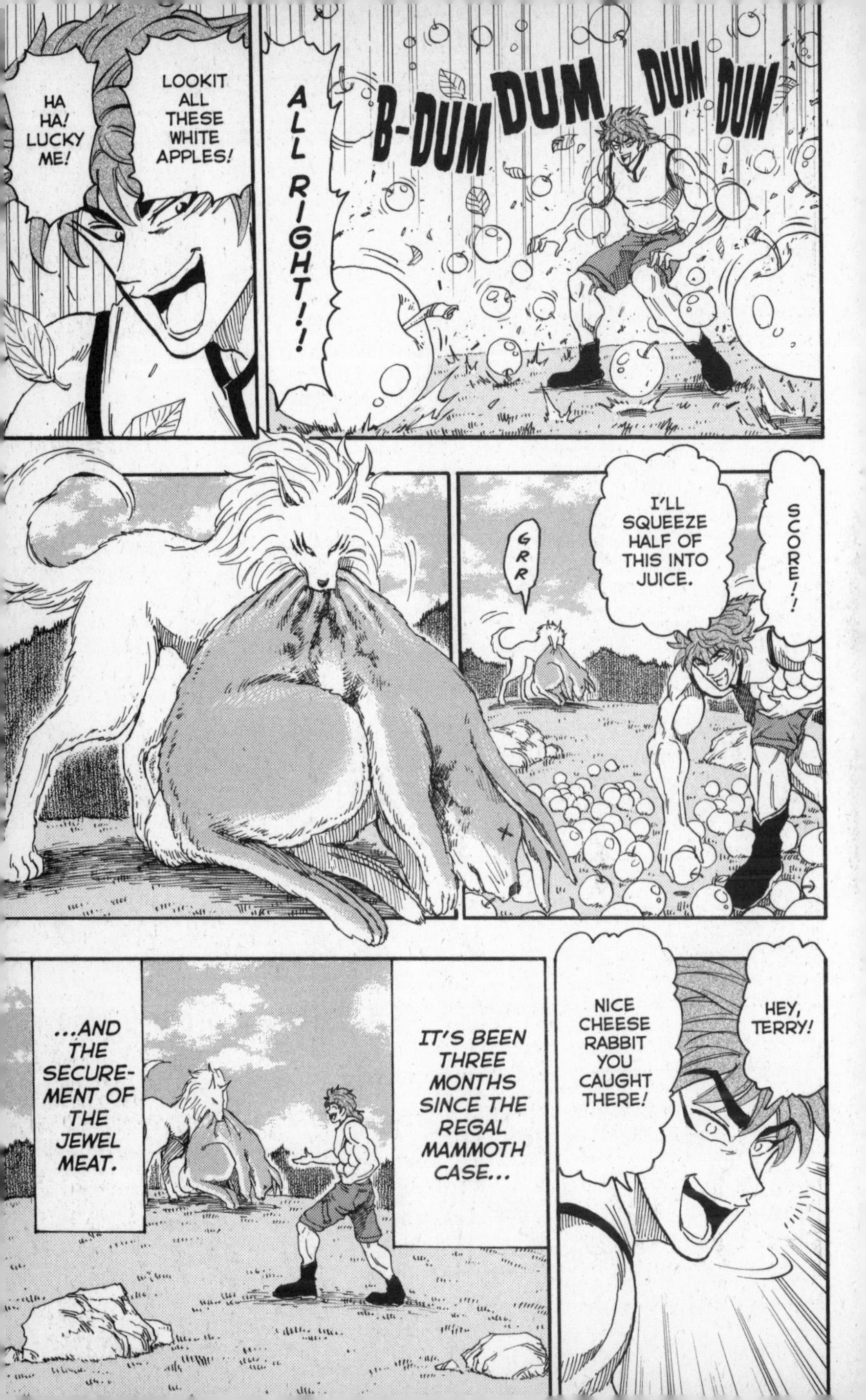
B-DUM DUM DUM DUM
ALL RIGHT!!
LOOKIT ALL THESE WHITE APPLES!
HA HA! LUCKY ME!
SCORE!!
I'LL SQUEEZE HALF OF THIS INTO JUICE.
GRR
HEY, TERRY!
NICE CHEESE RABBIT YOU CAUGHT THERE!
IT'S BEEN THREE MONTHS SINCE THE REGAL MAMMOTH CASE...
...AND THE SECUREMENT OF THE JEWEL MEAT.

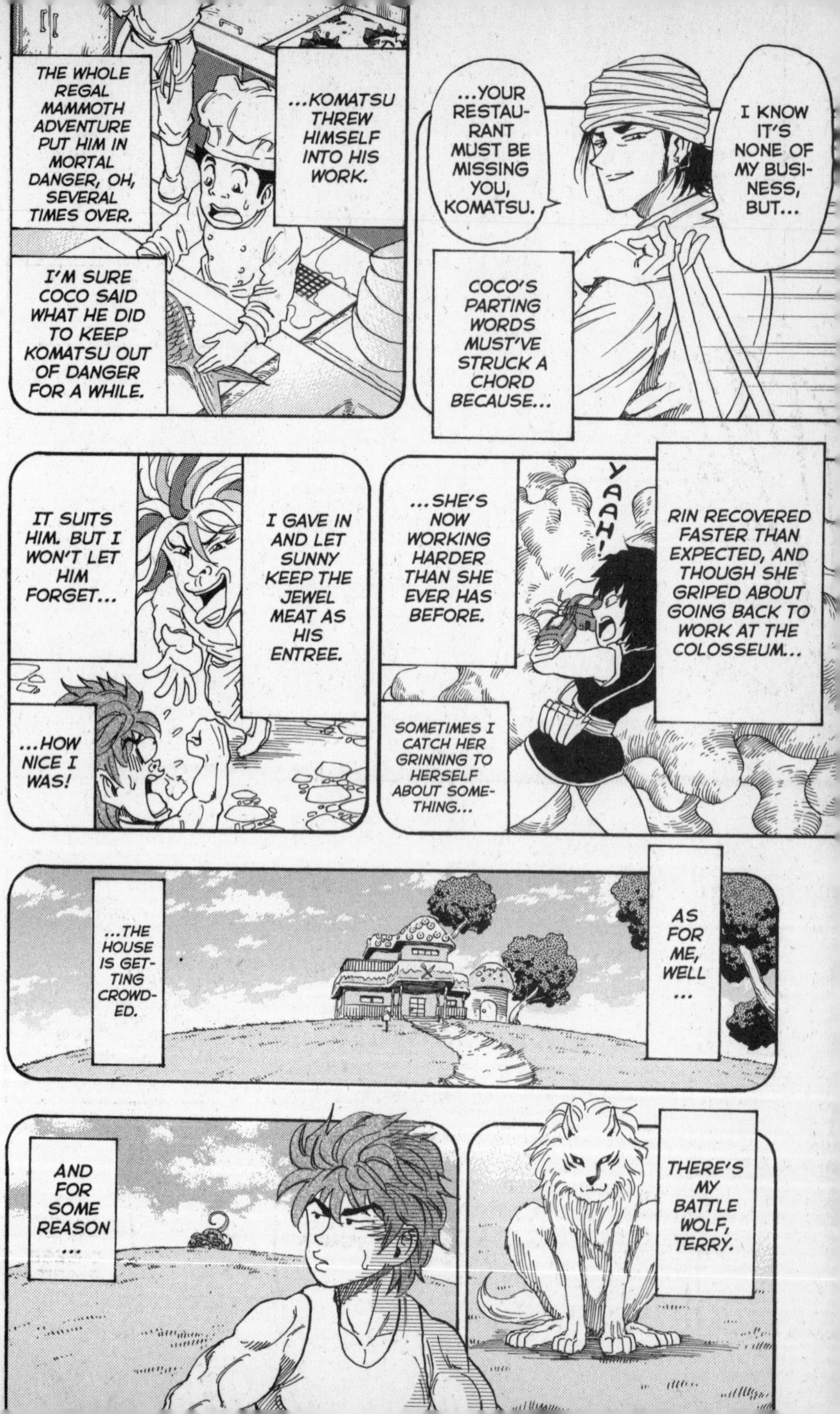
I KNOW IT'S NONE OF MY BUSINESS, BUT...
...YOUR RESTAURANT MUST BE MISSING YOU, KOMATSU.
COCO'S PARTING WORDS MUST'VE STRUCK A CHORD BECAUSE...
...KOMATSU THREW HIMSELF INTO HIS WORK.
THE WHOLE REGAL MAMMOTH ADVENTURE PUT HIM IN MORTAL DANGER, OH, SEVERAL TIMES OVER.
I'M SURE COCO SAID WHAT HE DID TO KEEP KOMATSU OUT OF DANGER FOR A WHILE.
RIN RECOVERED FASTER THAN EXPECTED, AND THOUGH SHE GRIPED ABOUT GOING BACK TO WORK AT THE COLOSSEUM...
YAAH!
...SHE'S NOW WORKING HARDER THAN SHE EVER HAS BEFORE.
SOMETIMES I CATCH HER GRINNING TO HERSELF ABOUT SOMETHING...
I GAVE IN AND LET SUNNY KEEP THE JEWEL MEAT AS HIS ENTREE.
IT SUITS HIM. BUT I WON'T LET HIM FORGET...
...HOW NICE I WAS!
AS FOR ME, WELL...
...THE HOUSE IS GETTING CROWDED.
THERE'S MY BATTLE WOLF, TERRY.
AND FOR SOME REASON...

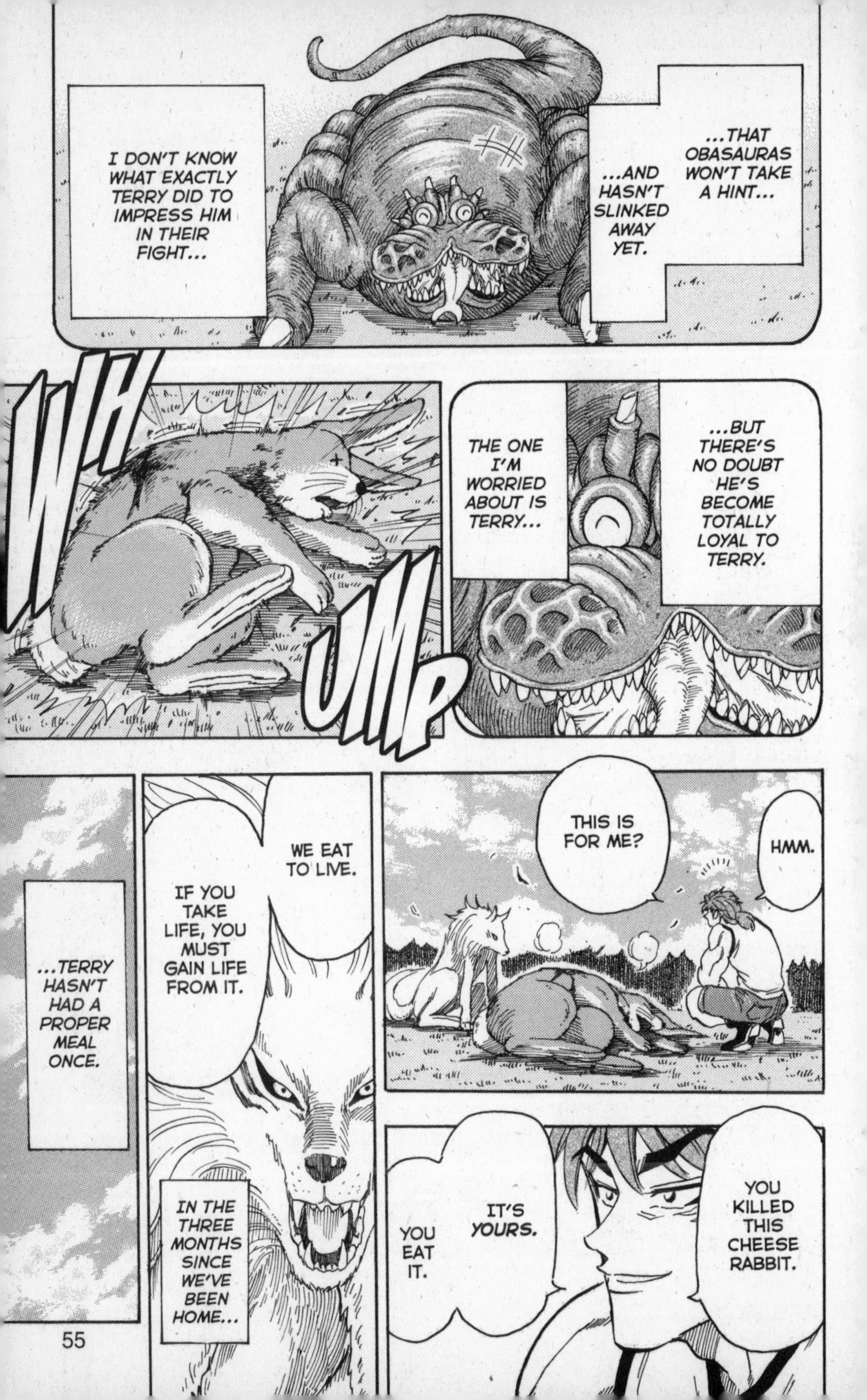
...THAT OBASAURAS WON'T TAKE A HINT...
...AND HASN'T SLINKED AWAY YET.
I DON'T KNOW WHAT EXACTLY TERRY DID TO IMPRESS HIM IN THEIR FIGHT...
...BUT THERE'S NO DOUBT HE'S BECOME TOTALLY LOYAL TO TERRY.
THE ONE I'M WORRIED ABOUT IS TERRY...
WHUMP
HMM.
THIS IS FOR ME?
YOU KILLED THIS CHEESE RABBIT.
IT'S YOURS.
YOU EAT IT.
WE EAT TO LIVE.
IF YOU TAKE LIFE, YOU MUST GAIN LIFE FROM IT.
IN THE THREE MONTHS SINCE WE'VE BEEN HOME...
...TERRY HASN'T HAD A PROPER MEAL ONCE.

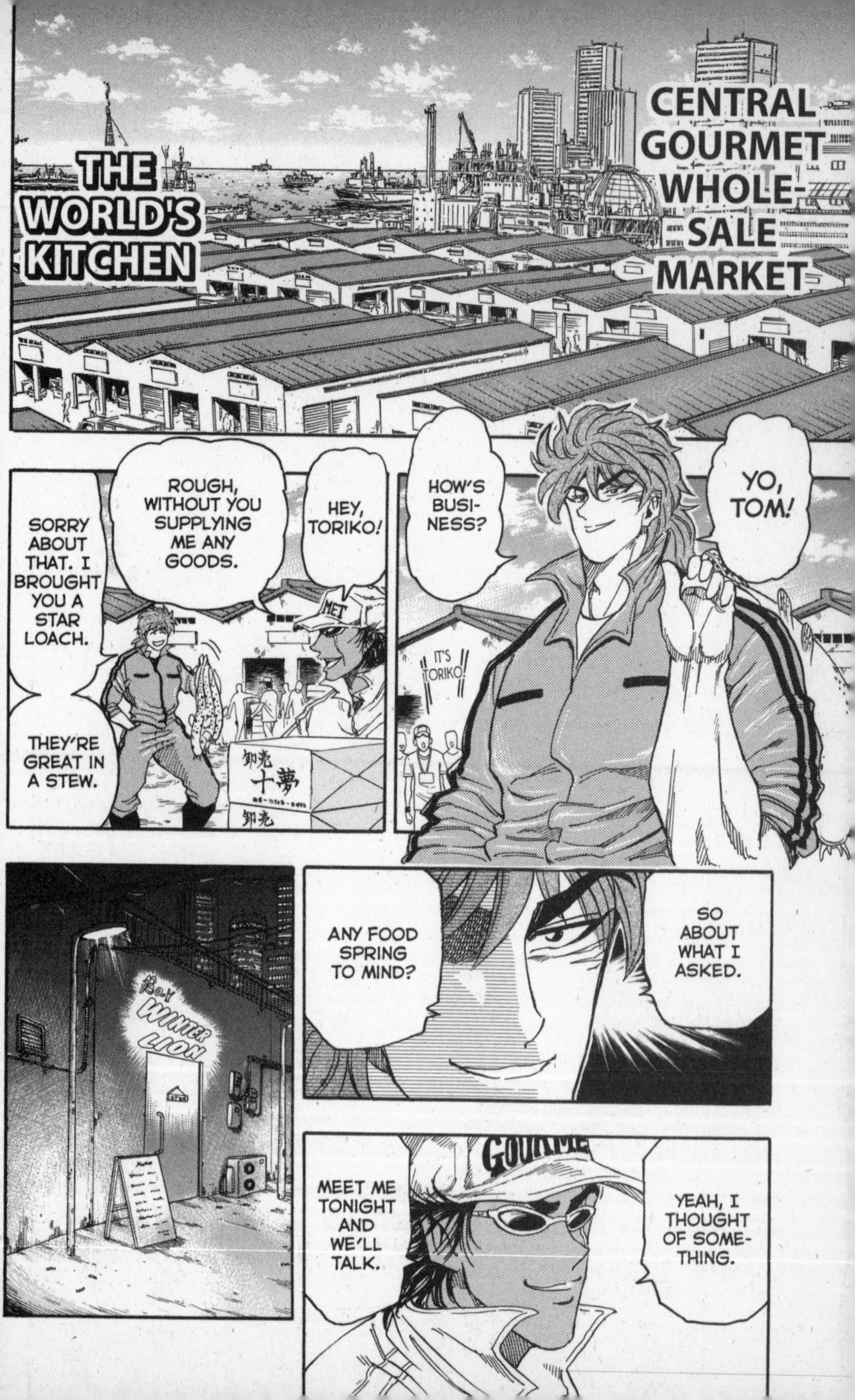
CENTRAL GOURMET WHOLE-SALE MARKET
THE WORLD'S KITCHEN
YO, TOM!
HOW'S BUSI-NESS?
IT'S TORIKO!
HEY, TORIKO!
ROUGH, WITHOUT YOU SUPPLYING ME ANY GOODS.
SORRY ABOUT THAT. I BROUGHT YOU A STAR LOACH.
THEY'RE GREAT IN A STEW.
卸売
十夢
卸売
SO ABOUT WHAT I ASKED.
ANY FOOD SPRING TO MIND?
YEAH, I THOUGHT OF SOME-THING.
MEET ME TONIGHT AND WE'LL TALK.
WINTER LION

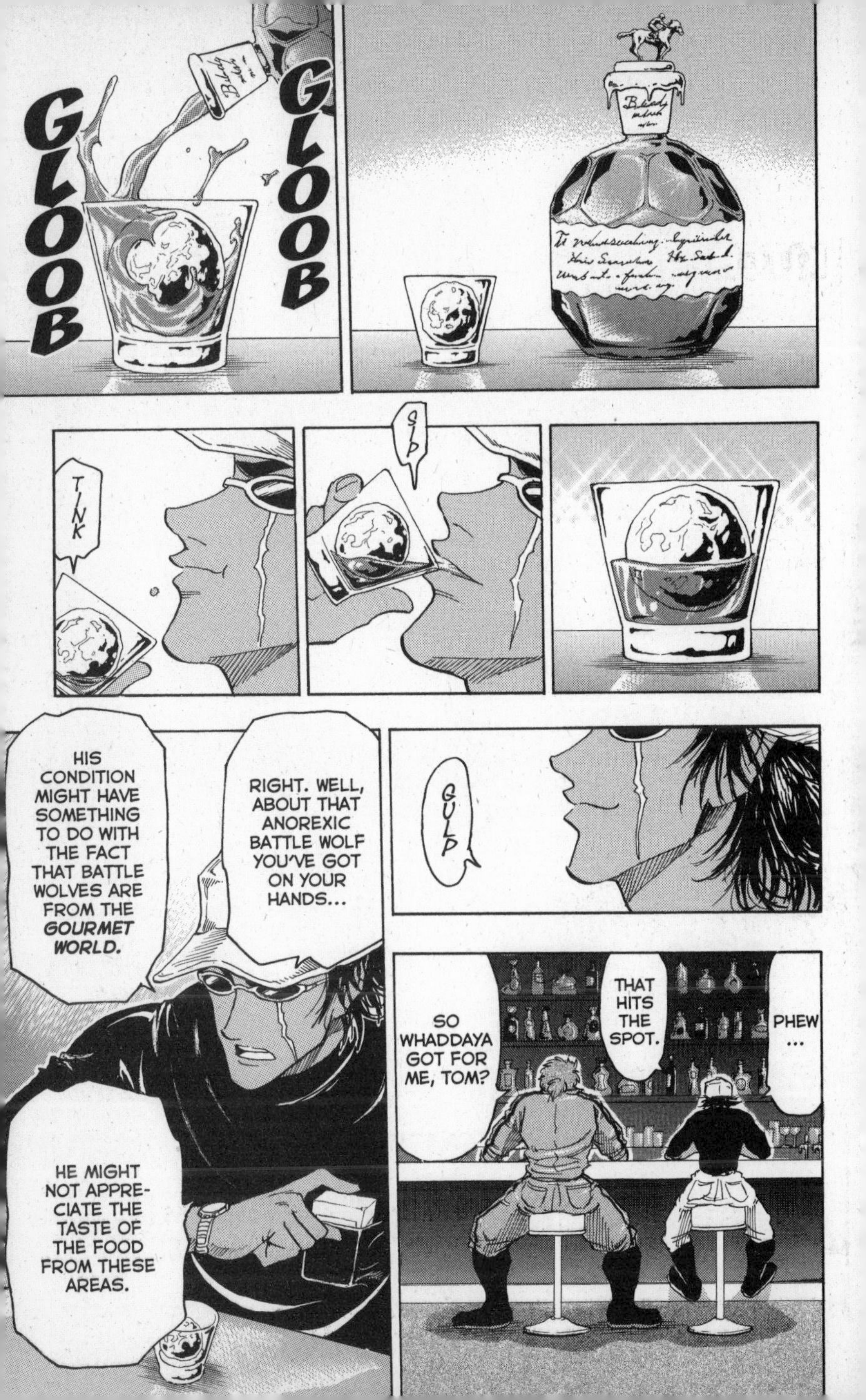
GLOOB
GLOOB
SIP
TINK
GULP
PHEW...
THAT HITS THE SPOT.
SO WHADDAYA GOT FOR ME, TOM?
RIGHT. WELL, ABOUT THAT ANOREXIC BATTLE WOLF YOU'VE GOT ON YOUR HANDS...
HIS CONDITION MIGHT HAVE SOMETHING TO DO WITH THE FACT THAT BATTLE WOLVES ARE FROM THE *GOURMET WORLD.*
HE MIGHT NOT APPRECIATE THE TASTE OF THE FOOD FROM THESE AREAS.

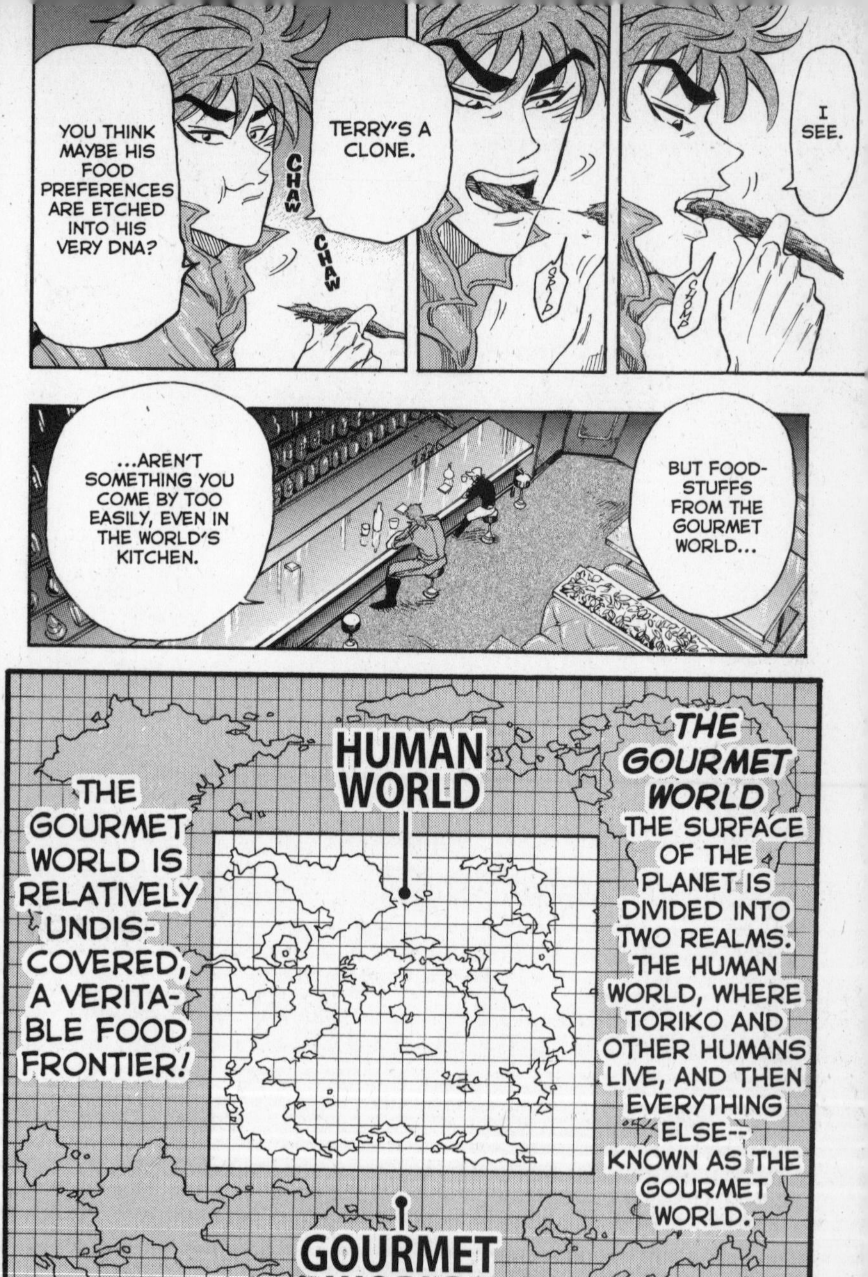
I SEE.
CHOMP
TERRY'S A CLONE.
GRIP
YOU THINK MAYBE HIS FOOD PREFERENCES ARE ETCHED INTO HIS VERY DNA?
CHAW
CHAW
BUT FOOD-STUFFS FROM THE GOURMET WORLD...
...AREN'T SOMETHING YOU COME BY TOO EASILY, EVEN IN THE WORLD'S KITCHEN.
THE GOURMET WORLD
THE SURFACE OF THE PLANET IS DIVIDED INTO TWO REALMS. THE HUMAN WORLD, WHERE TORIKO AND OTHER HUMANS LIVE, AND THEN EVERYTHING ELSE--KNOWN AS THE GOURMET WORLD.
HUMAN WORLD
THE GOURMET WORLD IS RELATIVELY UNDISCOVERED, A VERITABLE FOOD FRONTIER!
GOURMET WORLD

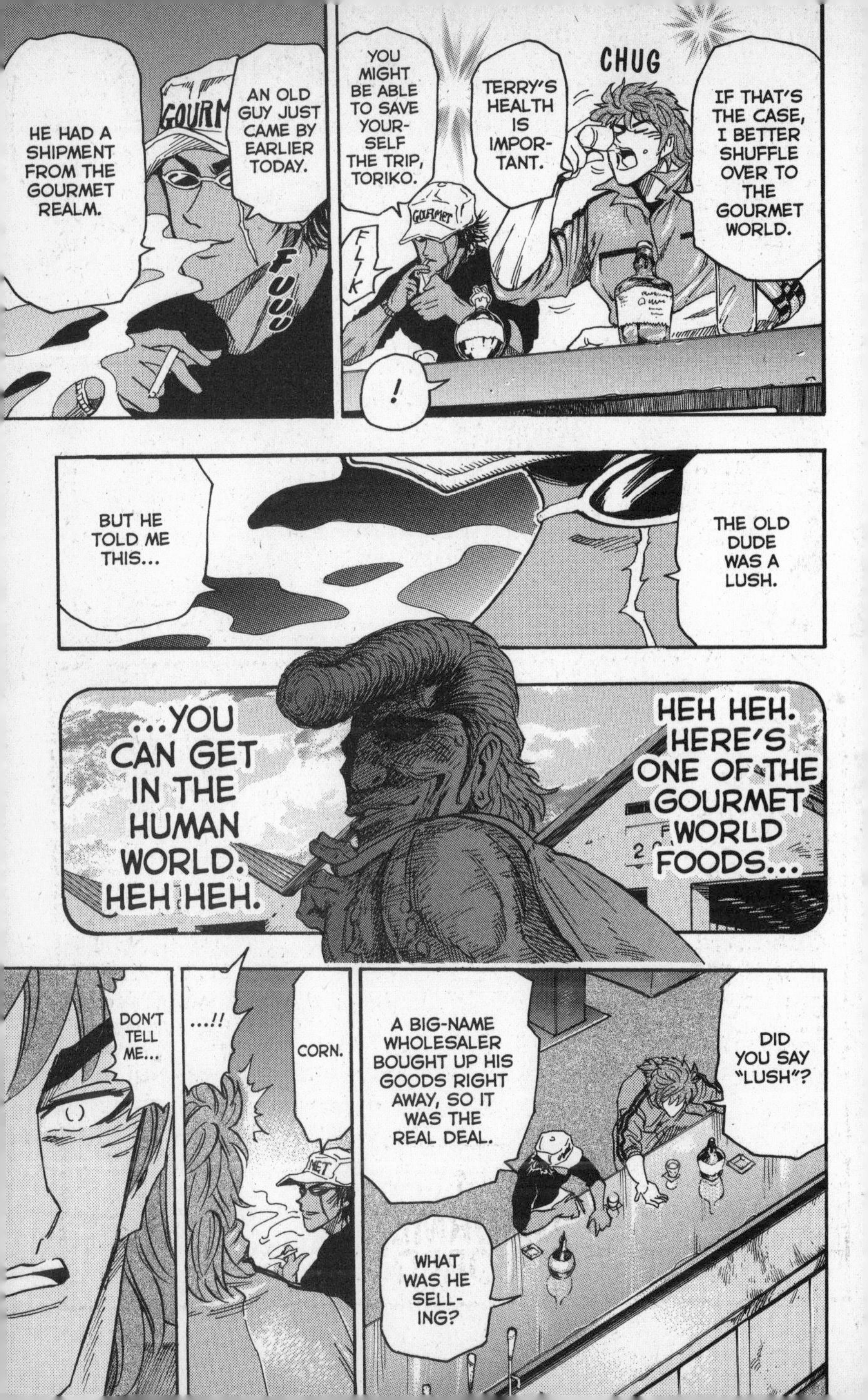
IF THAT'S THE CASE, I BETTER SHUFFLE OVER TO THE GOURMET WORLD.
CHUG
TERRY'S HEALTH IS IMPORTANT.
YOU MIGHT BE ABLE TO SAVE YOURSELF THE TRIP, TORIKO.
FLIK
!
AN OLD GUY JUST CAME BY EARLIER TODAY.
HE HAD A SHIPMENT FROM THE GOURMET REALM.
FUUU
THE OLD DUDE WAS A LUSH.
BUT HE TOLD ME THIS...
HEH HEH. HERE'S ONE OF THE GOURMET WORLD FOODS...
...YOU CAN GET IN THE HUMAN WORLD. HEH HEH.
DID YOU SAY "LUSH"?
A BIG-NAME WHOLESALER BOUGHT UP HIS GOODS RIGHT AWAY, SO IT WAS THE REAL DEAL.
WHAT WAS HE SELLING?
CORN.
...!!
DON'T TELL ME...

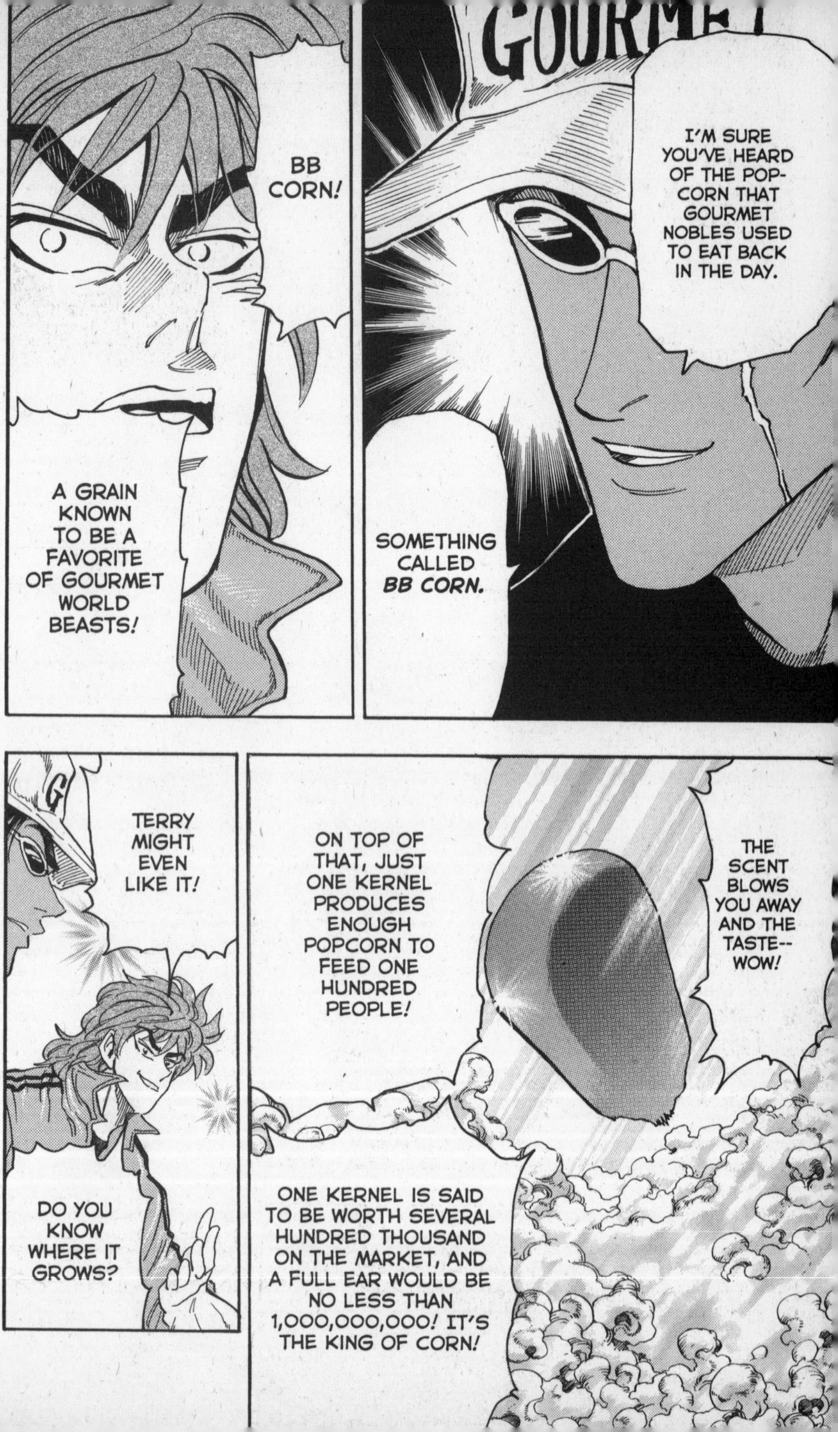
I'M SURE YOU'VE HEARD OF THE POP-CORN THAT GOURMET NOBLES USED TO EAT BACK IN THE DAY.
SOMETHING CALLED *BB CORN.*
BB CORN!
A GRAIN KNOWN TO BE A FAVORITE OF GOURMET WORLD BEASTS!
THE SCENT BLOWS YOU AWAY AND THE TASTE--WOW!
ON TOP OF THAT, JUST ONE KERNEL PRODUCES ENOUGH POPCORN TO FEED ONE HUNDRED PEOPLE!
ONE KERNEL IS SAID TO BE WORTH SEVERAL HUNDRED THOUSAND ON THE MARKET, AND A FULL EAR WOULD BE NO LESS THAN 1,000,000,000! IT'S THE KING OF CORN!
TERRY MIGHT EVEN LIKE IT!
DO YOU KNOW WHERE IT GROWS?

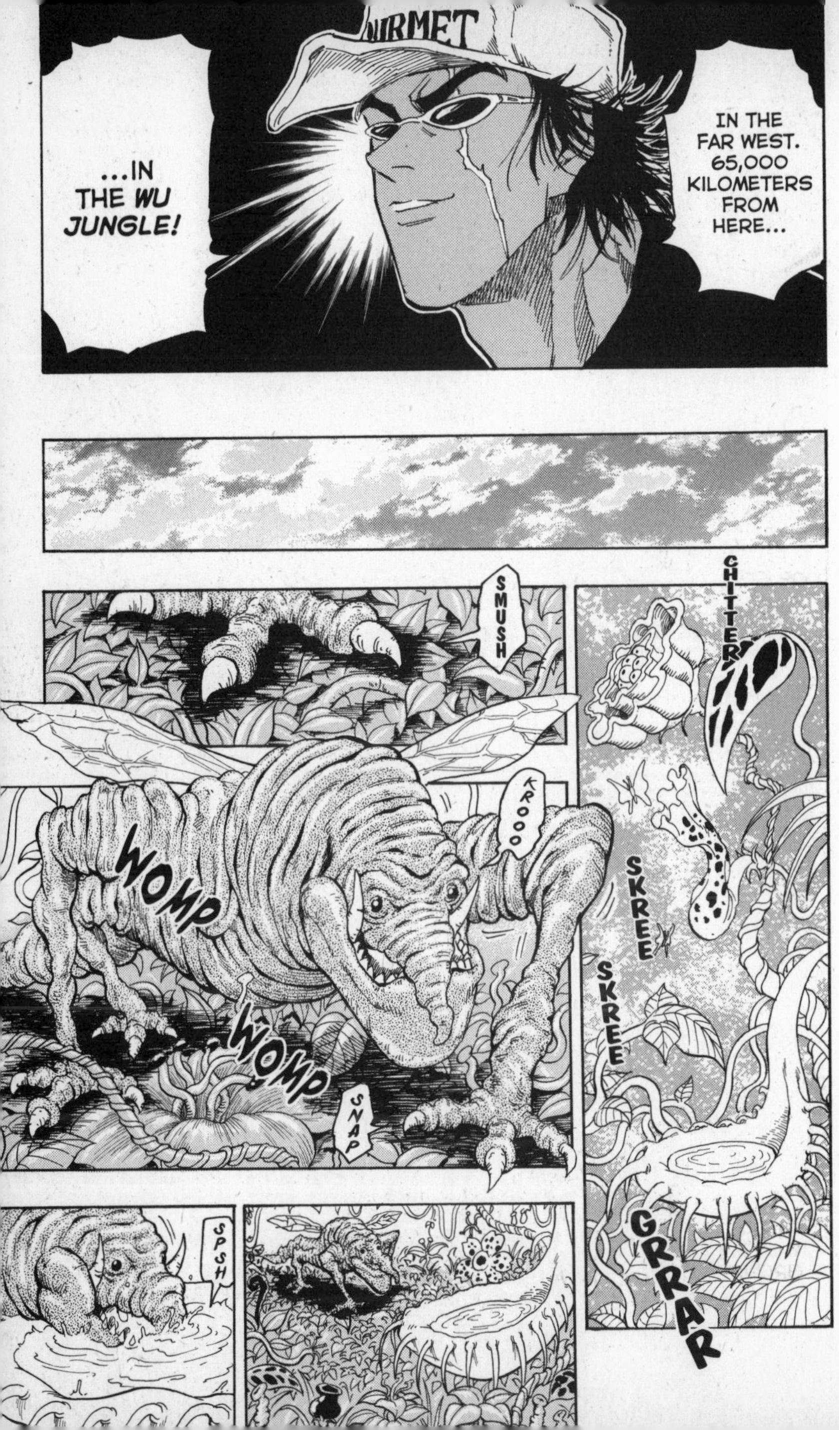
IN THE FAR WEST. 65,000 KILOMETERS FROM HERE...
...IN THE WU JUNGLE!
CHITTER
SKREE
SKREE
GRRAR
SMUSH
KROOO
WOMP
WOMP
SNAP
SPSH

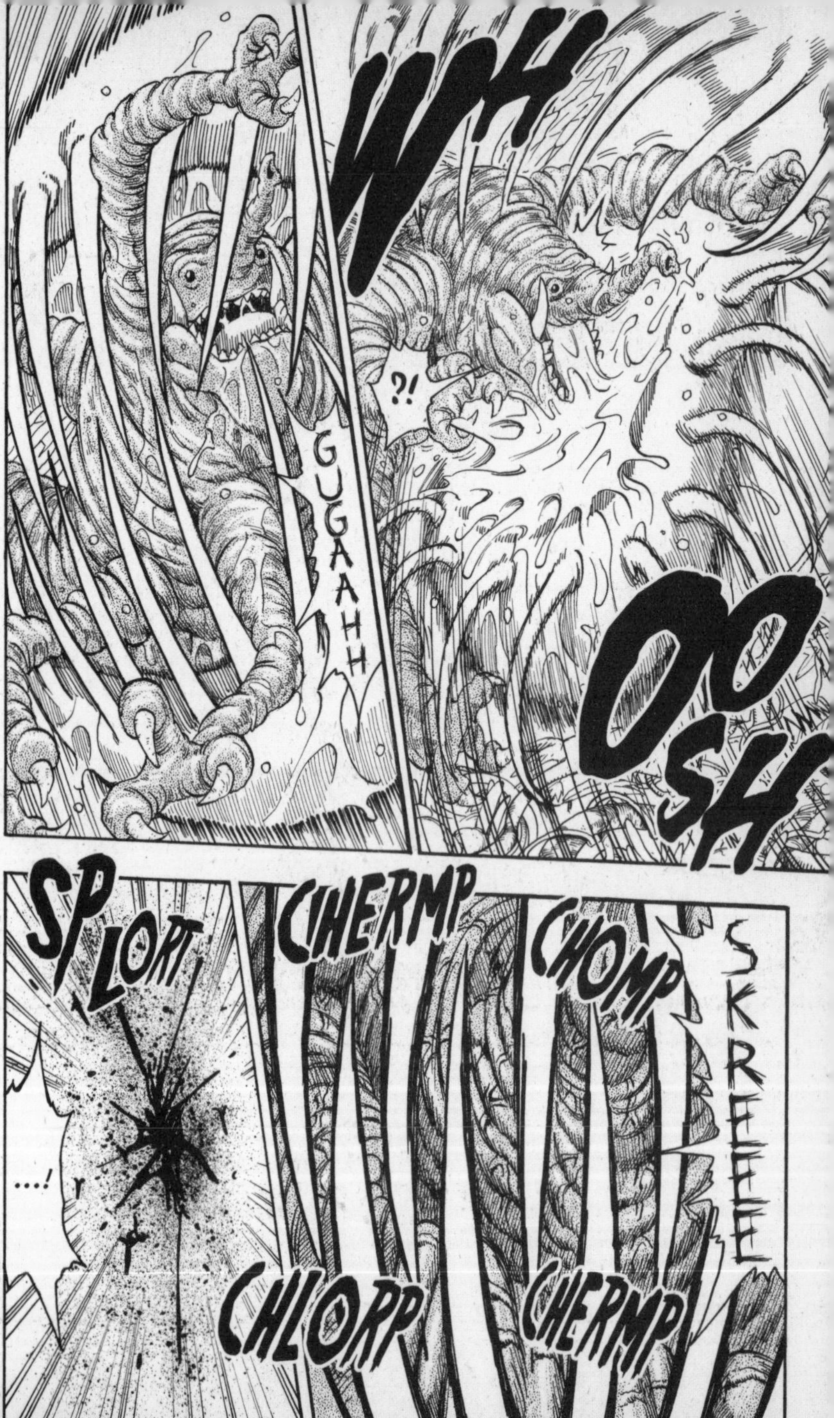
WHOOSH
?!
GUGAAHH
SKREEE
CHOMP
CHERMP
CHERMP
CHLORP
SPLORT
...!

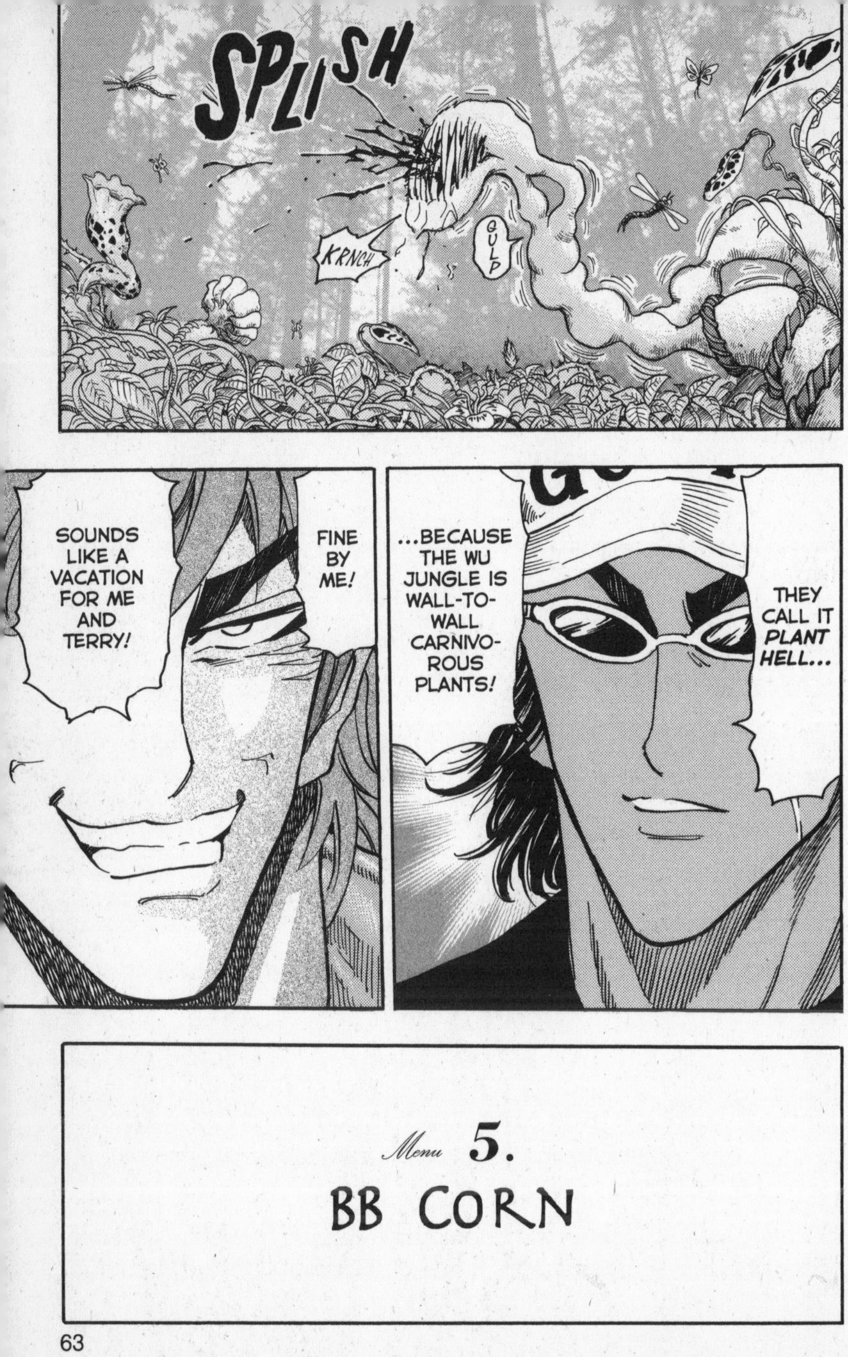
SPLISH
GULP
KRNCH
THEY CALL IT PLANT HELL...
...BECAUSE THE WU JUNGLE IS WALL-TO-WALL CARNIVOROUS PLANTS!
FINE BY ME!
SOUNDS LIKE A VACATION FOR ME AND TERRY!

Menu 5.

BB CORN

GOURMET CHECKLIST

Vol. 040

MARBLED TOFU
(PLANT)

**CAPTURE LEVEL: LESS THAN 1
(ARTIFICIALLY PRODUCED)**

HABITAT: IGO GOURMET LAB

LENGTH: ---

HEIGHT: ---

WEIGHT: ---

PRICE: 100 G / 5,000 YEN

SCALE

A FOOD DEVELOPED AT THE IGO GOURMET LABORATORY, MARBLED TOFU IS A HYBRID SUPER-FATTY SOYBEAN. IT'S LACED WITH GRADE-A FAT AKIN TO THAT OF A MARBLED HUNK OF STEAK, BUT WITH AN AFTERTASTE THAT'S FRESH LIKE TOFU. ALTHOUGH IT MIGHT LOOK AND TASTE LIKE MEAT, ALL THE FAT IS PLANT FAT, SO MARBLED TOFU IS QUITE POPULAR AMONG VEGETARIAN GOURMET HUNTERS.

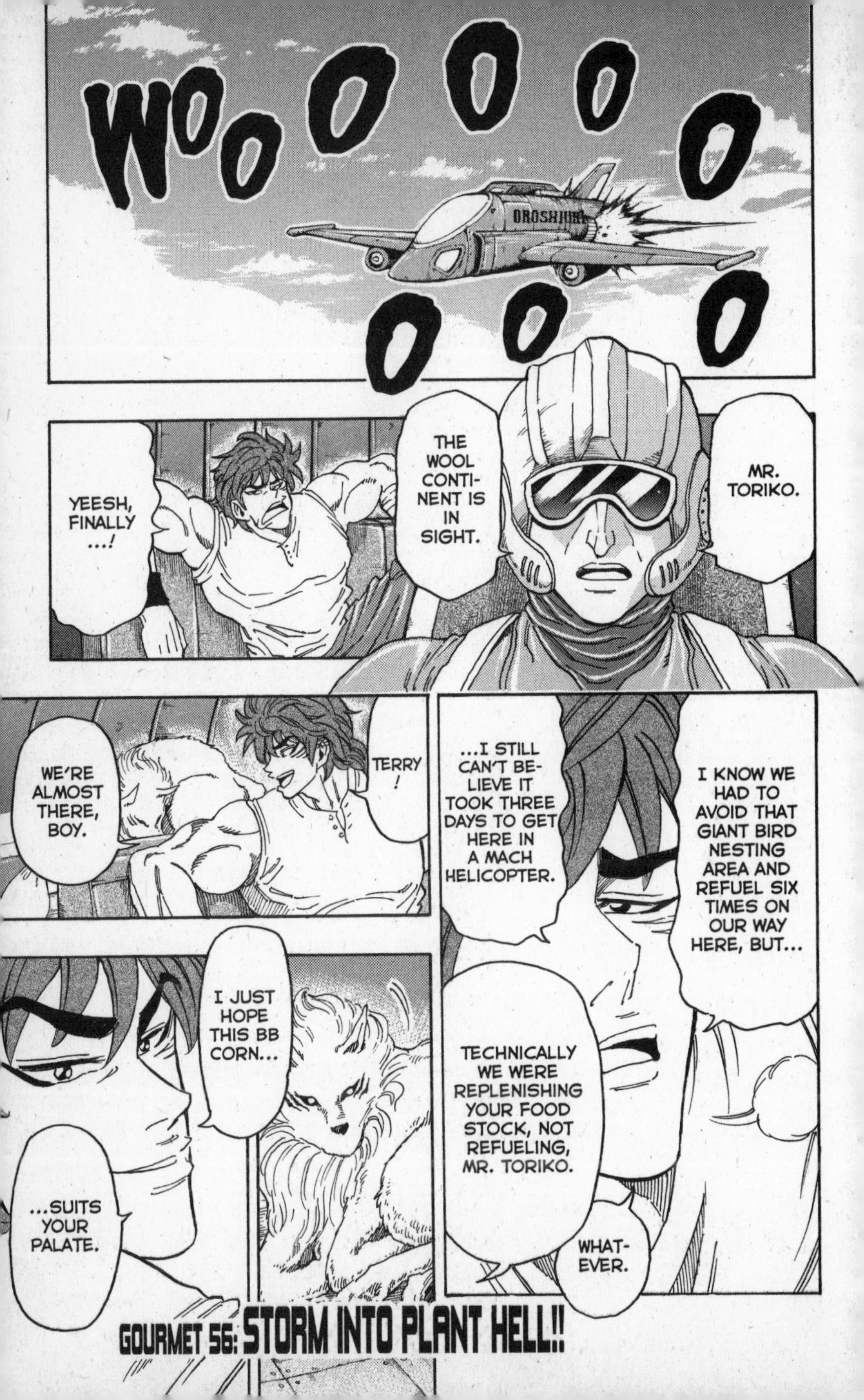
WOOOOOOOOOO
MR. TORIKO.
THE WOOL CONTINENT IS IN SIGHT.
YEESH, FINALLY...!
I KNOW WE HAD TO AVOID THAT GIANT BIRD NESTING AREA AND REFUEL SIX TIMES ON OUR WAY HERE, BUT...
...I STILL CAN'T BELIEVE IT TOOK THREE DAYS TO GET HERE IN A MACH HELICOPTER.
TECHNICALLY WE WERE REPLENISHING YOUR FOOD STOCK, NOT REFUELING, MR. TORIKO.
WHATEVER.
TERRY!
WE'RE ALMOST THERE, BOY.
I JUST HOPE THIS BB CORN...
...SUITS YOUR PALATE.
GOURMET 56: STORM INTO PLANT HELL!!

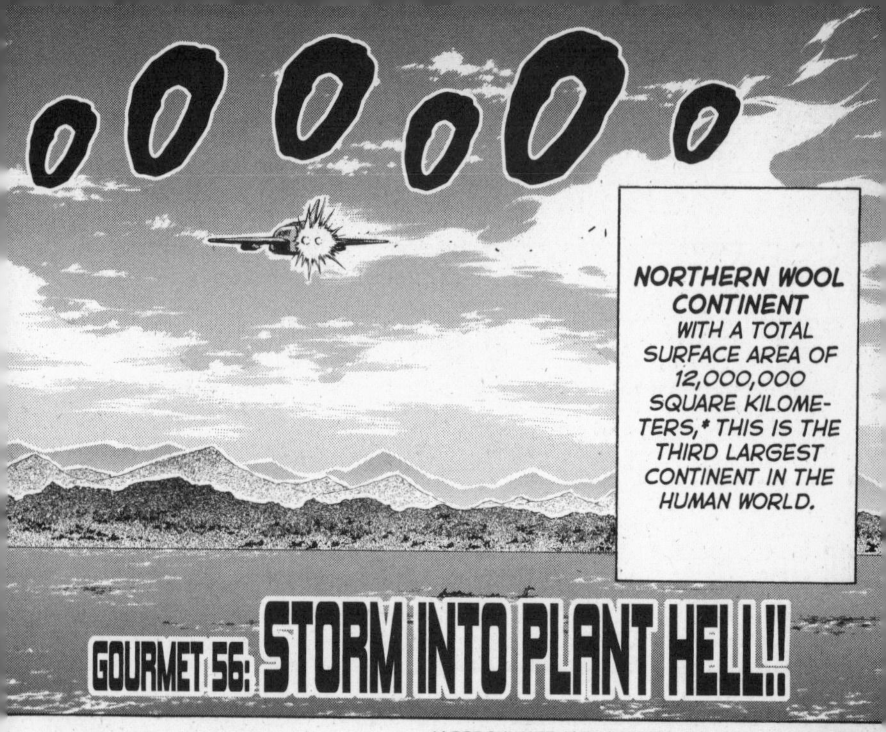
OOOOOO
NORTHERN WOOL CONTINENT WITH A TOTAL SURFACE AREA OF 12,000,000 SQUARE KILOMETERS,* THIS IS THE THIRD LARGEST CONTINENT IN THE HUMAN WORLD.
GOURMET 56: STORM INTO PLANT HELL!!

*APPROXIMATELY TWO TIMES THE SIZE OF EURASIA

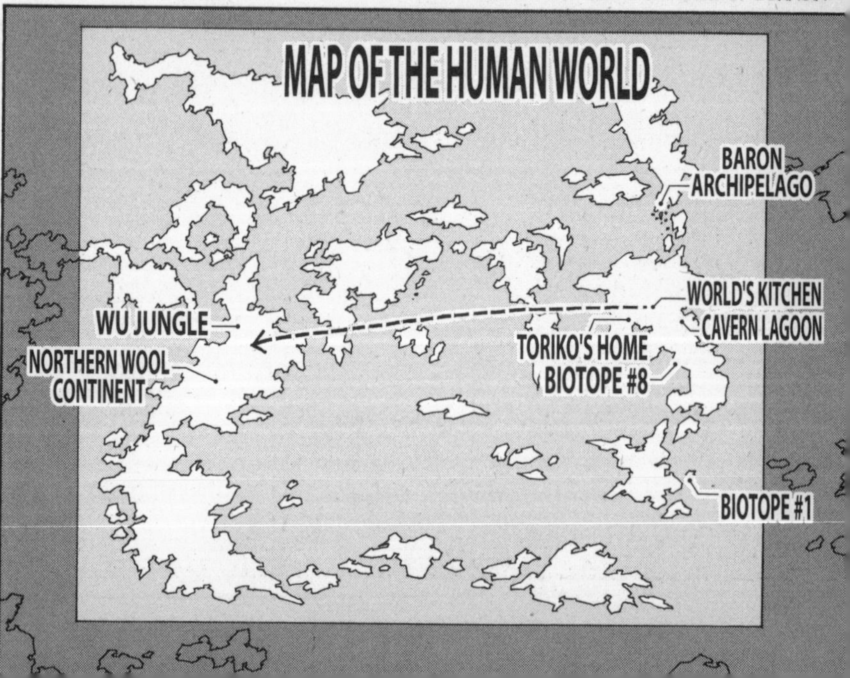
MAP OF THE HUMAN WORLD
BARON ARCHIPELAGO
WORLD'S KITCHEN
CAVERN LAGOON
TORIKO'S HOME
BIOTOPE #8
WU JUNGLE
NORTHERN WOOL CONTINENT
BIOTOPE #1

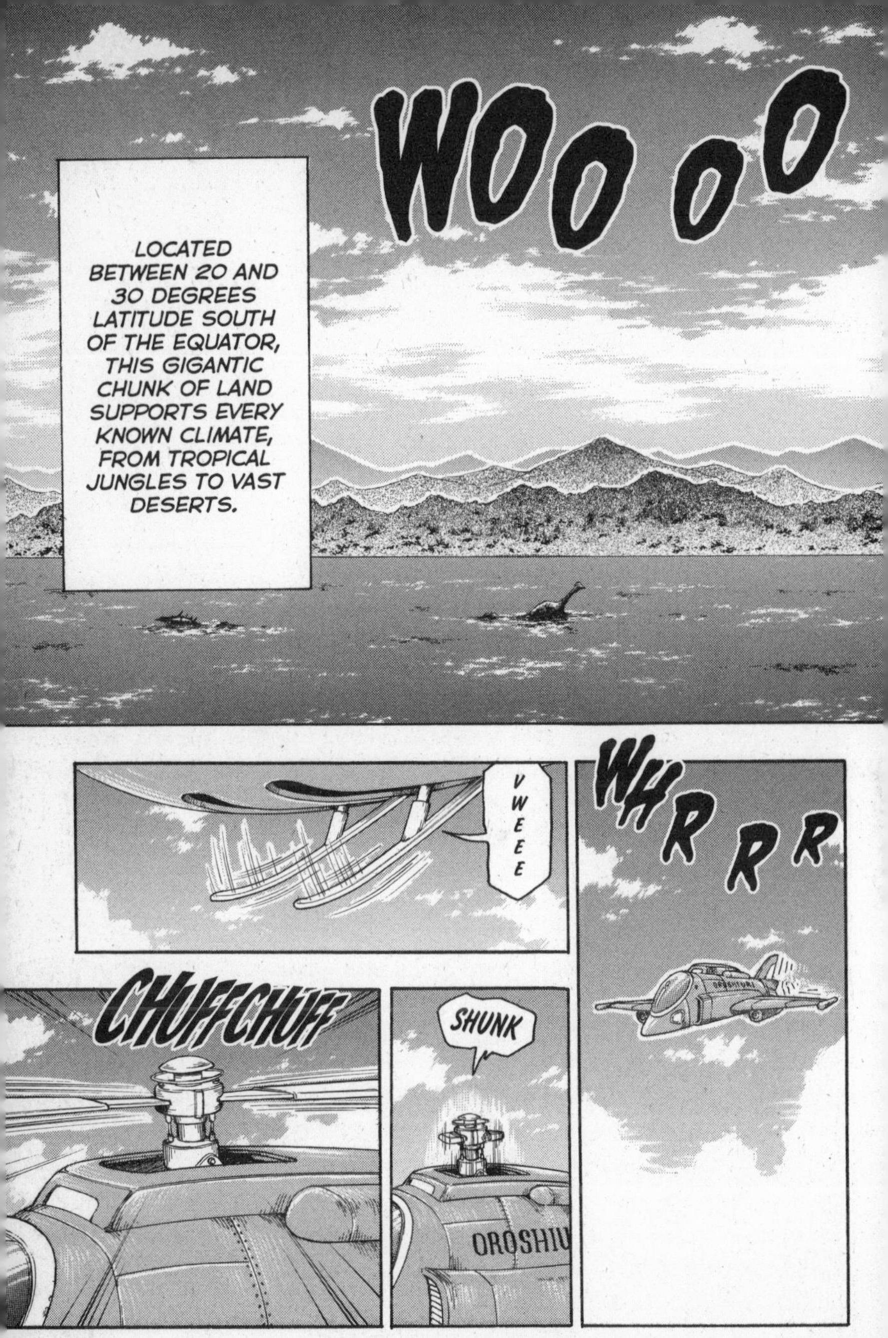
WOOOOO
LOCATED BETWEEN 20 AND 30 DEGREES LATITUDE SOUTH OF THE EQUATOR, THIS GIGANTIC CHUNK OF LAND SUPPORTS EVERY KNOWN CLIMATE, FROM TROPICAL JUNGLES TO VAST DESERTS.
WHRRR
VWEEE
SHUNK
OROSHIU
CHUFFCHUFF

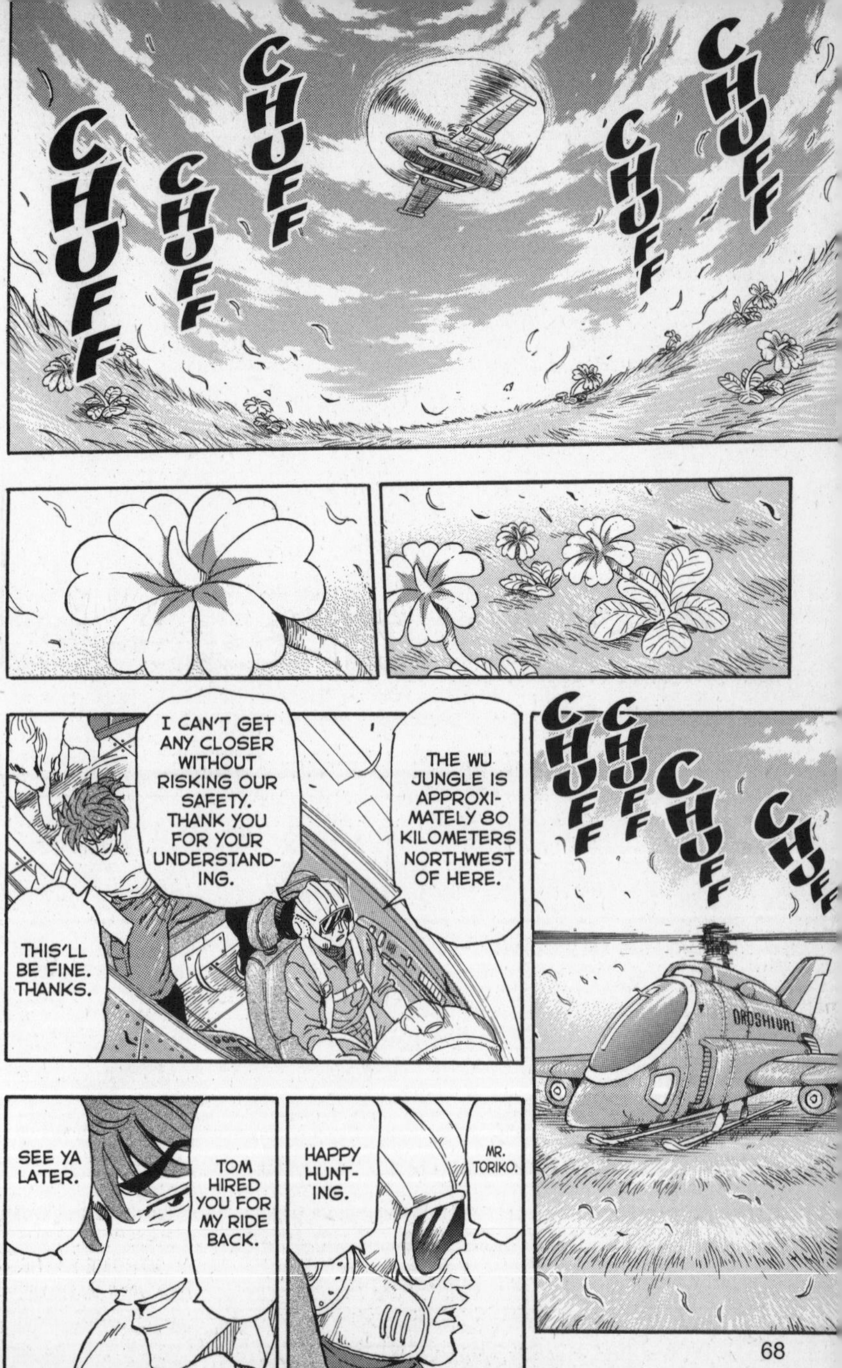
CHUFF
CHUFF
CHUFF
CHUFF
CHUFF
CHUFF
CHUFF
CHUFF
CHUFF
THE WU JUNGLE IS APPROXIMATELY 80 KILOMETERS NORTHWEST OF HERE.
I CAN'T GET ANY CLOSER WITHOUT RISKING OUR SAFETY. THANK YOU FOR YOUR UNDERSTANDING.
THIS'LL BE FINE. THANKS.
MR. TORIKO.
HAPPY HUNTING.
TOM HIRED YOU FOR MY RIDE BACK.
SEE YA LATER.
ORDSHIURI

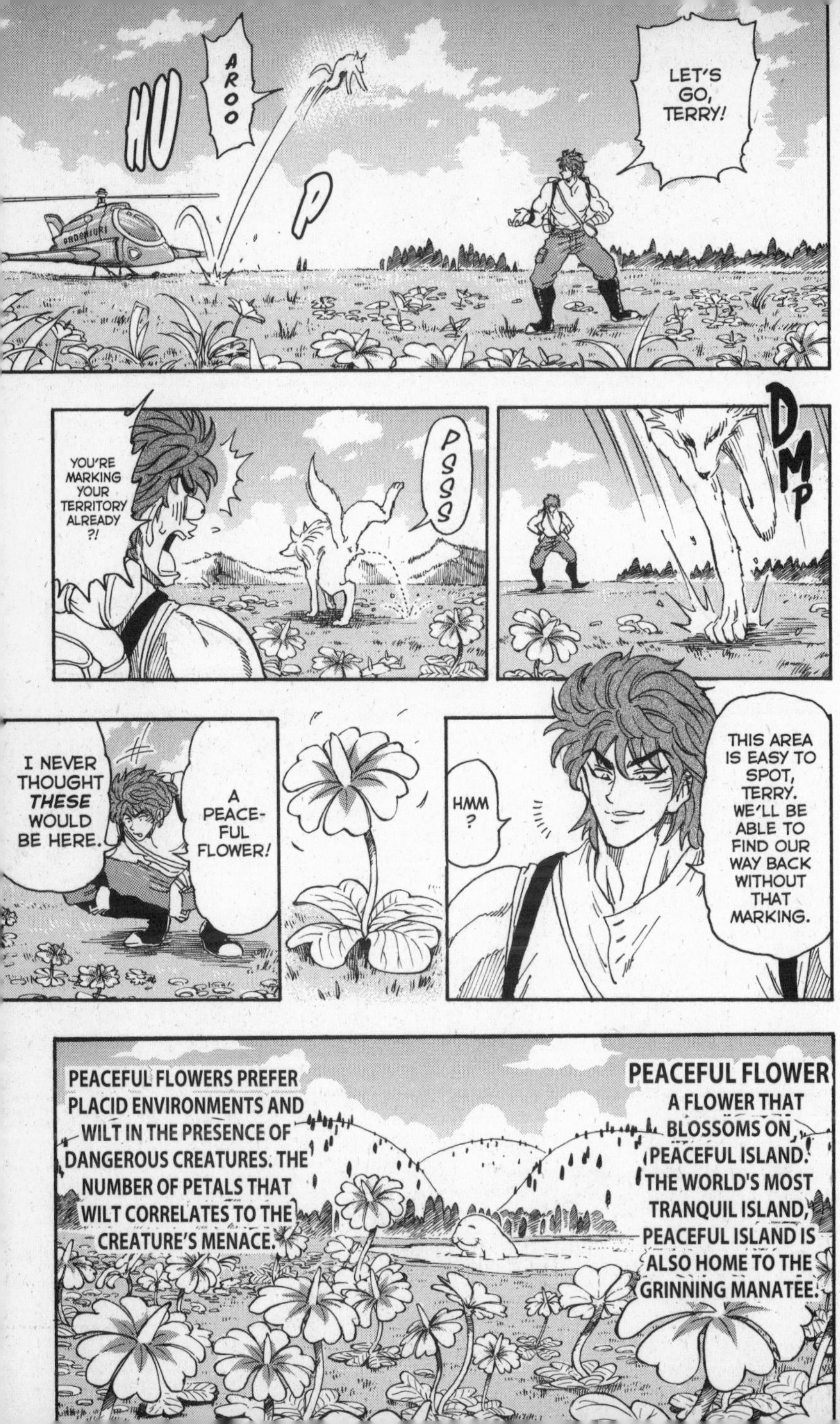
LET'S GO, TERRY!
AROO
HU
P
DMP
PSSS
YOU'RE MARKING YOUR TERRITORY ALREADY?!
THIS AREA IS EASY TO SPOT, TERRY. WE'LL BE ABLE TO FIND OUR WAY BACK WITHOUT THAT MARKING.
HMM?
A PEACE-FUL FLOWER!
I NEVER THOUGHT *THESE* WOULD BE HERE.
PEACEFUL FLOWER
A FLOWER THAT BLOSSOMS ON PEACEFUL ISLAND. THE WORLD'S MOST TRANQUIL ISLAND, PEACEFUL ISLAND IS ALSO HOME TO THE GRINNING MANATEE.
PEACEFUL FLOWERS PREFER PLACID ENVIRONMENTS AND WILT IN THE PRESENCE OF DANGEROUS CREATURES. THE NUMBER OF PETALS THAT WILT CORRELATES TO THE CREATURE'S MENACE.

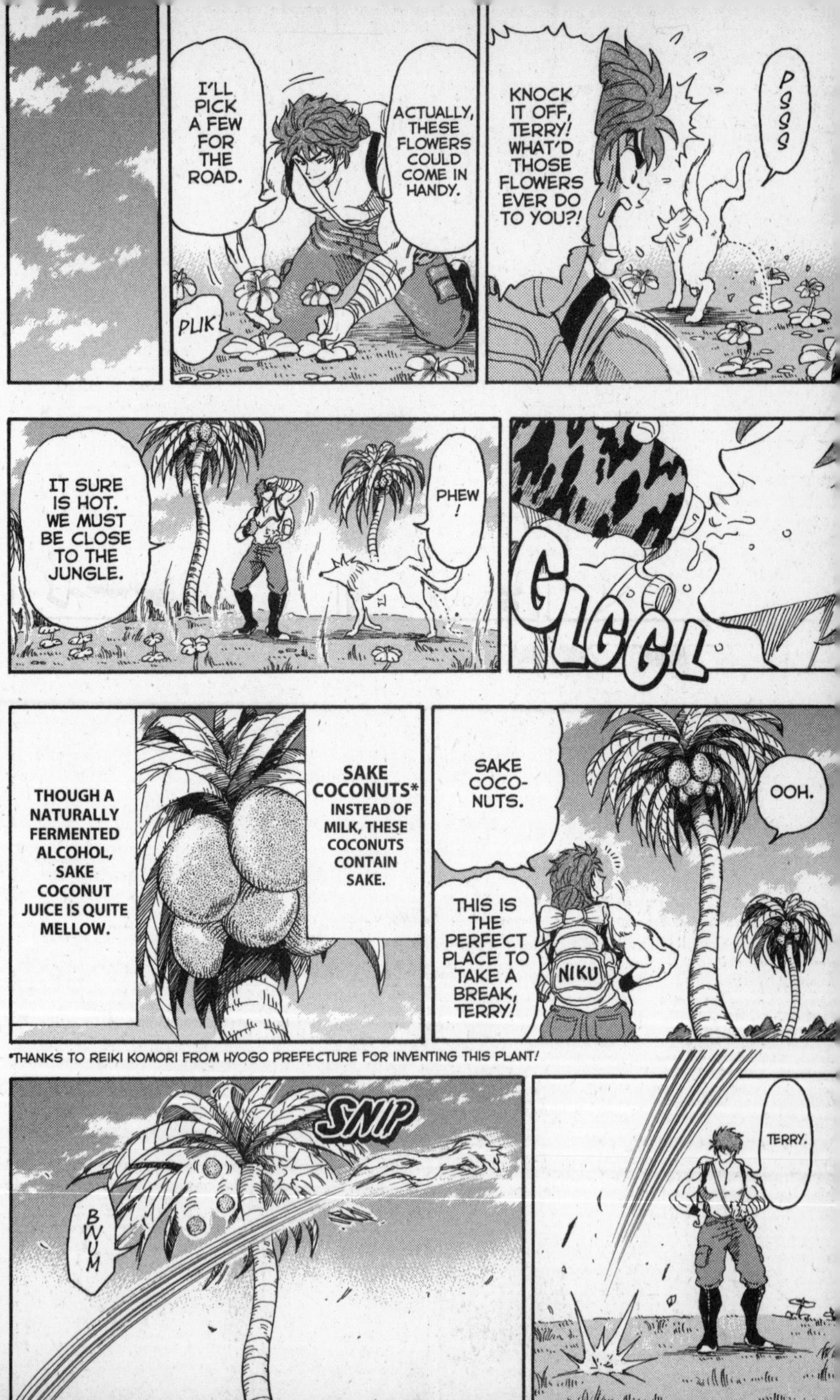
PSSS
KNOCK IT OFF, TERRY! WHAT'D THOSE FLOWERS EVER DO TO YOU?!
ACTUALLY, THESE FLOWERS COULD COME IN HANDY.
I'LL PICK A FEW FOR THE ROAD.
PLIK
GLGGL
PHEW!
IT SURE IS HOT. WE MUST BE CLOSE TO THE JUNGLE.
OOH.
SAKE COCONUTS.
THIS IS THE PERFECT PLACE TO TAKE A BREAK, TERRY!
NIKU
SAKE COCONUTS* INSTEAD OF MILK, THESE COCONUTS CONTAIN SAKE.
THOUGH A NATURALLY FERMENTED ALCOHOL, SAKE COCONUT JUICE IS QUITE MELLOW.
*THANKS TO REIKI KOMORI FROM HYOGO PREFECTURE FOR INVENTING THIS PLANT!
TERRY.
SNIP
BWUM

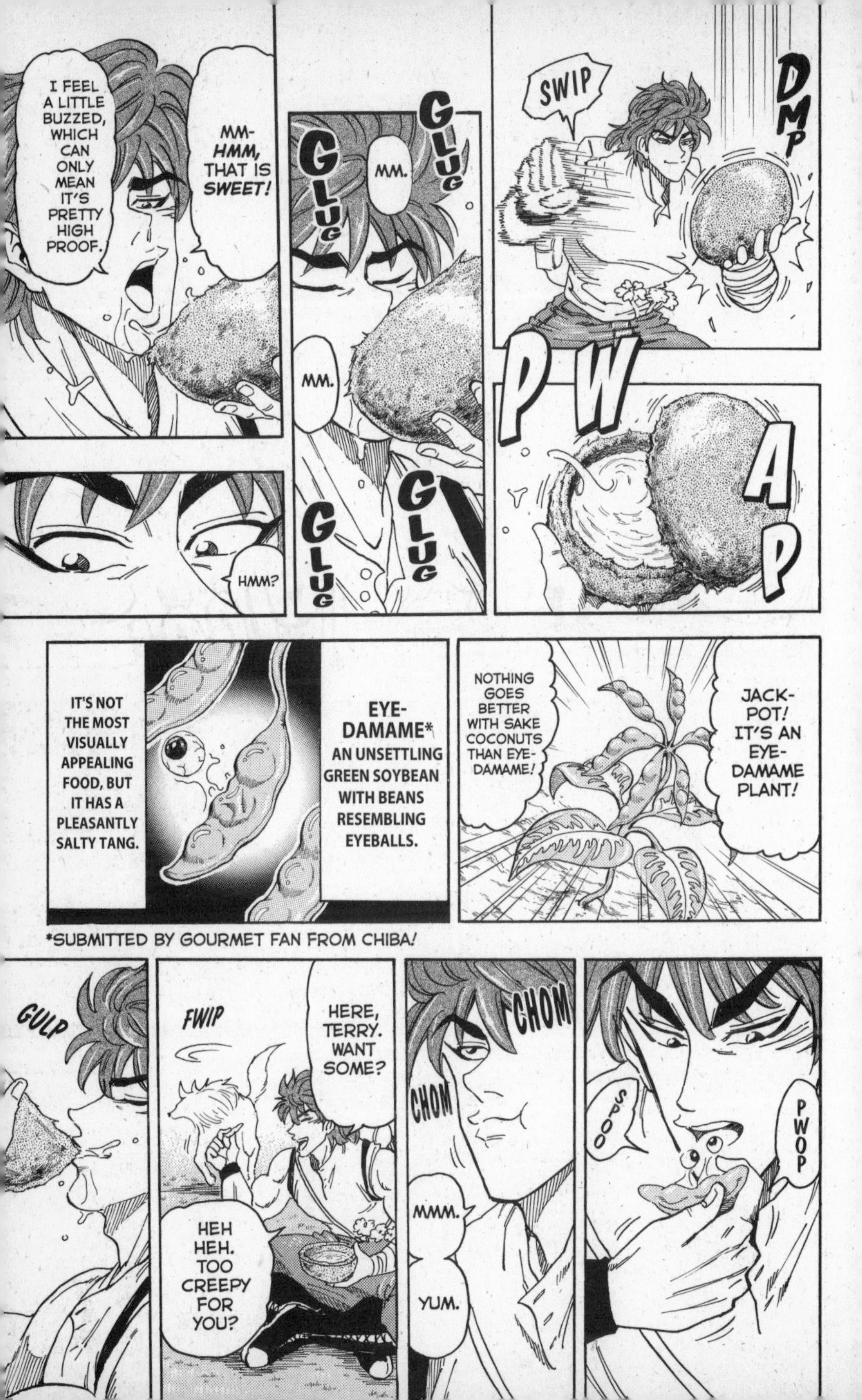
SWIP
DMP
PWAP
GLUG
GLUG
MM.
MM.
GLUG
GLUG
MM-HMM, THAT IS SWEET!
I FEEL A LITTLE BUZZED, WHICH CAN ONLY MEAN IT'S PRETTY HIGH PROOF.
HMM?
JACKPOT! IT'S AN EYE-DAMAME PLANT!
NOTHING GOES BETTER WITH SAKE COCONUTS THAN EYE-DAMAME!
EYE-DAMAME* AN UNSETTLING GREEN SOYBEAN WITH BEANS RESEMBLING EYEBALLS.
IT'S NOT THE MOST VISUALLY APPEALING FOOD, BUT IT HAS A PLEASANTLY SALTY TANG.
*SUBMITTED BY GOURMET FAN FROM CHIBA!
PWOP
SPOO
CHOM
CHOM
MMM.
YUM.
HERE, TERRY. WANT SOME?
FWIP
HEH HEH. TOO CREEPY FOR YOU?
GULP

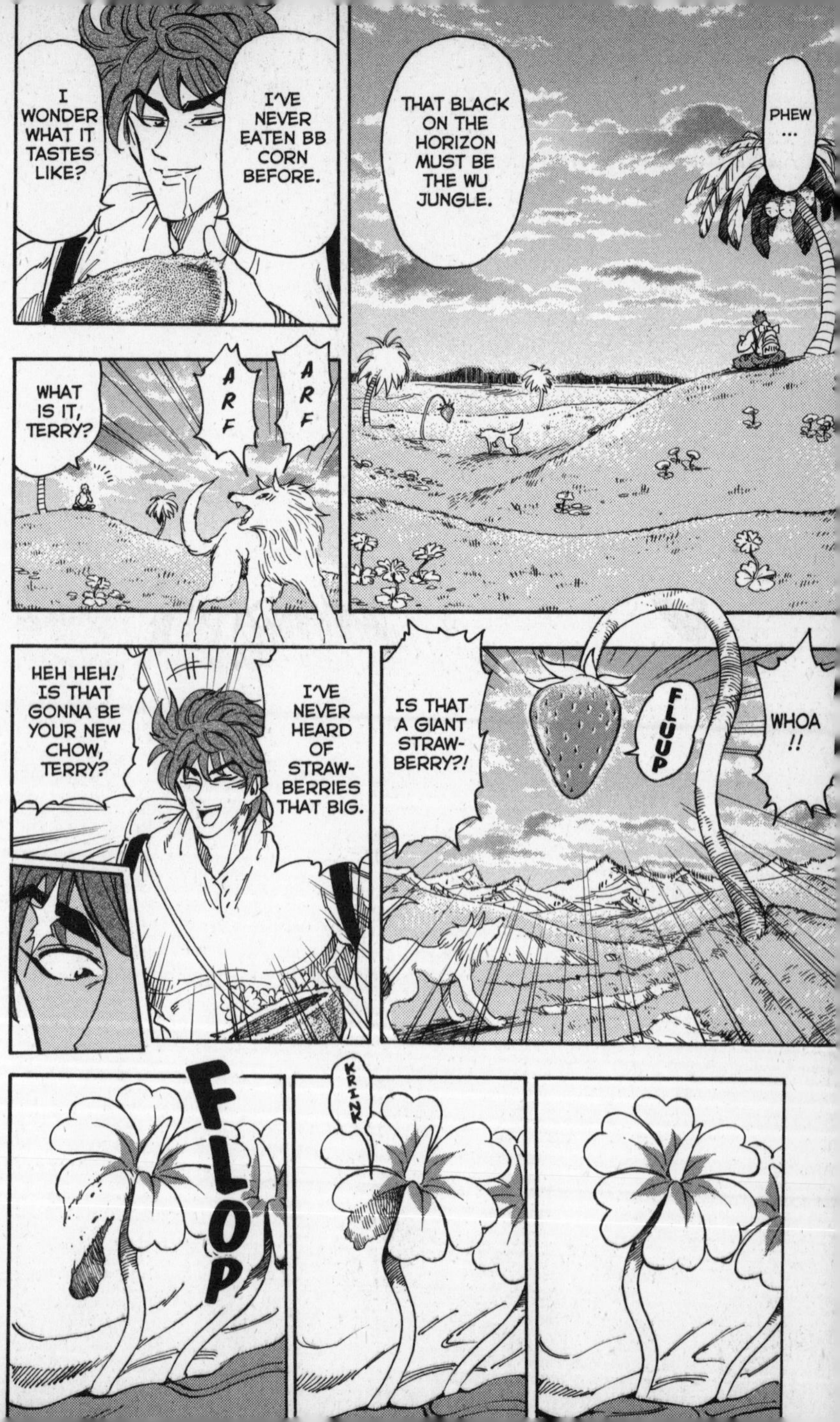

PHEW ...
THAT BLACK ON THE HORIZON MUST BE THE WU JUNGLE.
I'VE NEVER EATEN BB CORN BEFORE.
I WONDER WHAT IT TASTES LIKE?
ARF
ARF
WHAT IS IT, TERRY?
WHOA !!
FLUUP
IS THAT A GIANT STRAW-BERRY?!
I'VE NEVER HEARD OF STRAW-BERRIES THAT BIG.
HEH HEH! IS THAT GONNA BE YOUR NEW CHOW, TERRY?
KRINK
FLOP

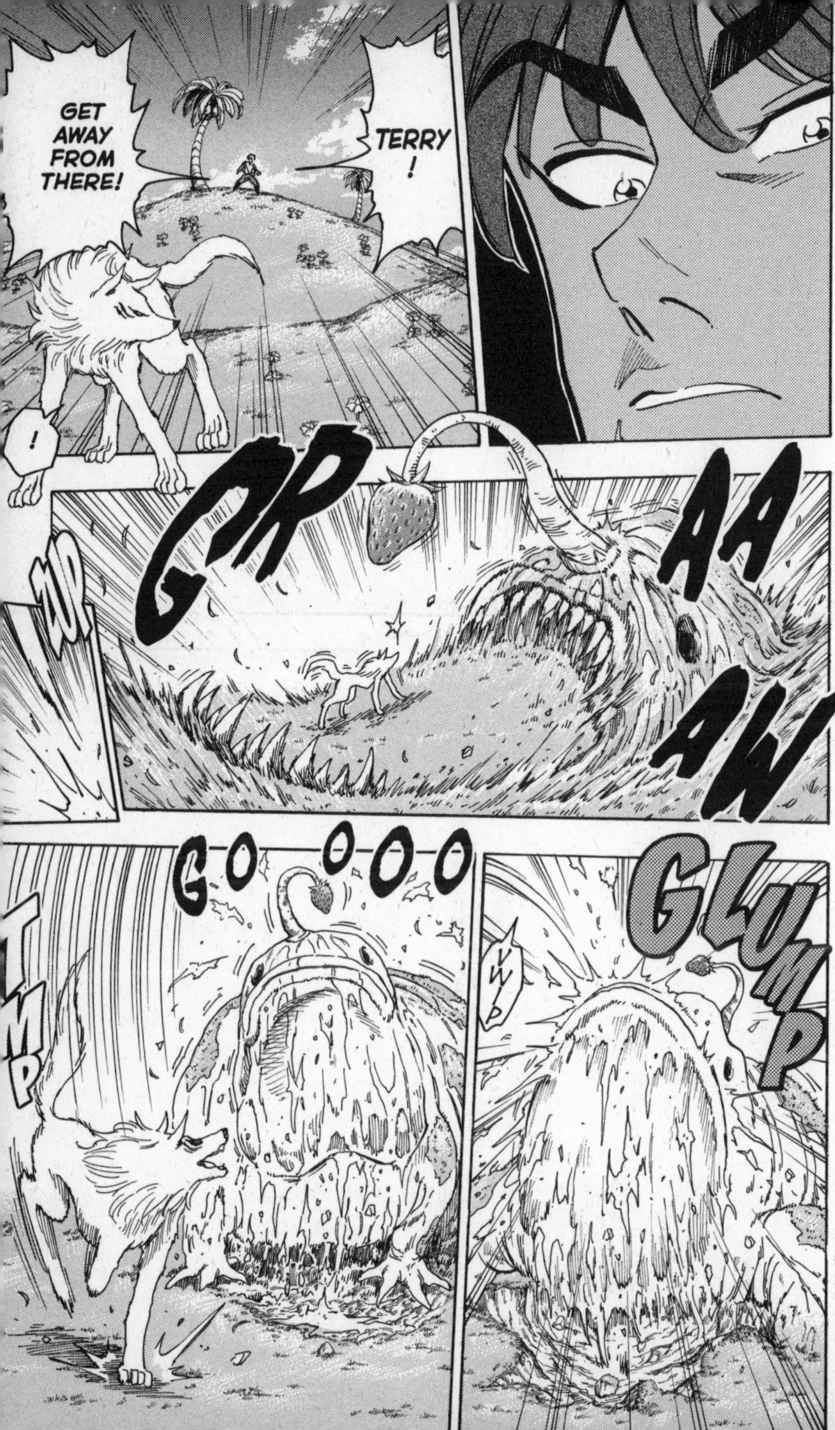
TERRY!
GET AWAY FROM THERE!
!
AA
AW
GOR
GLUMP
VWIP
GOOOO

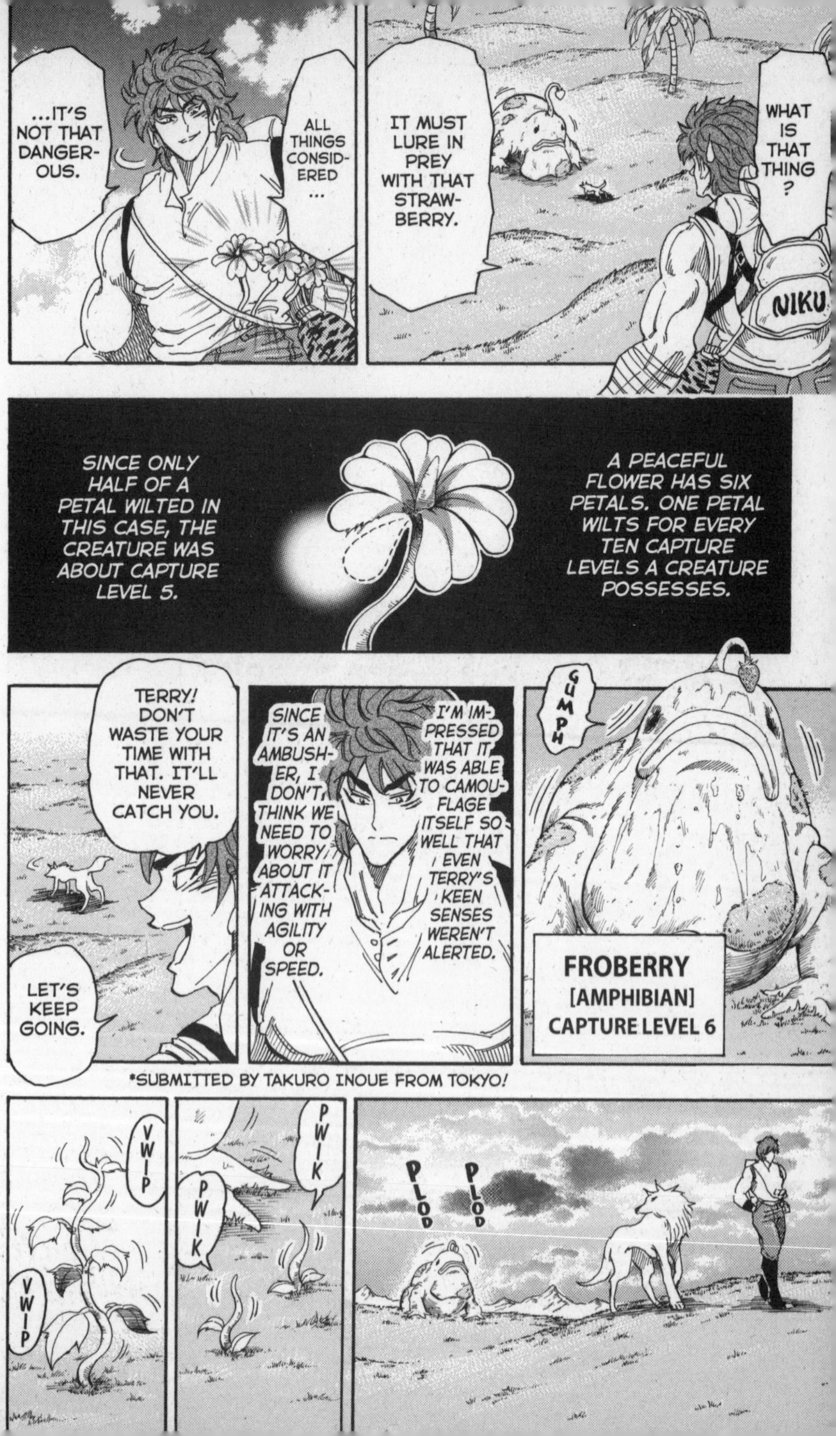
WHAT IS THAT THING?
NIKU
IT MUST LURE IN PREY WITH THAT STRAWBERRY.
ALL THINGS CONSIDERED ...
...IT'S NOT THAT DANGEROUS.
A PEACEFUL FLOWER HAS SIX PETALS. ONE PETAL WILTS FOR EVERY TEN CAPTURE LEVELS A CREATURE POSSESSES.
SINCE ONLY HALF OF A PETAL WILTED IN THIS CASE, THE CREATURE WAS ABOUT CAPTURE LEVEL 5.
GUMPH
FROBERRY [AMPHIBIAN] CAPTURE LEVEL 6
I'M IMPRESSED THAT IT WAS ABLE TO CAMOUFLAGE ITSELF SO WELL THAT EVEN TERRY'S KEEN SENSES WEREN'T ALERTED.
SINCE IT'S AN AMBUSHER, I DON'T THINK WE NEED TO WORRY ABOUT IT ATTACKING WITH AGILITY OR SPEED.
TERRY! DON'T WASTE YOUR TIME WITH THAT. IT'LL NEVER CATCH YOU.
LET'S KEEP GOING.
*SUBMITTED BY TAKURO INOUE FROM TOKYO!
PLOD
PLOD
PWIK
PWIK
VWIP
VWIP

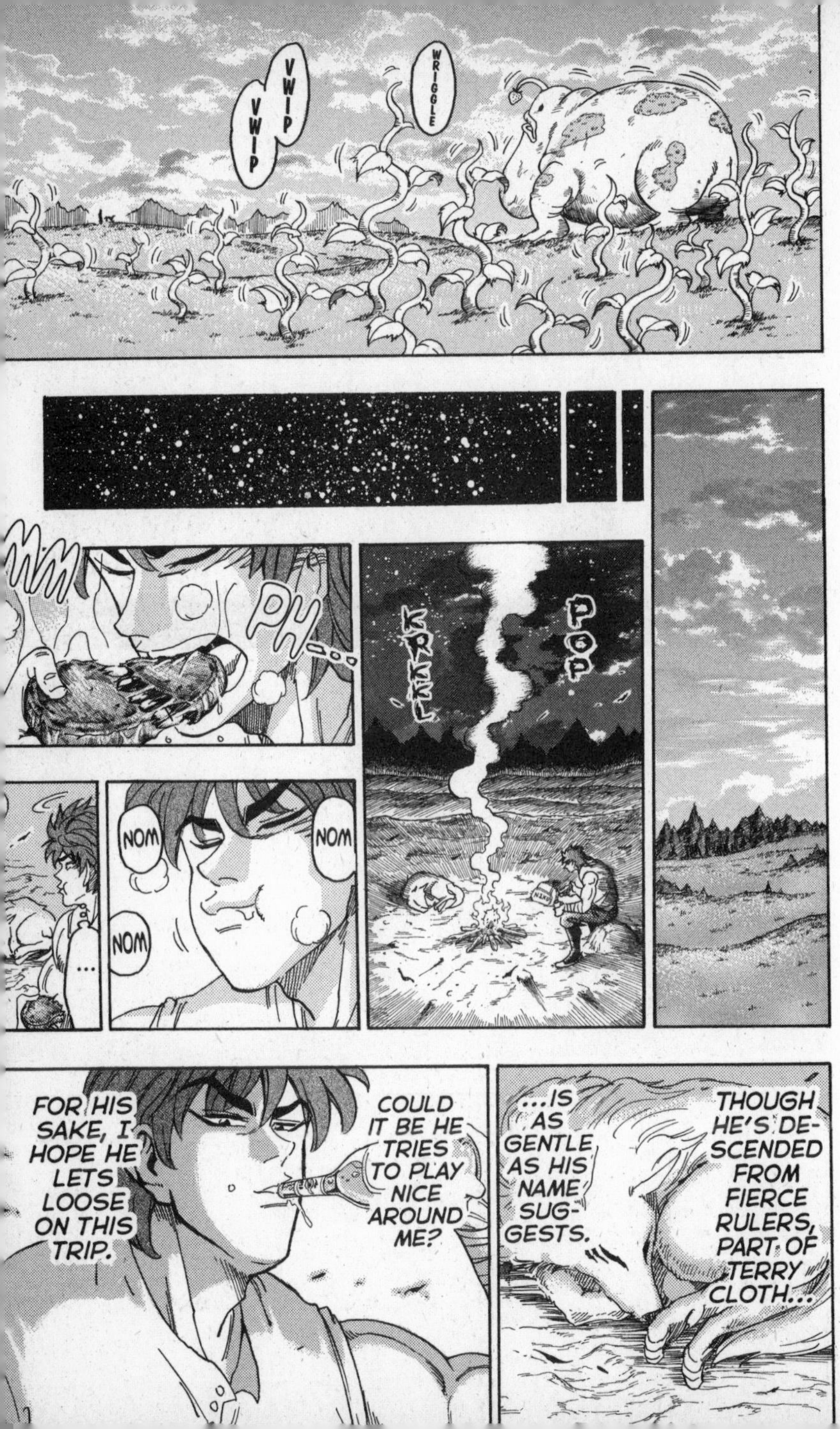
WRIGGLE
VWIP
VWIP
POP
KRAKKL
MMMPH...
NOM
NOM
NOM
...
THOUGH HE'S DESCENDED FROM FIERCE RULERS, PART OF TERRY CLOTH...
...IS AS GENTLE AS HIS NAME SUGGESTS.
COULD IT BE HE TRIES TO PLAY NICE AROUND ME?
FOR HIS SAKE, I HOPE HE LETS LOOSE ON THIS TRIP.

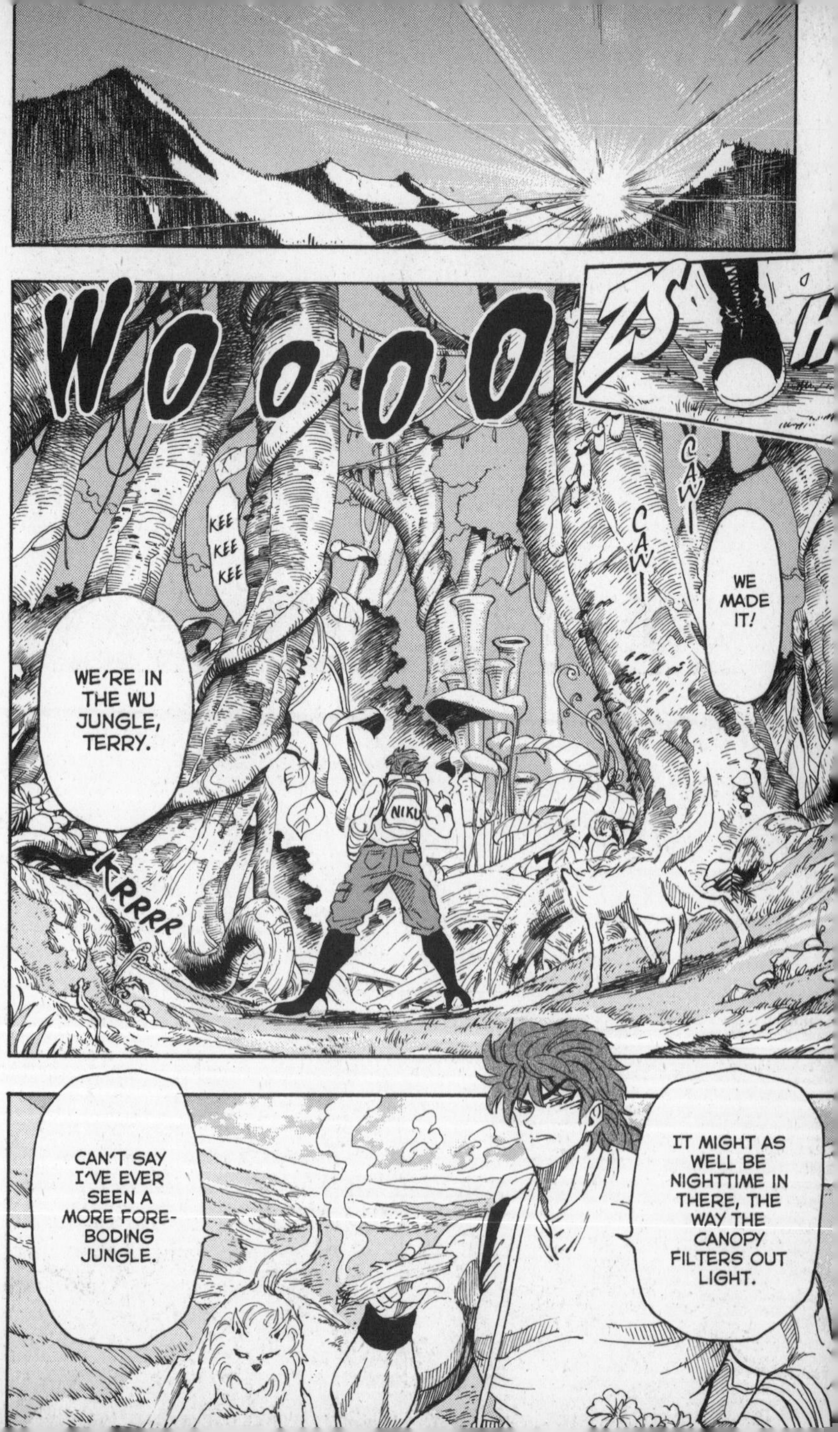
ZSH
CAW
CAW
WE MADE IT!
WOOOOO
KEE KEE KEE
WE'RE IN THE WU JUNGLE, TERRY.
KRRRR
IT MIGHT AS WELL BE NIGHTTIME IN THERE, THE WAY THE CANOPY FILTERS OUT LIGHT.
CAN'T SAY I'VE EVER SEEN A MORE FORE-BODING JUNGLE.

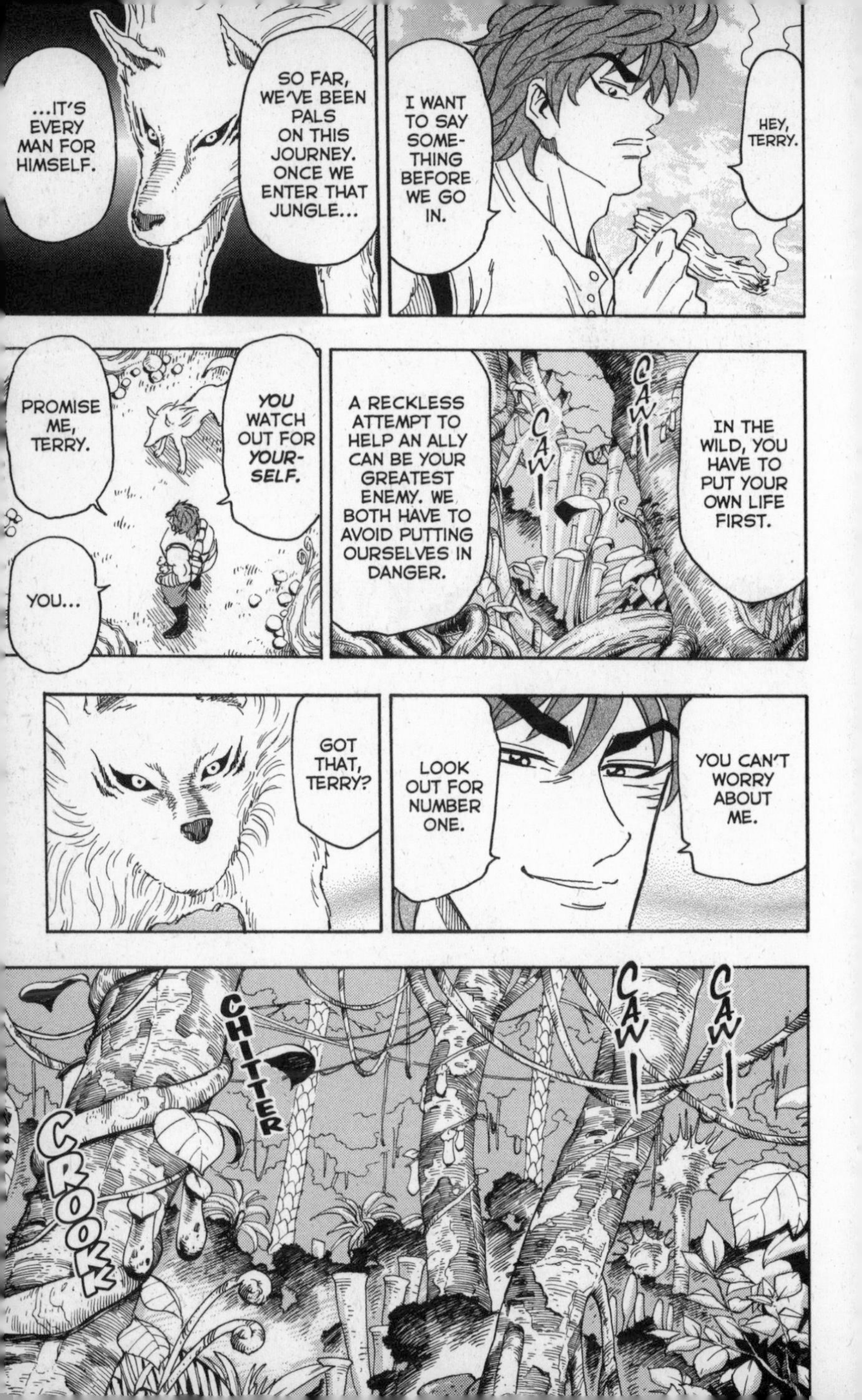
HEY, TERRY.
I WANT TO SAY SOME-THING BEFORE WE GO IN.
SO FAR, WE'VE BEEN PALS ON THIS JOURNEY. ONCE WE ENTER THAT JUNGLE...
...IT'S EVERY MAN FOR HIMSELF.
CAW!
CAW!
IN THE WILD, YOU HAVE TO PUT YOUR OWN LIFE FIRST.
A RECKLESS ATTEMPT TO HELP AN ALLY CAN BE YOUR GREATEST ENEMY. WE BOTH HAVE TO AVOID PUTTING OURSELVES IN DANGER.
YOU WATCH OUT FOR *YOURSELF.*
PROMISE ME, TERRY.
YOU...
YOU CAN'T WORRY ABOUT ME.
LOOK OUT FOR NUMBER ONE.
GOT THAT, TERRY?
CAW!
CAW!
CHITTER
CROOK

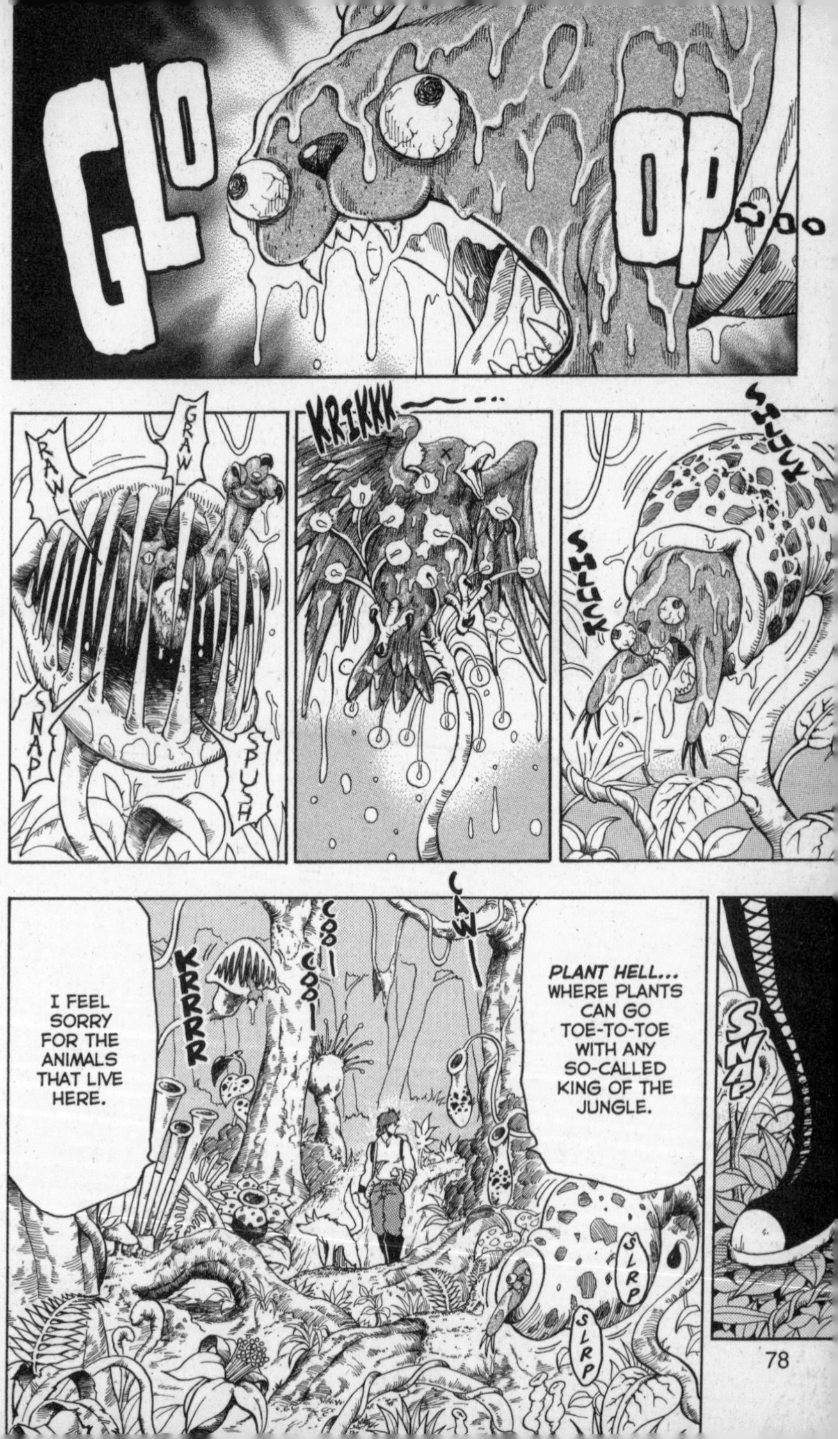

GLOOPOOO
SHLUCK
SHLUCK
KRIKKK
GRAW
RAW
SNAP
SPUSH
SNAP
CAW
PLANT HELL... WHERE PLANTS CAN GO TOE-TO-TOE WITH ANY SO-CALLED KING OF THE JUNGLE.
COO COO
KRRRR
I FEEL SORRY FOR THE ANIMALS THAT LIVE HERE.
SLRP
SLRP

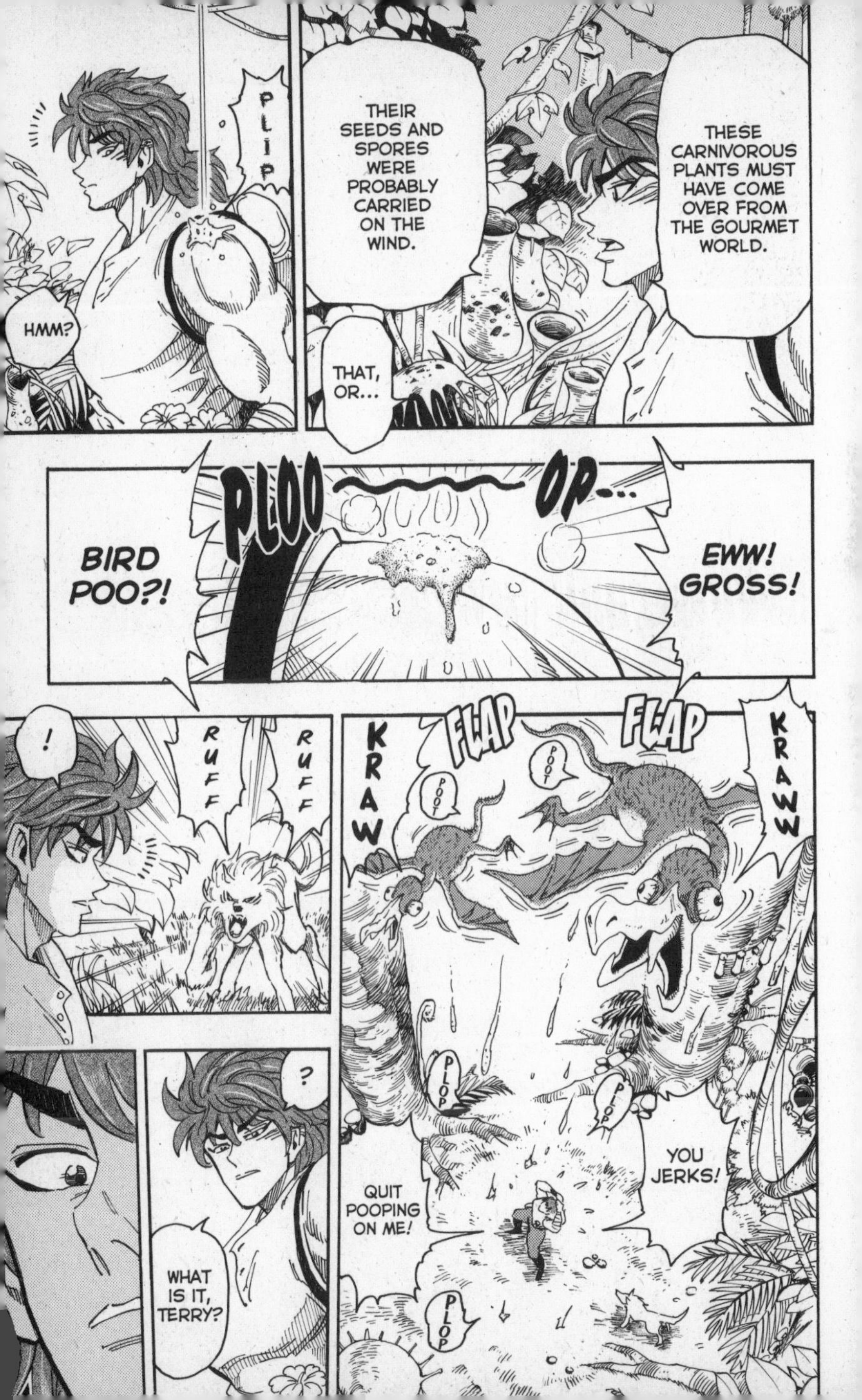
THESE CARNIVOROUS PLANTS MUST HAVE COME OVER FROM THE GOURMET WORLD.
THEIR SEEDS AND SPORES WERE PROBABLY CARRIED ON THE WIND.
THAT, OR...
PLIP
HMM?
PLOO~~~OP...
EWW! GROSS!
BIRD POO?!
KRAWW
FLAP
FLAP
KRAW
POOT
POOT
PLOP
PLOP
YOU JERKS!
QUIT POOPING ON ME!
PLOP
!
RUFF
RUFF
?
WHAT IS IT, TERRY?

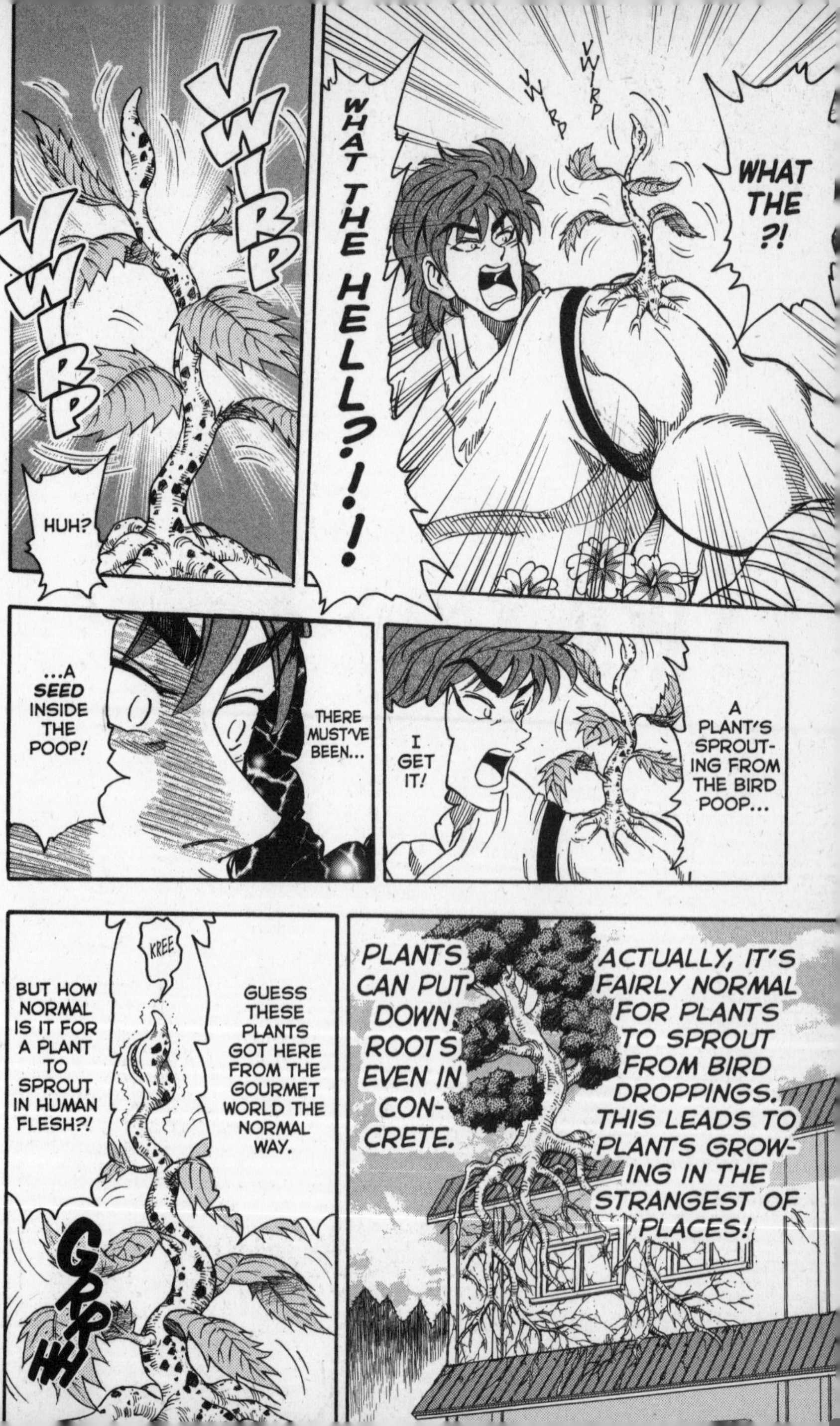
WHAT THE ?!
VWIRP VWIRP
WHAT THE HELL?!!!
VWIRP
VWIRP
HUH?
A PLANT'S SPROUTING FROM THE BIRD POOP...
I GET IT!
THERE MUST'VE BEEN...
...A SEED INSIDE THE POOP!
ACTUALLY, IT'S FAIRLY NORMAL FOR PLANTS TO SPROUT FROM BIRD DROPPINGS. THIS LEADS TO PLANTS GROWING IN THE STRANGEST OF PLACES!
PLANTS CAN PUT DOWN ROOTS EVEN IN CONCRETE.
KREE
GUESS THESE PLANTS GOT HERE FROM THE GOURMET WORLD THE NORMAL WAY.
BUT HOW NORMAL IS IT FOR A PLANT TO SPROUT IN HUMAN FLESH?!
GRRHH

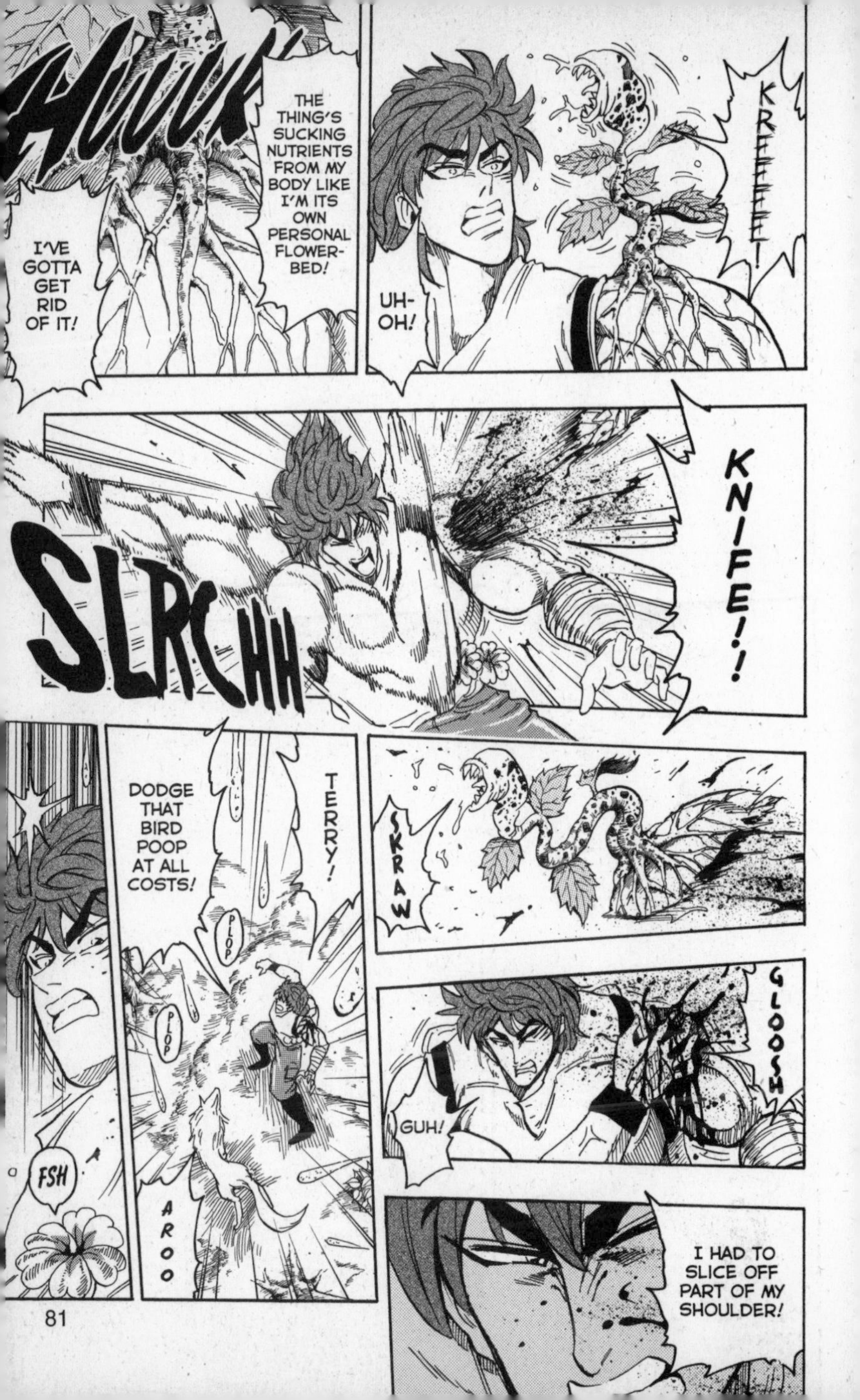
KREEEEE!
UH-OH!
THE THING'S SUCKING NUTRIENTS FROM MY BODY LIKE I'M ITS OWN PERSONAL FLOWER-BED!
I'VE GOTTA GET RID OF IT!
KNIFE!!!
SLRCHH
SKRAW
GLOOSH
GUH!
I HAD TO SLICE OFF PART OF MY SHOULDER!
TERRY!
DODGE THAT BIRD POOP AT ALL COSTS!
PLOP
PLOP
AROO
FSH

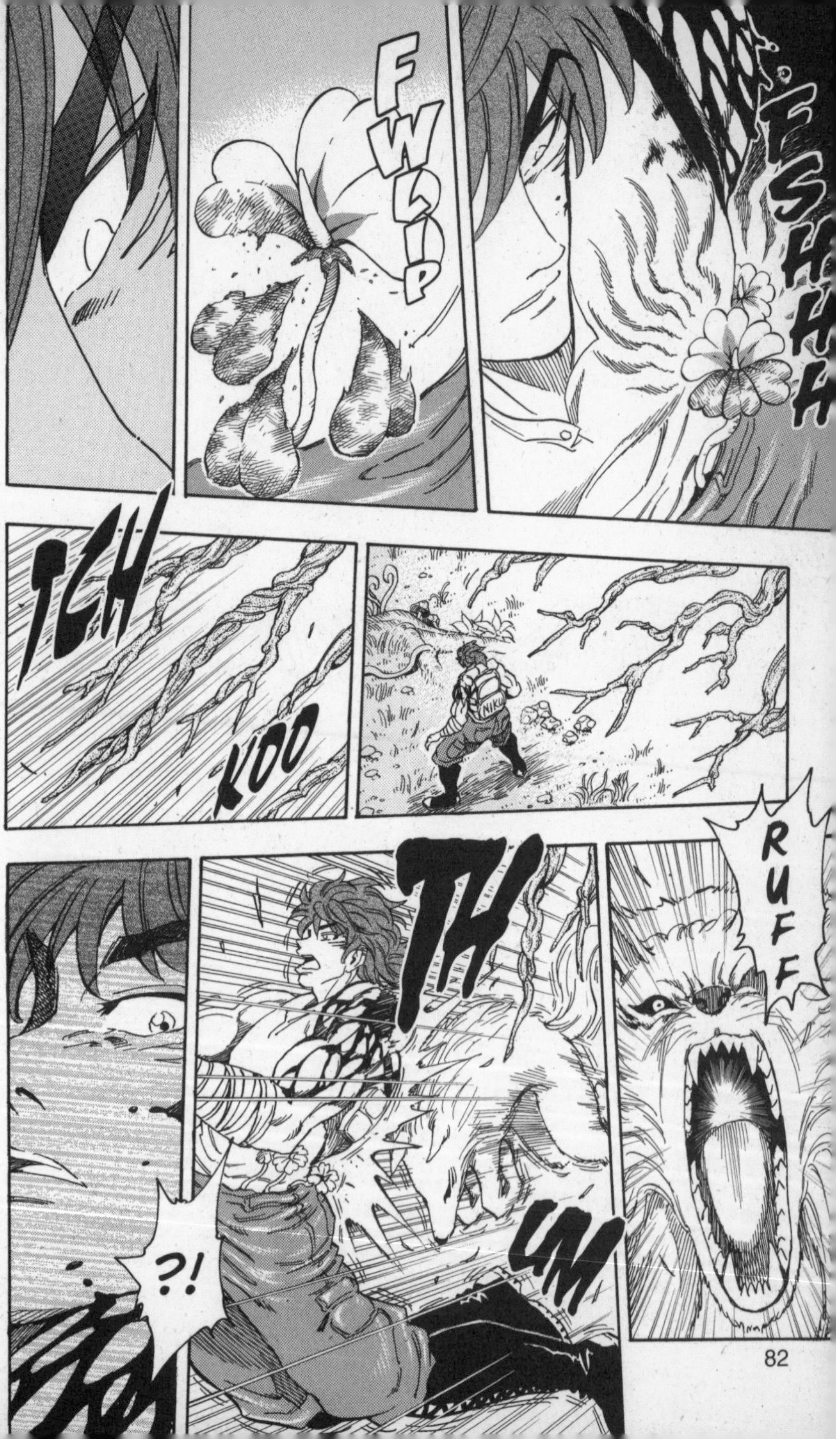
FSHHHH
FWLIP
ICH
KOO
RUFF
TH
UM
?!

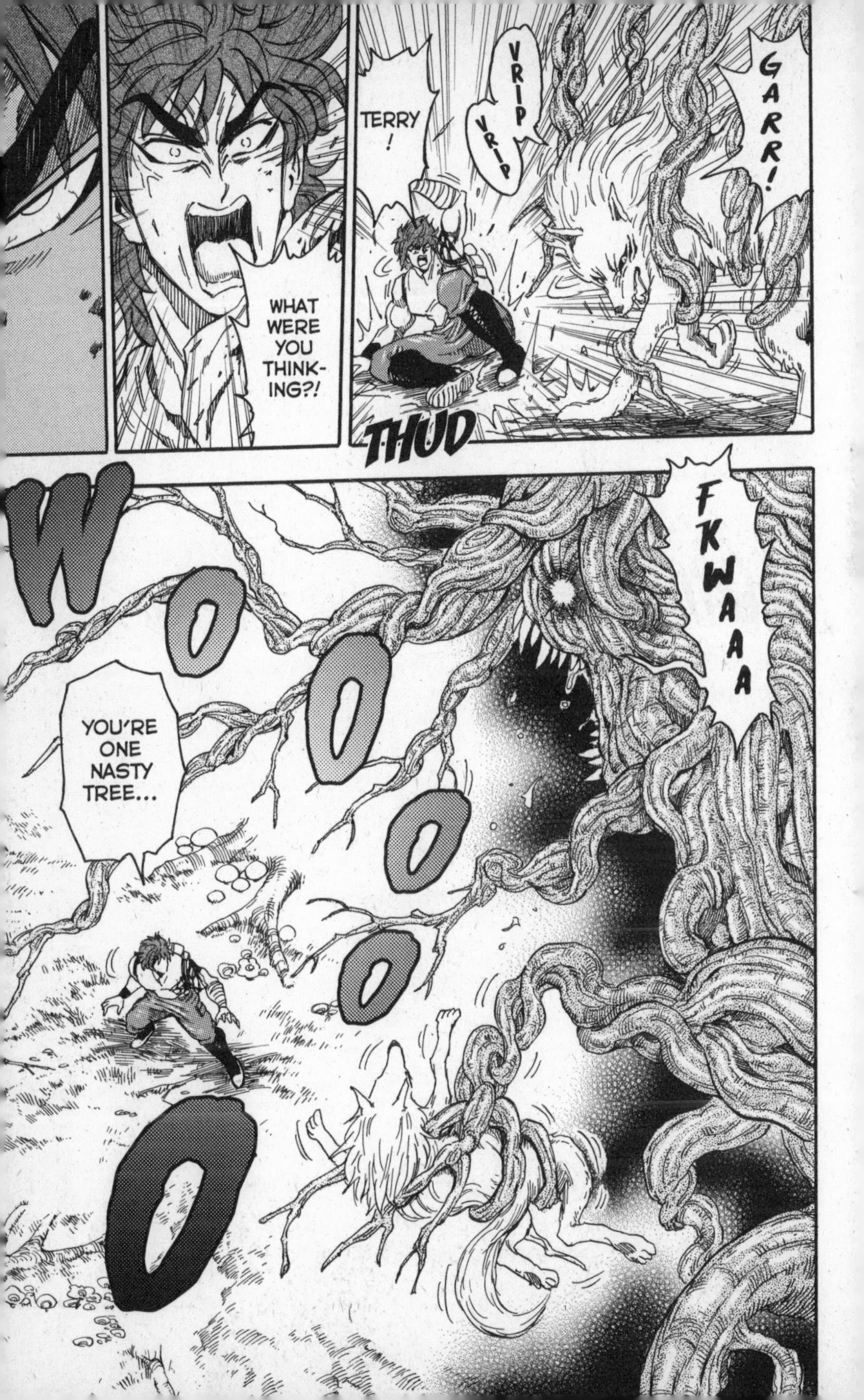
GARR!
VRIP VRIP
TERRY!
THUD
WHAT WERE YOU THINKING?!
FKWAAA
WOOOOO
YOU'RE ONE NASTY TREE...

TORIKO

GOURMET CHECKLIST

Vol. 041

DRUNKEN COW

(MAMMAL)

CAPTURE LEVEL: 30

HABITAT: BACCHUS ISLE

LENGTH: 9 METERS

HEIGHT: 3.5 METERS

WEIGHT: 8 TONS

PRICE: 100 G / 25,000 YEN

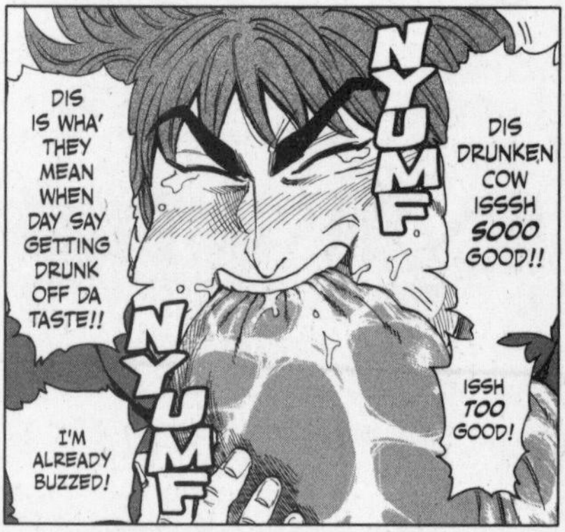
DIS DRUNKEN COW ISSSH SOOO GOOD!!
NYUMF
DIS IS WHA' THEY MEAN WHEN DAY SAY GETTING DRUNK OFF DA TASTE!!
ISSH TOO GOOD!
NYUMF
I'M ALREADY BUZZED!

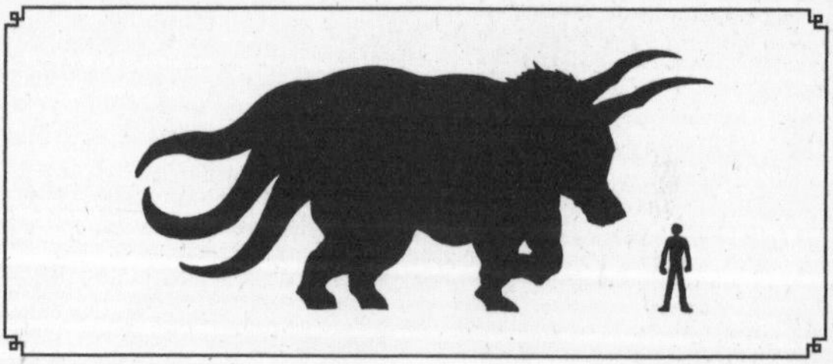

SCALE

LIKE ALL ANIMALS ON BACCHUS ISLE, THIS BOVINE'S MAIN WATER SUPPLY IS ALCOHOL-STEEPED LAKE WATER. TRUE TO THEIR NAME, DRUNKEN COWS CAN ALWAYS BE FOUND TEETERING AROUND IN DRUNKEN STUPORS. THE DRUNKER ONE GETS, THE MORE VIOLENT IT GETS. A DEEPLY INEBRIATED DRUNKEN COW GIVES A WHOLE NEW MEANING TO "RAGING BULL."

GOURMET 57: A GLIMPSE OF ROYALTY!!

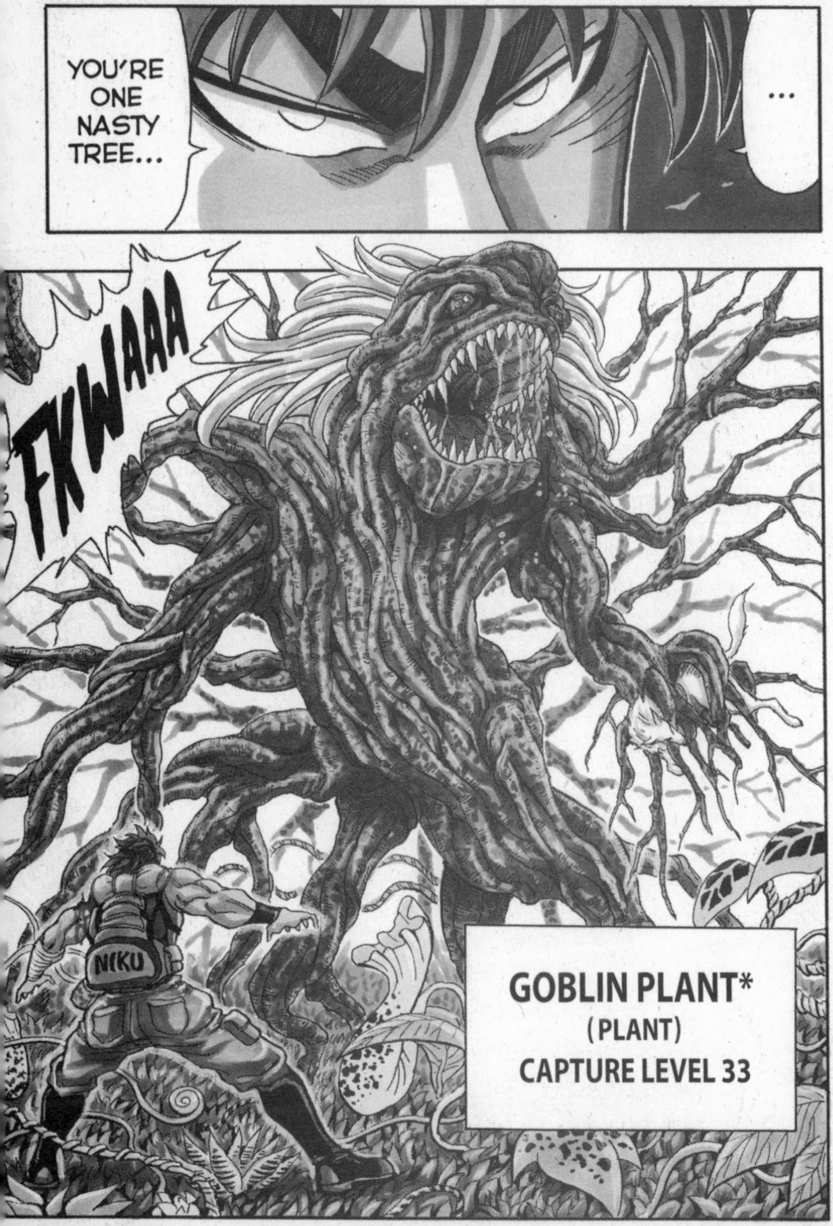
...
YOU'RE ONE NASTY TREE...
FKWAAA
GOBLIN PLANT*
(PLANT)
CAPTURE LEVEL 33

*THANKS TO ASAKI UCHINO FROM FUKUOKA FOR CREATING THE GOBLIN PLANT!

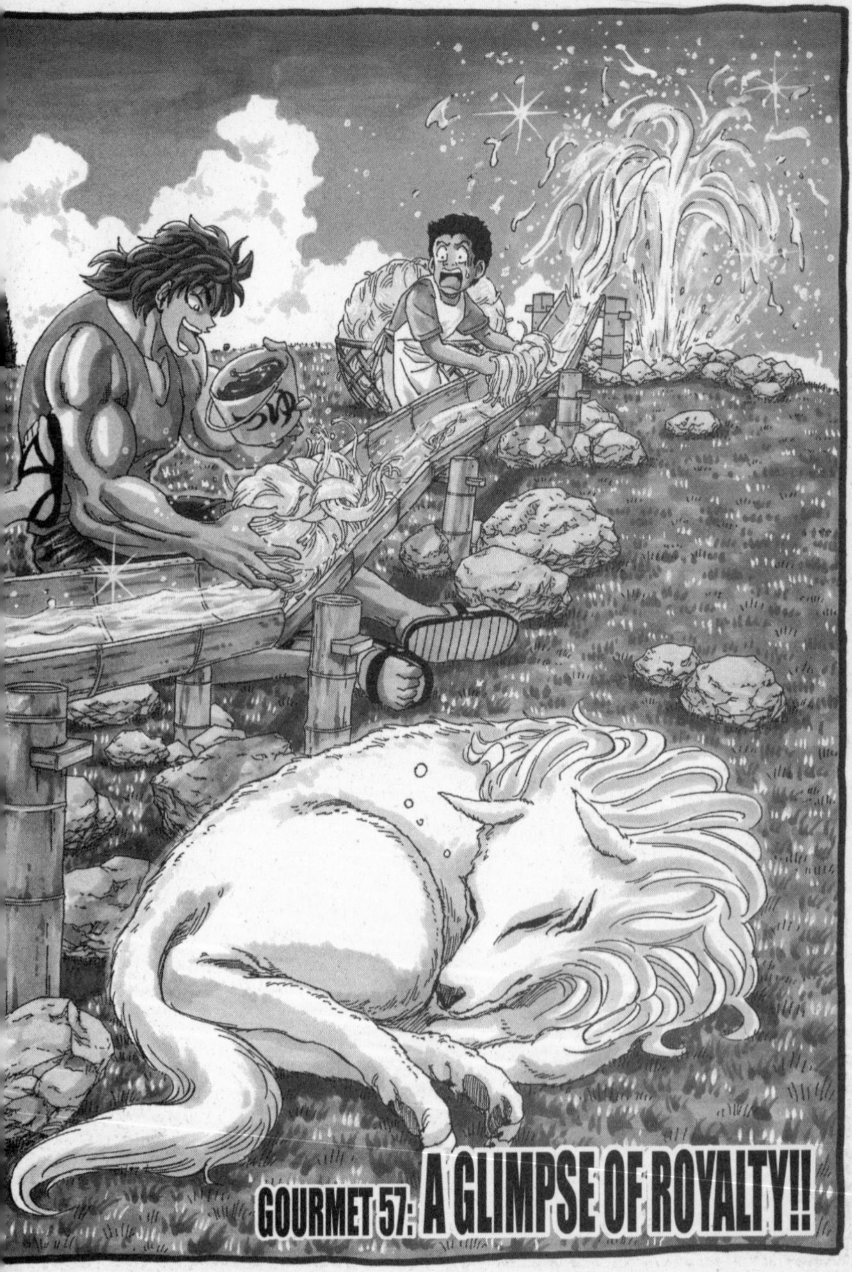
GOURMET 57: A GLIMPSE OF ROYALTY!!

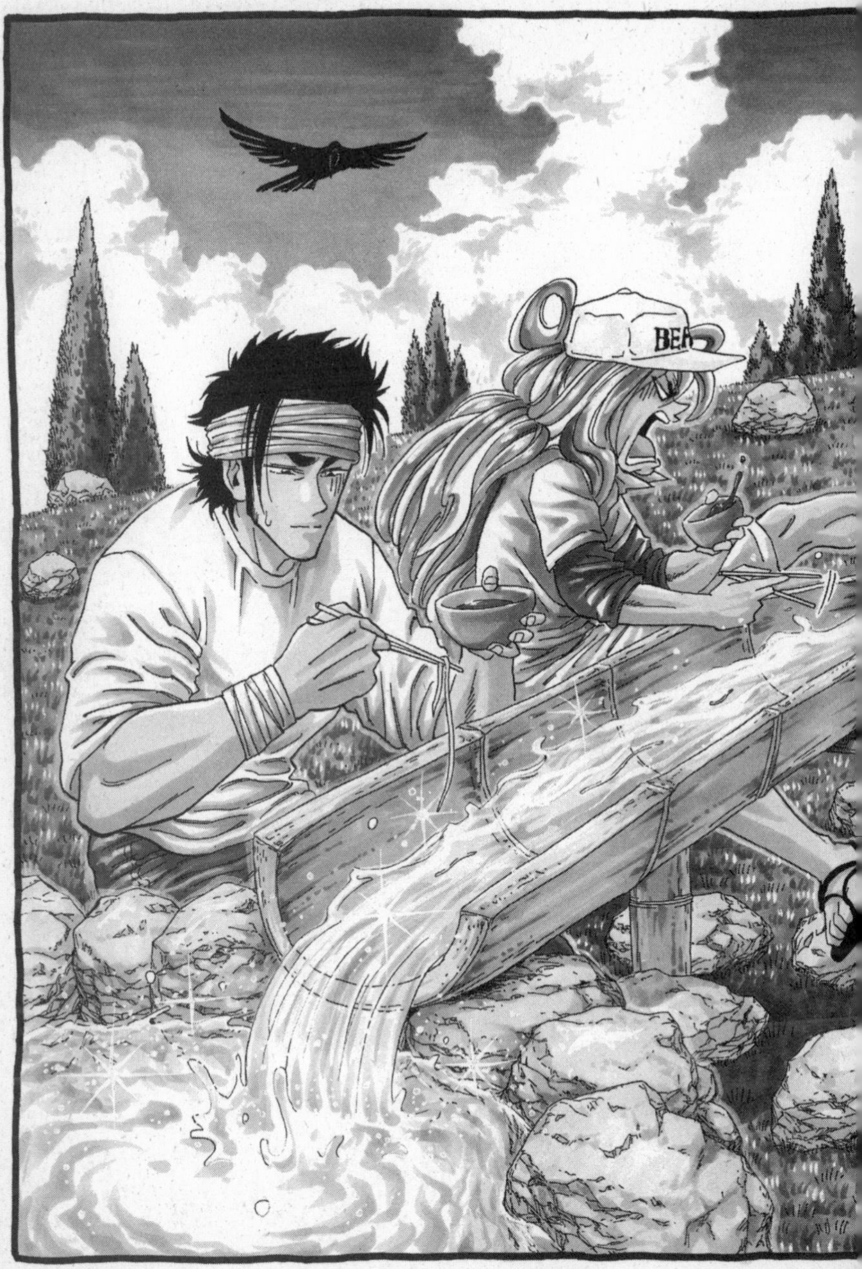
BEA

TORIKO

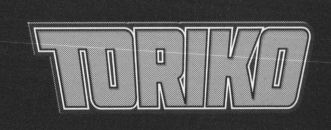

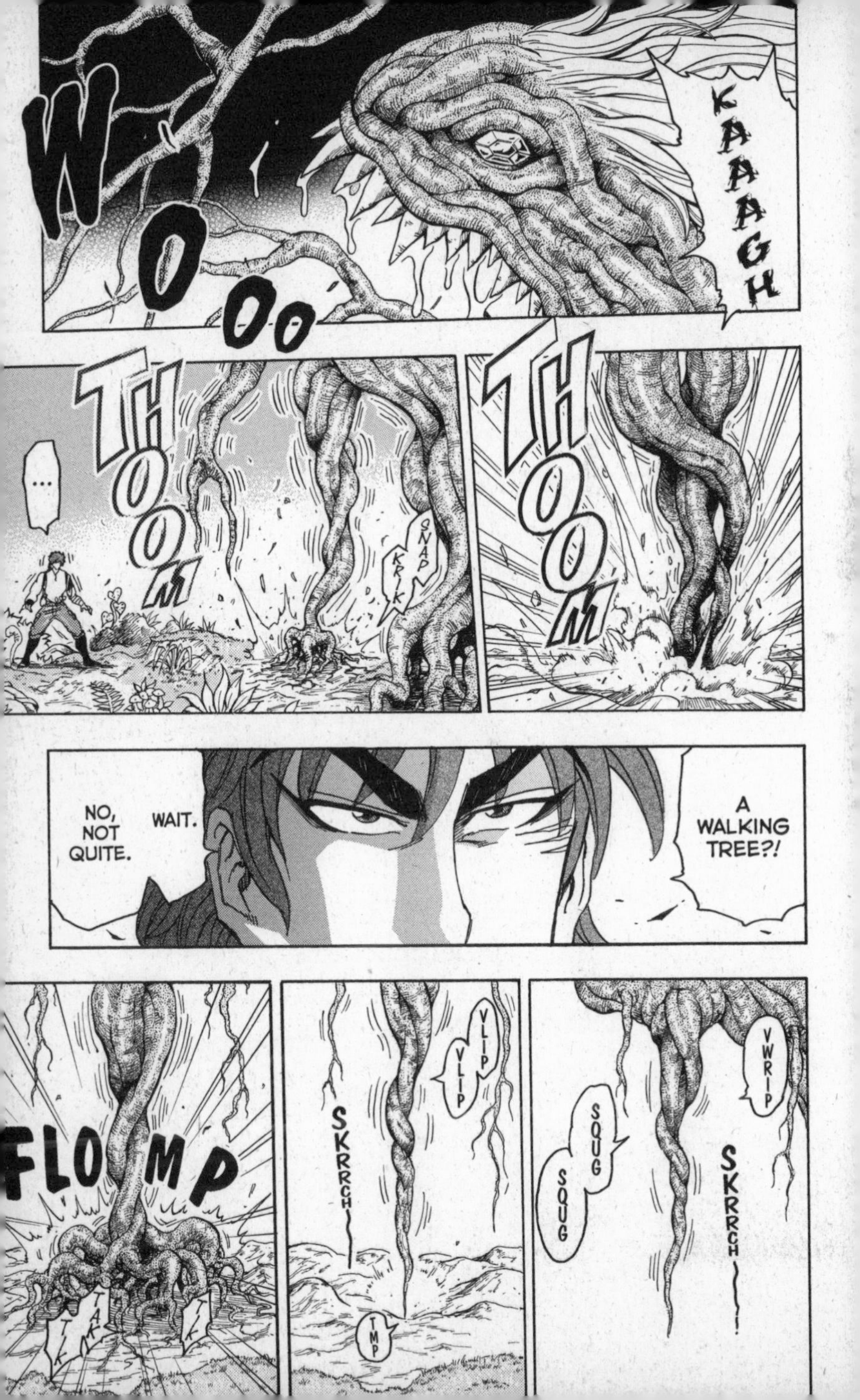
KAAAGH
WOOOO
THOOOM
SNAP KRIK
THOOOM
...
A WALKING TREE?!
WAIT.
NO, NOT QUITE.
VWRIP
SKRRCH
SQUG SQUG
VLIP VLIP
SKRRCH
TMP
FLOMP
TIK TAK TIK

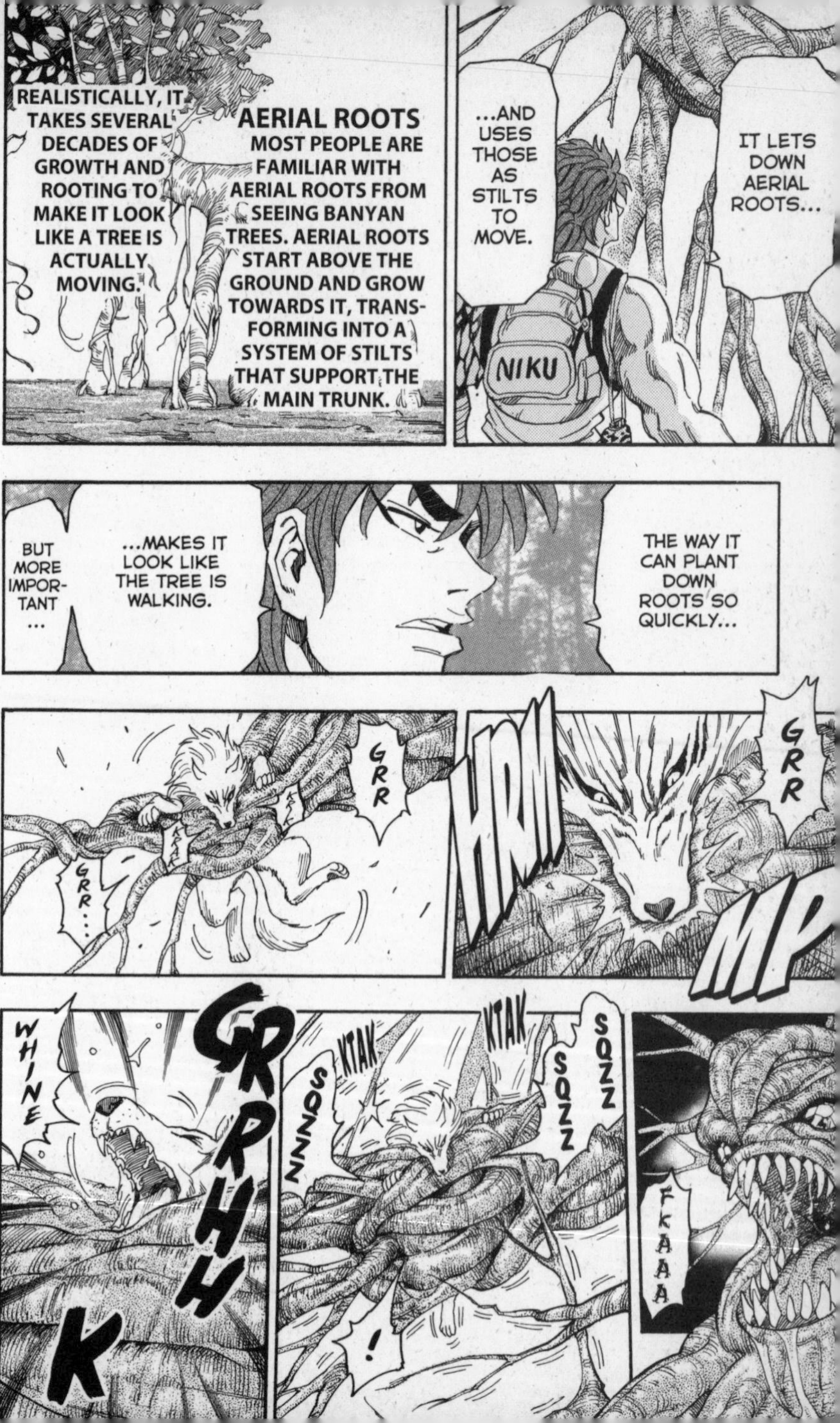
IT LETS DOWN AERIAL ROOTS...
...AND USES THOSE AS STILTS TO MOVE.
NIKU
AERIAL ROOTS
MOST PEOPLE ARE FAMILIAR WITH AERIAL ROOTS FROM SEEING BANYAN TREES. AERIAL ROOTS START ABOVE THE GROUND AND GROW TOWARDS IT, TRANSFORMING INTO A SYSTEM OF STILTS THAT SUPPORT THE MAIN TRUNK.
REALISTICALLY, IT TAKES SEVERAL DECADES OF GROWTH AND ROOTING TO MAKE IT LOOK LIKE A TREE IS ACTUALLY MOVING.
THE WAY IT CAN PLANT DOWN ROOTS SO QUICKLY...
...MAKES IT LOOK LIKE THE TREE IS WALKING.
BUT MORE IMPORTANT ...
GRR
HRMMP
GRR
GRR...
FKAAA
SQZZ
SQZZ
KTAK
KTAK
SQNNNZ
!
GRRHHK
WHINE

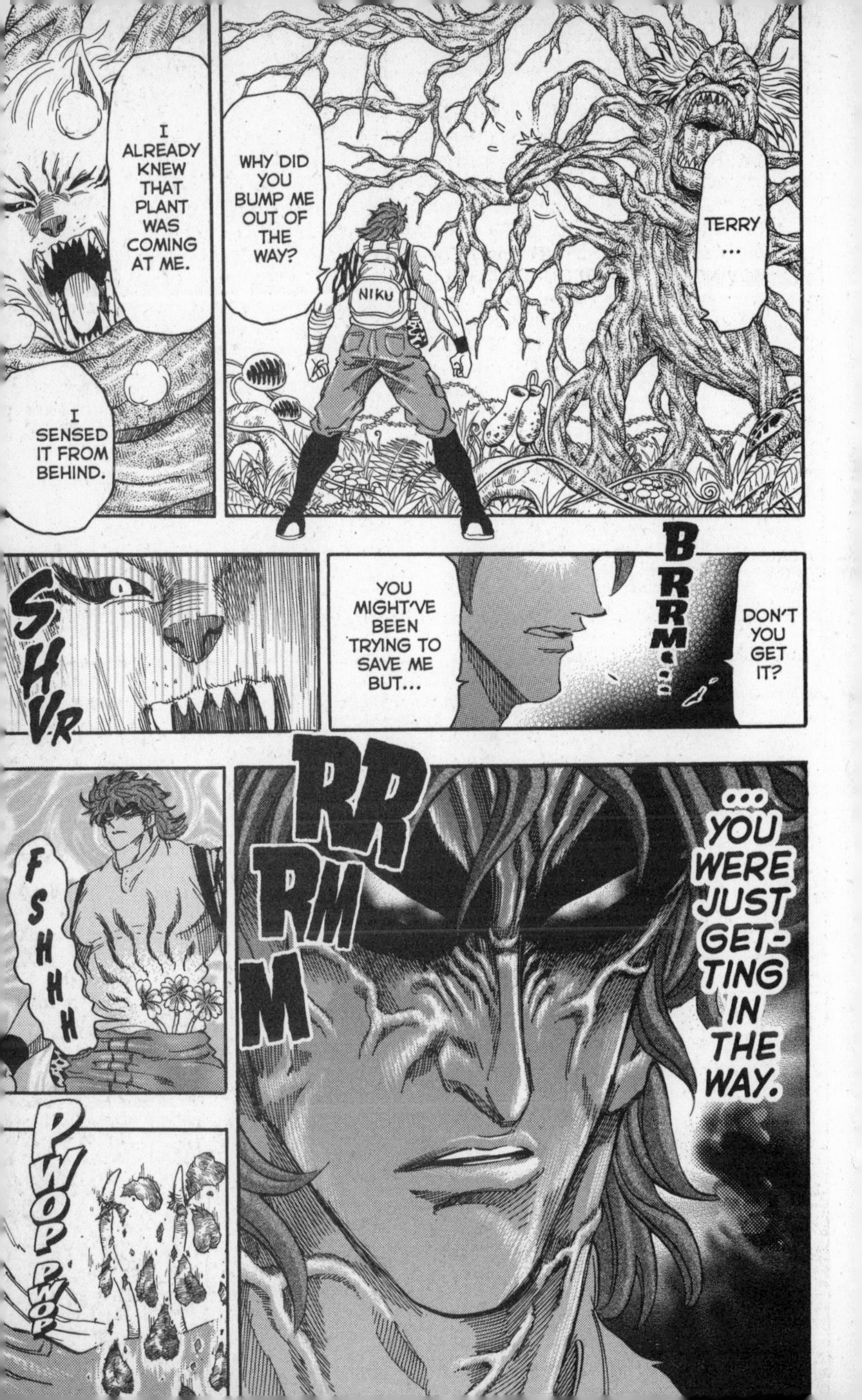
TERRY ...
WHY DID YOU BUMP ME OUT OF THE WAY?
I ALREADY KNEW THAT PLANT WAS COMING AT ME.
I SENSED IT FROM BEHIND.
DON'T YOU GET IT?
BRRM...
YOU MIGHT'VE BEEN TRYING TO SAVE ME BUT...
SHVR
RRRMM
...YOU WERE JUST GET-TING IN THE WAY.
FSHHH
PWOP PWOP

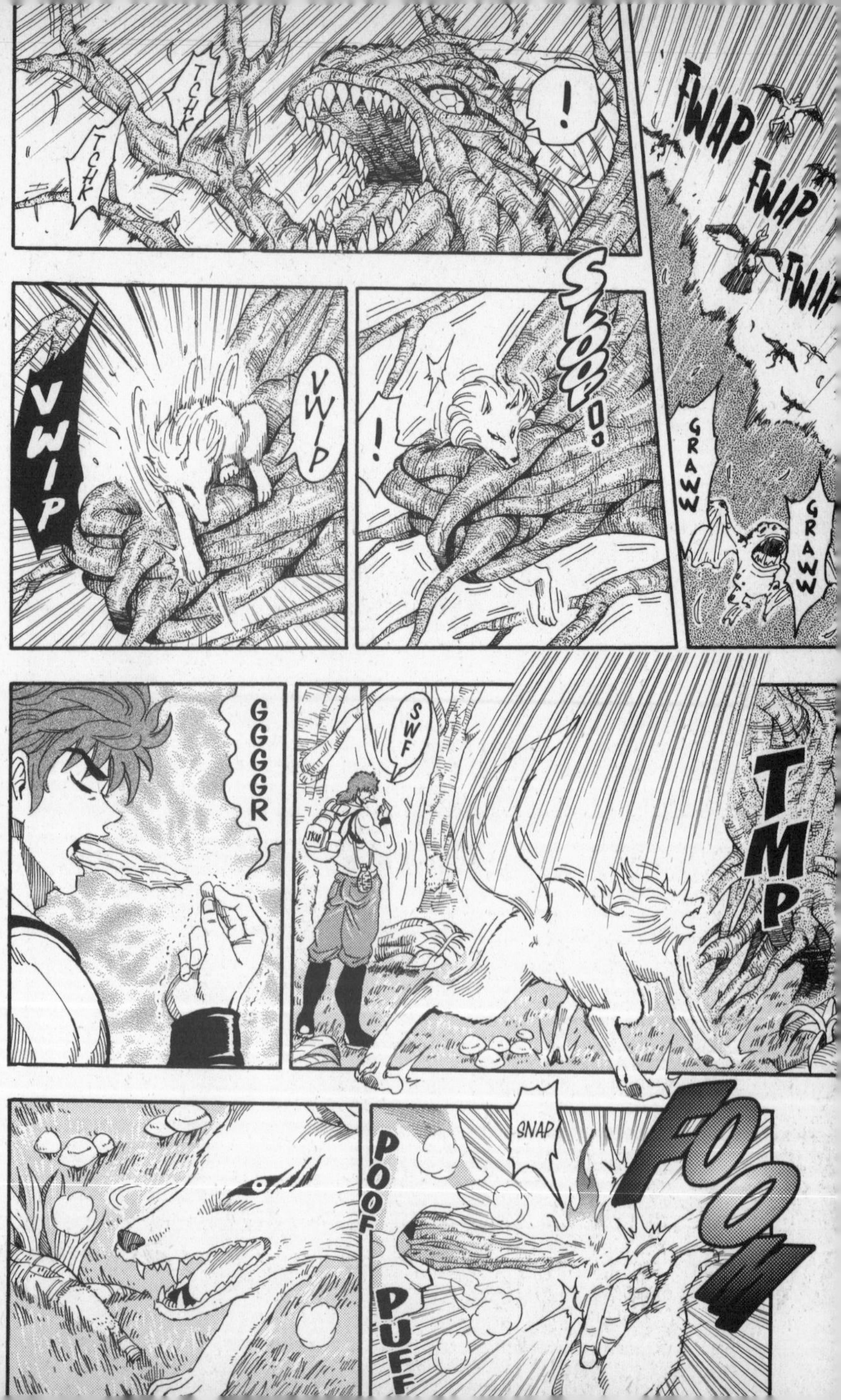
FWAP
FWAP
FWAP
GRAWW
GRAWW
!
TCHK
TCHK
SLOOOP
!
VWIP
VWIP
TMP
SWF
GGGGR
SNAP
POOOM
POOF
PUFF

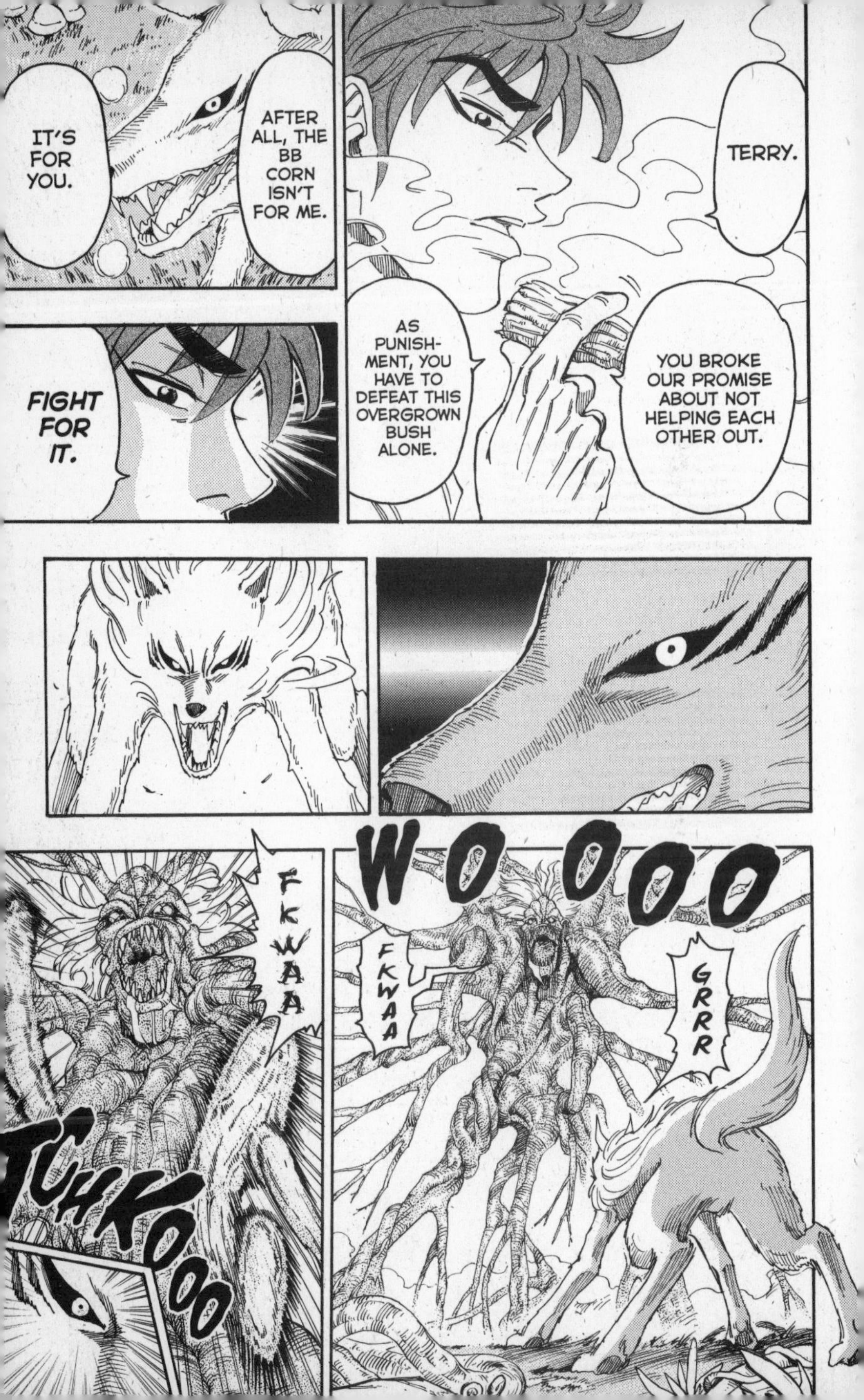

TERRY.
YOU BROKE OUR PROMISE ABOUT NOT HELPING EACH OTHER OUT.
AS PUNISH-MENT, YOU HAVE TO DEFEAT THIS OVERGROWN BUSH ALONE.
AFTER ALL, THE BB CORN ISN'T FOR ME.
IT'S FOR YOU.
FIGHT FOR IT.
WOOOO
GRRR
FKWAA
FKWAA
TCHKOOO

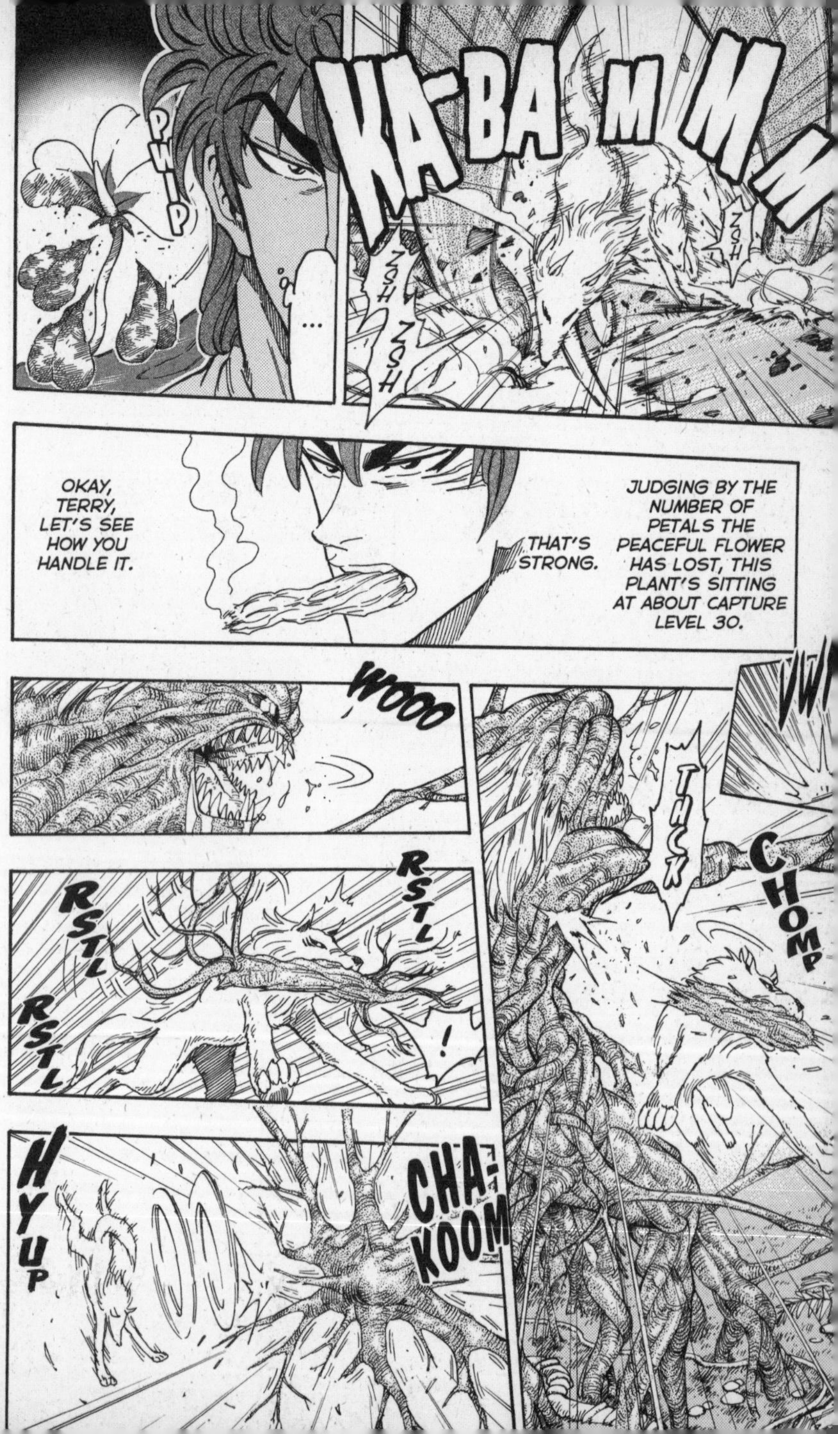

KA-BA M M M
ZSH
ZSH
ZSH ZSH
PWIP
...
JUDGING BY THE NUMBER OF PETALS THE PEACEFUL FLOWER HAS LOST, THIS PLANT'S SITTING AT ABOUT CAPTURE LEVEL 30.
THAT'S STRONG.
OKAY, TERRY, LET'S SEE HOW YOU HANDLE IT.
THCK
CHOMP
WOOO
RSTL
RSTL
RSTL
!
CHA-KOOM
HYUP

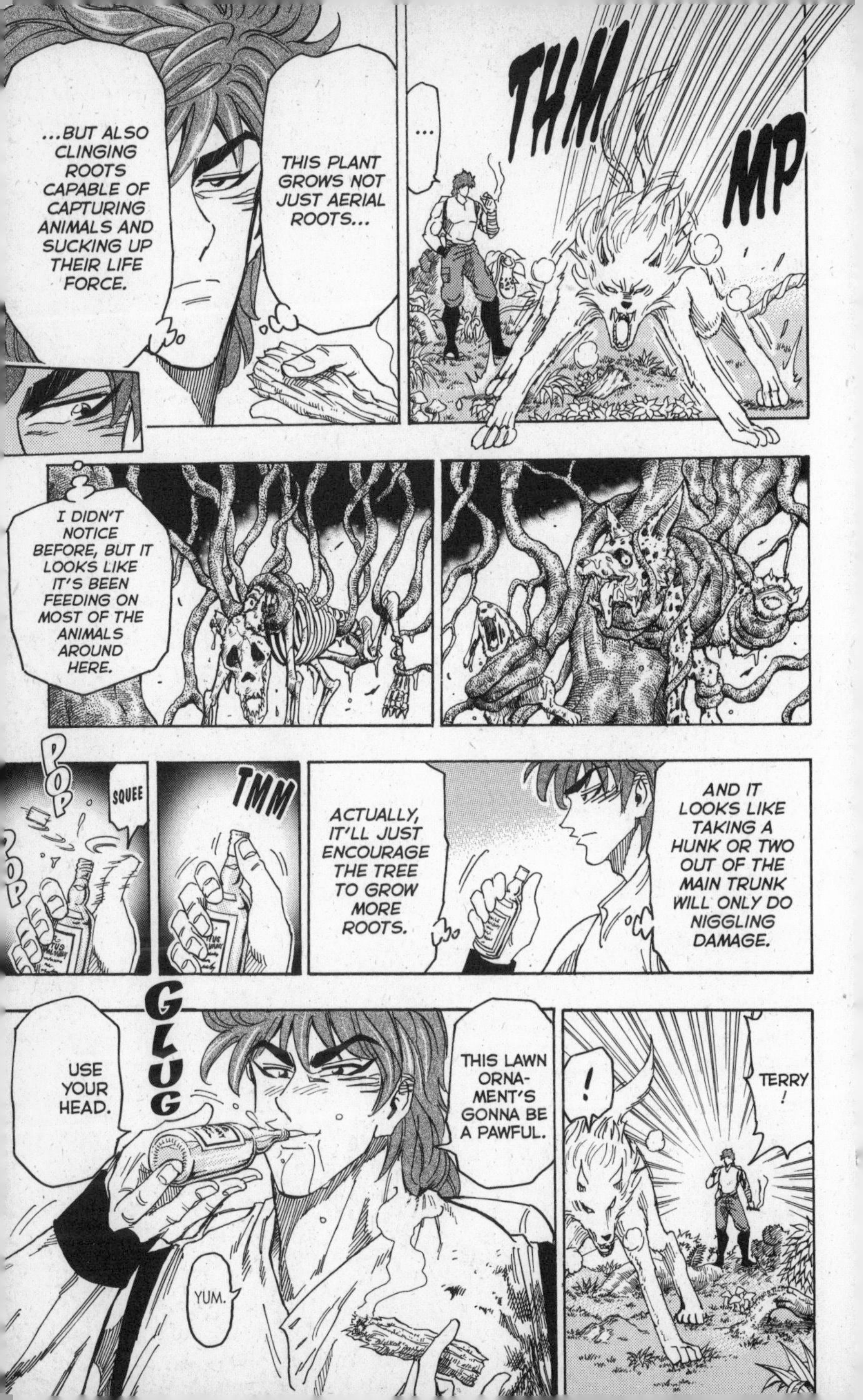
THMMP
...
THIS PLANT GROWS NOT JUST AERIAL ROOTS...
...BUT ALSO CLINGING ROOTS CAPABLE OF CAPTURING ANIMALS AND SUCKING UP THEIR LIFE FORCE.
I DIDN'T NOTICE BEFORE, BUT IT LOOKS LIKE IT'S BEEN FEEDING ON MOST OF THE ANIMALS AROUND HERE.
AND IT LOOKS LIKE TAKING A HUNK OR TWO OUT OF THE MAIN TRUNK WILL ONLY DO NIGGLING DAMAGE.
ACTUALLY, IT'LL JUST ENCOURAGE THE TREE TO GROW MORE ROOTS.
TMM
SQUEE
POP
POP
TERRY !
!
THIS LAWN ORNA-MENT'S GONNA BE A PAWFUL.
USE YOUR HEAD.
GLUG
YUM.

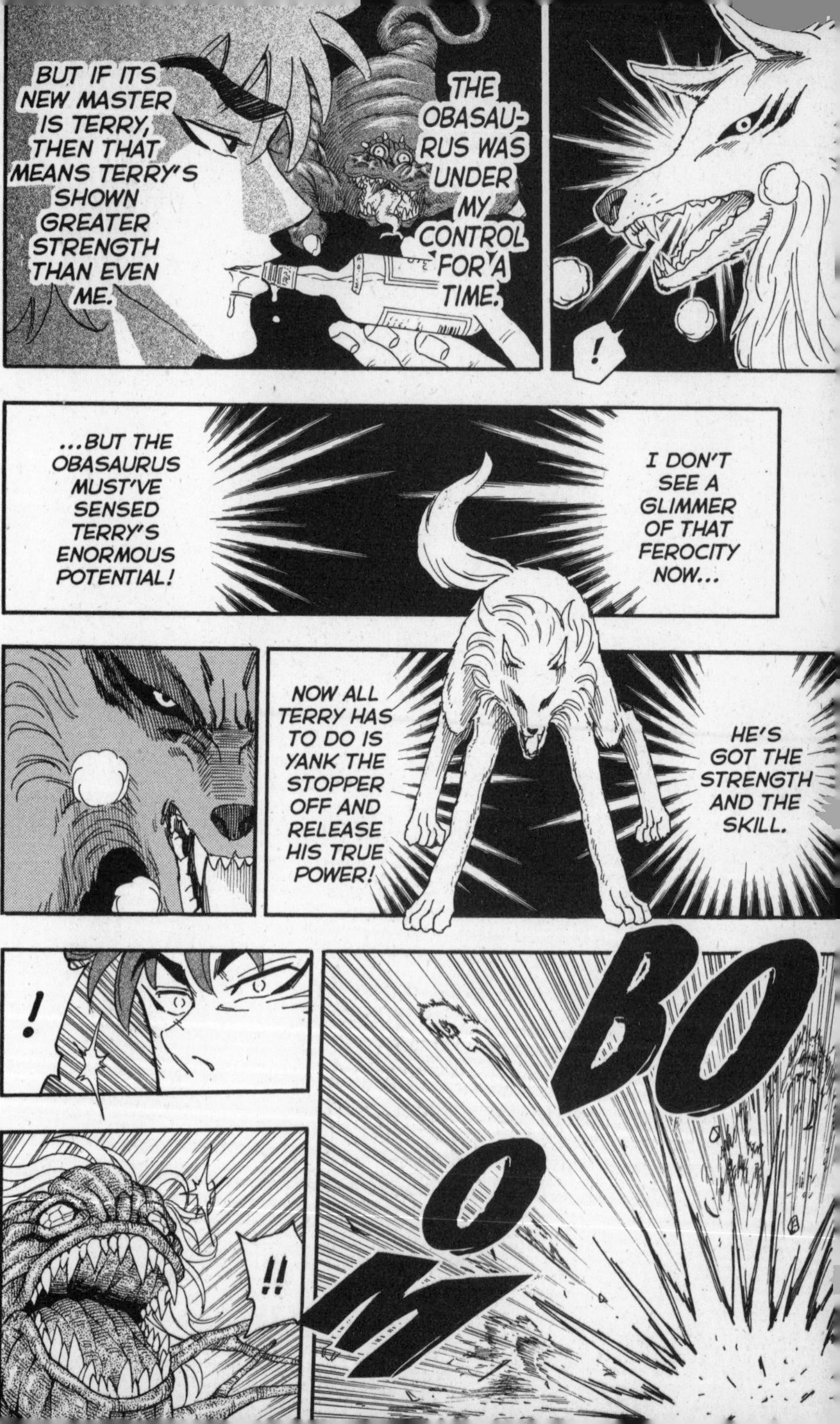
!
THE OBASAURUS WAS UNDER MY CONTROL FOR A TIME.
BUT IF ITS NEW MASTER IS TERRY, THEN THAT MEANS TERRY'S SHOWN GREATER STRENGTH THAN EVEN ME.
I DON'T SEE A GLIMMER OF THAT FEROCITY NOW...
...BUT THE OBASAURUS MUST'VE SENSED TERRY'S ENORMOUS POTENTIAL!
HE'S GOT THE STRENGTH AND THE SKILL.
NOW ALL TERRY HAS TO DO IS YANK THE STOPPER OFF AND RELEASE HIS TRUE POWER!
BOOM
!
!!

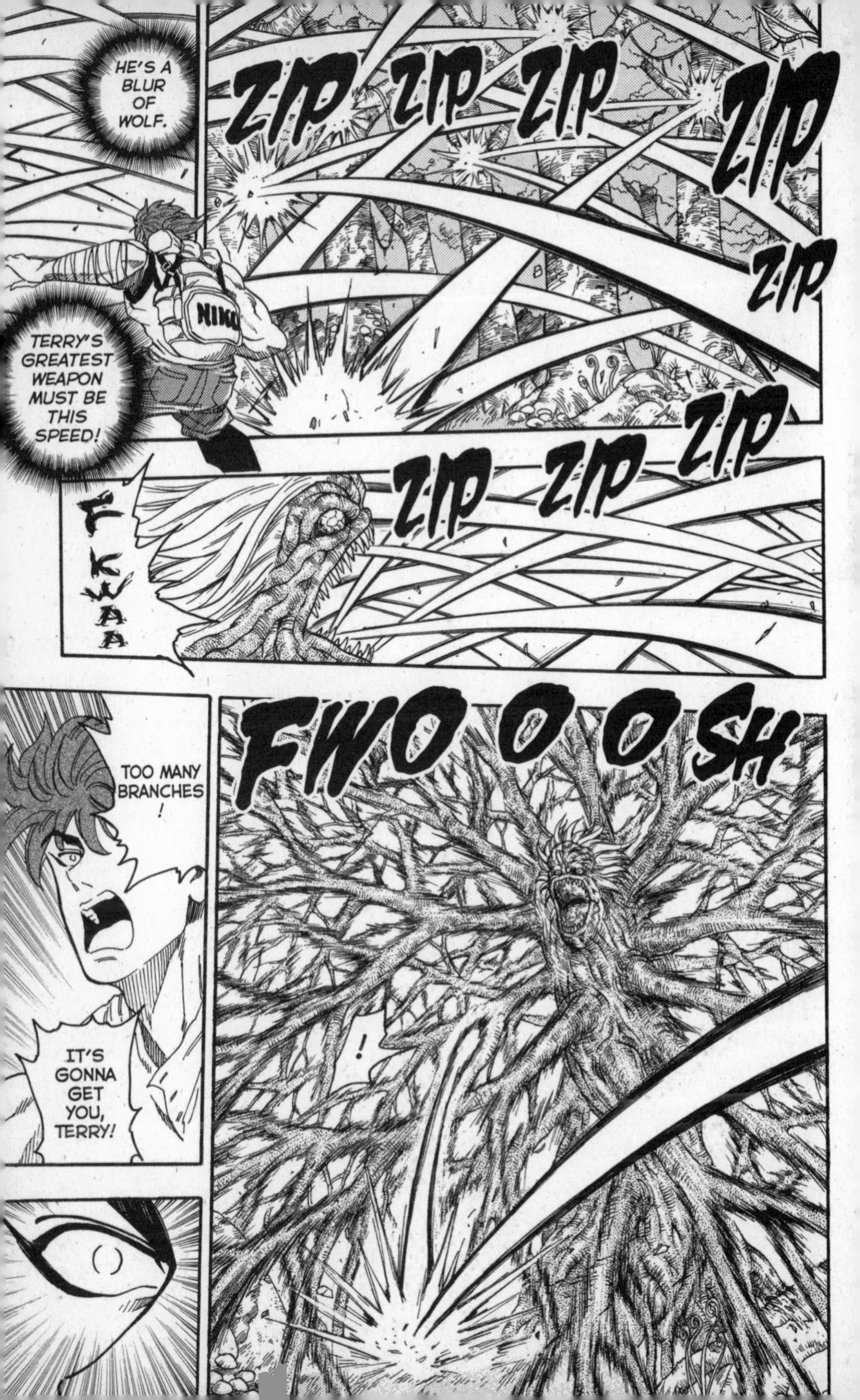
ZIP ZIP ZIP ZIP
ZIP
HE'S A BLUR OF WOLF.
TERRY'S GREATEST WEAPON MUST BE THIS SPEED!
NIKU
ZIP ZIP ZIP
FKWAA
FWOOOSH
!
TOO MANY BRANCHES!
IT'S GONNA GET YOU, TERRY!

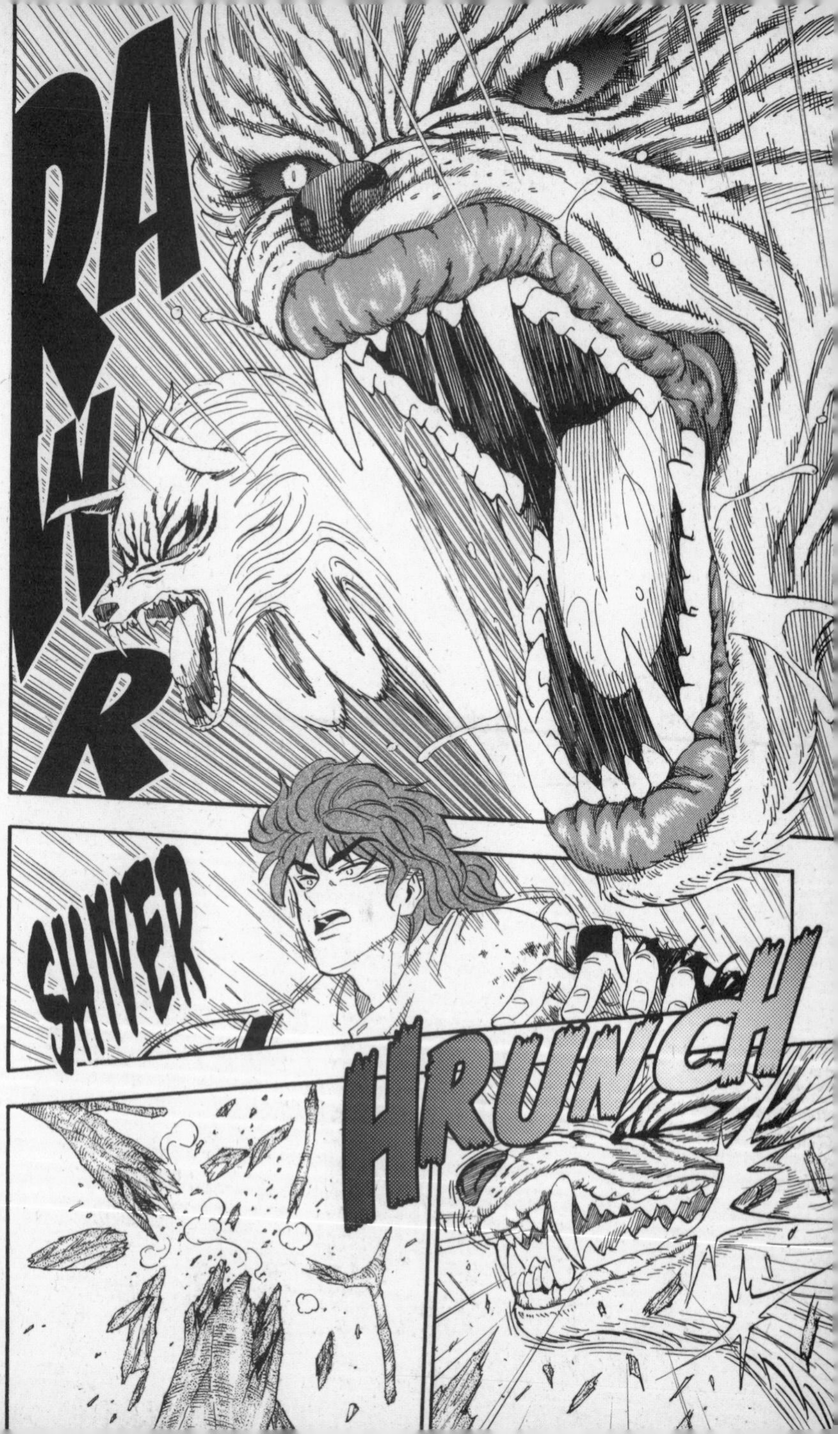
RAWR
SHIVER
HRUNCH

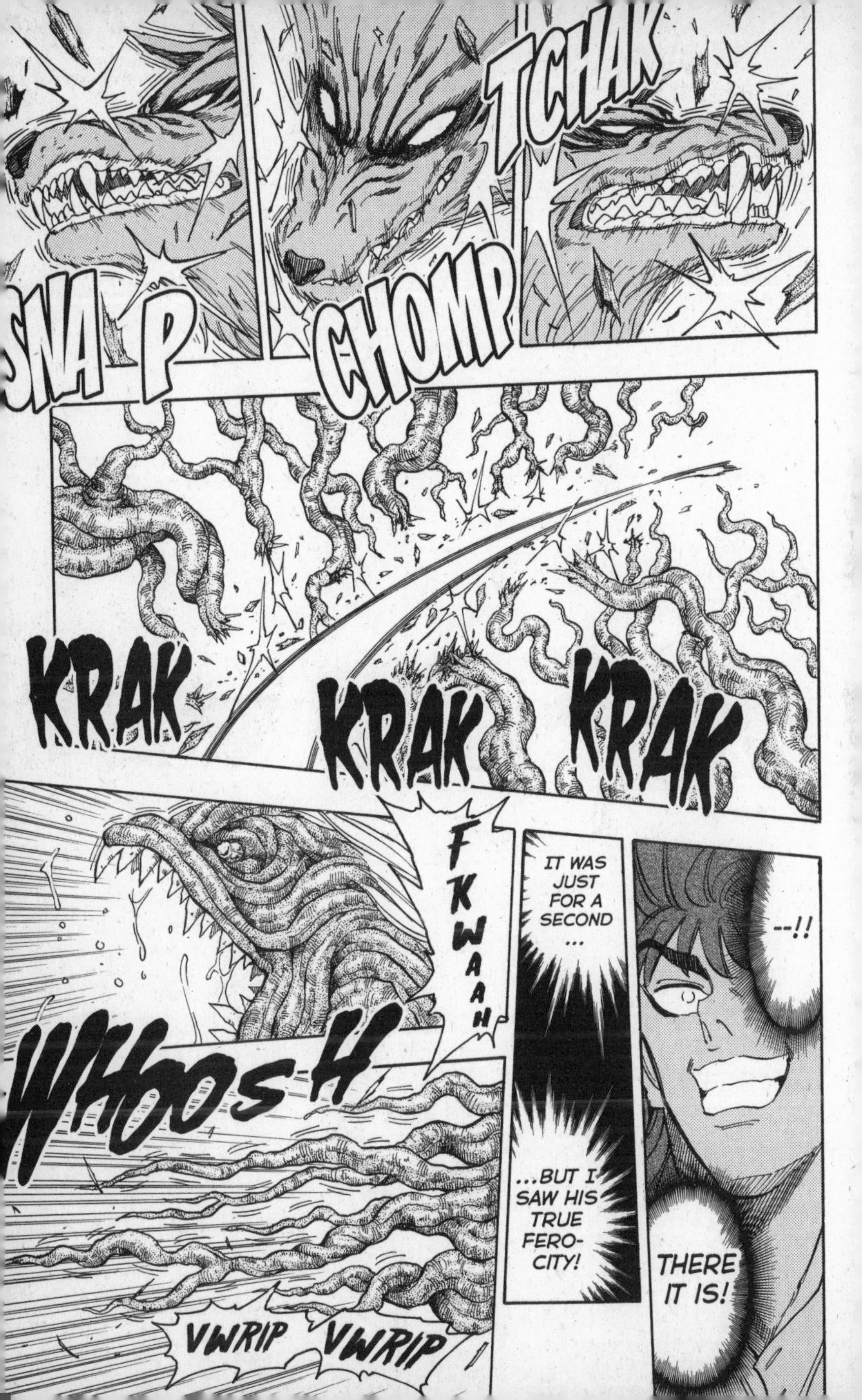
TCHAK
CHOMP
SNA P
KRAK
KRAK
KRAK
--!!
THERE IT IS!
IT WAS JUST FOR A SECOND ...
...BUT I SAW HIS TRUE FERO-CITY!
FKWAAAH
WHOOSH
VWRIP
VWRIP

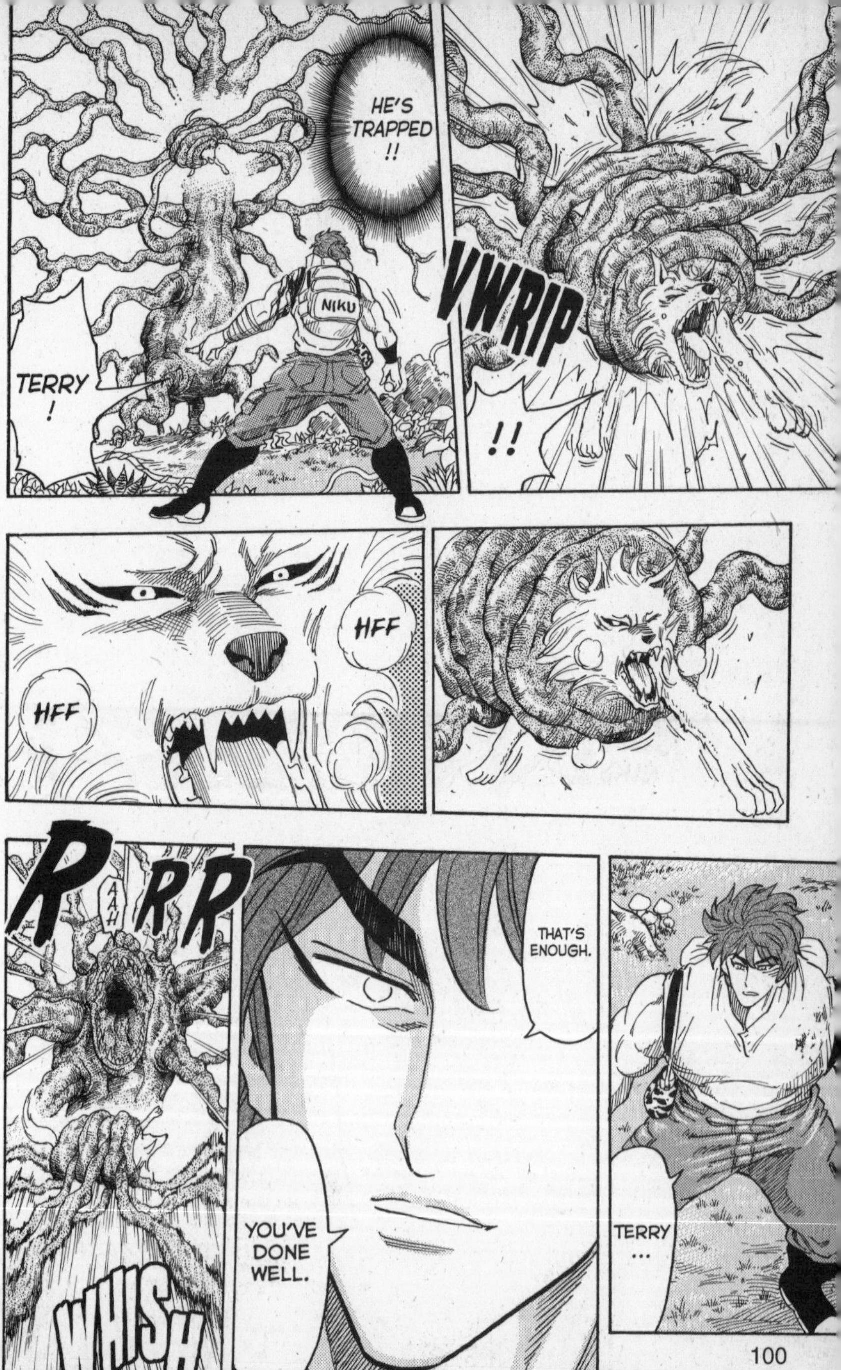
VWRIP
!!
HE'S TRAPPED !!
TERRY !
HFF
HFF
TERRY ...
THAT'S ENOUGH.
YOU'VE DONE WELL.
RRRR
AAH
WHISH

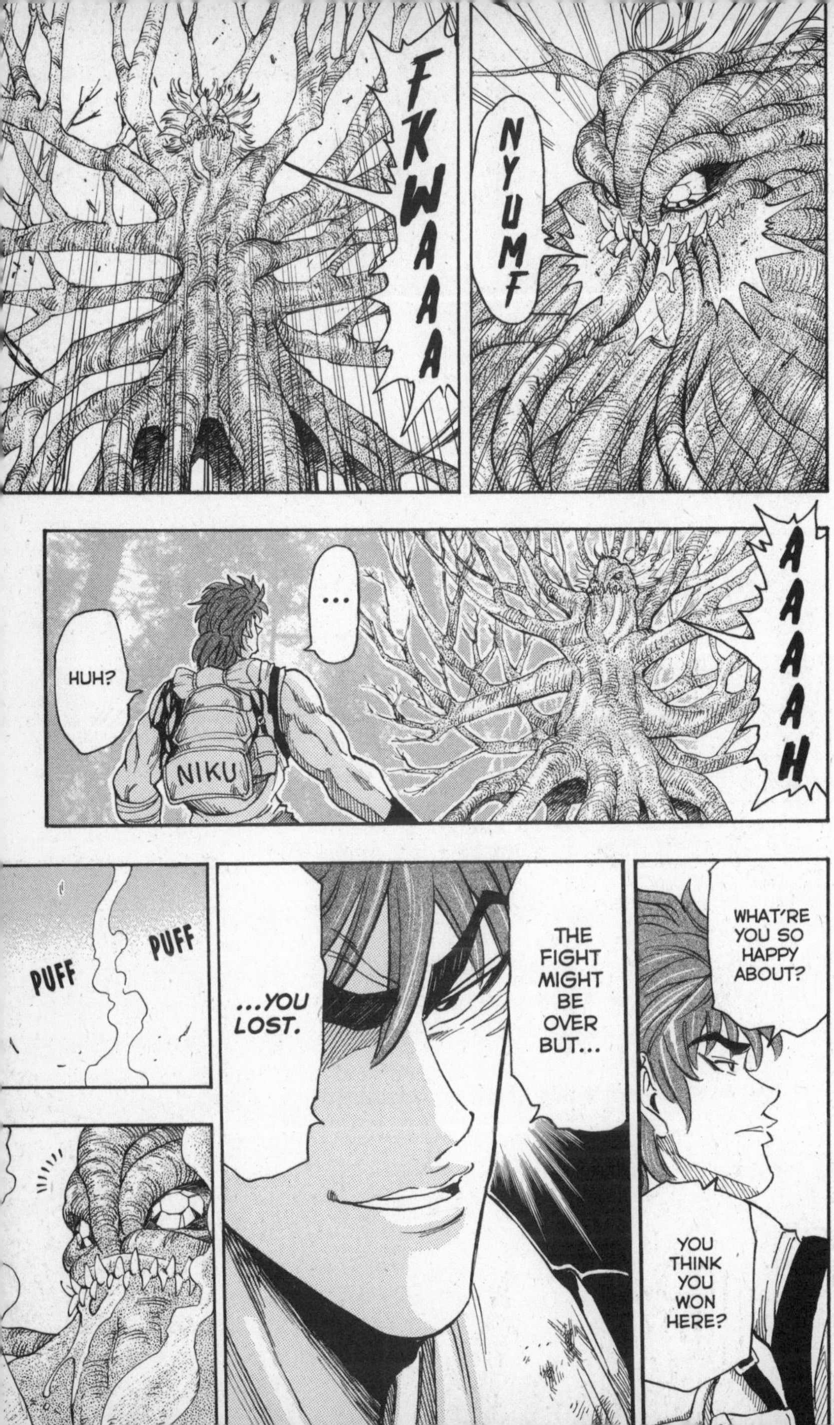
NYUMF
FKWAAAA
AAAAAH
...
HUH?
NIKU
WHAT'RE YOU SO HAPPY ABOUT?
YOU THINK YOU WON HERE?
THE FIGHT MIGHT BE OVER BUT...
...YOU LOST.
PUFF
PUFF

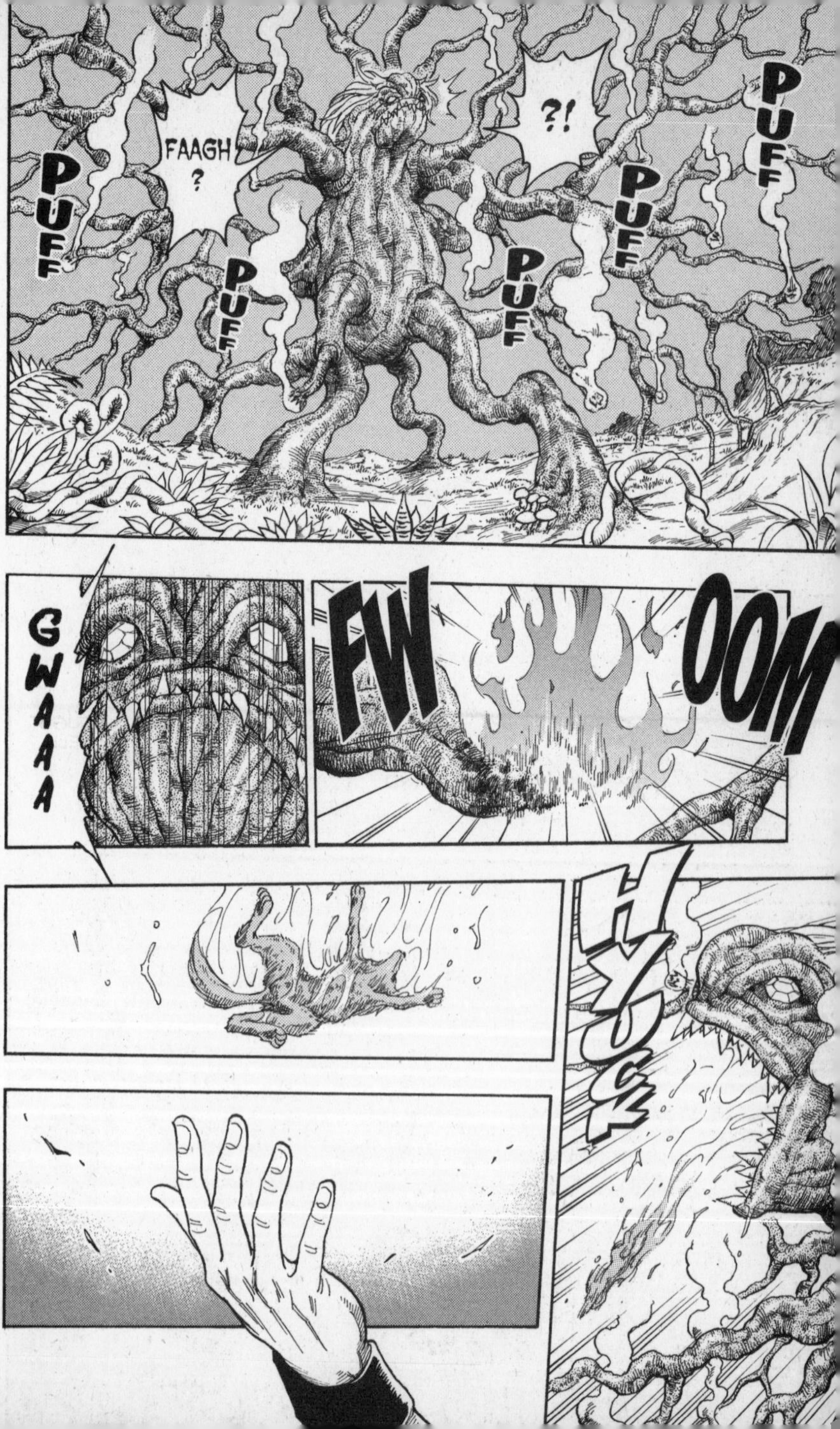
PUFF
?!
PUFF
PUFF
FAAGH ?
PUFF
PUFF
FWOOM
GWAAA
HYUCK

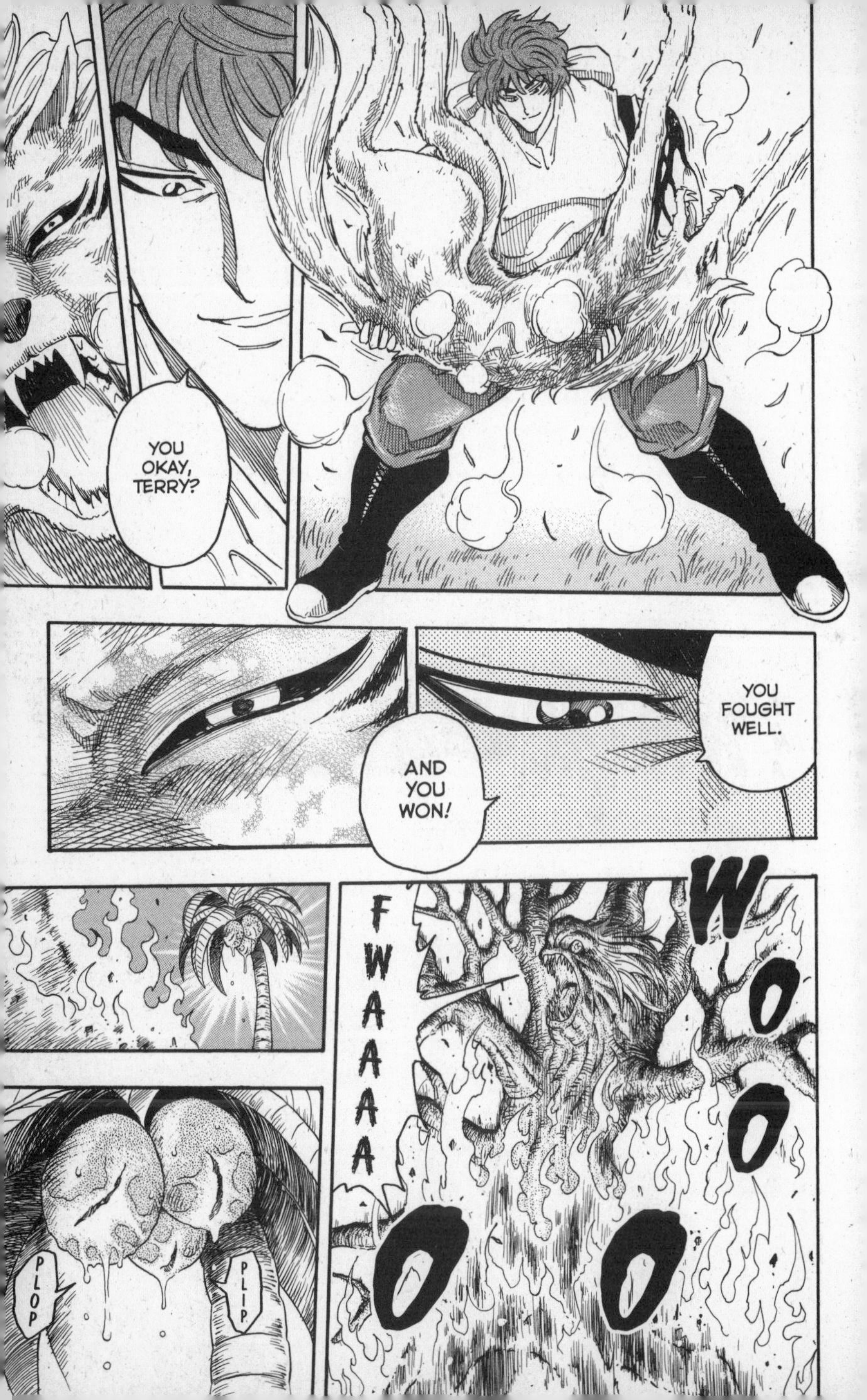
YOU OKAY, TERRY?
YOU FOUGHT WELL.
AND YOU WON!
WOOO
FWAAAAA
OOO
PLIP
PLOP

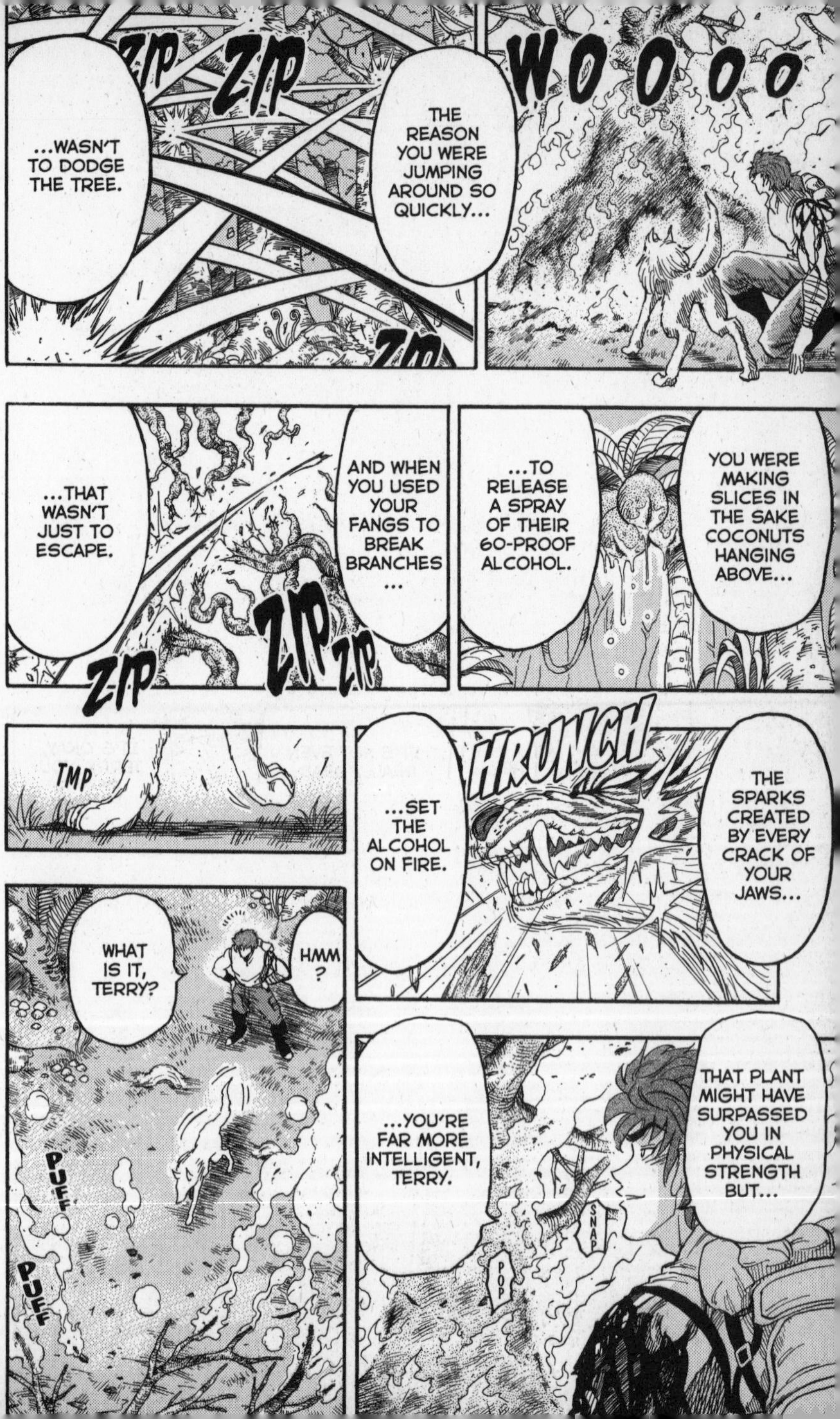
WOOOO
THE REASON YOU WERE JUMPING AROUND SO QUICKLY...
...WASN'T TO DODGE THE TREE.
ZIP
ZIP
ZIP
YOU WERE MAKING SLICES IN THE SAKE COCONUTS HANGING ABOVE...
...TO RELEASE A SPRAY OF THEIR 60-PROOF ALCOHOL.
AND WHEN YOU USED YOUR FANGS TO BREAK BRANCHES...
...THAT WASN'T JUST TO ESCAPE.
ZIP
ZIP
ZIP
HRUNCH
THE SPARKS CREATED BY EVERY CRACK OF YOUR JAWS...
...SET THE ALCOHOL ON FIRE.
TMP
THAT PLANT MIGHT HAVE SURPASSED YOU IN PHYSICAL STRENGTH BUT...
...YOU'RE FAR MORE INTELLIGENT, TERRY.
SNAP
POP
HMM?
WHAT IS IT, TERRY?
PUFF
PUFF

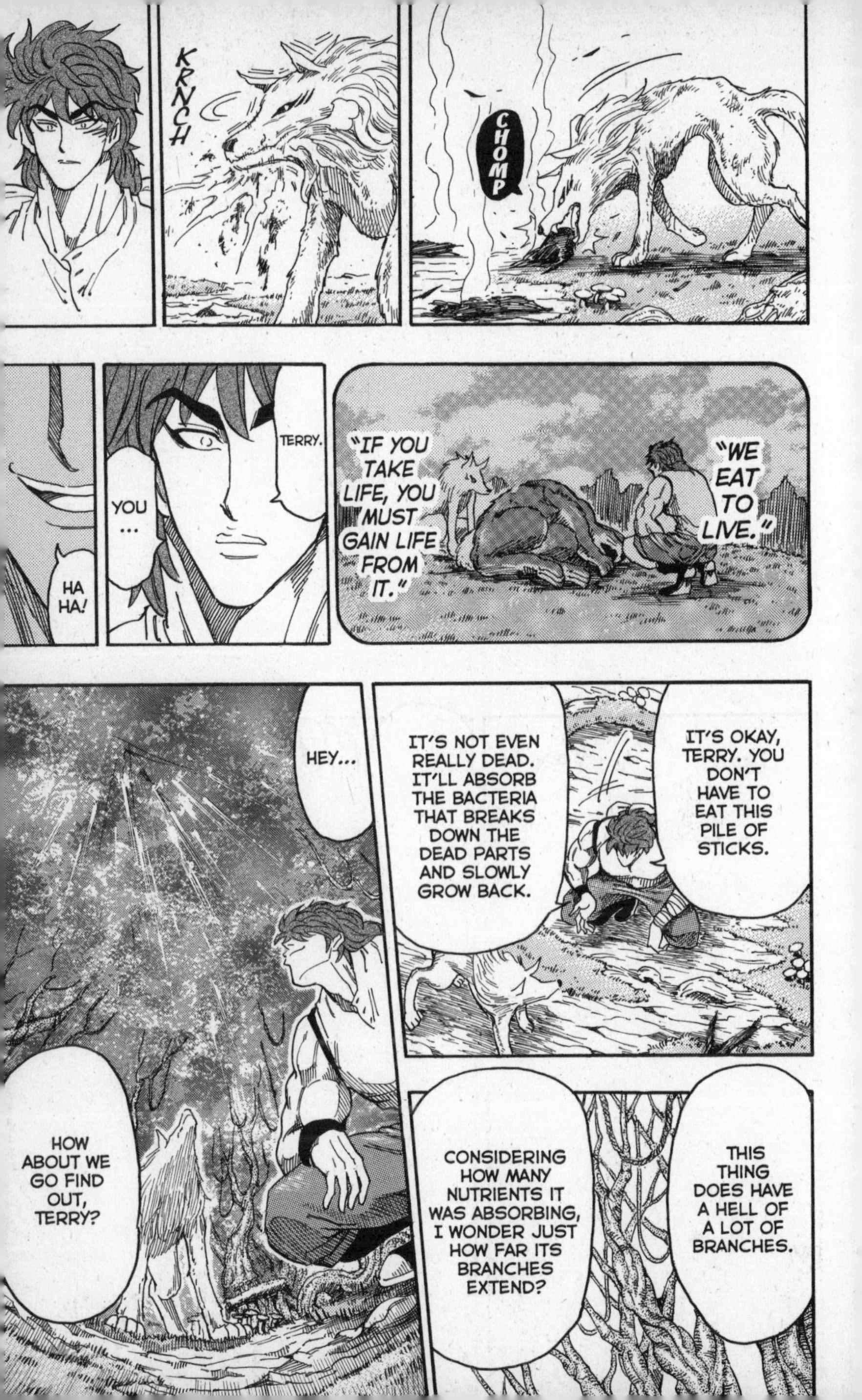
CHOMP
KRNCH
"WE EAT TO LIVE."
"IF YOU TAKE LIFE, YOU MUST GAIN LIFE FROM IT."
TERRY.
YOU ...
HA HA!
IT'S OKAY, TERRY. YOU DON'T HAVE TO EAT THIS PILE OF STICKS.
IT'S NOT EVEN REALLY DEAD. IT'LL ABSORB THE BACTERIA THAT BREAKS DOWN THE DEAD PARTS AND SLOWLY GROW BACK.
THIS THING DOES HAVE A HELL OF A LOT OF BRANCHES.
CONSIDERING HOW MANY NUTRIENTS IT WAS ABSORBING, I WONDER JUST HOW FAR ITS BRANCHES EXTEND?
HEY...
HOW ABOUT WE GO FIND OUT, TERRY?

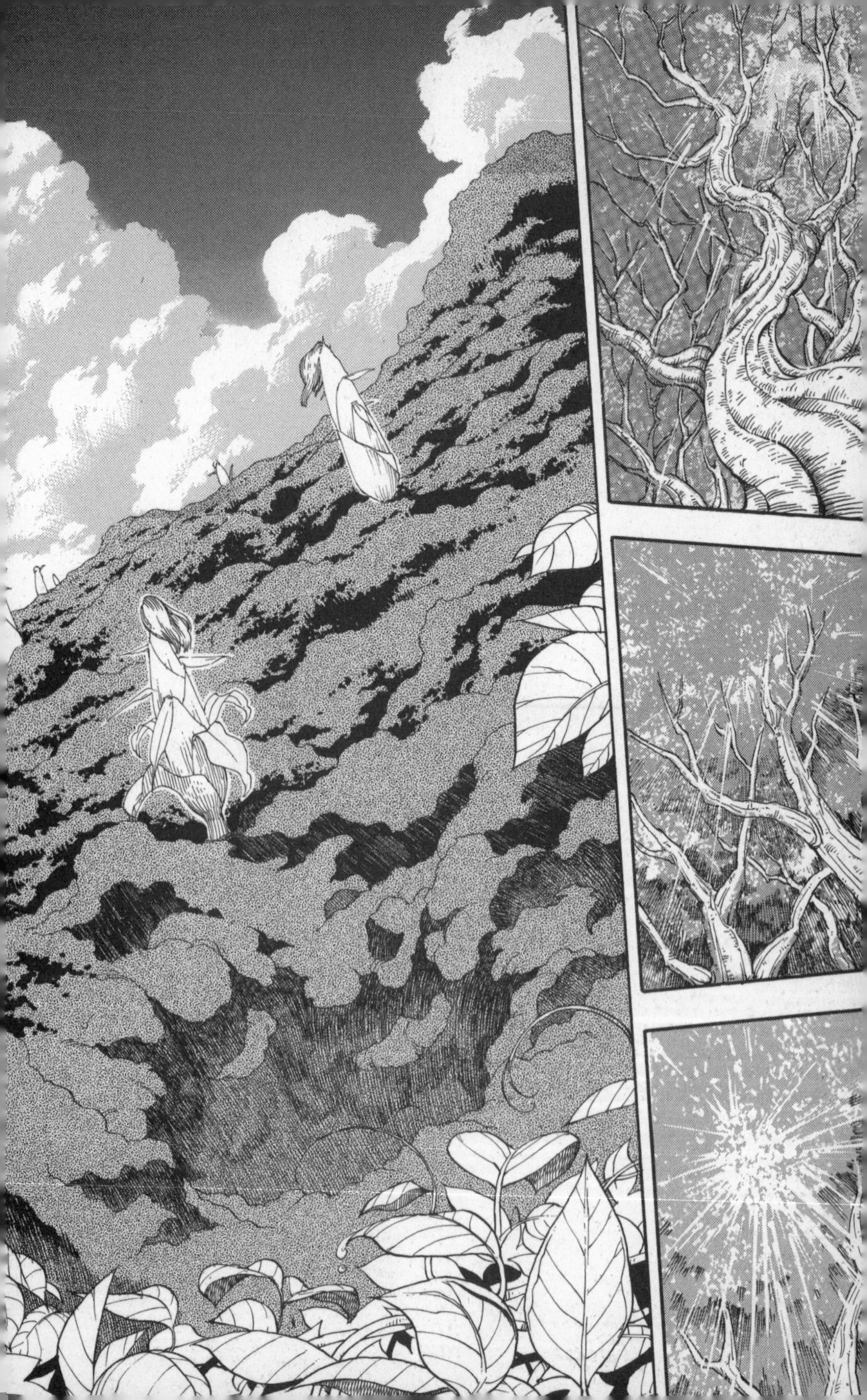

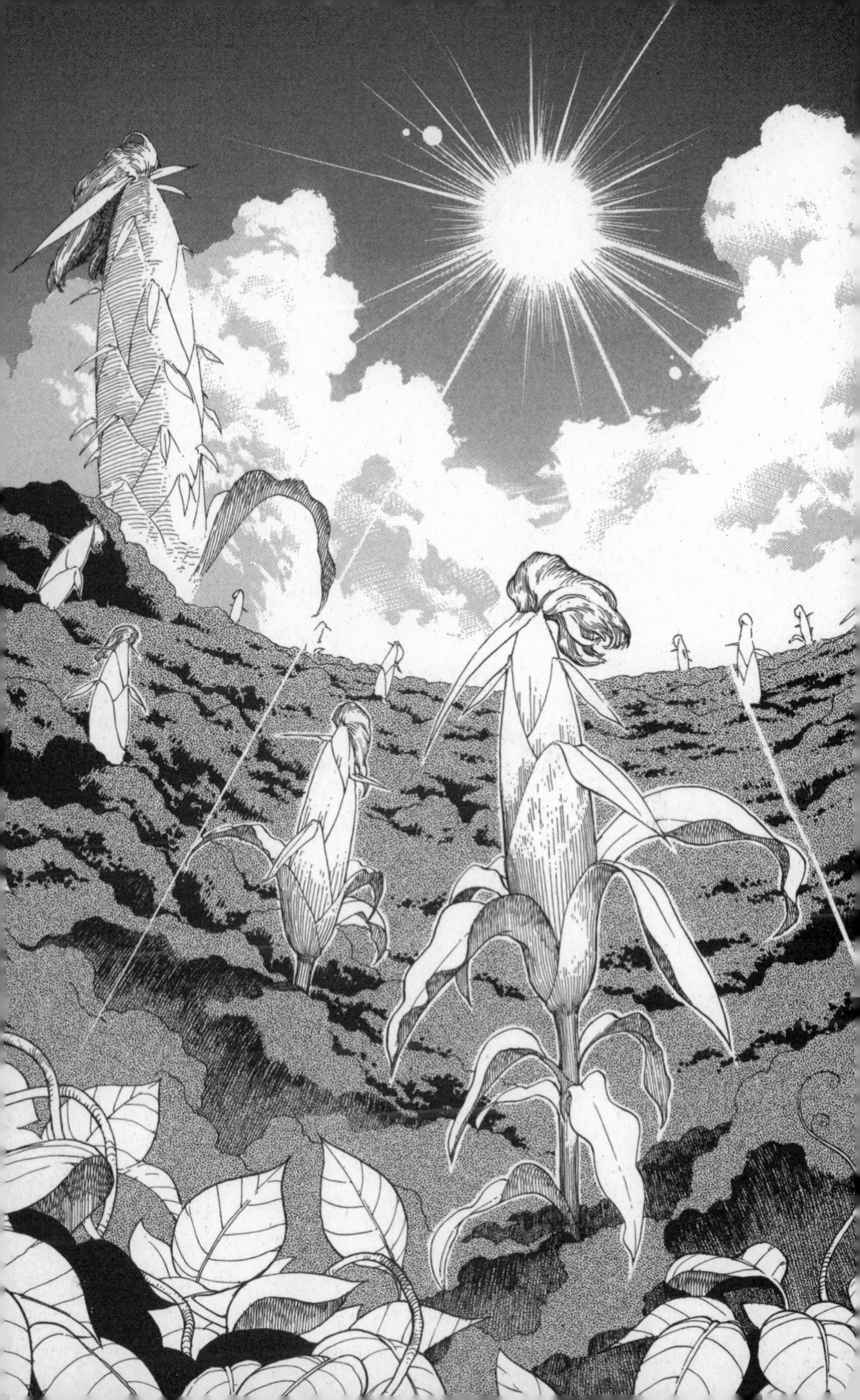

TORIKO

GOURMET CHECKLIST

Vol. 042

GANGHOOD

(REPTILE)

CAPTURE LEVEL: 15

HABITAT: REGAL ISLE (BIOTOPE #1)

LENGTH: 4 METERS

HEIGHT: 3.5 METERS

WEIGHT: 1.5 TONS

PRICE: (INEDIBLE)

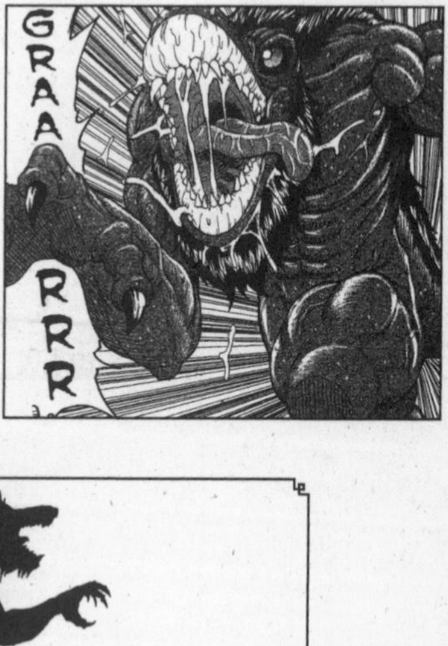
GRAARRR

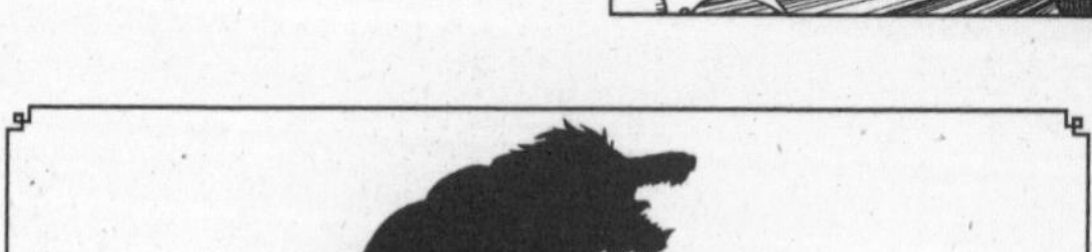

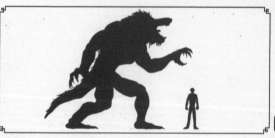

SCALE

A VIOLENT AND INSATIABLE REPTILIAN BEAST THAT TRAVELS IN PACKS KNOWN AS REGAL ISLE'S GANGS. GANGHOODS ARE SCAVENGERS, FEASTING ON PREY THAT OTHER ANIMALS HAVE TAKEN DOWN. INDIVIDUALLY, THEY'RE NOT MUCH OF A THREAT, BUT IN PACKS THEY WORK AS A TEAM, MAKING THEM FORMIDABLE ENEMIES.

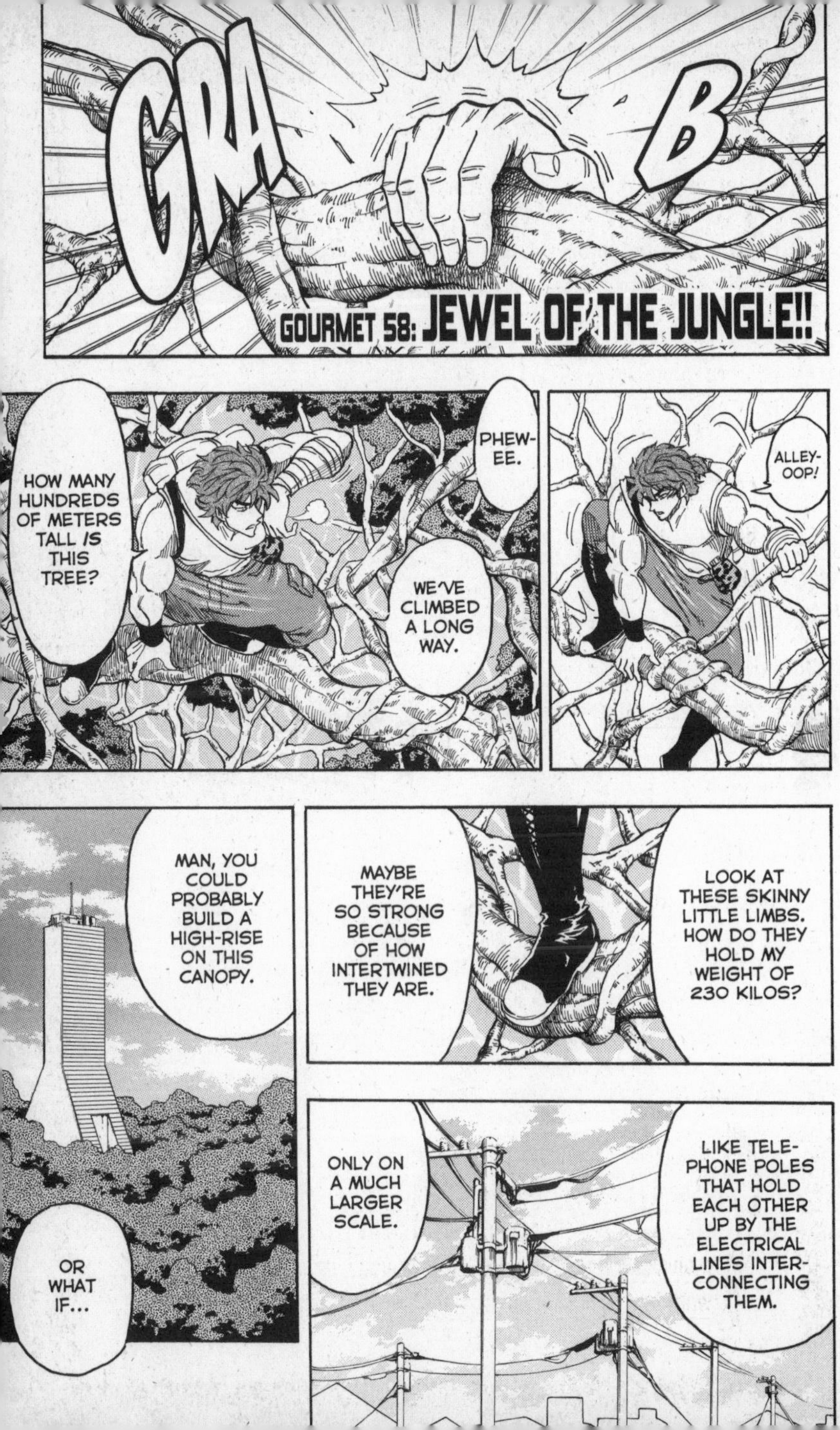
GRAB
GOURMET 58: JEWEL OF THE JUNGLE!!
ALLEY-OOP!
PHEW-EE.
WE'VE CLIMBED A LONG WAY.
HOW MANY HUNDREDS OF METERS TALL *IS* THIS TREE?
LOOK AT THESE SKINNY LITTLE LIMBS. HOW DO THEY HOLD MY WEIGHT OF 230 KILOS?
MAYBE THEY'RE SO STRONG BECAUSE OF HOW INTERTWINED THEY ARE.
MAN, YOU COULD PROBABLY BUILD A HIGH-RISE ON THIS CANOPY.
OR WHAT IF...
LIKE TELEPHONE POLES THAT HOLD EACH OTHER UP BY THE ELECTRICAL LINES INTERCONNECTING THEM.
ONLY ON A MUCH LARGER SCALE.

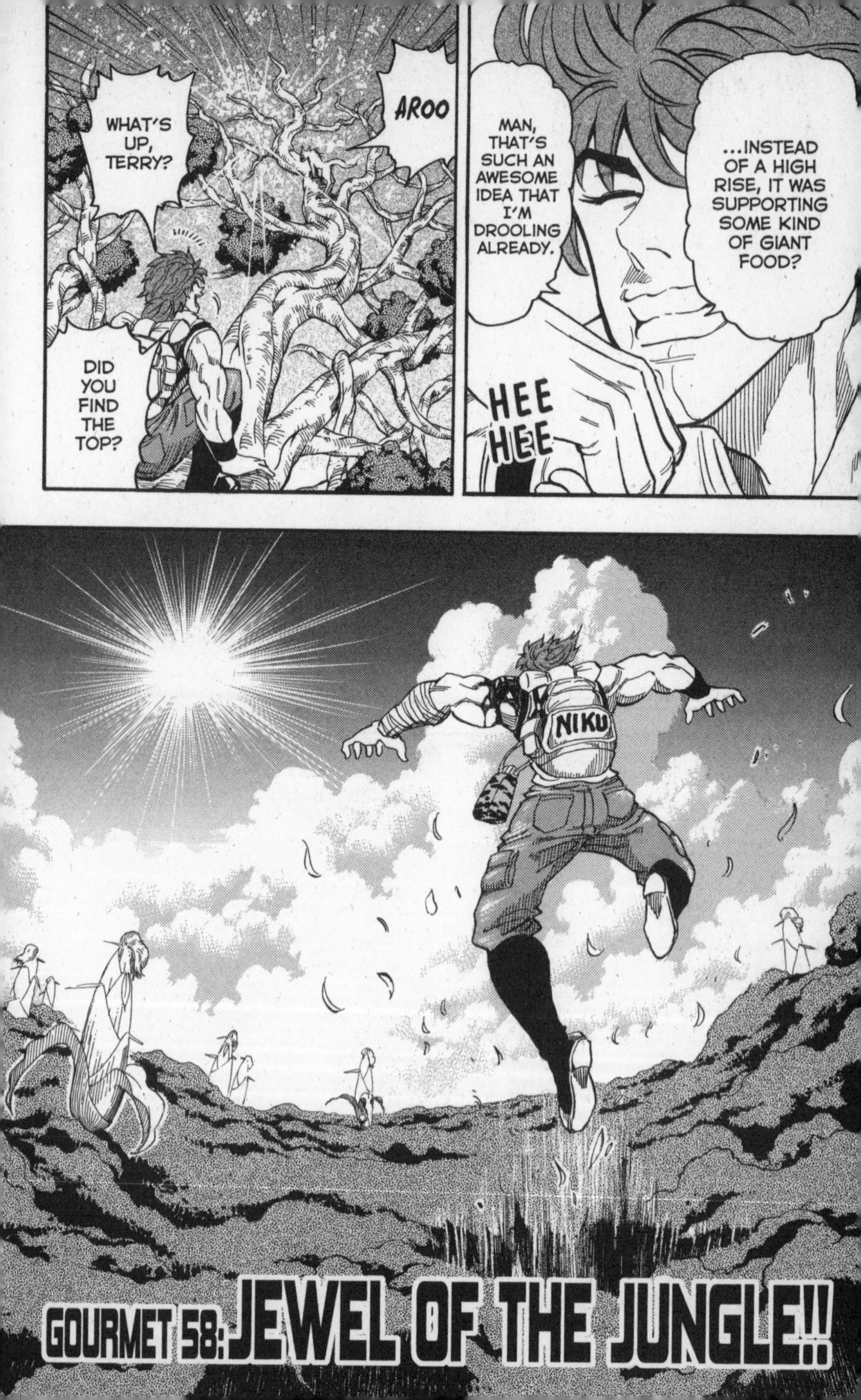
...INSTEAD OF A HIGH RISE, IT WAS SUPPORTING SOME KIND OF GIANT FOOD?
MAN, THAT'S SUCH AN AWESOME IDEA THAT I'M DROOLING ALREADY.
HEE HEE
AROO
WHAT'S UP, TERRY?
DID YOU FIND THE TOP?
GOURMET 58: JEWEL OF THE JUNGLE!!

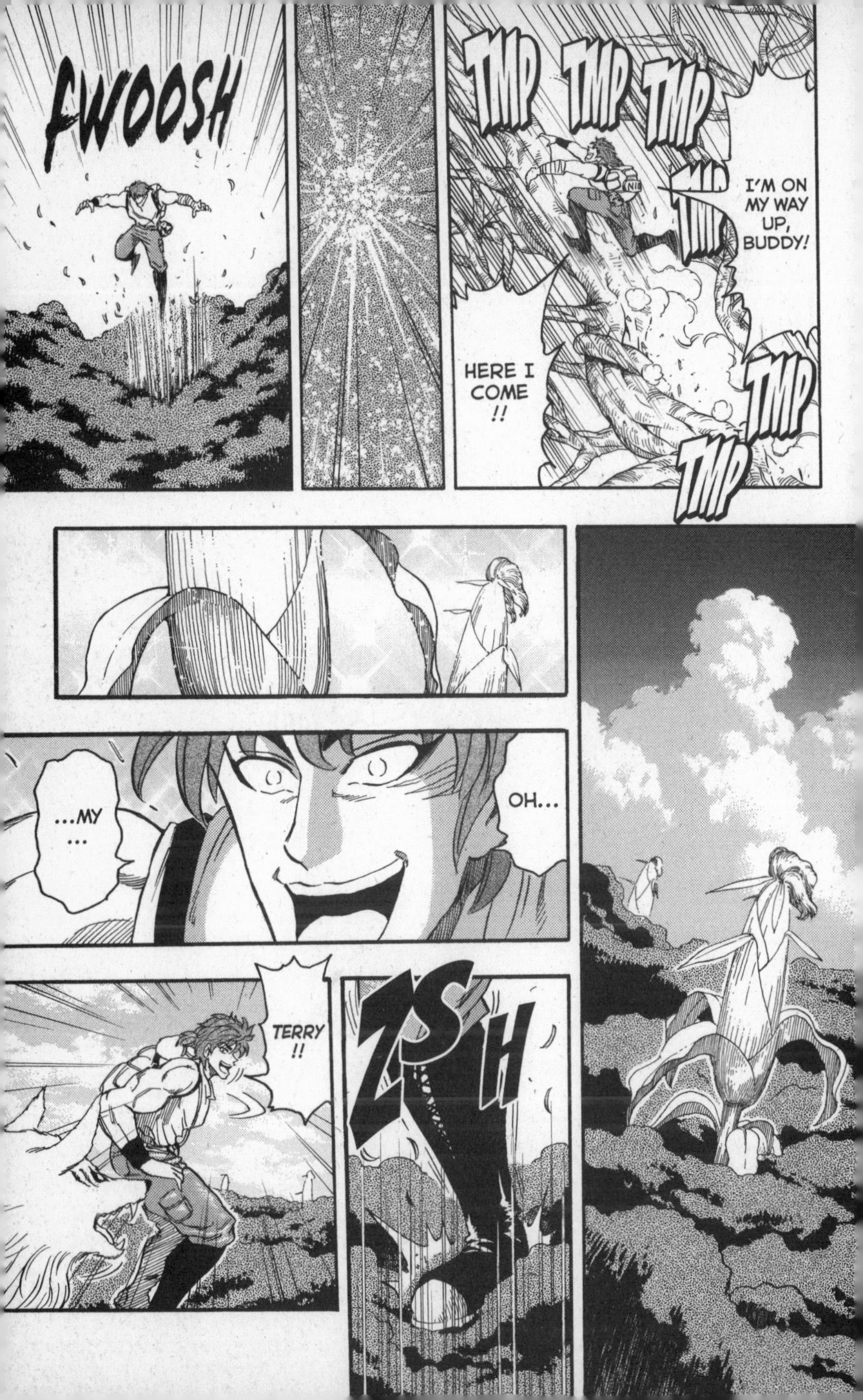
TMP TMP TMP
I'M ON MY WAY UP, BUDDY!
TMP TMP
HERE I COME !!
TMP TMP
FWOOSH
OH...
...MY ...
ZSH
TERRY !!

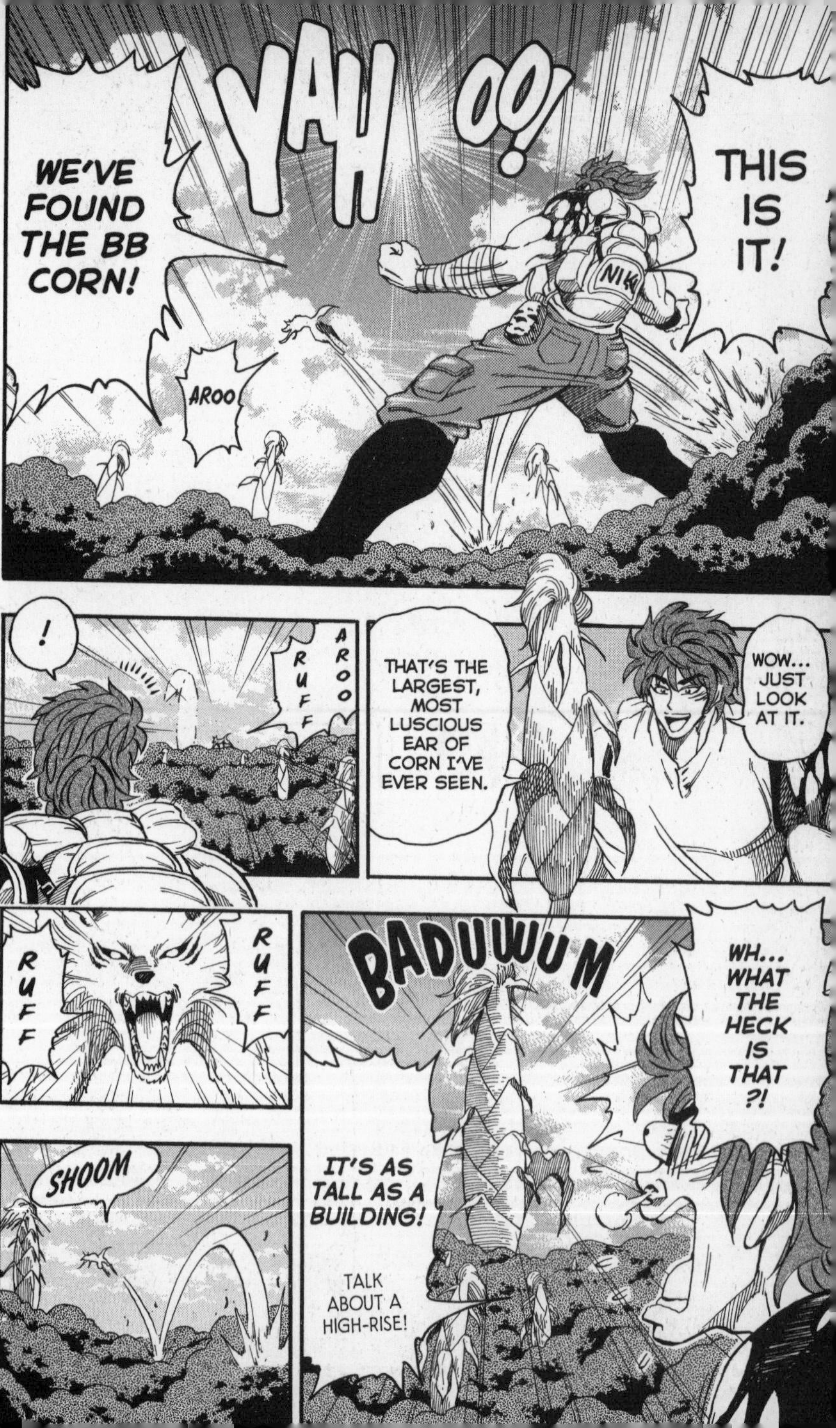
YAHOO!
THIS IS IT!
WE'VE FOUND THE BB CORN!
AROO
WOW... JUST LOOK AT IT.
THAT'S THE LARGEST, MOST LUSCIOUS EAR OF CORN I'VE EVER SEEN.
AROO
RUFF
!
BADUWUUM
WH... WHAT THE HECK IS THAT?!
IT'S AS TALL AS A BUILDING!
TALK ABOUT A HIGH-RISE!
RUFF
RUFF
SHOOM

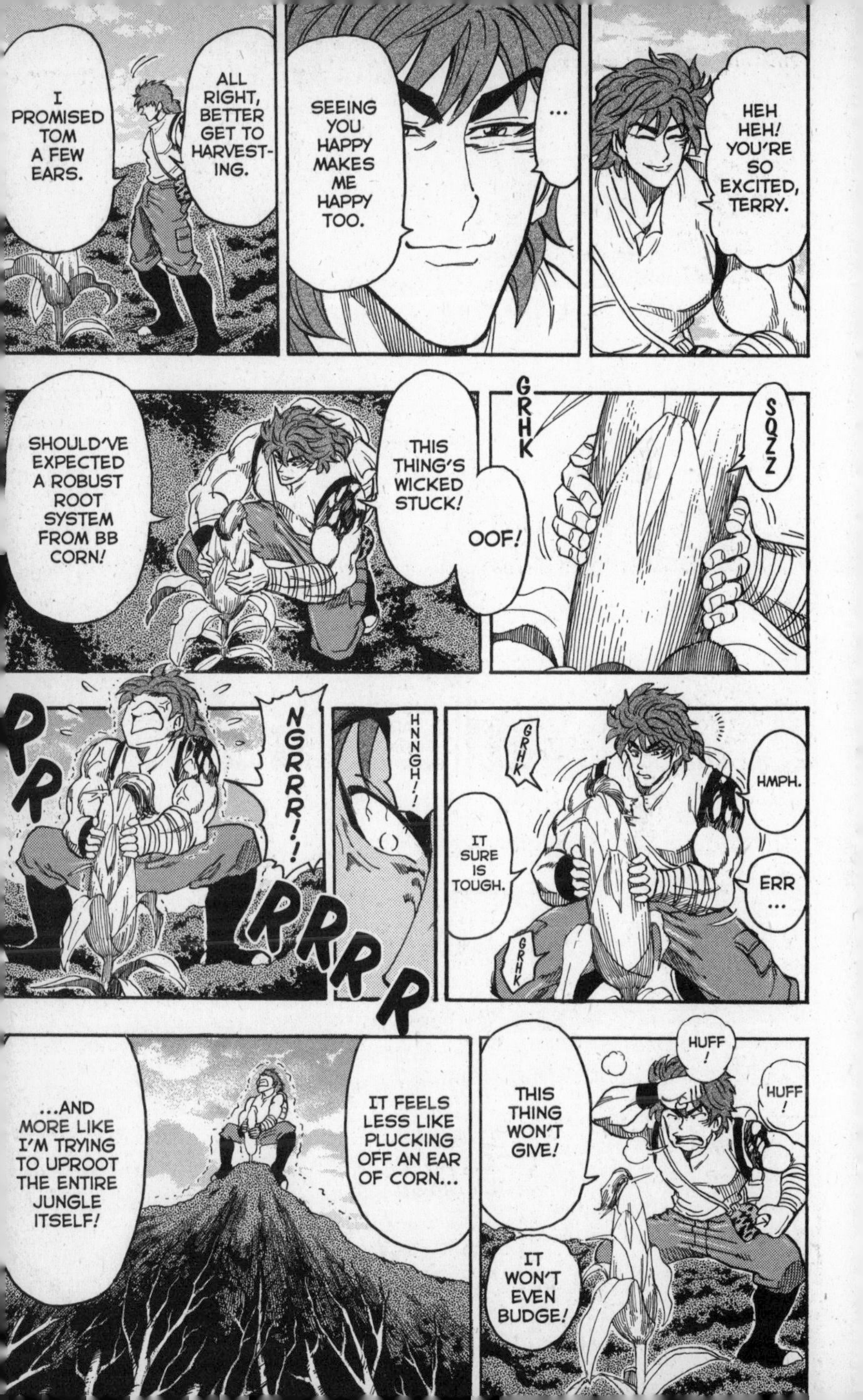
HEH HEH! YOU'RE SO EXCITED, TERRY.
...
SEEING YOU HAPPY MAKES ME HAPPY TOO.
ALL RIGHT, BETTER GET TO HARVESTING.
I PROMISED TOM A FEW EARS.
SQZZ
GRHK
OOF!
THIS THING'S WICKED STUCK!
SHOULD'VE EXPECTED A ROBUST ROOT SYSTEM FROM BB CORN!
HMPH.
GRHK
ERR...
IT SURE IS TOUGH.
GRHK
HNNGH!!
NGRRR!!
PR
RRRR
HUFF!
HUFF!
THIS THING WON'T GIVE!
IT WON'T EVEN BUDGE!
IT FEELS LESS LIKE PLUCKING OFF AN EAR OF CORN...
...AND MORE LIKE I'M TRYING TO UPROOT THE ENTIRE JUNGLE ITSELF!

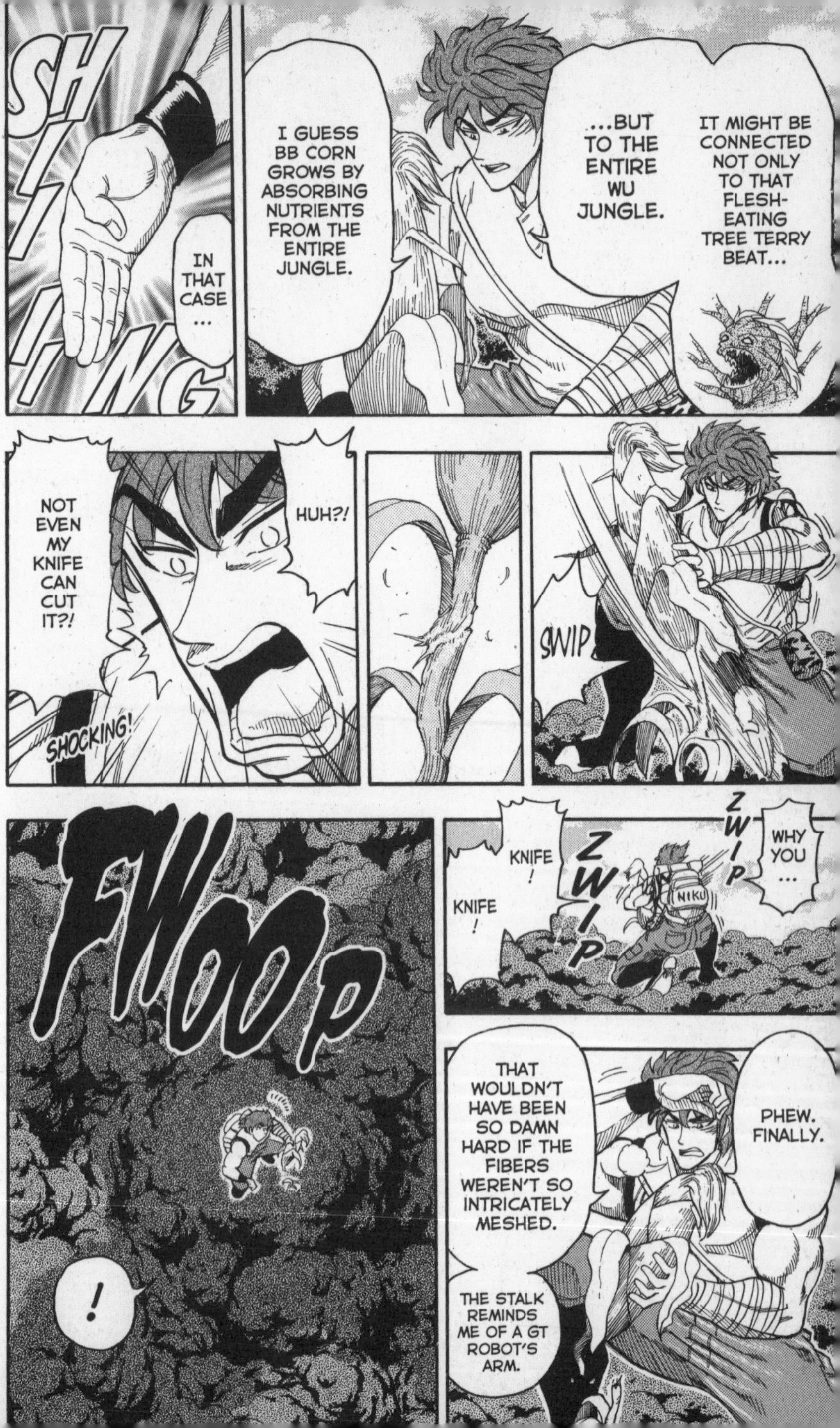
IT MIGHT BE CONNECTED NOT ONLY TO THAT FLESH-EATING TREE TERRY BEAT...
....BUT TO THE ENTIRE WU JUNGLE.
I GUESS BB CORN GROWS BY ABSORBING NUTRIENTS FROM THE ENTIRE JUNGLE.
SHIIIING
IN THAT CASE ...
SWIP
HUH?!
NOT EVEN MY KNIFE CAN CUT IT?!
SHOCKING!
WHY YOU ...
ZWIP
NIKU
ZWIP
KNIFE!
KNIFE!
PHEW. FINALLY.
THAT WOULDN'T HAVE BEEN SO DAMN HARD IF THE FIBERS WEREN'T SO INTRICATELY MESHED.
THE STALK REMINDS ME OF A GT ROBOT'S ARM.
FWOOP
!

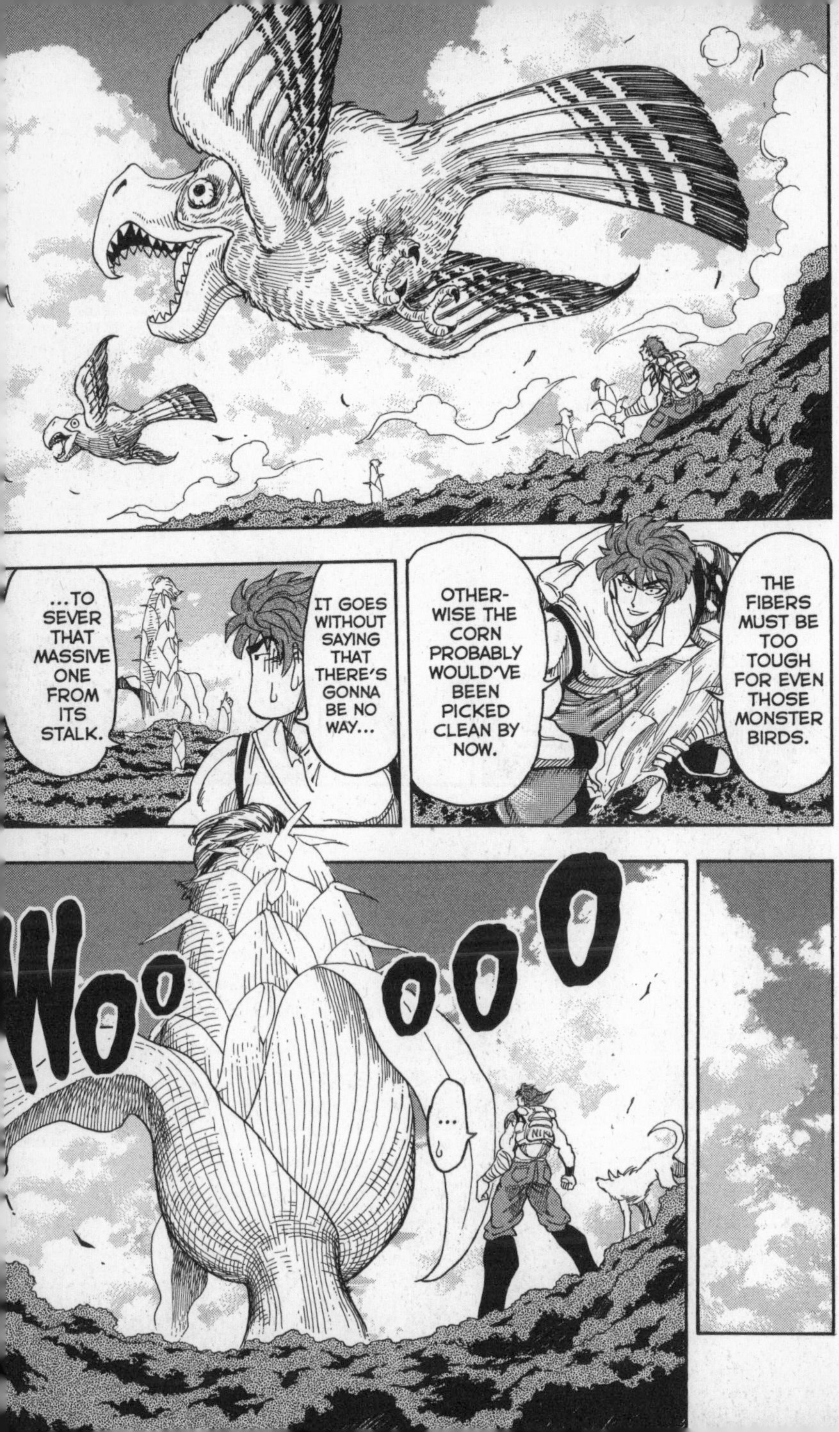
THE FIBERS MUST BE TOO TOUGH FOR EVEN THOSE MONSTER BIRDS.
OTHER-WISE THE CORN PROBABLY WOULD'VE BEEN PICKED CLEAN BY NOW.
IT GOES WITHOUT SAYING THAT THERE'S GONNA BE NO WAY...
...TO SEVER THAT MASSIVE ONE FROM ITS STALK.
WOOOOO
...

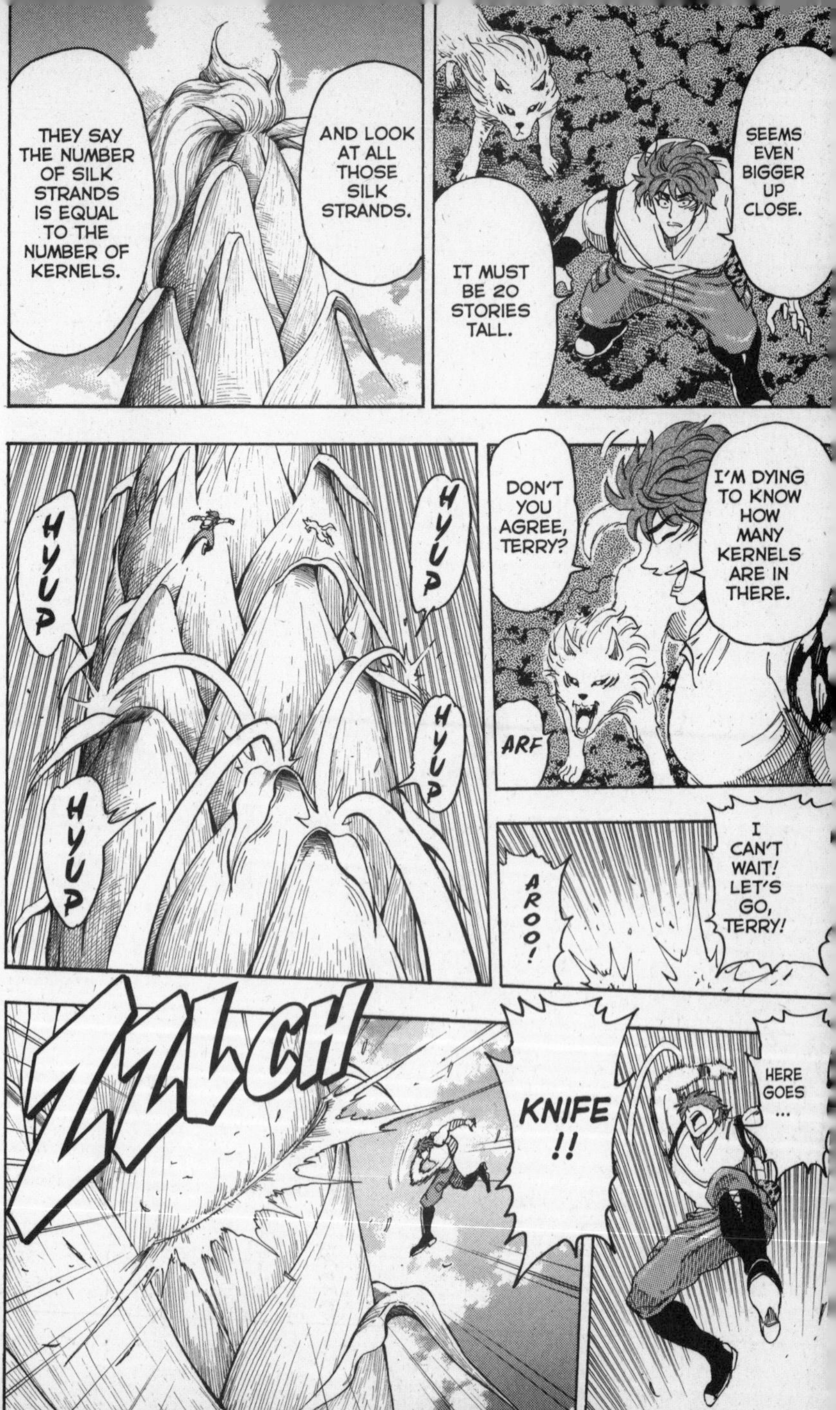
SEEMS EVEN BIGGER UP CLOSE.
IT MUST BE 20 STORIES TALL.
AND LOOK AT ALL THOSE SILK STRANDS.
THEY SAY THE NUMBER OF SILK STRANDS IS EQUAL TO THE NUMBER OF KERNELS.
I'M DYING TO KNOW HOW MANY KERNELS ARE IN THERE.
DON'T YOU AGREE, TERRY?
ARF
I CAN'T WAIT! LET'S GO, TERRY!
AROO!
HYUUP
HYUUP
HYUUP
HYUUP
HERE GOES ...
KNIFE !!
ZZLCH

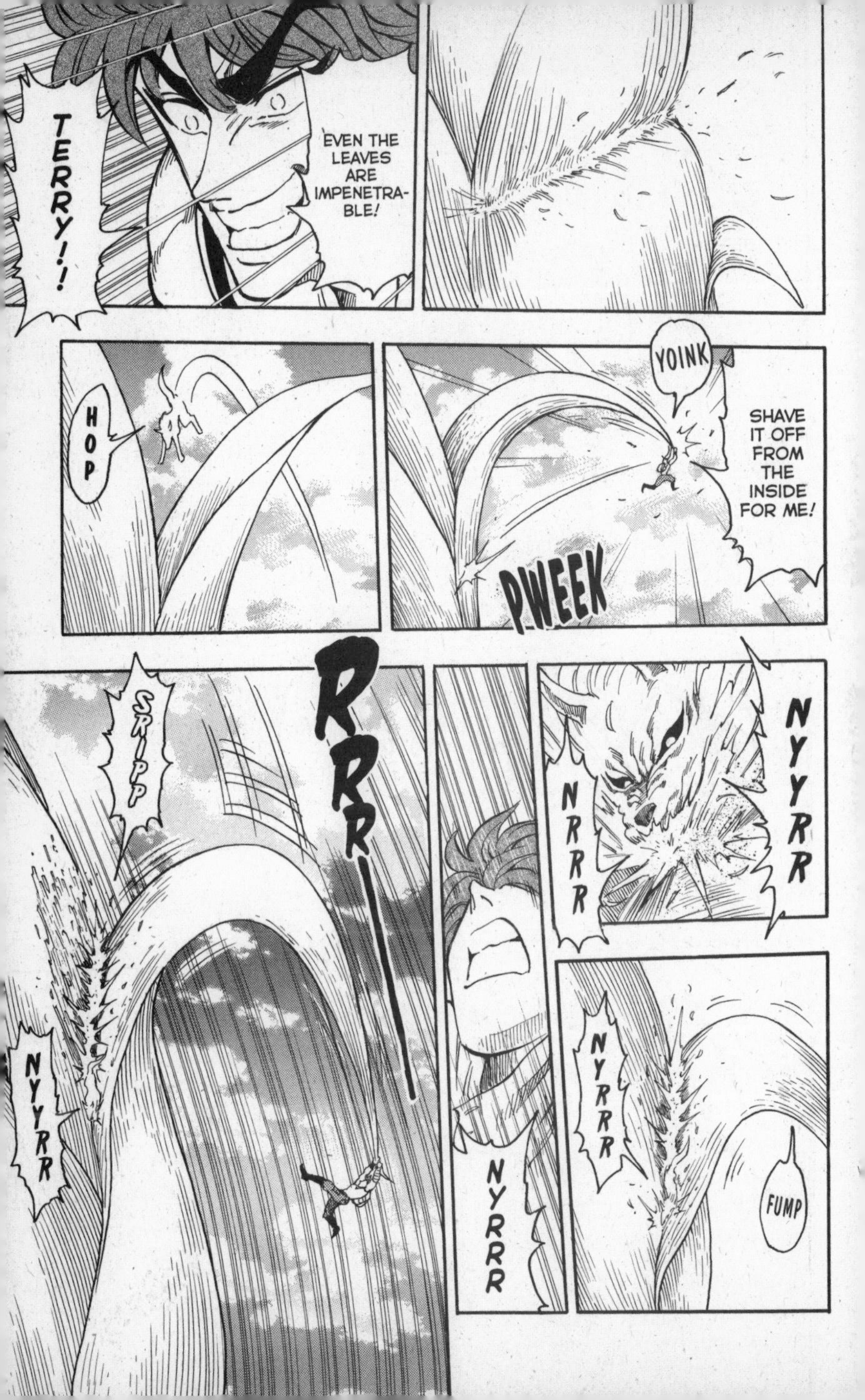
EVEN THE LEAVES ARE IMPENETRABLE!
TERRY!!!
YOINK
SHAVE IT OFF FROM THE INSIDE FOR ME!
PWEEK
HOP
NYYRR
NRRR
NYRRR
FUMP
NYRRR
RRR
SRIPP
NYYRR

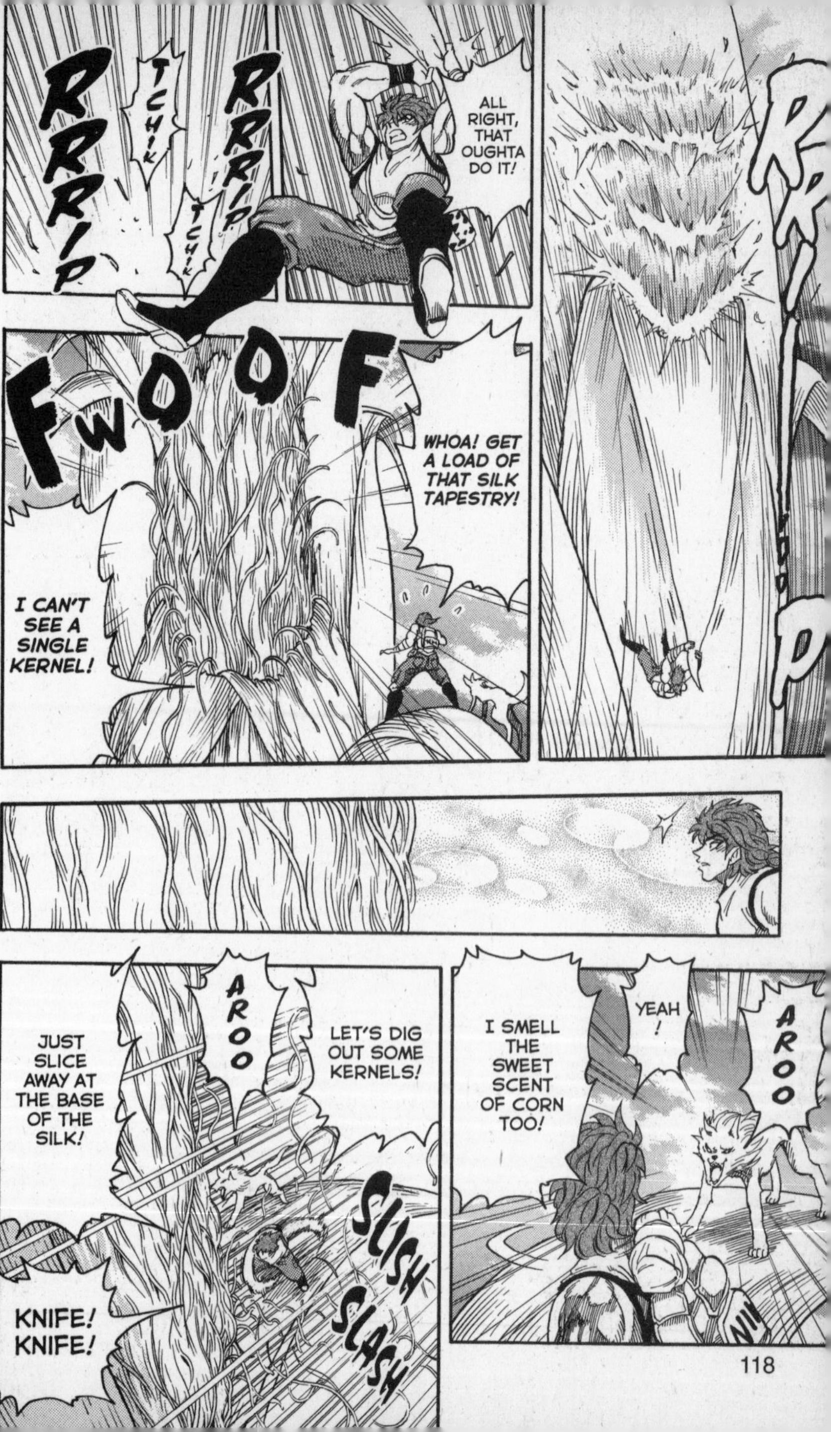
ALL RIGHT, THAT OUGHTA DO IT!
RRRIP
TCHIK
RRRIP
TCHIK
WHOA! GET A LOAD OF THAT SILK TAPESTRY!
FWOOF
I CAN'T SEE A SINGLE KERNEL!
AROO
YEAH!
I SMELL THE SWEET SCENT OF CORN TOO!
AROO
LET'S DIG OUT SOME KERNELS!
JUST SLICE AWAY AT THE BASE OF THE SILK!
SLISH
SLASH
KNIFE! KNIFE!

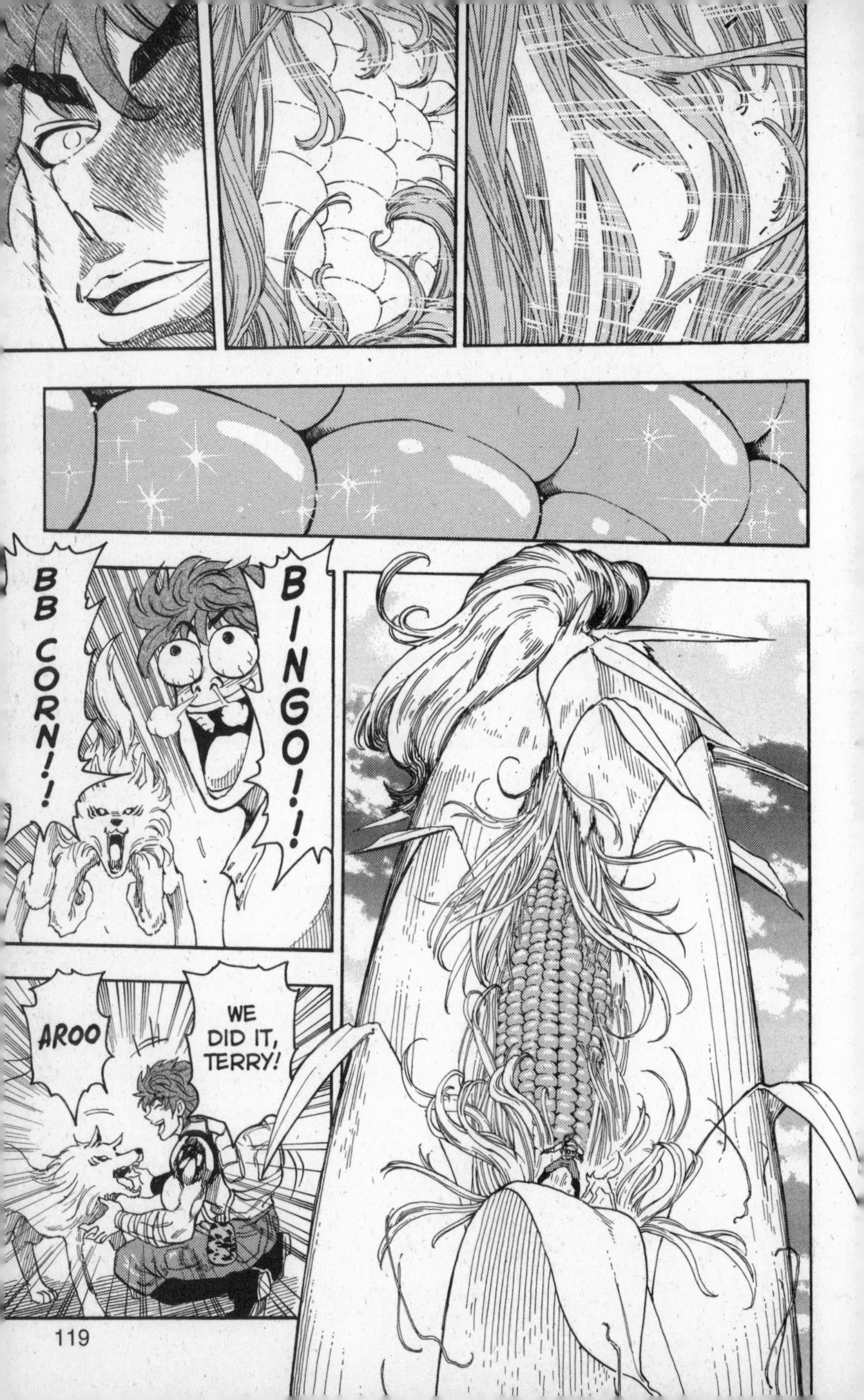
BINGO!!!
BB CORN!!!
WE DID IT, TERRY!
AROO

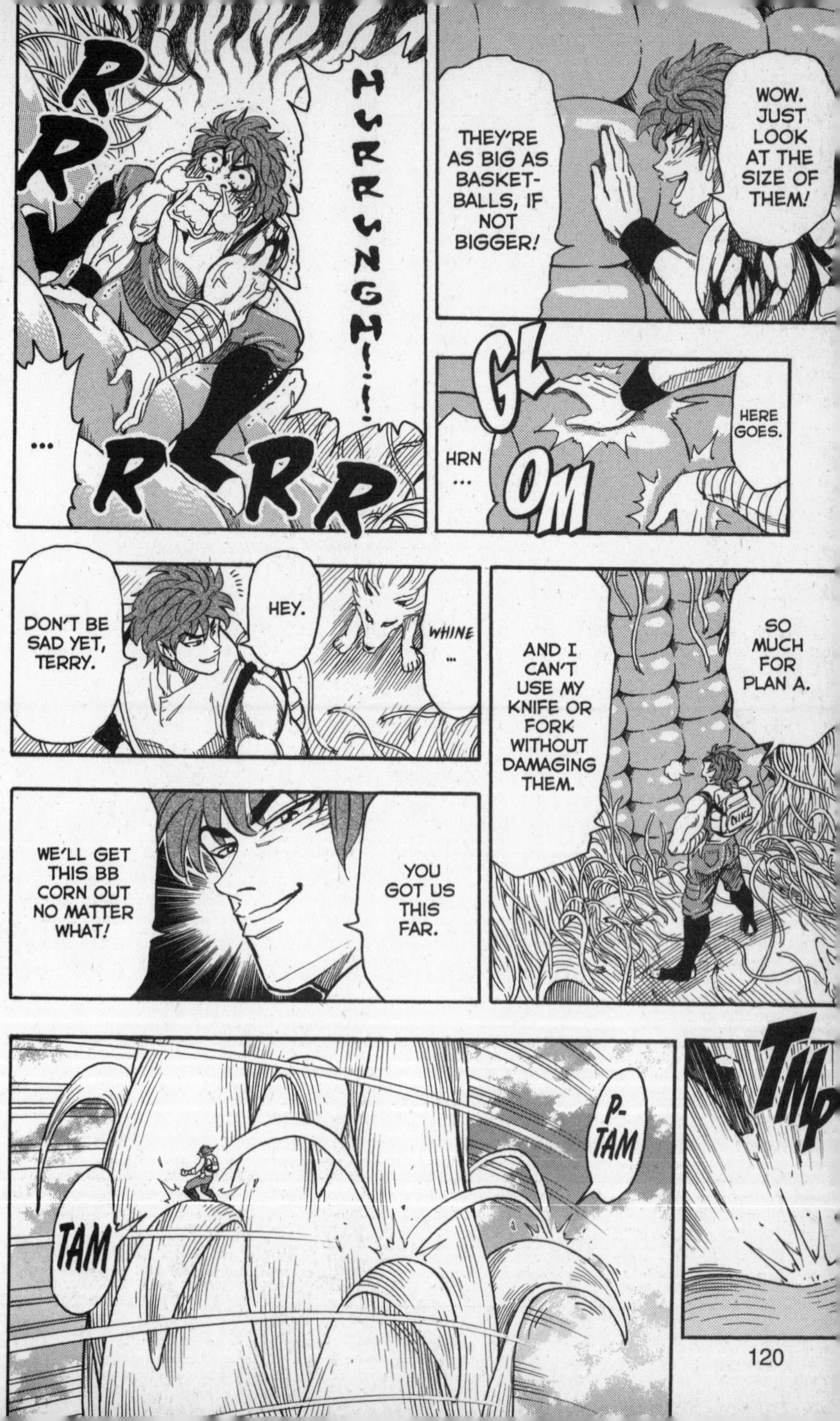
WOW. JUST LOOK AT THE SIZE OF THEM!
THEY'RE AS BIG AS BASKET-BALLS, IF NOT BIGGER!
HERE GOES.
GLOM
HRN ...
HURRUNGH!!!
RRR
RRRR
...
SO MUCH FOR PLAN A.
AND I CAN'T USE MY KNIFE OR FORK WITHOUT DAMAGING THEM.
WHINE ...
HEY.
DON'T BE SAD YET, TERRY.
YOU GOT US THIS FAR.
WE'LL GET THIS BB CORN OUT NO MATTER WHAT!
TMP
P-TAM
TAM

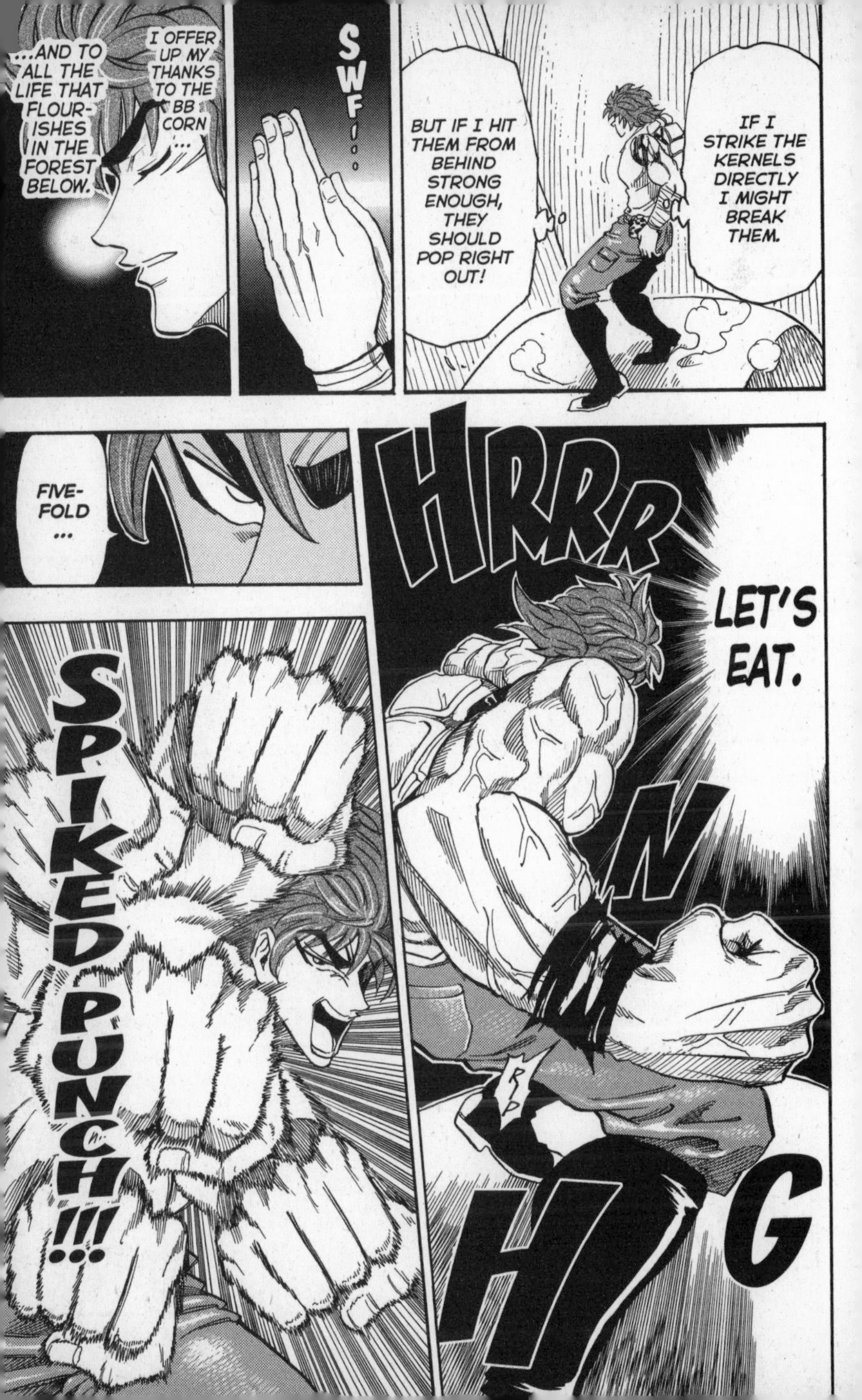

IF I STRIKE THE KERNELS DIRECTLY I MIGHT BREAK THEM.
BUT IF I HIT THEM FROM BEHIND STRONG ENOUGH, THEY SHOULD POP RIGHT OUT!
SWF!...
I OFFER UP MY THANKS TO THE BB CORN...
...AND TO ALL THE LIFE THAT FLOURISHES IN THE FOREST BELOW.
HRRR
LET'S EAT.
N
RIP
H
G
FIVE-FOLD...
SPIKED PUNCH!!!

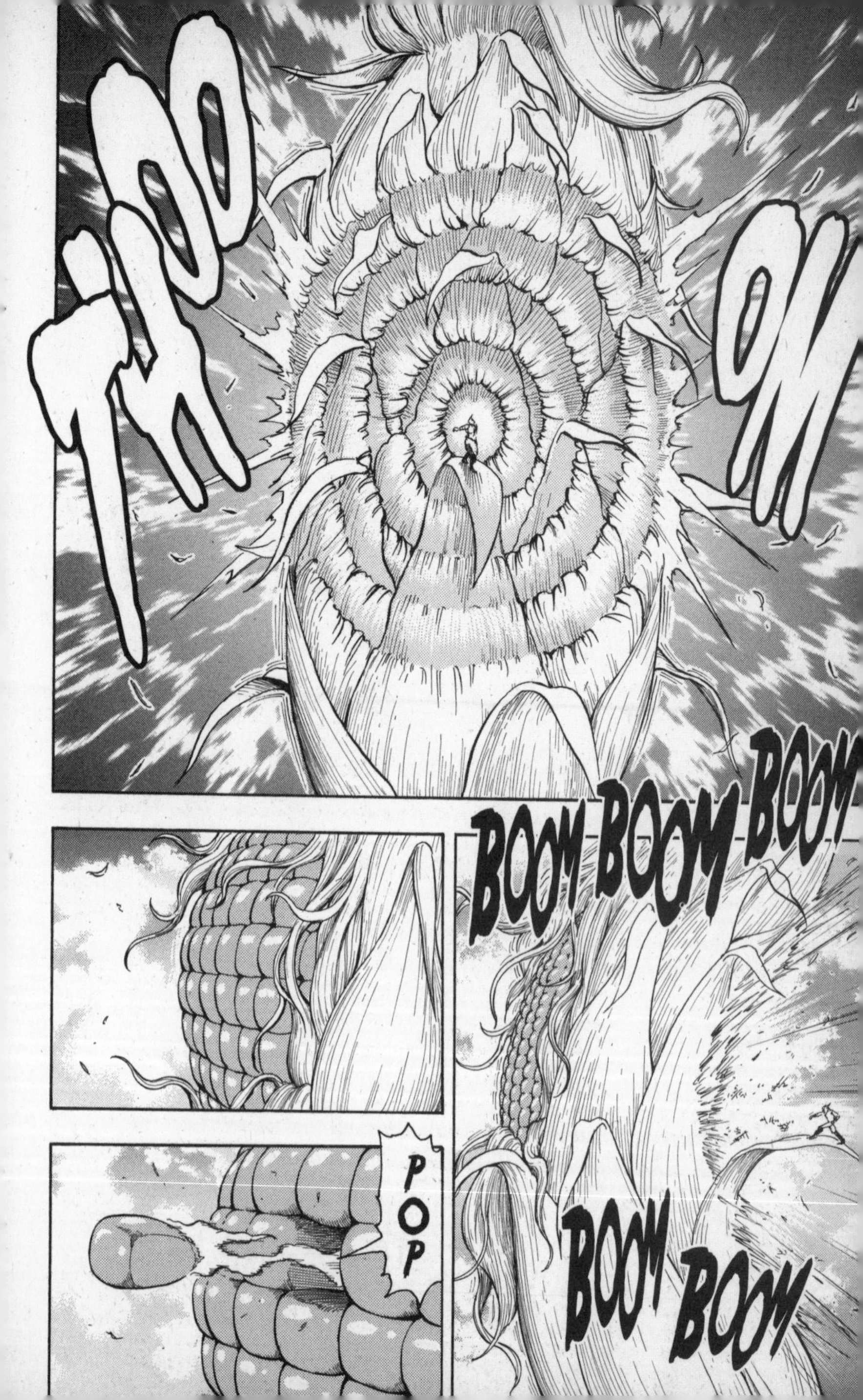
BOOM BOOM BOOM
BOOM BOOM
POP

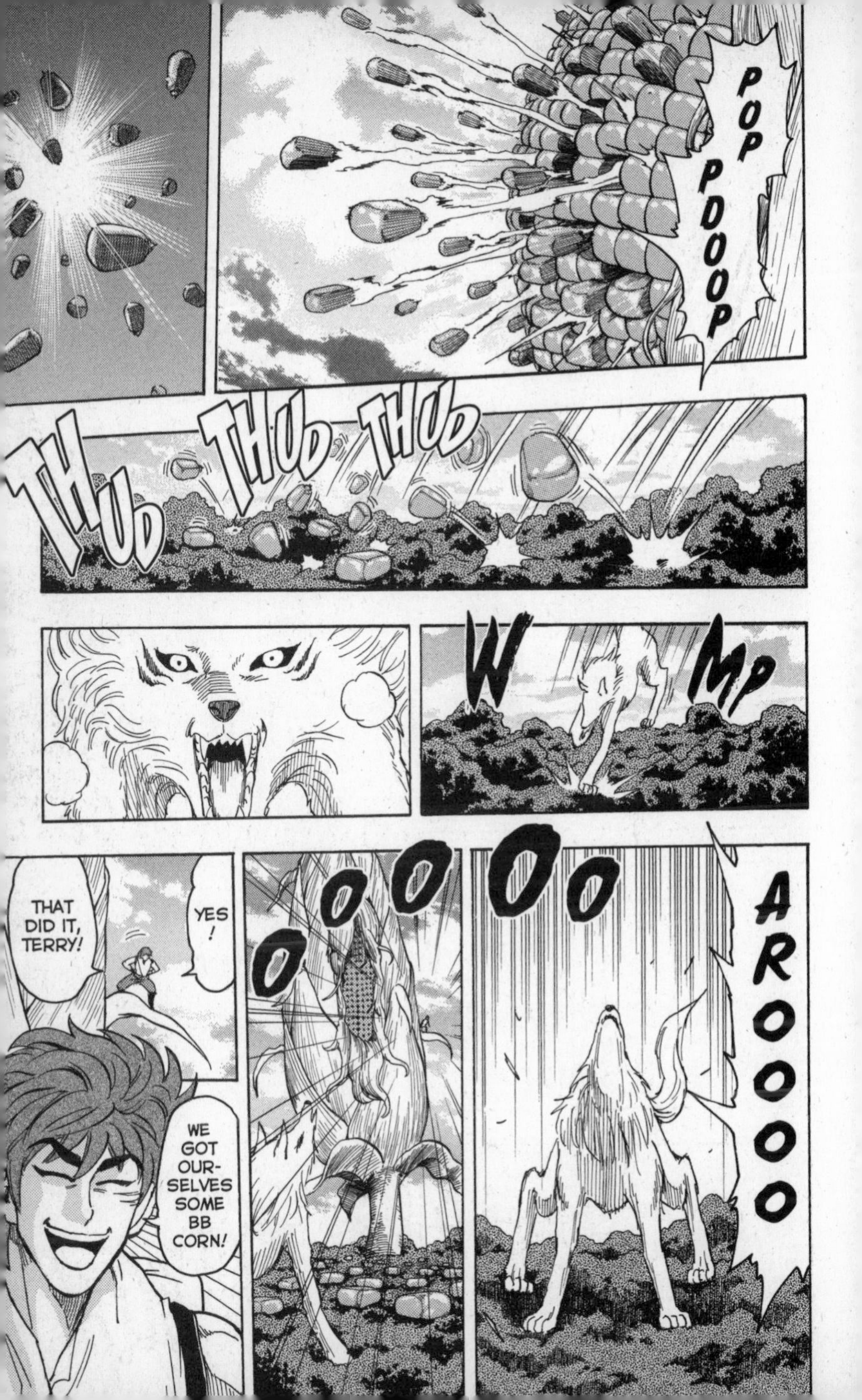

POP
PDOOP
THUD THUD THUD
WMP
AROOOOO
OOOOO
YES!
THAT DID IT, TERRY!
WE GOT OURSELVES SOME BB CORN!

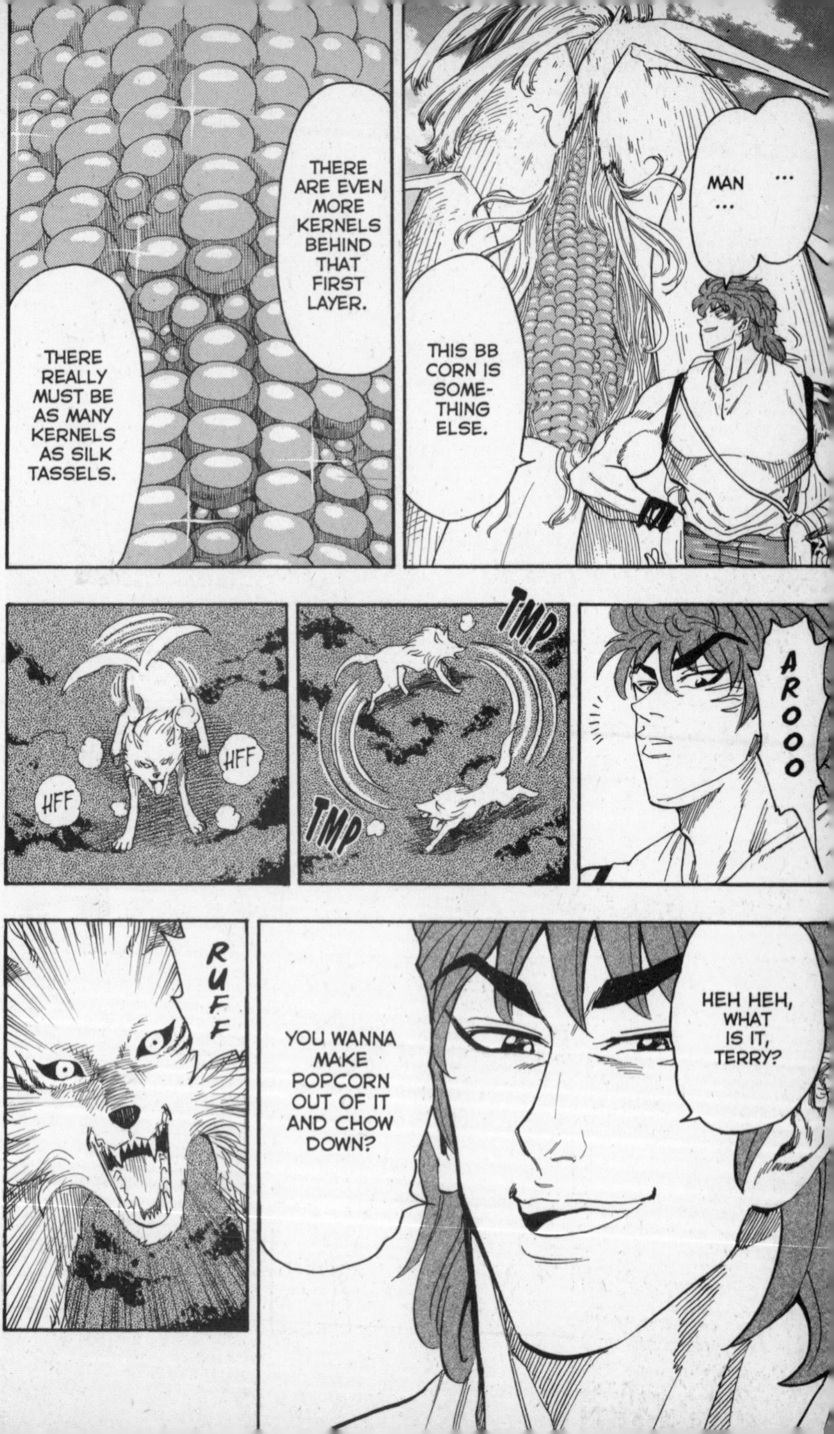
MAN ... ...
THIS BB CORN IS SOME-THING ELSE.
THERE ARE EVEN MORE KERNELS BEHIND THAT FIRST LAYER.
THERE REALLY MUST BE AS MANY KERNELS AS SILK TASSELS.
AROOOO
TMP
TMP
HFF
HFF
HEH HEH, WHAT IS IT, TERRY?
YOU WANNA MAKE POPCORN OUT OF IT AND CHOW DOWN?
RUFF

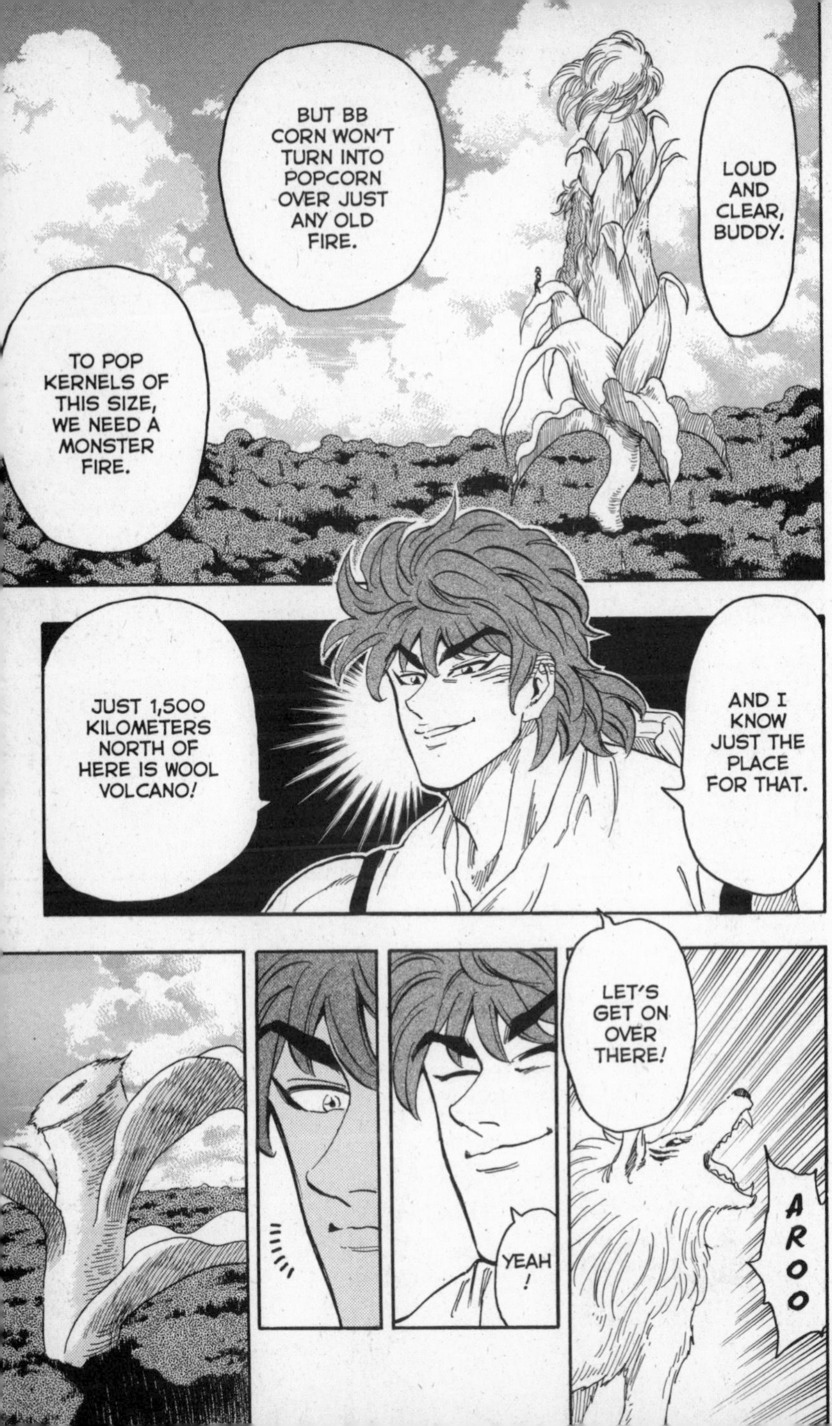
LOUD AND CLEAR, BUDDY.
BUT BB CORN WON'T TURN INTO POPCORN OVER JUST ANY OLD FIRE.
TO POP KERNELS OF THIS SIZE, WE NEED A MONSTER FIRE.
AND I KNOW JUST THE PLACE FOR THAT.
JUST 1,500 KILOMETERS NORTH OF HERE IS WOOL VOLCANO!
LET'S GET ON OVER THERE!
AROO
YEAH!

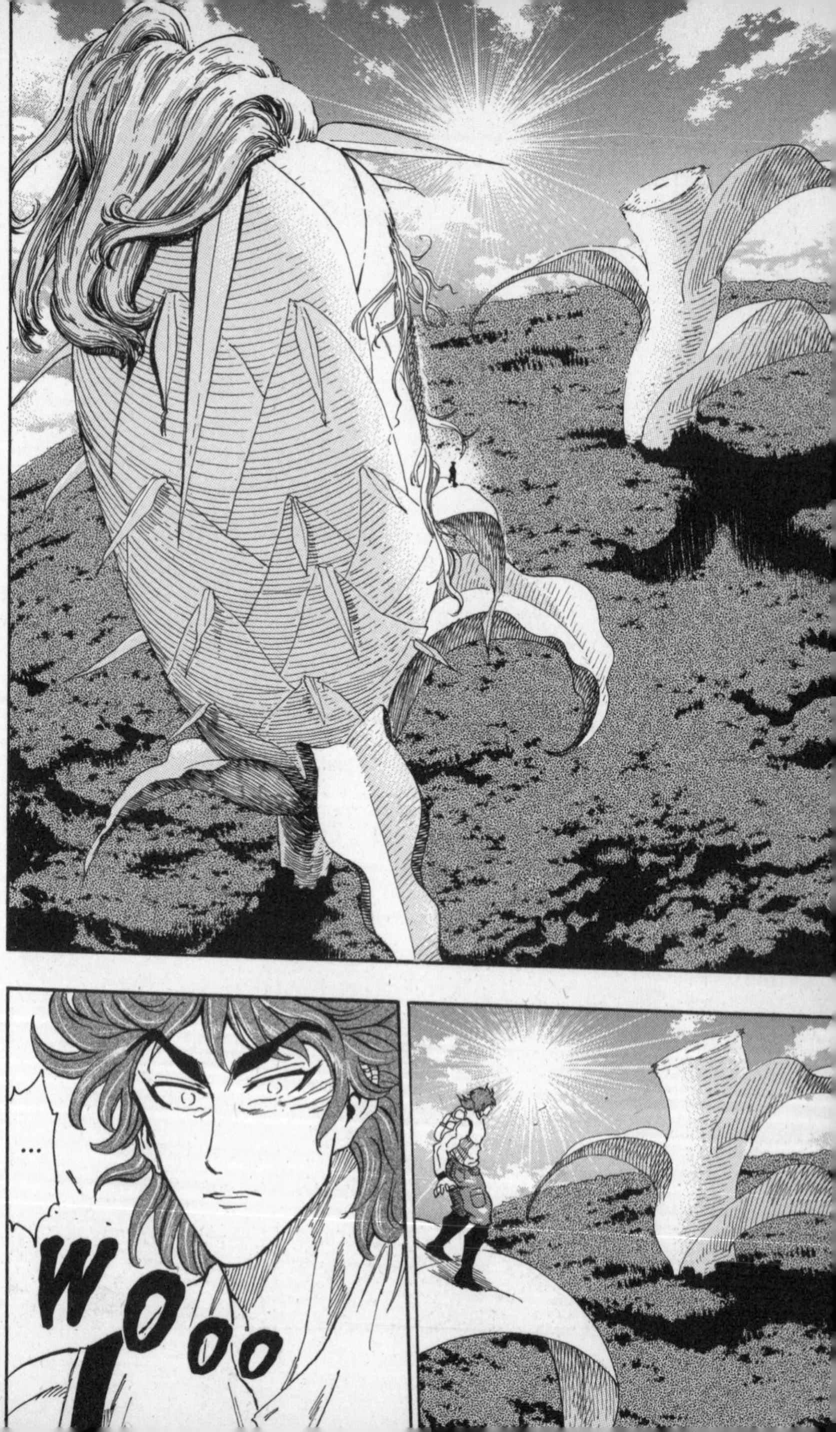
...
WOOO

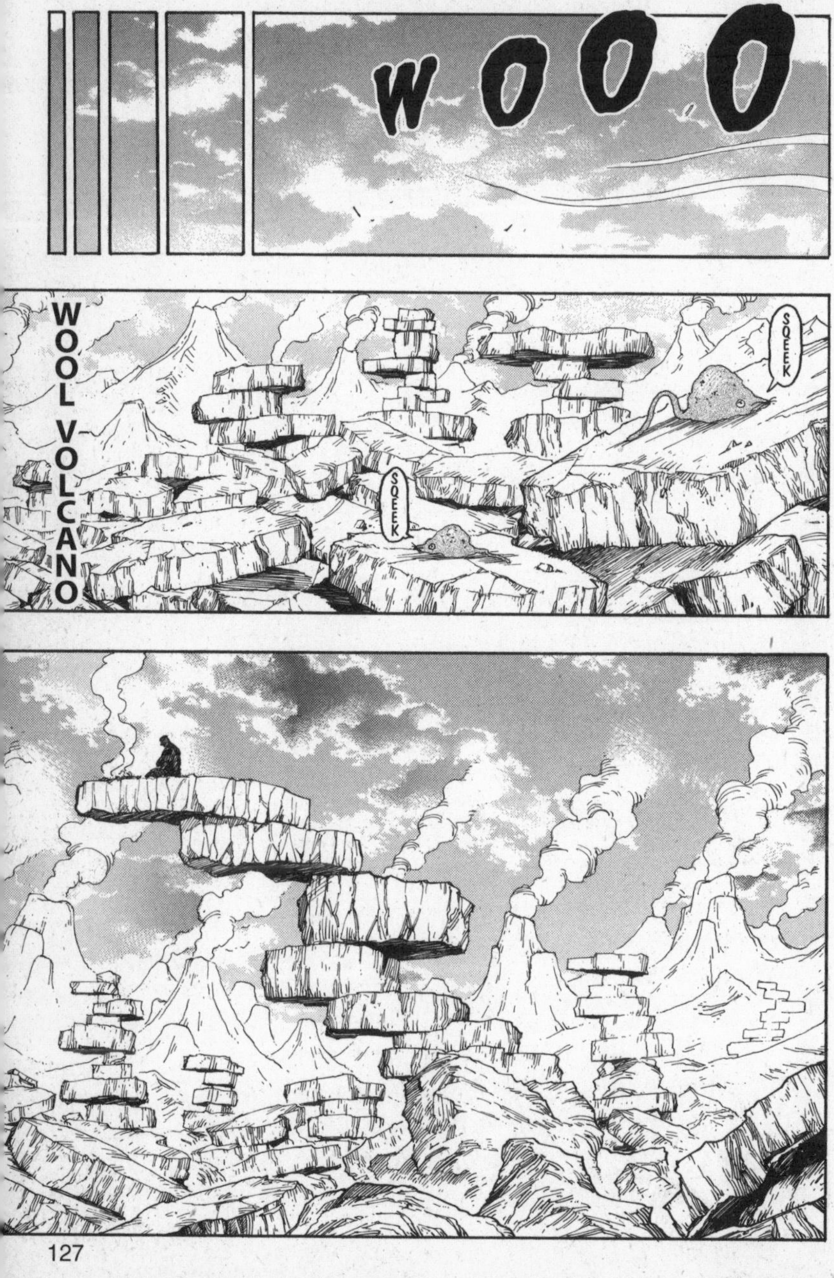
WOOO
SQEEK
SQEEK
WOOL VOLCANO

TORIKO

GOURMET CHECKLIST

Vol. 043

BUTT BUG
(INSECT)

CAPTURE LEVEL: LESS THAN 1

HABITAT: DARK, DAMP PLACES

LENGTH: 60 CM

HEIGHT: ---

WEIGHT: 2.5 KG

PRICE: 20,000 YEN EACH (AS A PET)

BDDA BDDA

HURBL DURBL DYAH

SQUEEE

BUTT BUG
(INSECT)
CAPTURE LEVEL: LESS THAN 1

SCALE

A TYPE OF BAGWORM, THIS INSECT'S POSTERIOR RESEMBLES A BUTT, HENCE THE NAME. BECAUSE OF THAT, THERE ARE FEW WHO WILL EAT IT, AND THOSE WHO DO TEND TO BE PRETTY BIZARRE IN THEIR CULINARY TASTES. SPEAKING OF BIZARRE, THERE'S ALSO A SUBCULTURE OF BUTT-FETISHISTS WHO APPARENTLY LIKE TO OWN THESE THINGS AS PETS.

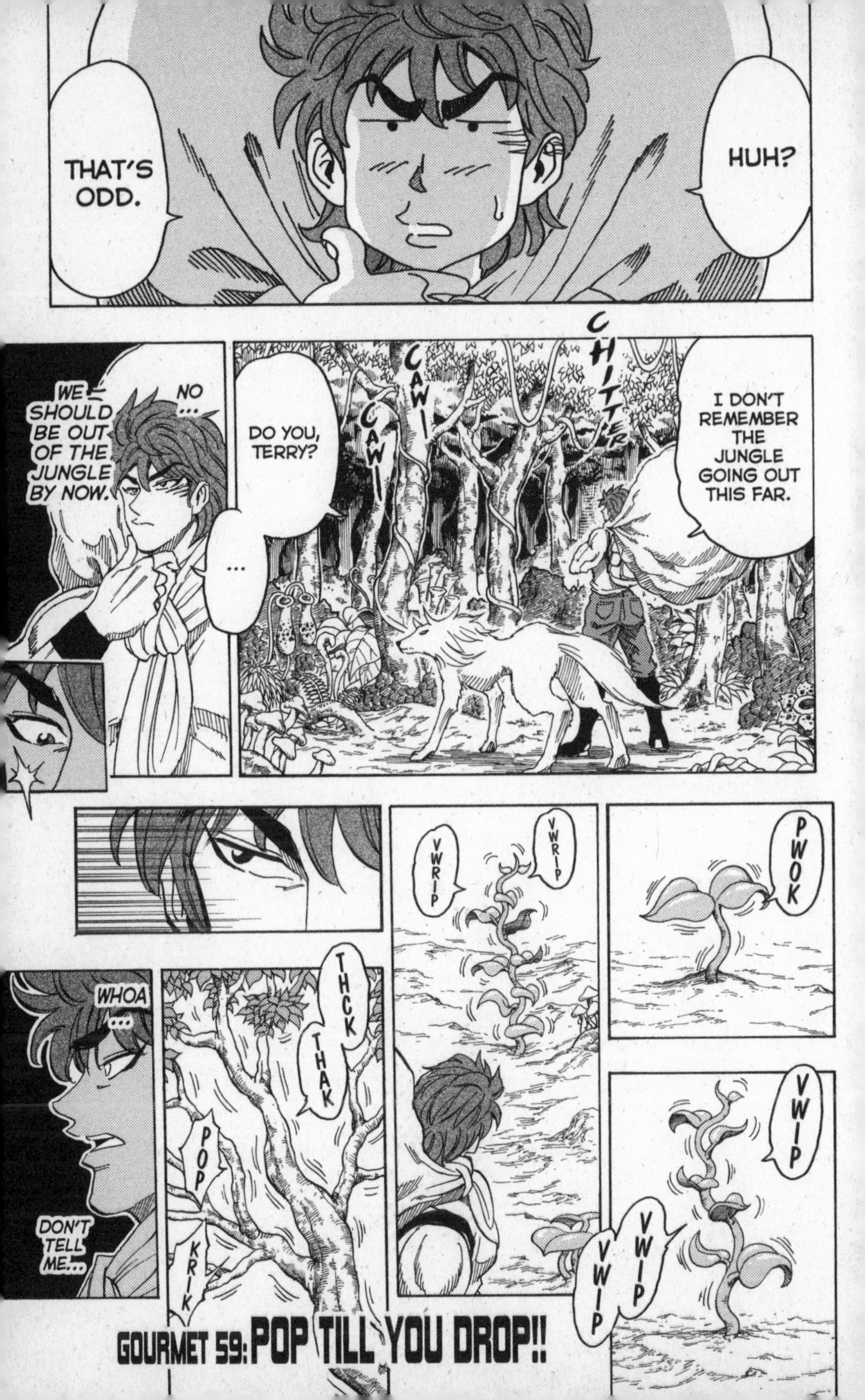
HUH?
THAT'S ODD.
CHITTER
CAW! CAW!
I DON'T REMEMBER THE JUNGLE GOING OUT THIS FAR.
DO YOU, TERRY?
...
NO...
WE SHOULD BE OUT OF THE JUNGLE BY NOW.
PWOK
VWRIP
VWRIP
VWIP
VWIP
VWIP
THCK
THAK
POP
KRIK
WHOA...
DON'T TELL ME...
GOURMET 59: POP TILL YOU DROP!!

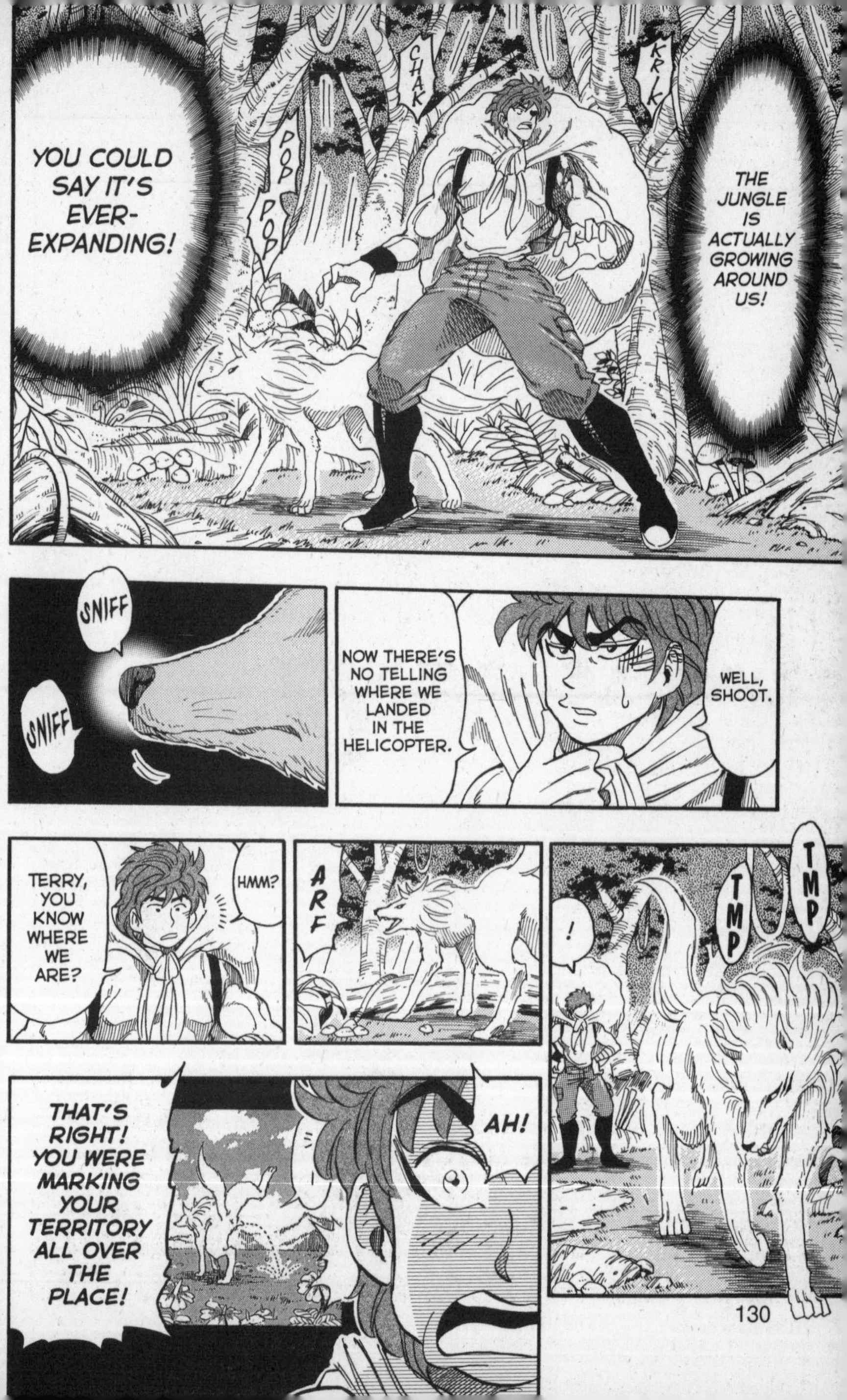
THE JUNGLE IS ACTUALLY GROWING AROUND US!
KRIK
CHAK
POP POP POP
YOU COULD SAY IT'S EVER-EXPANDING!
WELL, SHOOT.
NOW THERE'S NO TELLING WHERE WE LANDED IN THE HELICOPTER.
SNIFF
SNIFF
TMP
TMP
TMP
!
ARF
HMM?
TERRY, YOU KNOW WHERE WE ARE?
AH!
THAT'S RIGHT! YOU WERE MARKING YOUR TERRITORY ALL OVER THE PLACE!

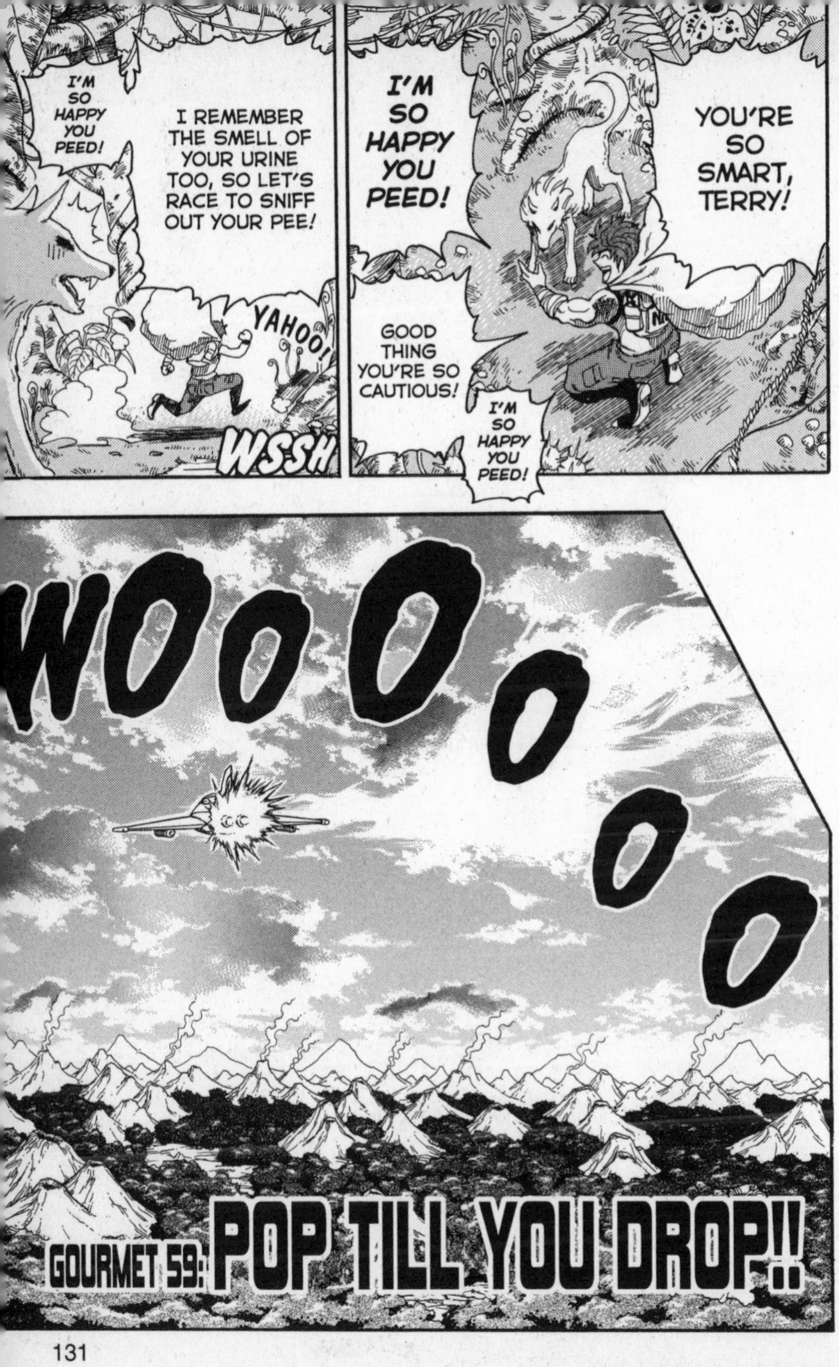
YOU'RE SO SMART, TERRY!
I'M SO HAPPY YOU PEED!
GOOD THING YOU'RE SO CAUTIOUS!
I'M SO HAPPY YOU PEED!
I REMEMBER THE SMELL OF YOUR URINE TOO, SO LET'S RACE TO SNIFF OUT YOUR PEE!
I'M SO HAPPY YOU PEED!
YAHOO!
WSSH
WOOOOOOO
GOURMET 59: POP TILL YOU DROP!!

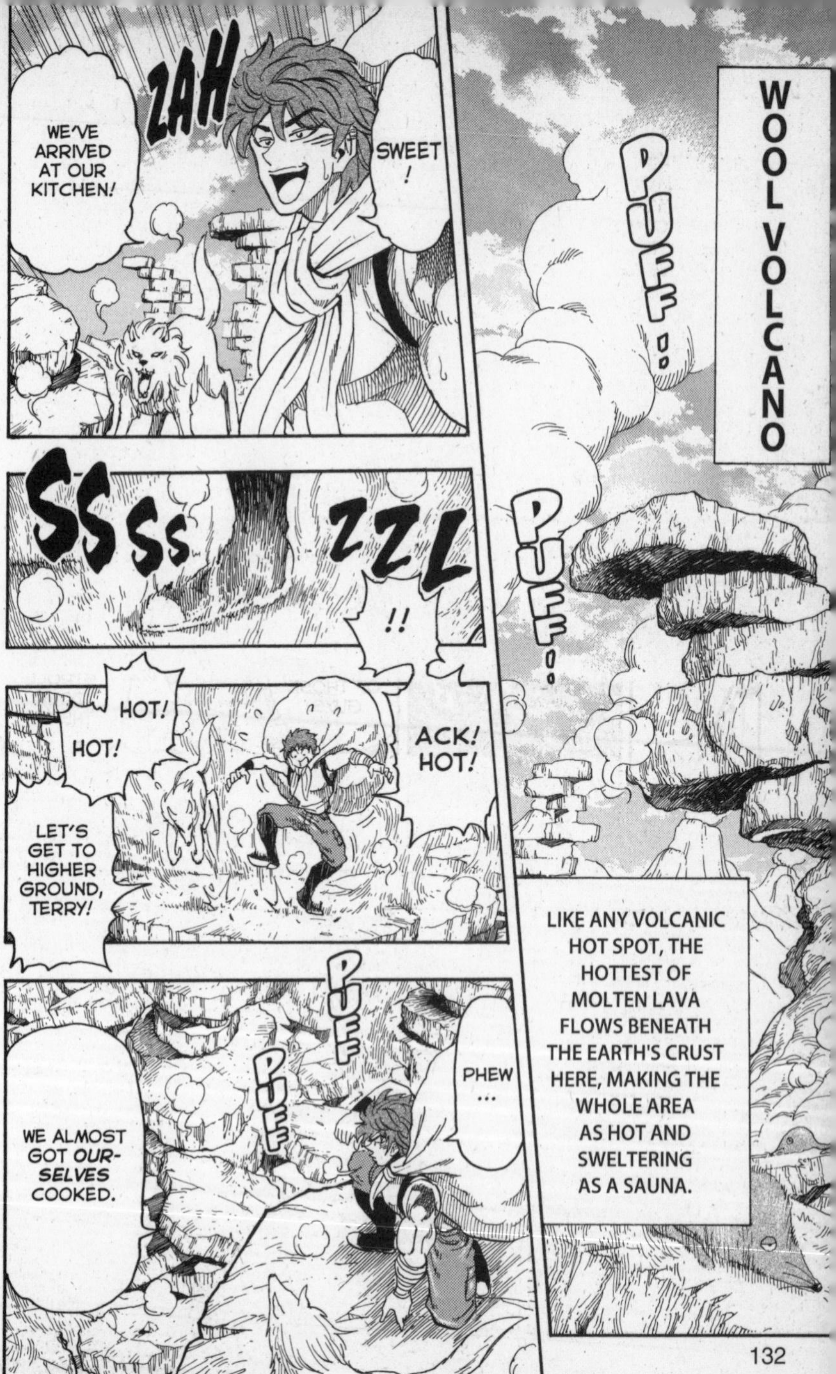
WOOL VOLCANO
PUFF!!
PUFF!!
LIKE ANY VOLCANIC HOT SPOT, THE HOTTEST OF MOLTEN LAVA FLOWS BENEATH THE EARTH'S CRUST HERE, MAKING THE WHOLE AREA AS HOT AND SWELTERING AS A SAUNA.
SWEET!
ZAH
WE'VE ARRIVED AT OUR KITCHEN!
!!
ZZZL
SSSS
ACK! HOT!
HOT!
HOT!
LET'S GET TO HIGHER GROUND, TERRY!
PHEW...
PUFF
PUFF
WE ALMOST GOT *OURSELVES* COOKED.

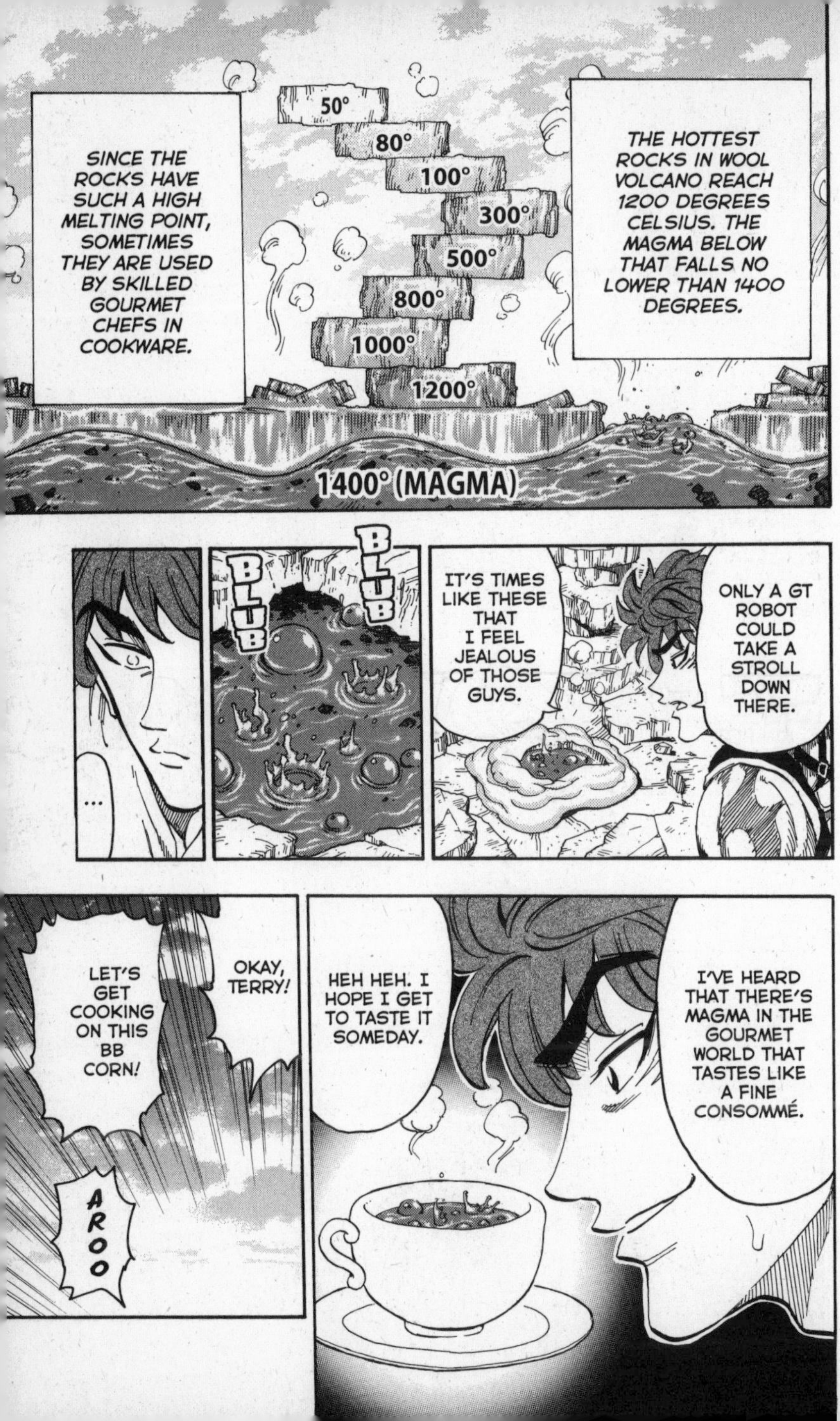
THE HOTTEST ROCKS IN WOOL VOLCANO REACH 1200 DEGREES CELSIUS. THE MAGMA BELOW THAT FALLS NO LOWER THAN 1400 DEGREES.
50°
80°
100°
300°
500°
800°
1000°
1200°
SINCE THE ROCKS HAVE SUCH A HIGH MELTING POINT, SOMETIMES THEY ARE USED BY SKILLED GOURMET CHEFS IN COOKWARE.
1400° (MAGMA)
ONLY A GT ROBOT COULD TAKE A STROLL DOWN THERE.
IT'S TIMES LIKE THESE THAT I FEEL JEALOUS OF THOSE GUYS.
BLUB
BLUB
...
I'VE HEARD THAT THERE'S MAGMA IN THE GOURMET WORLD THAT TASTES LIKE A FINE CONSOMMÉ.
HEH HEH. I HOPE I GET TO TASTE IT SOMEDAY.
OKAY, TERRY!
LET'S GET COOKING ON THIS BB CORN!
AROO

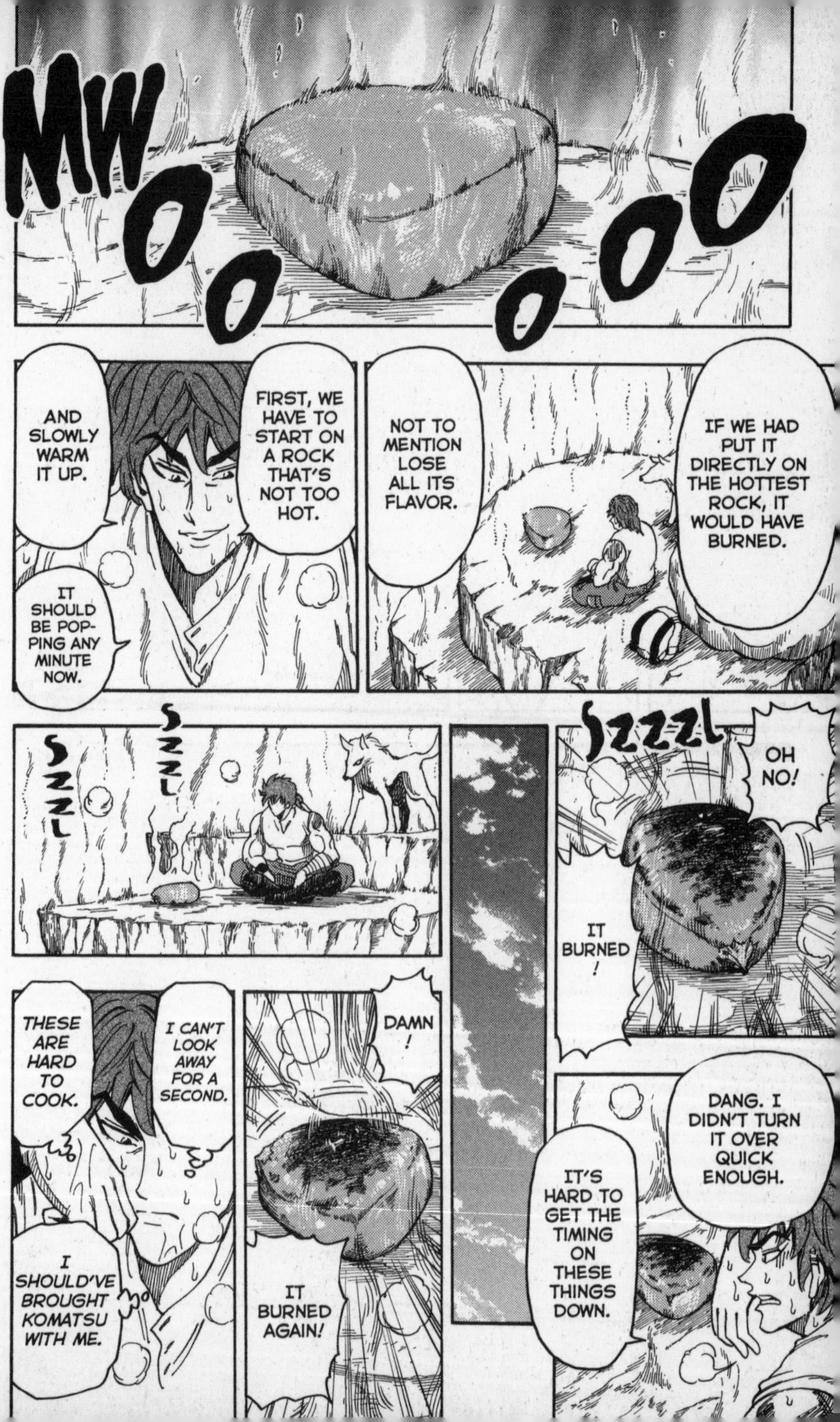
MWOOOOOOO
IF WE HAD PUT IT DIRECTLY ON THE HOTTEST ROCK, IT WOULD HAVE BURNED.
NOT TO MENTION LOSE ALL ITS FLAVOR.
FIRST, WE HAVE TO START ON A ROCK THAT'S NOT TOO HOT.
AND SLOWLY WARM IT UP.
IT SHOULD BE POPPING ANY MINUTE NOW.
SZZZL
OH NO!
IT BURNED!
DANG. I DIDN'T TURN IT OVER QUICK ENOUGH.
IT'S HARD TO GET THE TIMING ON THESE THINGS DOWN.
SZZZL
SZZZL
DAMN!
IT BURNED AGAIN!
I CAN'T LOOK AWAY FOR A SECOND.
THESE ARE HARD TO COOK.
I SHOULD'VE BROUGHT KOMATSU WITH ME.

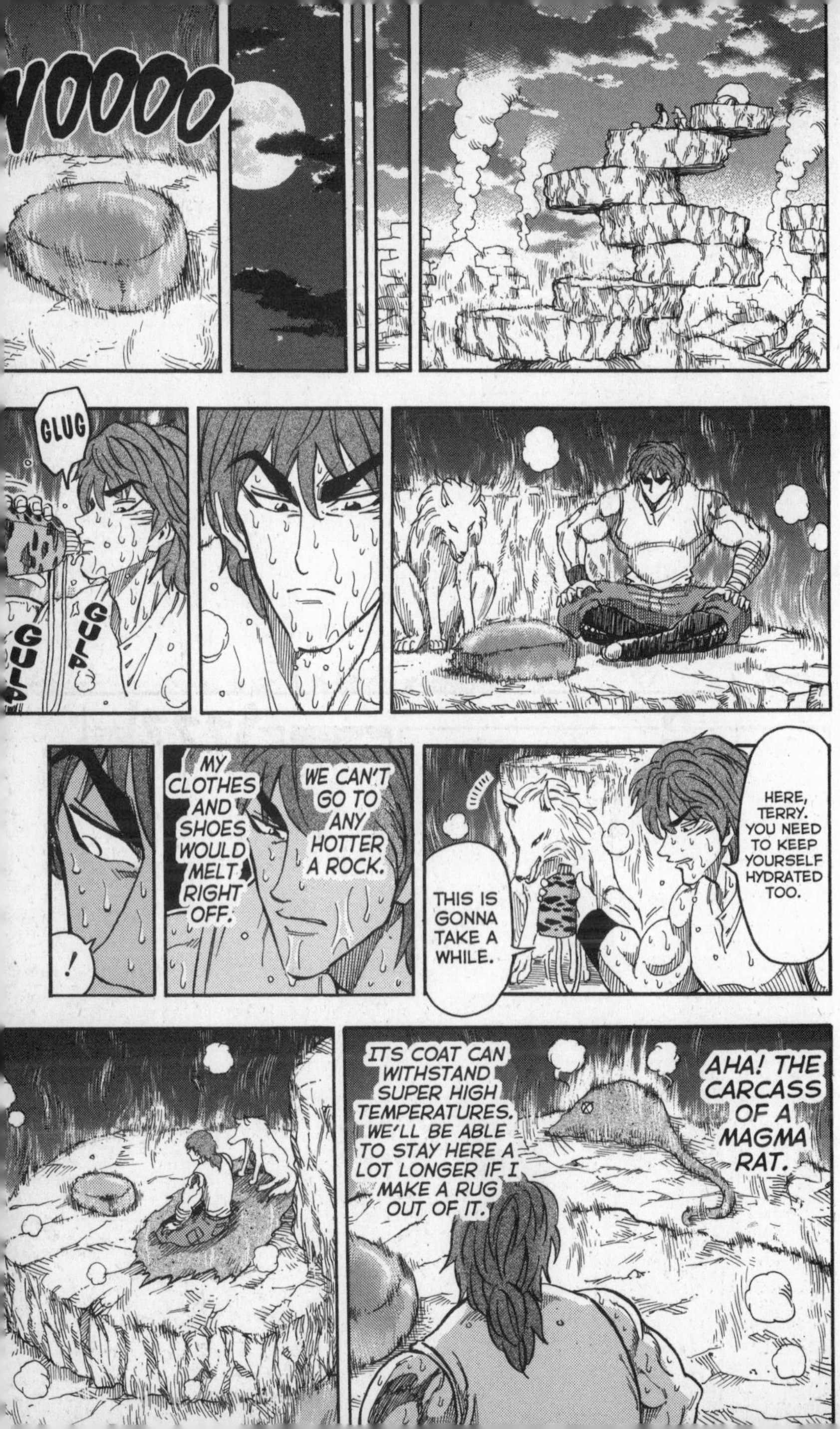
VOOOO
GLUG
GULP
GULP
HERE, TERRY. YOU NEED TO KEEP YOURSELF HYDRATED TOO.
THIS IS GONNA TAKE A WHILE.
WE CAN'T GO TO ANY HOTTER A ROCK.
MY CLOTHES AND SHOES WOULD MELT RIGHT OFF.
!
AHA! THE CARCASS OF A MAGMA RAT.
ITS COAT CAN WITHSTAND SUPER HIGH TEMPERATURES. WE'LL BE ABLE TO STAY HERE A LOT LONGER IF I MAKE A RUG OUT OF IT.

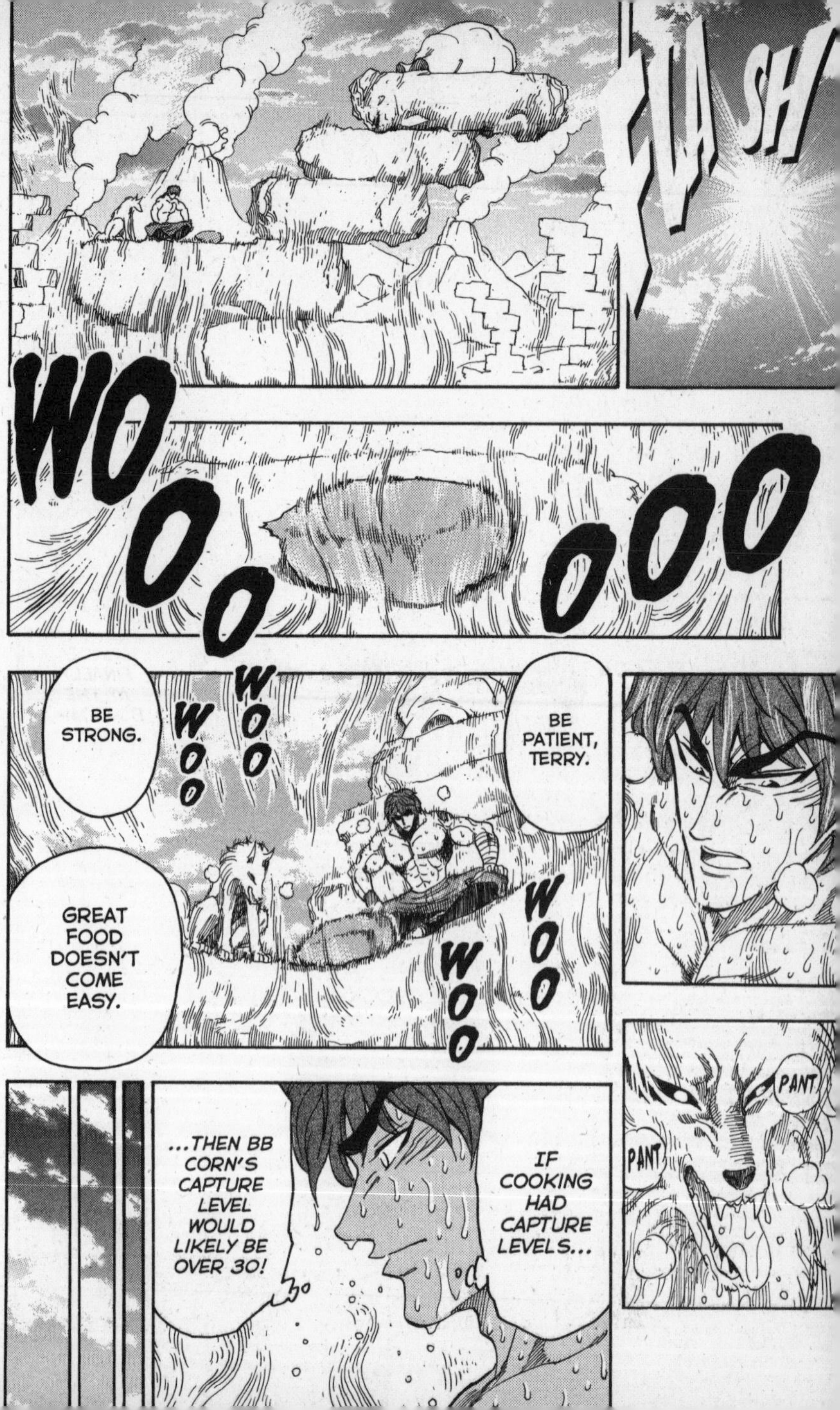
FLASH
WOOOOOOOOO
BE PATIENT, TERRY.
BE STRONG.
WOOO
WOOO
GREAT FOOD DOESN'T COME EASY.
WOOO
WOOO
PANT
PANT
IF COOKING HAD CAPTURE LEVELS...
...THEN BB CORN'S CAPTURE LEVEL WOULD LIKELY BE OVER 30!

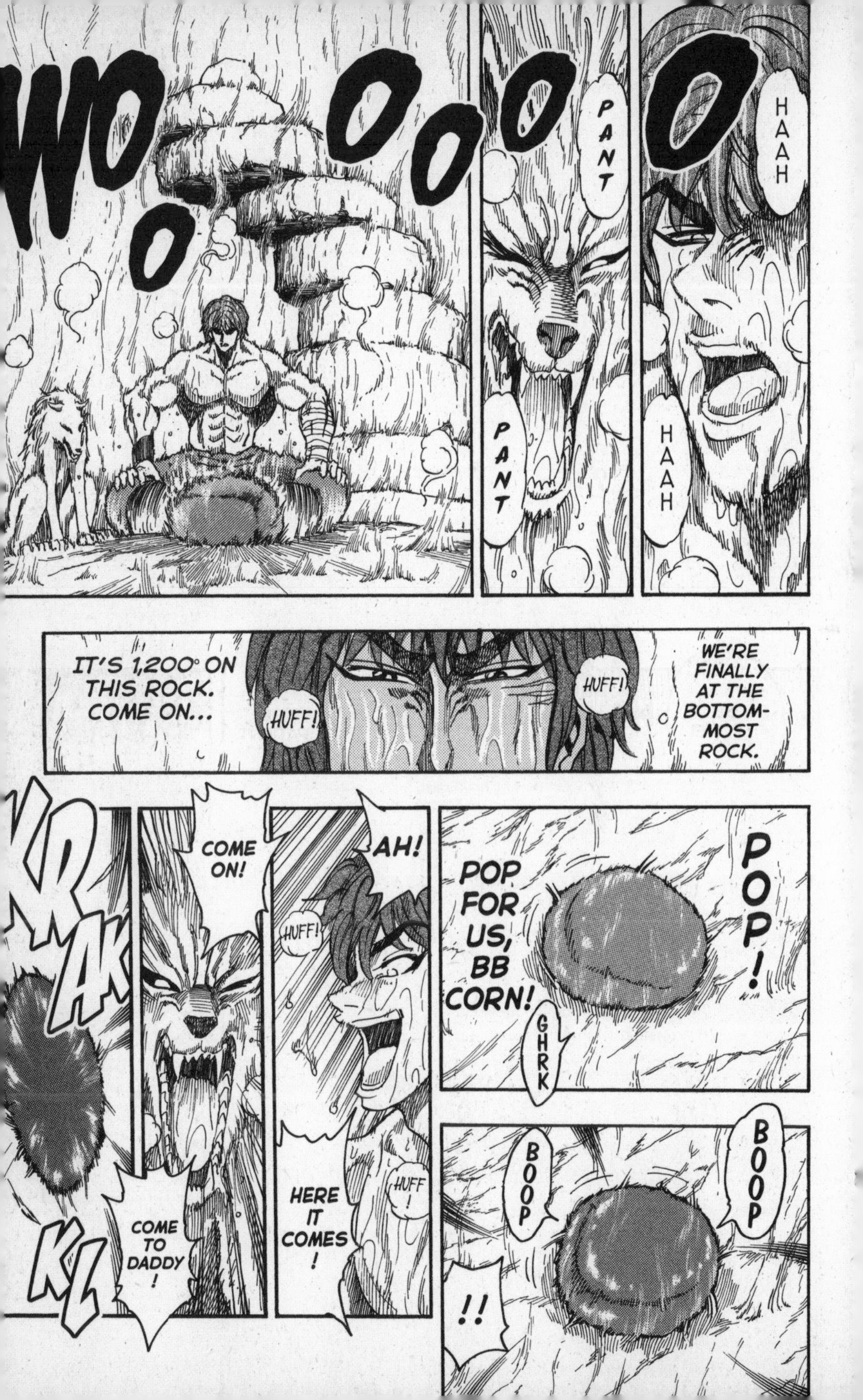
WOOOOOO
HAAH
HAAH
PANT
PANT
WE'RE FINALLY AT THE BOTTOM-MOST ROCK.
HUFF!
HUFF!
IT'S 1,200° ON THIS ROCK. COME ON...
POP!
POP FOR US, BB CORN!
GHRK
BOOP
BOOP
!!
AH!
HUFF!
HUFF!
HERE IT COMES!
COME ON!
COME TO DADDY!
KRAK
KL

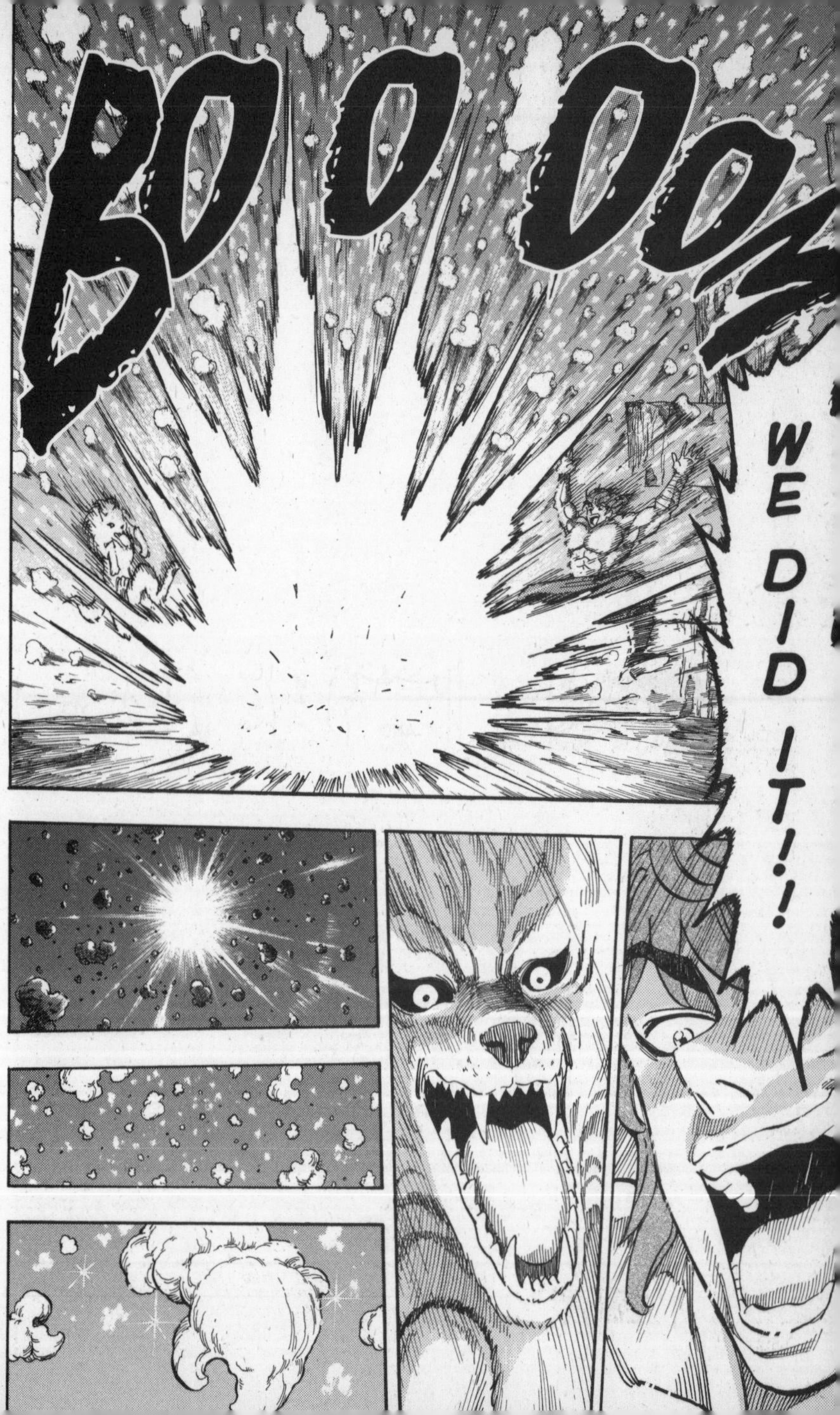
BOOOOM
WE DID IT!!!

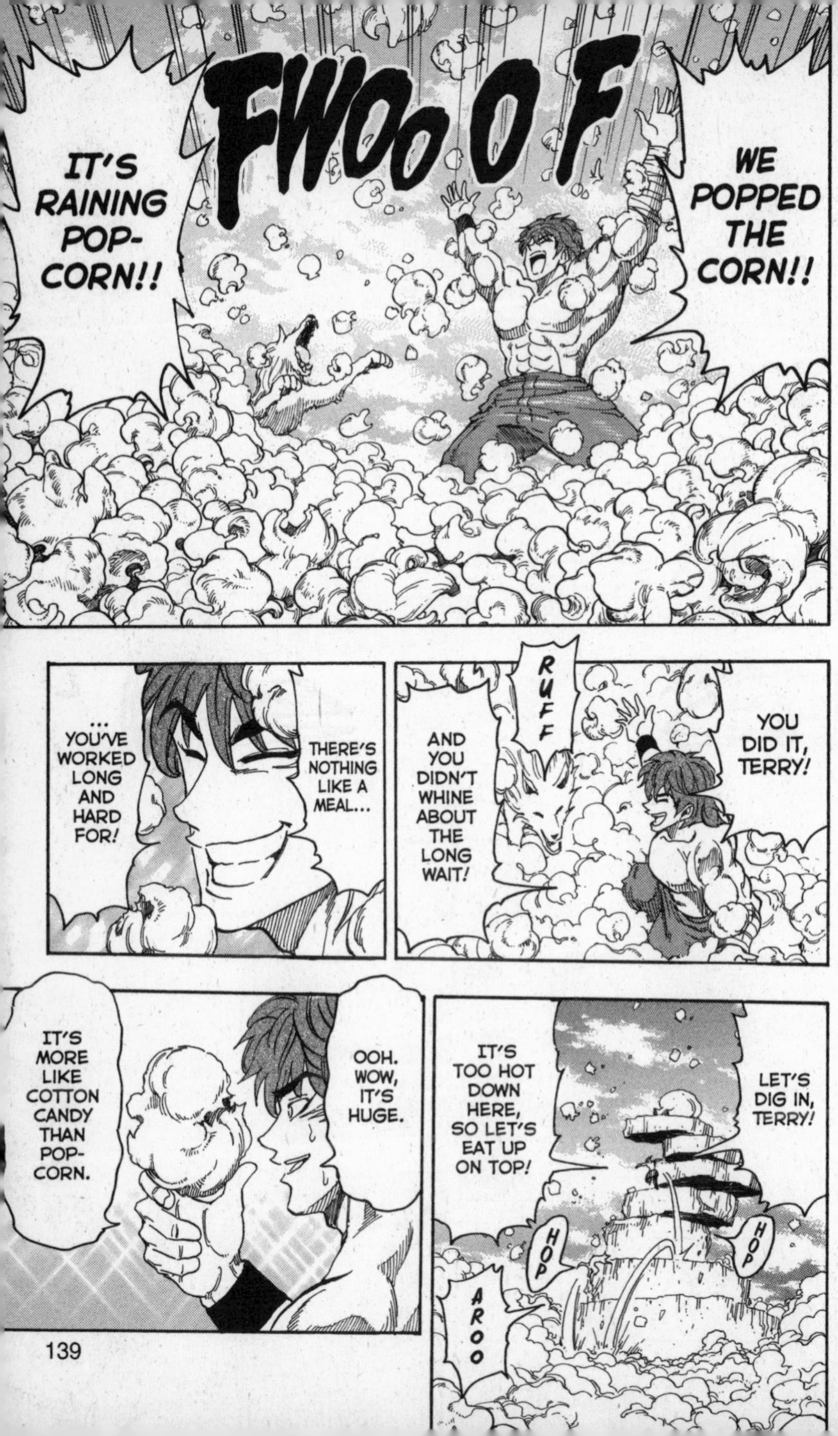
FWOOOF
WE POPPED THE CORN!!
IT'S RAINING POP-CORN!!
YOU DID IT, TERRY!
RUFF
AND YOU DIDN'T WHINE ABOUT THE LONG WAIT!
THERE'S NOTHING LIKE A MEAL...
...YOU'VE WORKED LONG AND HARD FOR!
LET'S DIG IN, TERRY!
IT'S TOO HOT DOWN HERE, SO LET'S EAT UP ON TOP!
HOP
HOP
AROO
OOH. WOW, IT'S HUGE.
IT'S MORE LIKE COTTON CANDY THAN POP-CORN.

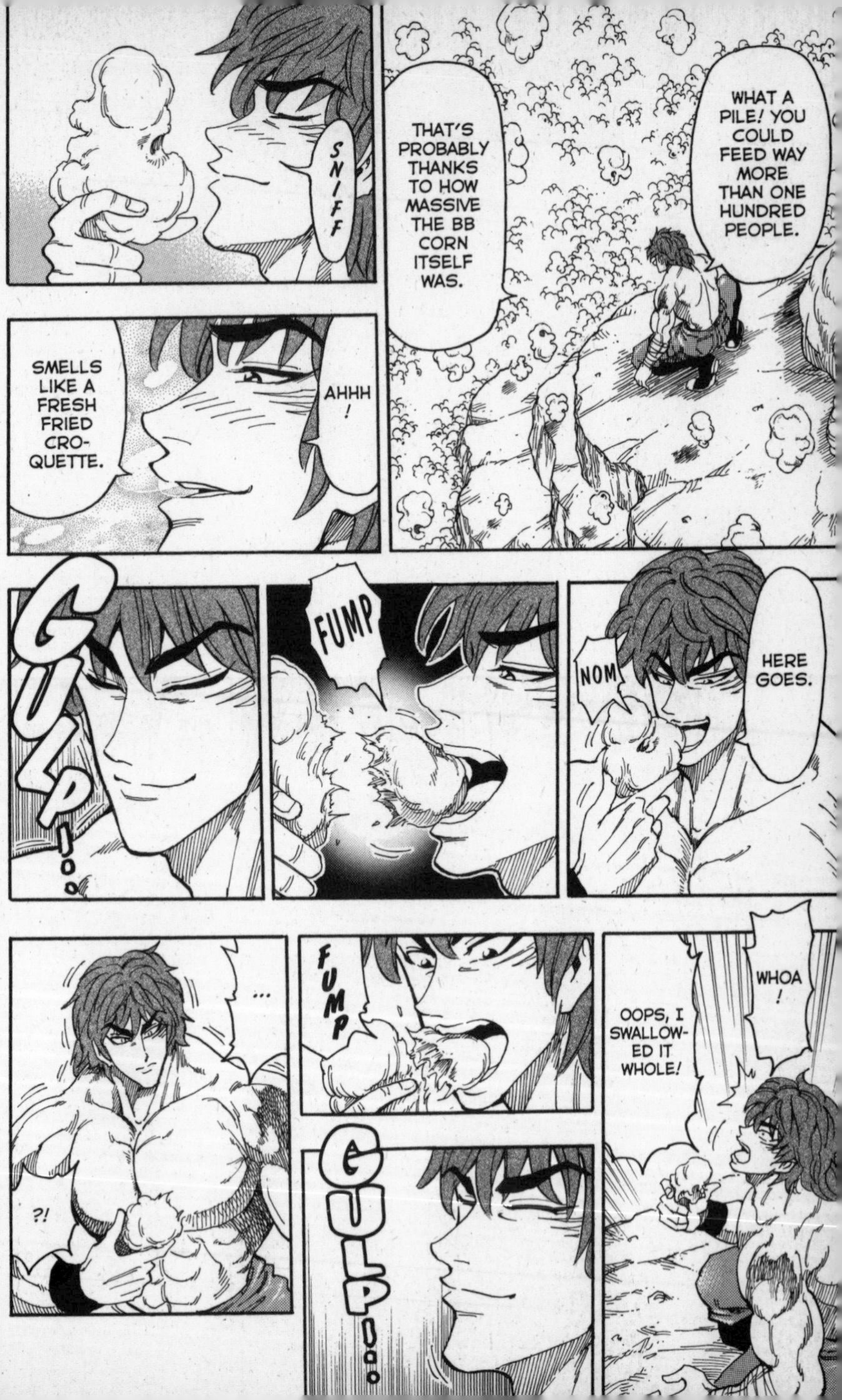
WHAT A PILE! YOU COULD FEED WAY MORE THAN ONE HUNDRED PEOPLE.
THAT'S PROBABLY THANKS TO HOW MASSIVE THE BB CORN ITSELF WAS.
SNIFF
AHHH!
SMELLS LIKE A FRESH FRIED CRO-QUETTE.
HERE GOES.
NOM
FUMP
GULP!..
WHOA!
OOPS, I SWALLOW-ED IT WHOLE!
FUMP
GULP!..
...
?!

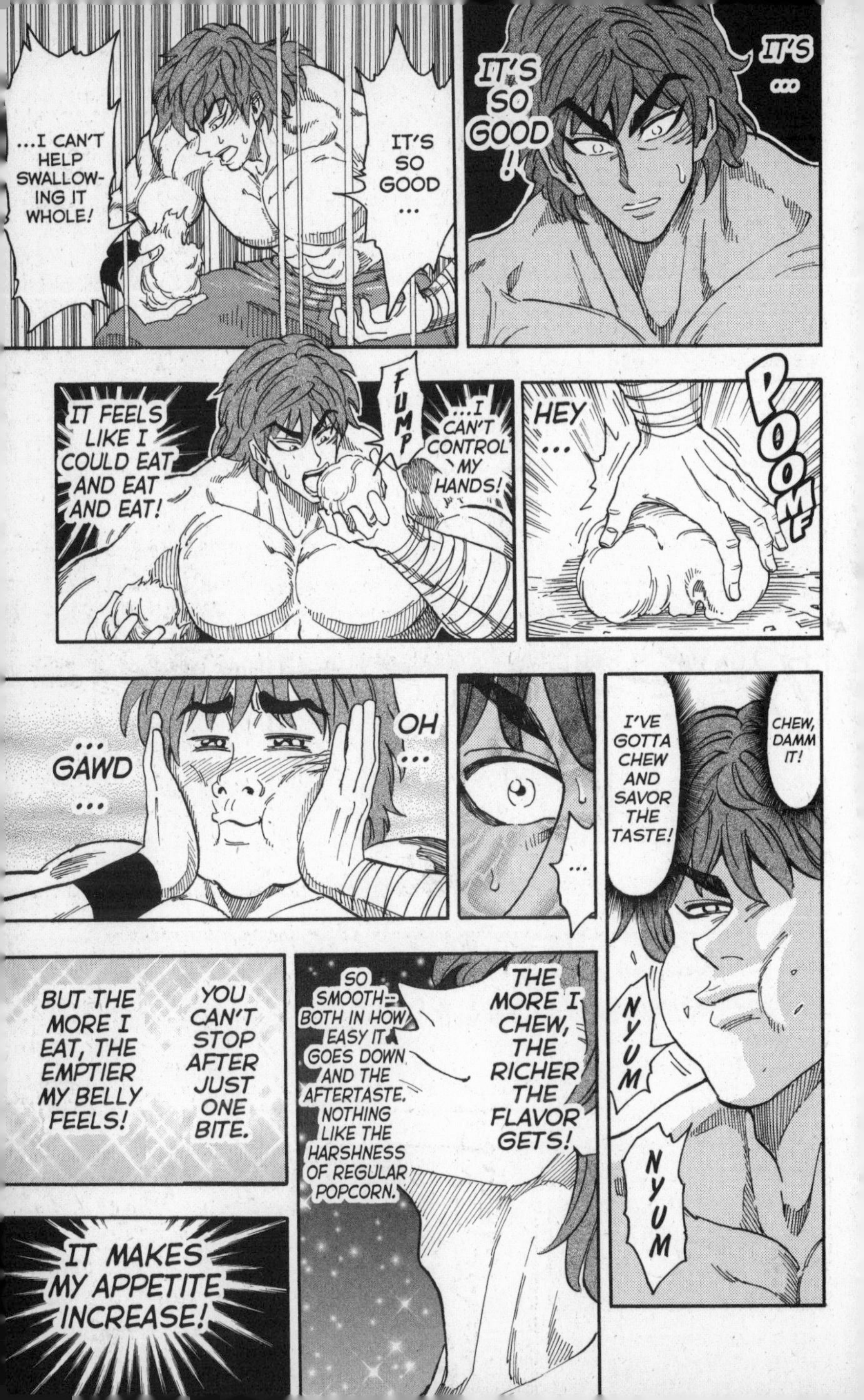

IT'S ...
IT'S SO GOOD!
IT'S SO GOOD ...
...I CAN'T HELP SWALLOWING IT WHOLE!
POOMF
HEY ...
...I CAN'T CONTROL MY HANDS!
FUMP
IT FEELS LIKE I COULD EAT AND EAT AND EAT!
CHEW, DAMM IT!
I'VE GOTTA CHEW AND SAVOR THE TASTE!
NYUM
NYUM
...
OH ...
... GAWD ...
THE MORE I CHEW, THE RICHER THE FLAVOR GETS!
SO SMOOTH-- BOTH IN HOW EASY IT GOES DOWN AND THE AFTERTASTE. NOTHING LIKE THE HARSHNESS OF REGULAR POPCORN.
YOU CAN'T STOP AFTER JUST ONE BITE.
BUT THE MORE I EAT, THE EMPTIER MY BELLY FEELS!
IT MAKES MY APPETITE INCREASE!

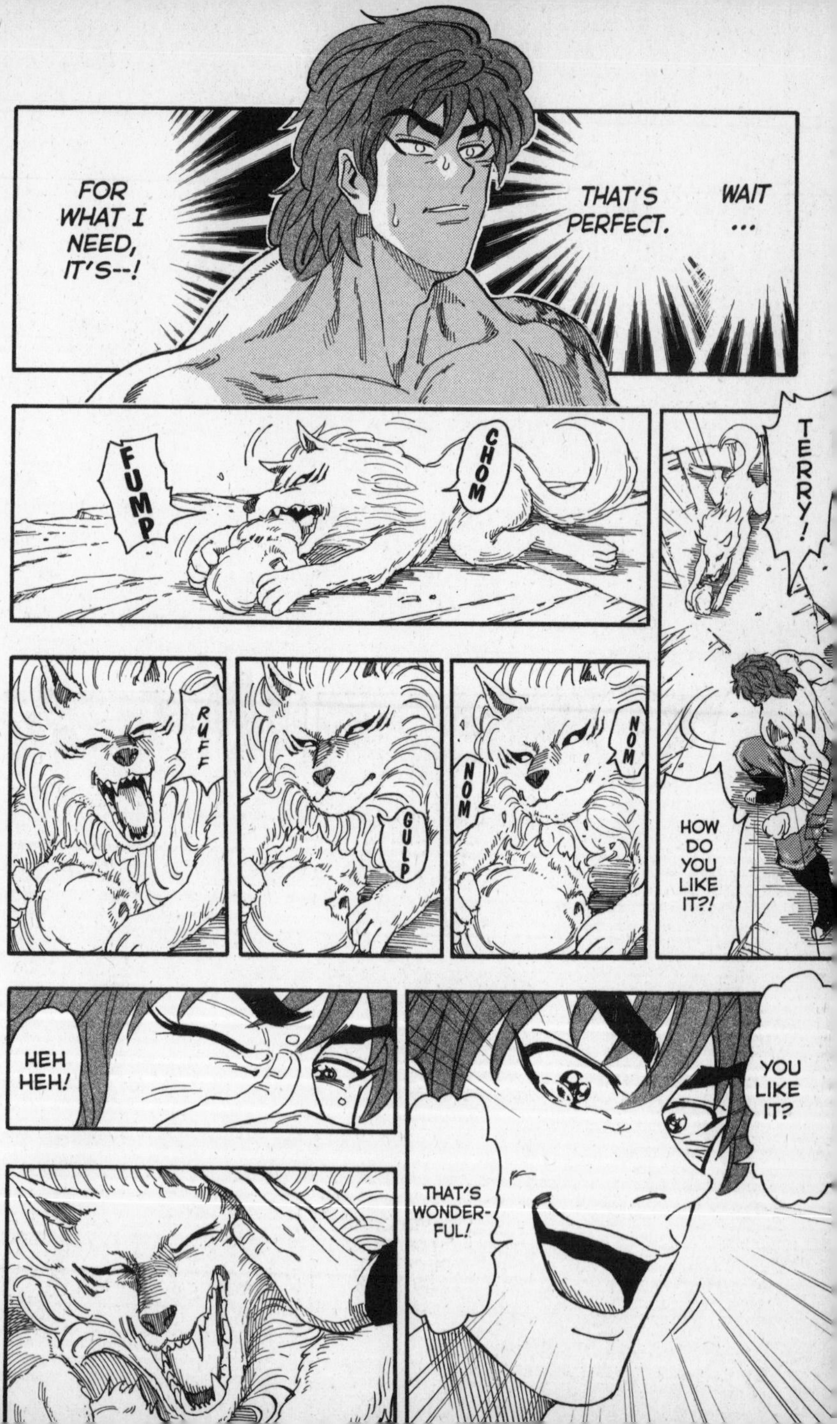
WAIT ...
THAT'S PERFECT.
FOR WHAT I NEED, IT'S--!
TERRY!
HOW DO YOU LIKE IT?!
CHOM
FUMP!
NOM NOM
GULP
RUFF
YOU LIKE IT?
THAT'S WONDER-FUL!
HEH HEH!

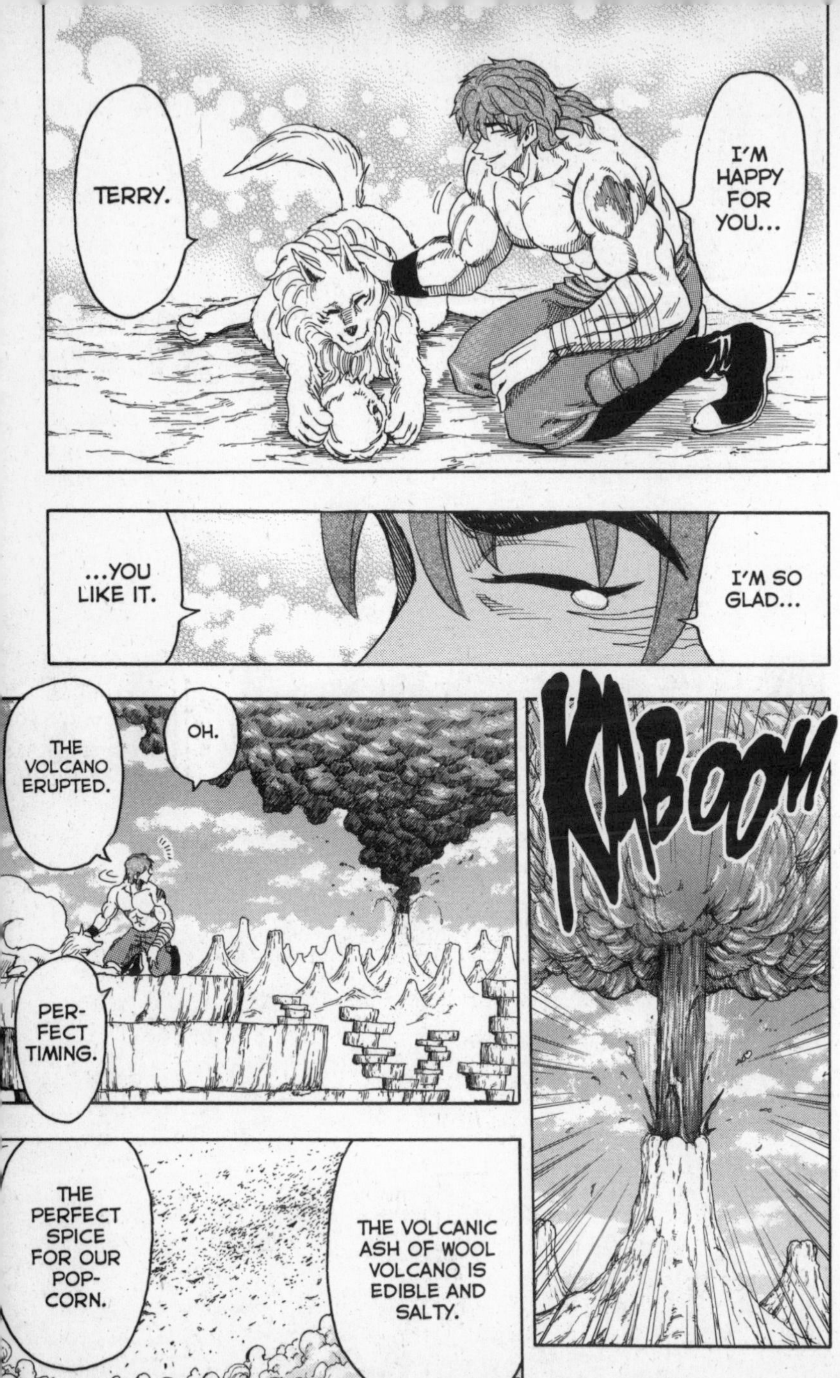
I'M HAPPY FOR YOU...
TERRY.
I'M SO GLAD...
...YOU LIKE IT.
KABOOM
OH.
THE VOLCANO ERUPTED.
PER-FECT TIMING.
THE VOLCANIC ASH OF WOOL VOLCANO IS EDIBLE AND SALTY.
THE PERFECT SPICE FOR OUR POP-CORN.

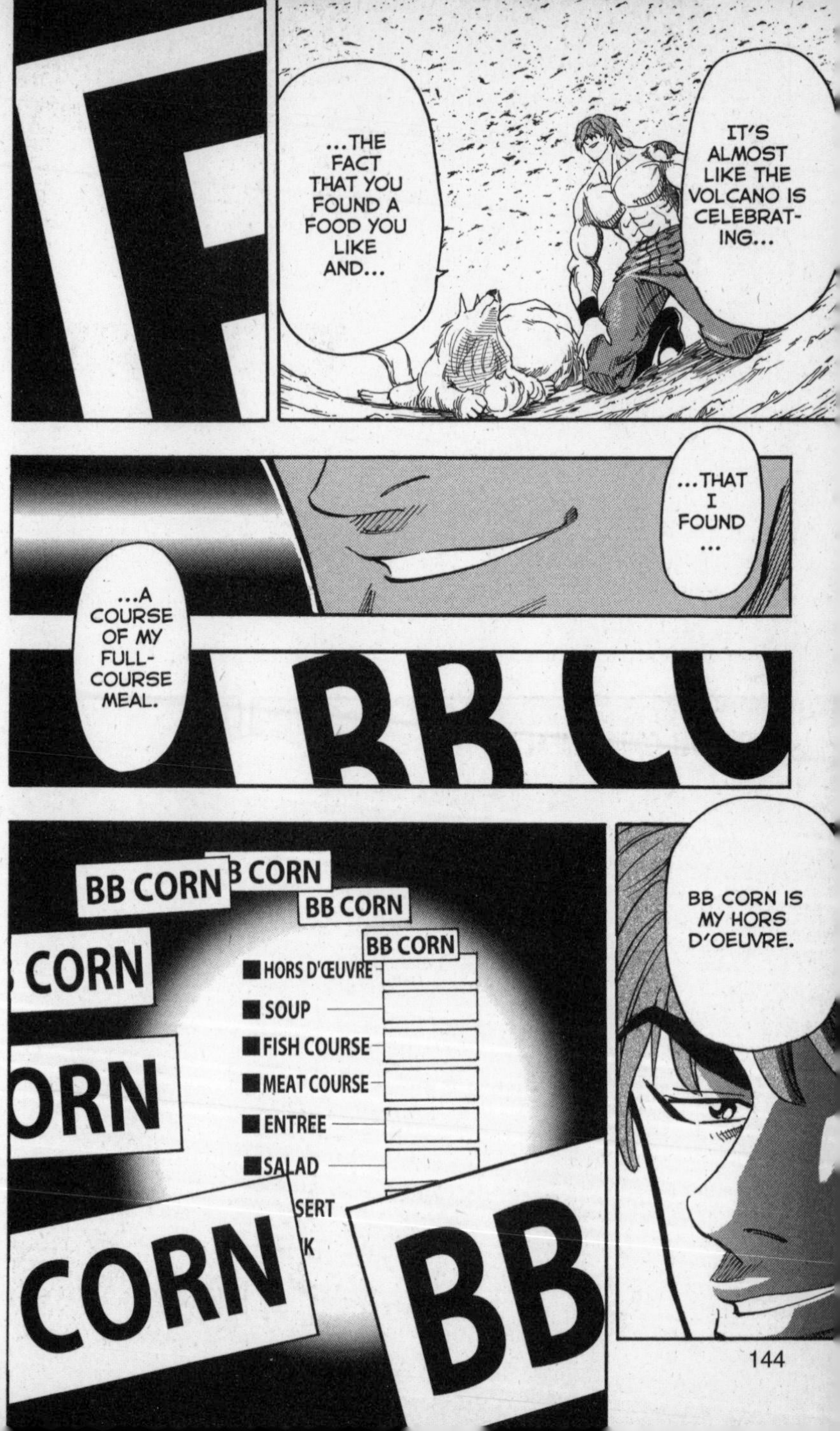

IT'S ALMOST LIKE THE VOLCANO IS CELEBRATING...
...THE FACT THAT YOU FOUND A FOOD YOU LIKE AND...
...THAT I FOUND...
...A COURSE OF MY FULL-COURSE MEAL.
BB CO
BB CORN IS MY HORS D'OEUVRE.
BB CORN
B CORN
BB CORN
BB CORN
CORN
ORN
HORS D'ŒUVRE
SOUP
FISH COURSE
MEAT COURSE
ENTREE
SALAD
CORN
BB

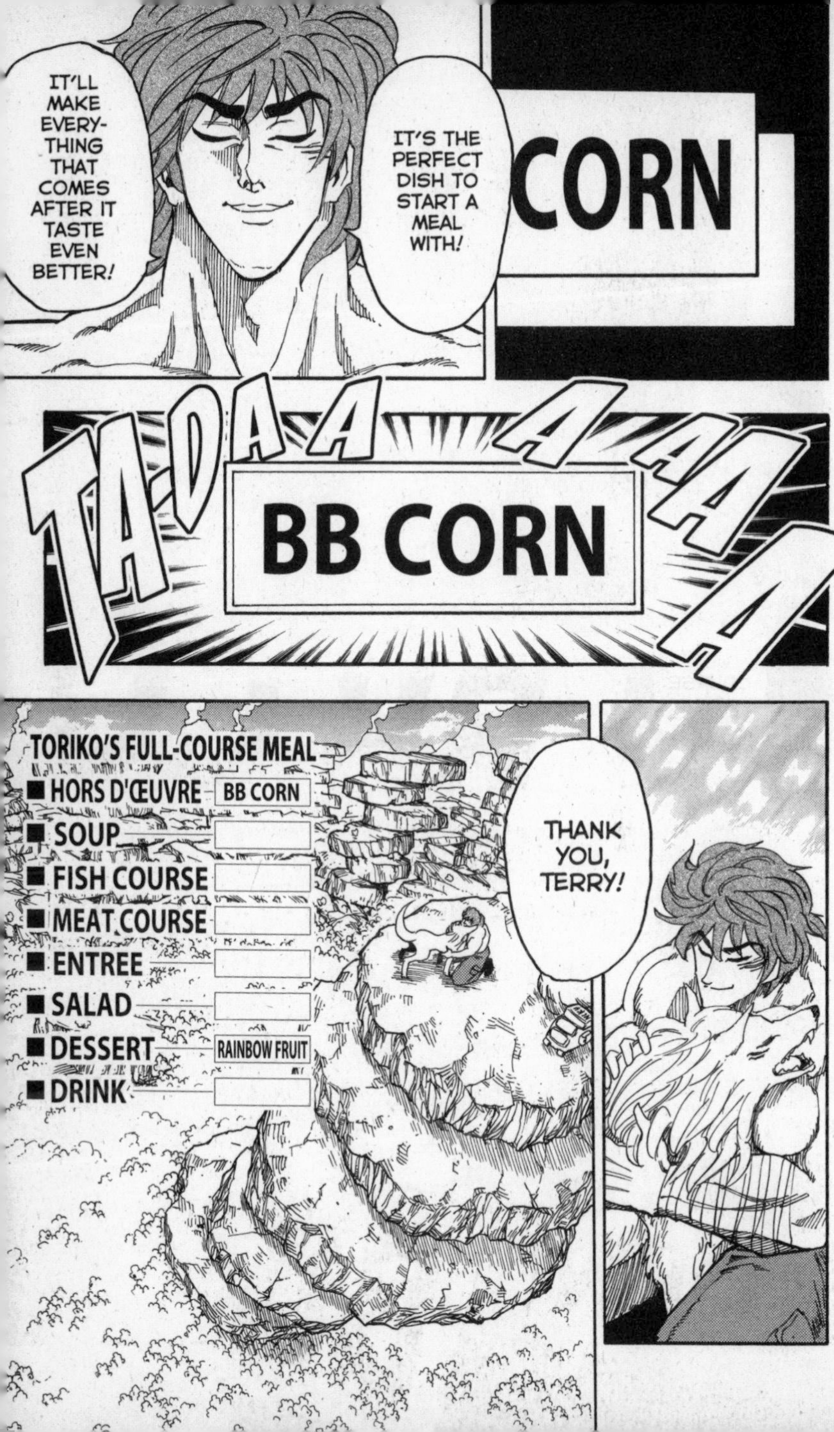
CORN
IT'S THE PERFECT DISH TO START A MEAL WITH!
IT'LL MAKE EVERY-THING THAT COMES AFTER IT TASTE EVEN BETTER!
TA-DA-A-A-A-A-A-A
BB CORN
THANK YOU, TERRY!
TORIKO'S FULL-COURSE MEAL
HORS D'ŒUVRE BB CORN
SOUP
FISH COURSE
MEAT COURSE
ENTREE
SALAD
DESSERT RAINBOW FRUIT
DRINK

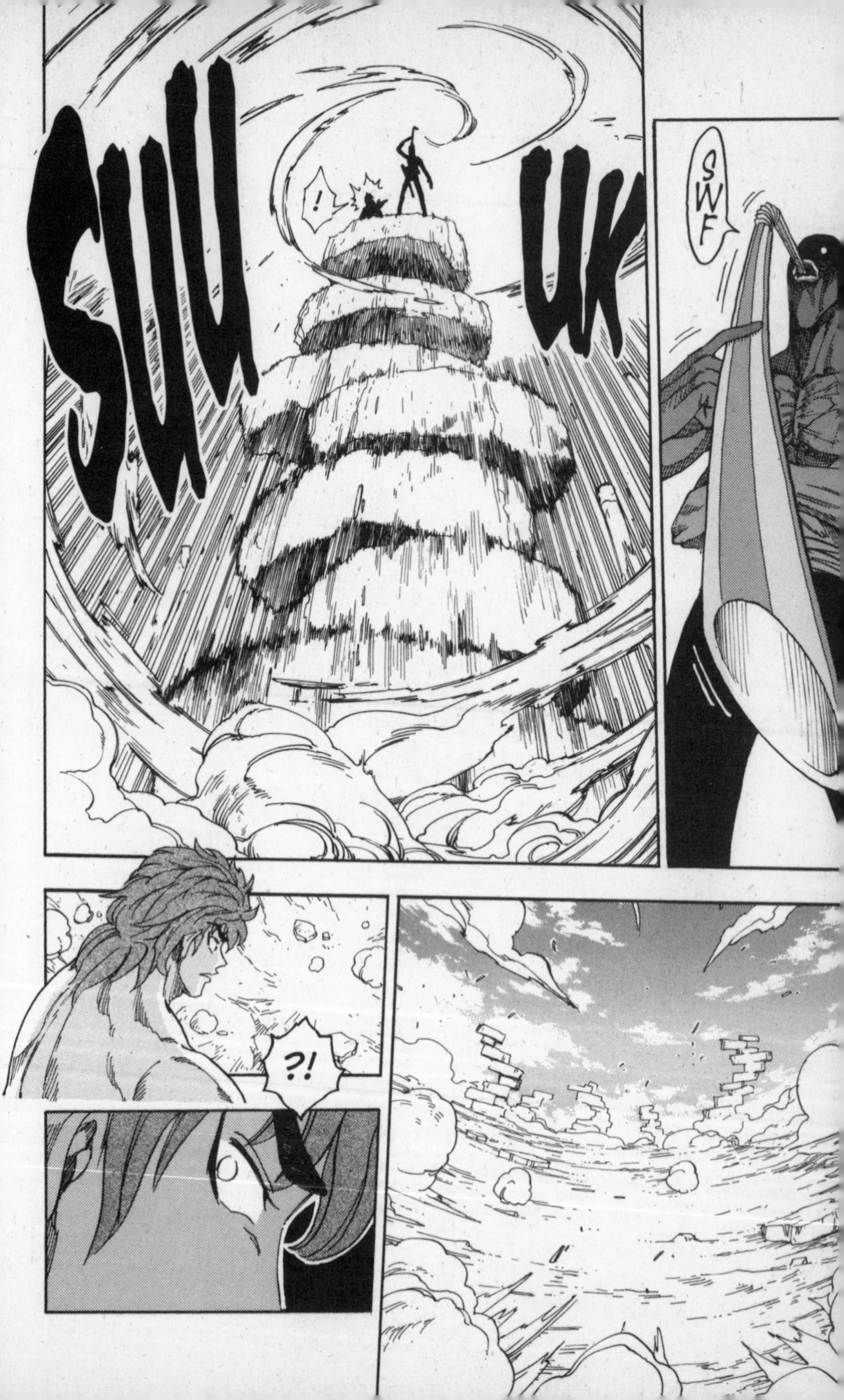
SWF
SUU
UK
!
?!

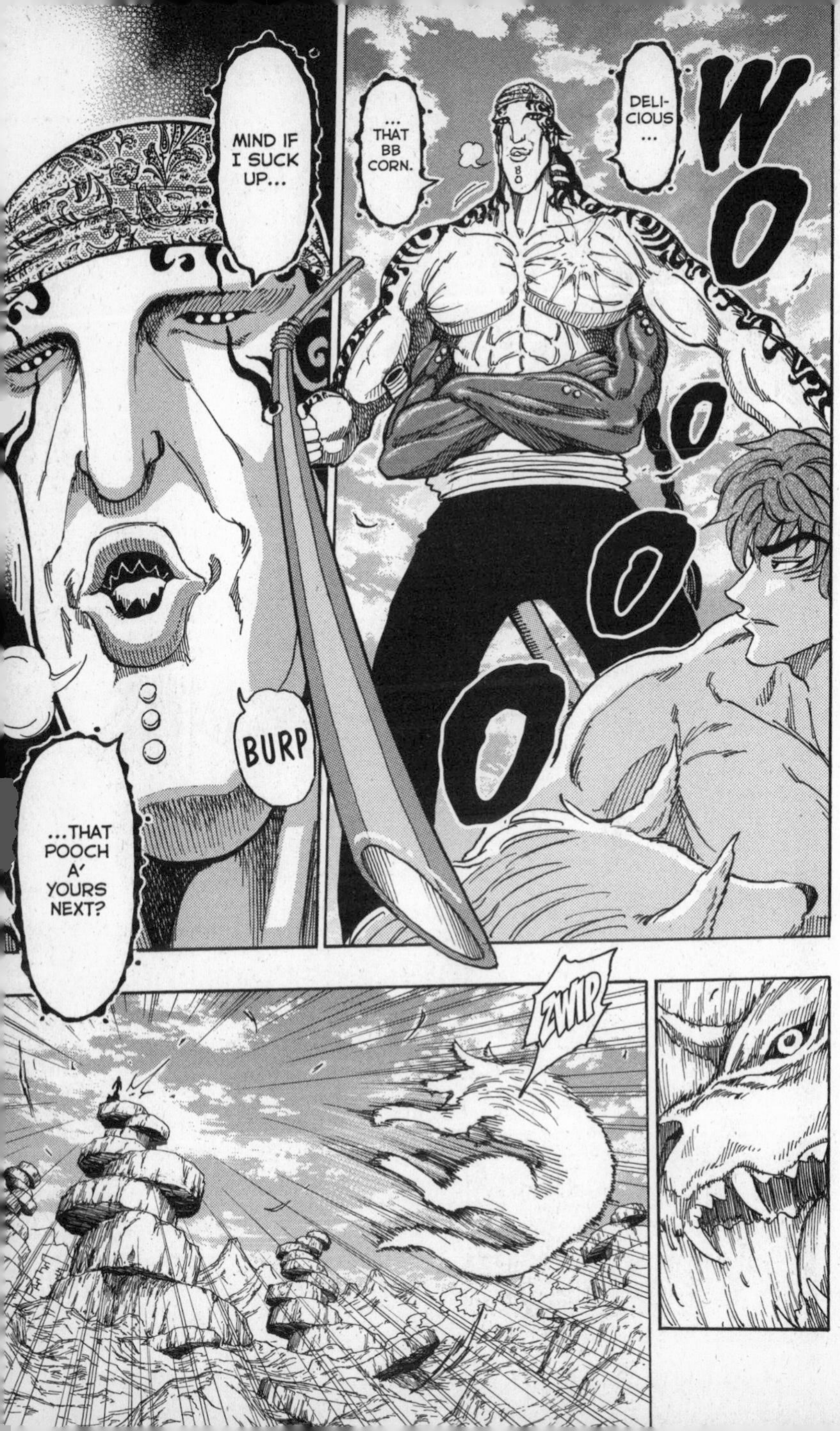
DELI-
CIOUS
...
WOOOOO
... THAT BB CORN.
MIND IF I SUCK UP...
BURP
...THAT POOCH A' YOURS NEXT?
ZWIP

TORIKO

GOURMET CHECKLIST

Vol. 044

BLACK GRASS
(PLANT)

CAPTURE LEVEL: LESS THAN 1

HABITAT: MILD, NUTRIENT-RICH SOIL

LENGTH: APPR. 30 CM

HEIGHT: ---

WEIGHT: ---

PRICE: 1 BUNDLE OF 50 BLADES / 1200 YEN

SCALE

BLACK GRASS SOUNDS PRETTY GROSS, HUH? BUT THAT'S JUST THE IMAGE THIS PERENNIAL NETTLE IS TRYING TO PROJECT. WITH TEXTURE AKIN TO LEEKS OR GREEN ONIONS BUT CRUNCHIER, THIS GRASS IS ACTUALLY PRETTY TASTY. WHEN IT SPREADS, IT LOOKS JUST LIKE A BLACK CARPET AND CAN SUSTAIN AN ENTIRE ECOSYSTEM.

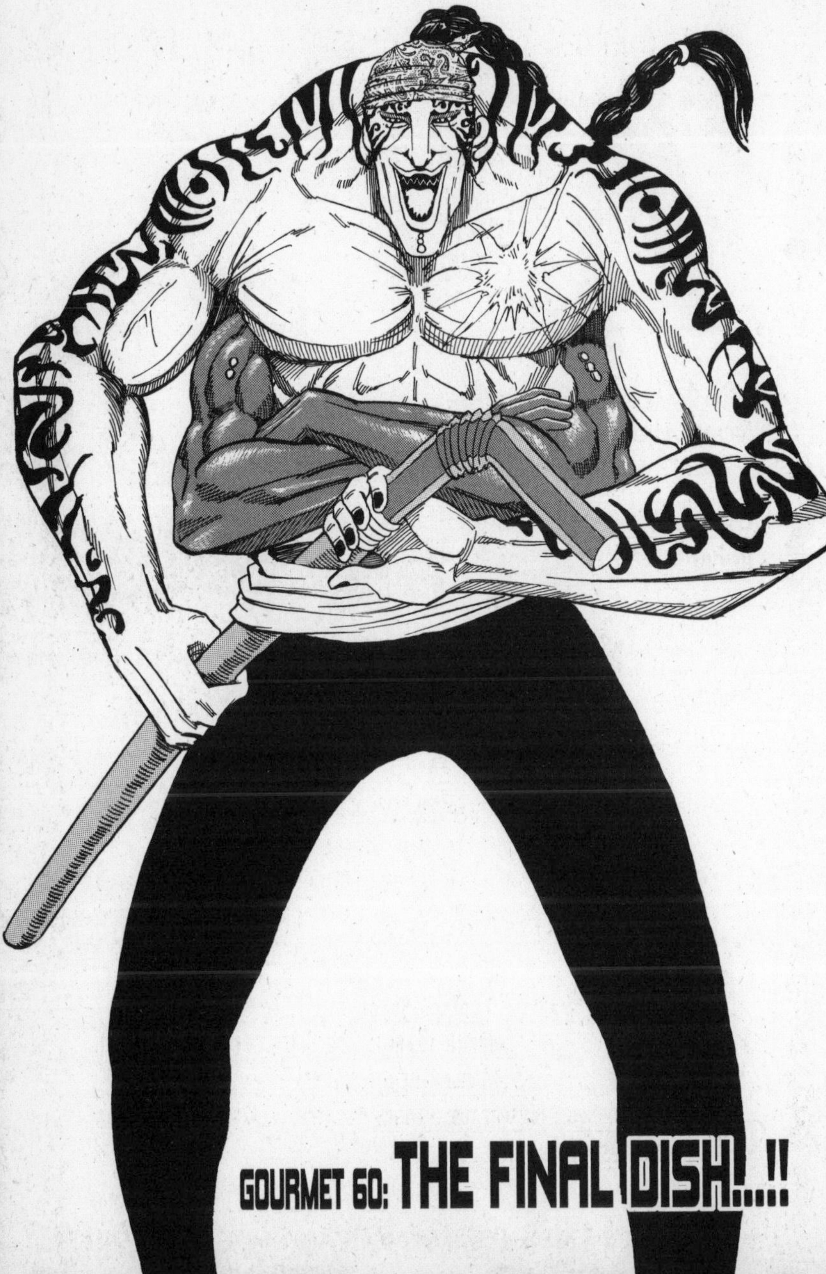

GOURMET 60: THE FINAL DISH...!!

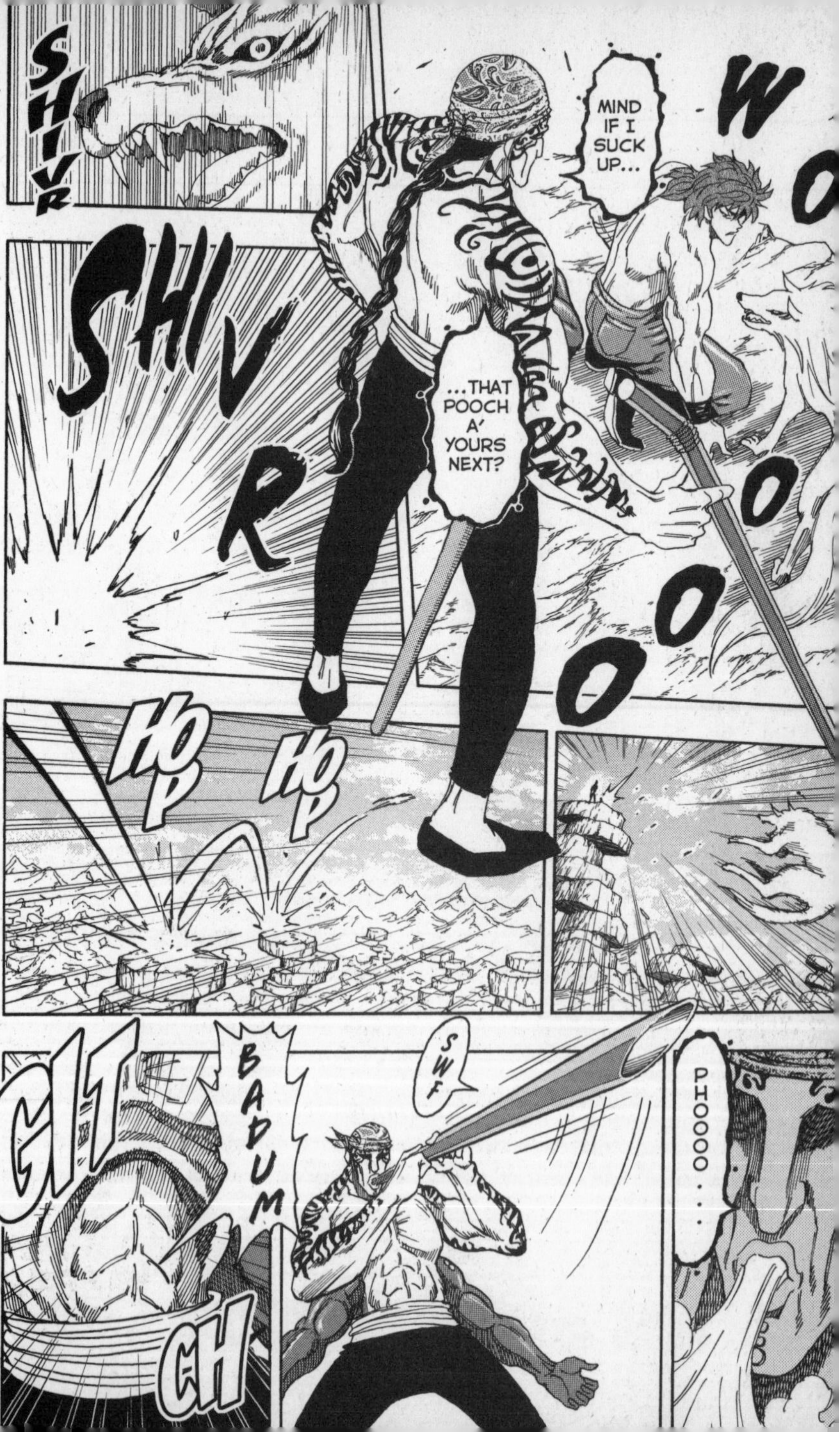
WOOOOOO
MIND IF I SUCK UP...
SHIVR
SHIVR
...THAT POOCH A' YOURS NEXT?
HOP HOP
PHOOOO...
SWF
BADUM
GITCH

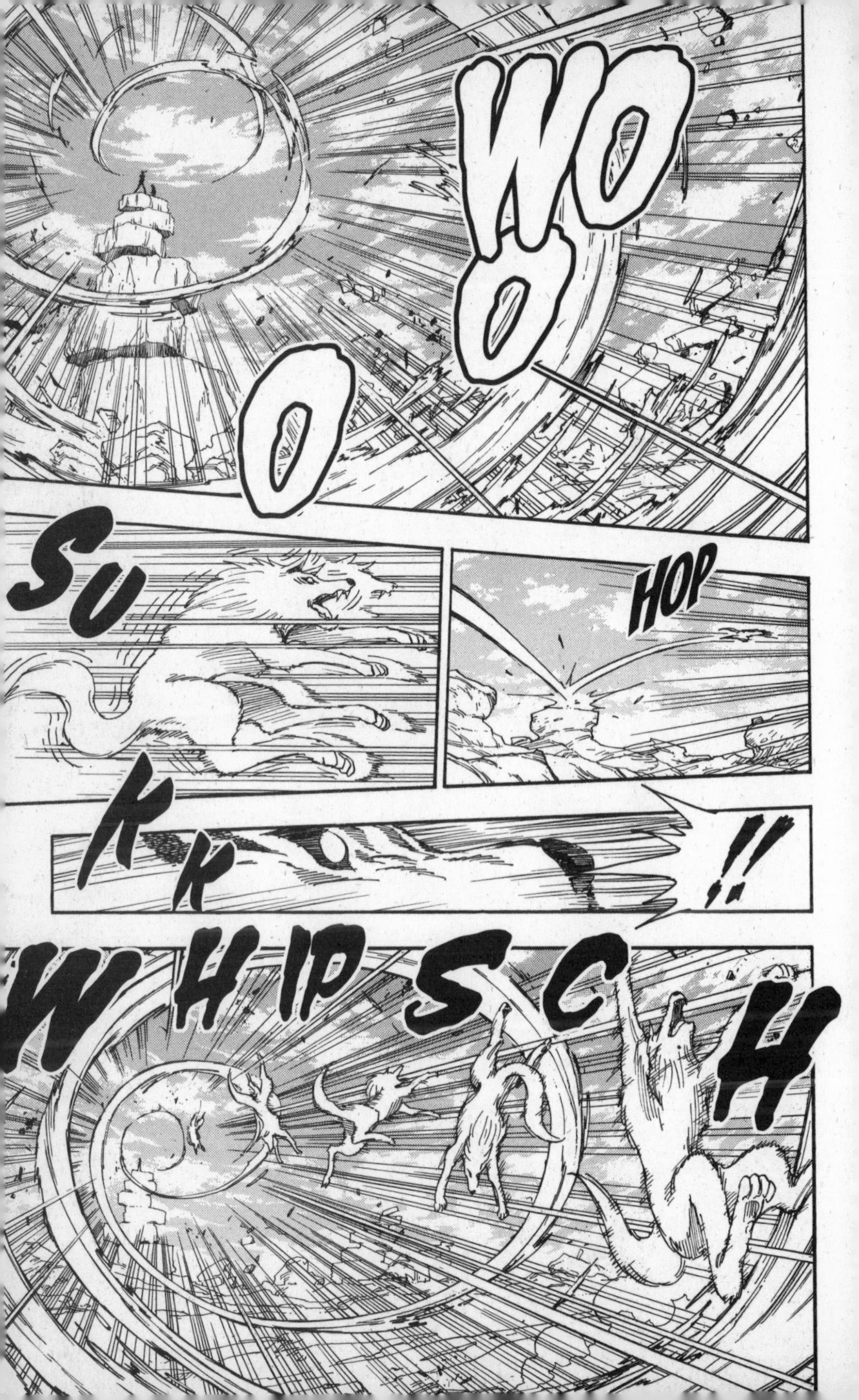
WOOO
HOP
SUKK
!!
WHIPSCH

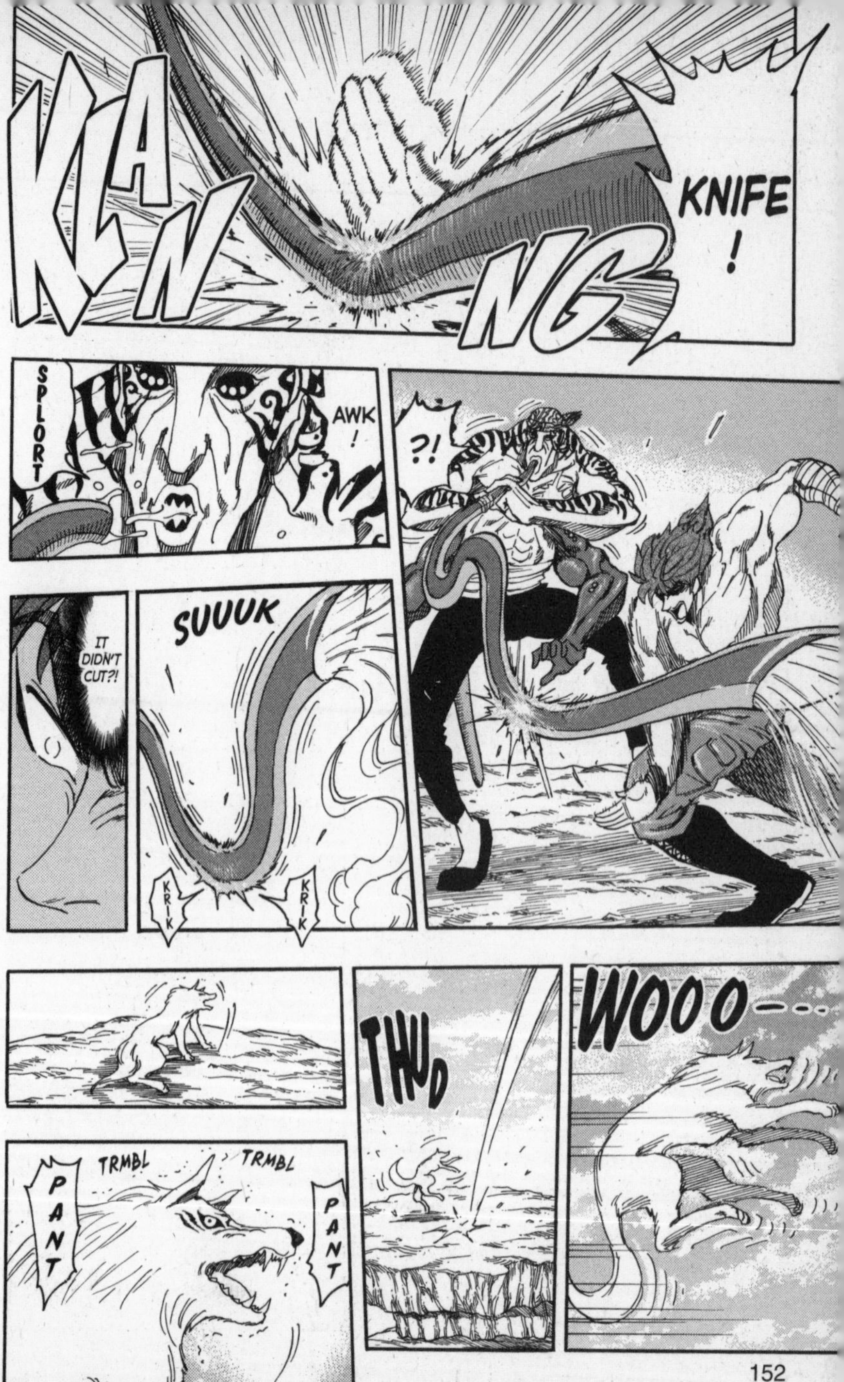
KNIFE!
KLANNG
?!
AWK!
SPLORT
SUUUK
KRIK
KRIK
IT DIDN'T CUT?!
WOOO---
THUD
PANT
TRMBL
TRMBL
PANT

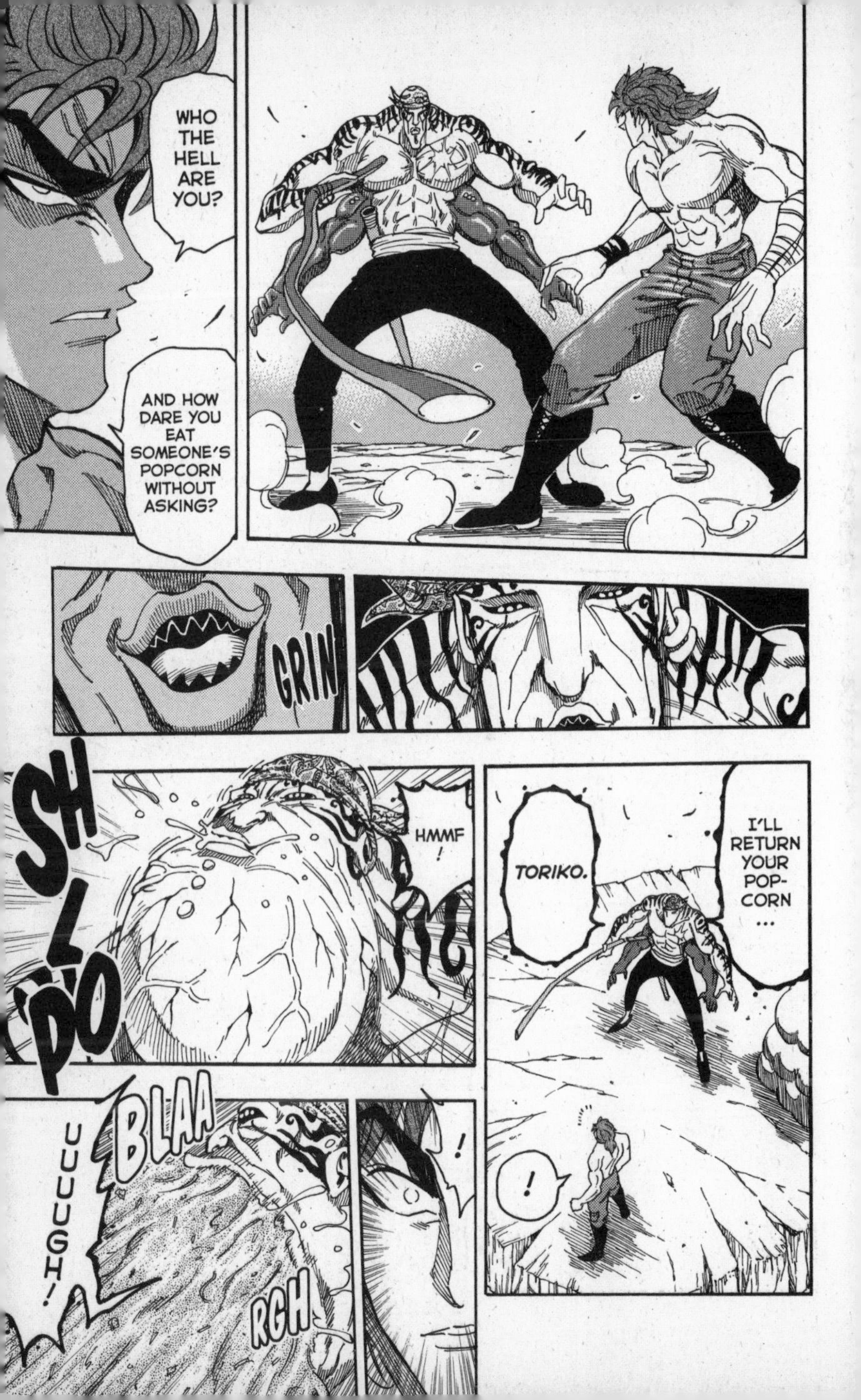
WHO THE HELL ARE YOU?
AND HOW DARE YOU EAT SOMEONE'S POPCORN WITHOUT ASKING?
GRIN
I'LL RETURN YOUR POP-CORN...
TORIKO.
!
SHLOP
HMMF!
!
RGH
BLAA
UUUUGH!

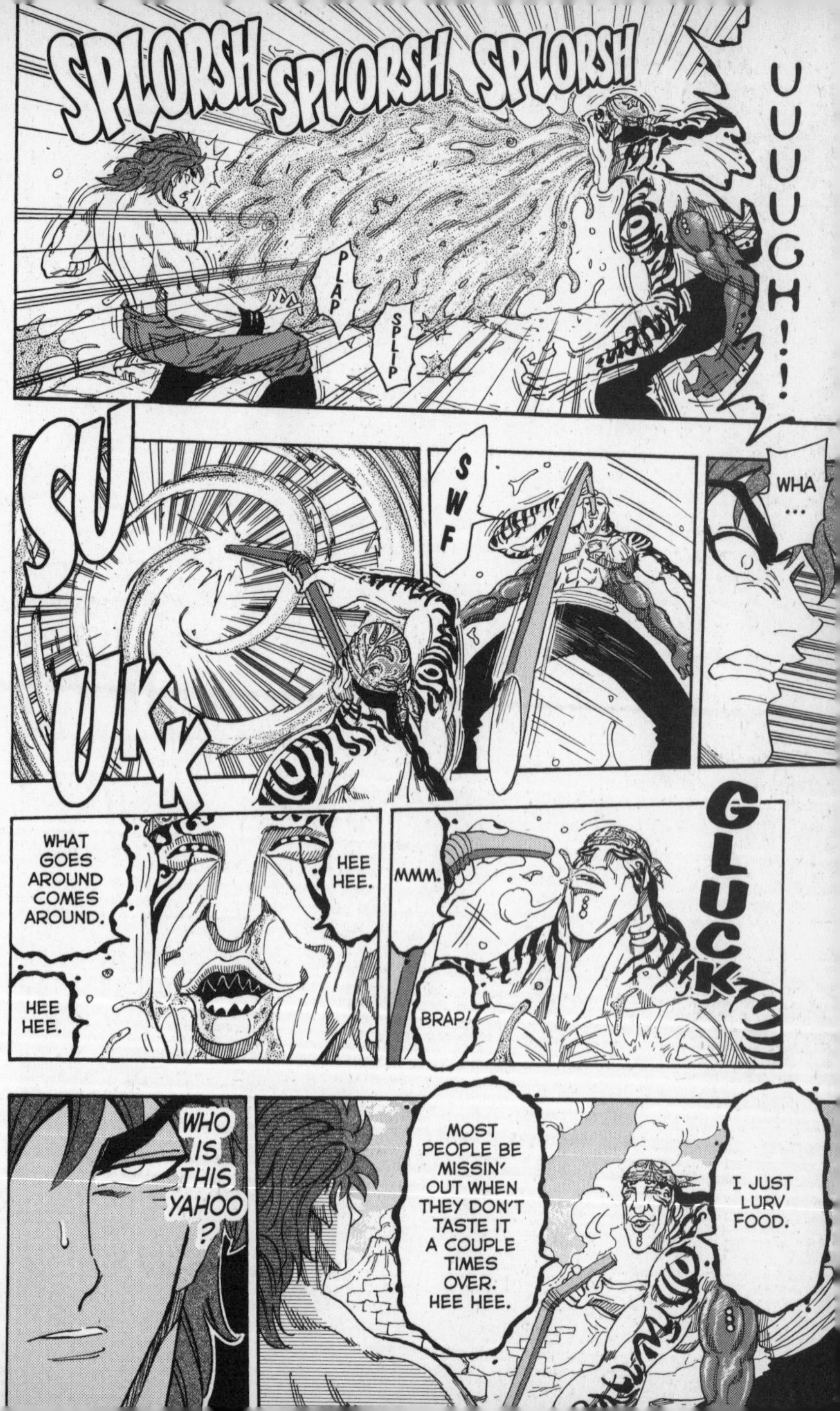
UUUUGH!!
SPLORSH SPLORSH SPLORSH
PLAP
SPLIP
WHA...
SWF
SUUKK
GLUCK
MMM.
BRAP!
HEE HEE.
WHAT GOES AROUND COMES AROUND.
HEE HEE.
I JUST LURV FOOD.
MOST PEOPLE BE MISSIN' OUT WHEN THEY DON'T TASTE IT A COUPLE TIMES OVER. HEE HEE.
WHO IS THIS YAHOO?

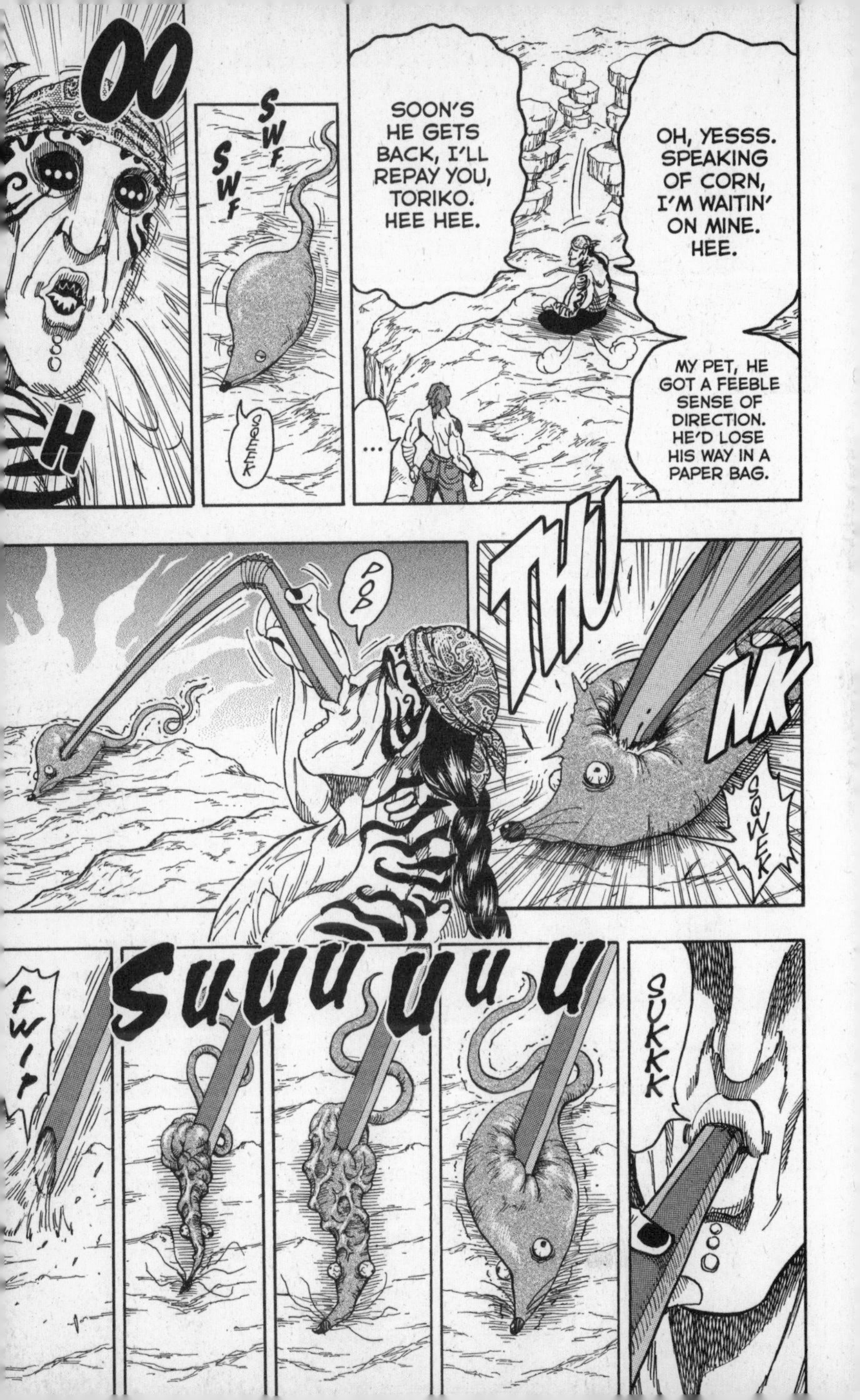
OH, YESSS. SPEAKING OF CORN, I'M WAITIN' ON MINE. HEE.
SOON'S HE GETS BACK, I'LL REPAY YOU, TORIKO. HEE HEE.
MY PET, HE GOT A FEEBLE SENSE OF DIRECTION. HE'D LOSE HIS WAY IN A PAPER BAG.
...
SWF
SWF
SQEEK
OO
H
THU
NK
SQWEK
POP
SUKKK
SUUUUUU
FWIP

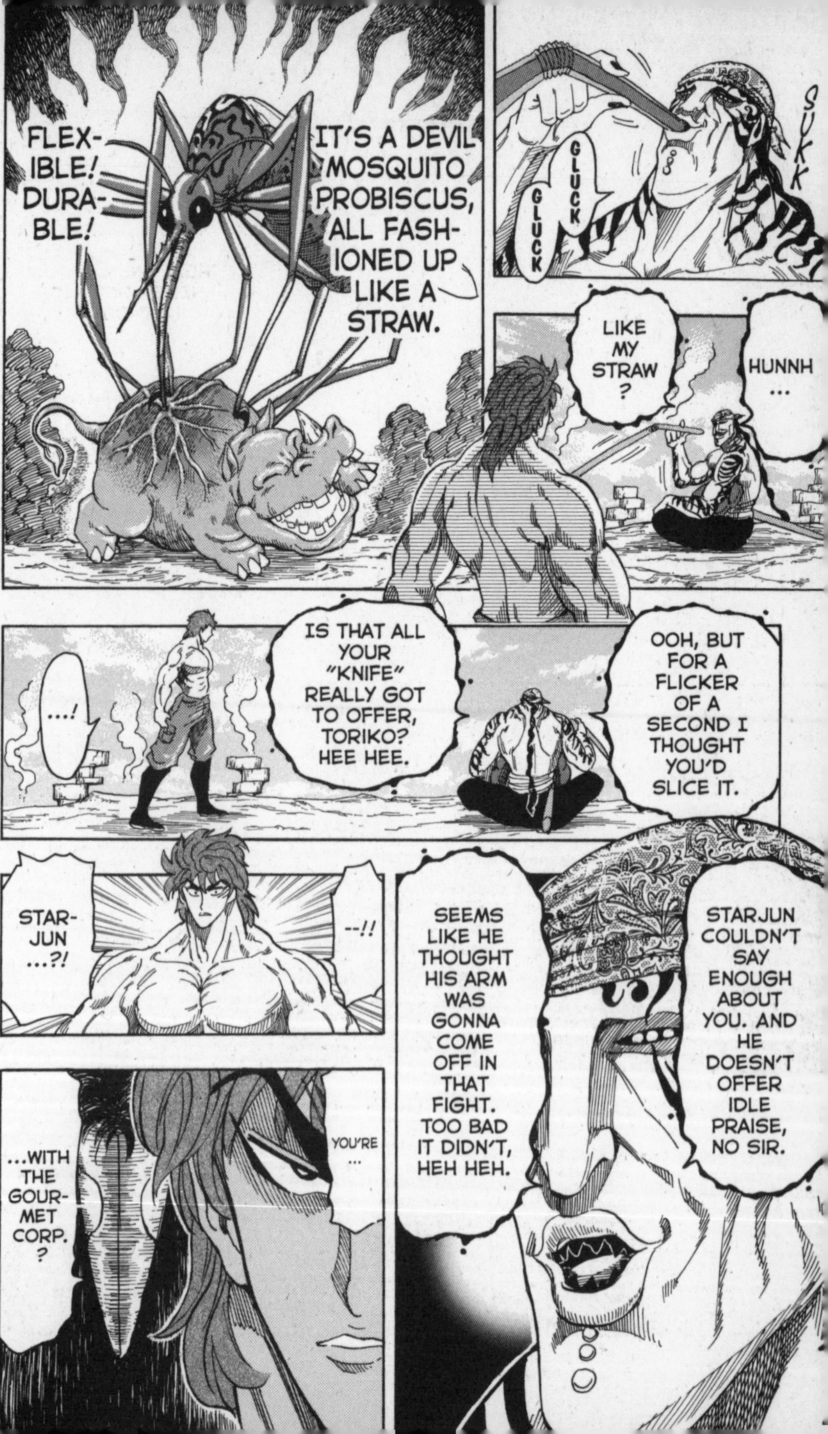
SUKK
GLUCK
GLUCK
HUNNH...
LIKE MY STRAW?
IT'S A DEVIL MOSQUITO PROBISCUS, ALL FASHIONED UP LIKE A STRAW.
FLEX-IBLE! DURA-BLE!
OOH, BUT FOR A FLICKER OF A SECOND I THOUGHT YOU'D SLICE IT.
IS THAT ALL YOUR "KNIFE" REALLY GOT TO OFFER, TORIKO? HEE HEE.
...!
STARJUN COULDN'T SAY ENOUGH ABOUT YOU. AND HE DOESN'T OFFER IDLE PRAISE, NO SIR.
SEEMS LIKE HE THOUGHT HIS ARM WAS GONNA COME OFF IN THAT FIGHT. TOO BAD IT DIDN'T, HEH HEH.
--!!
STAR-JUN...?!
YOU'RE...
...WITH THE GOUR-MET CORP.?

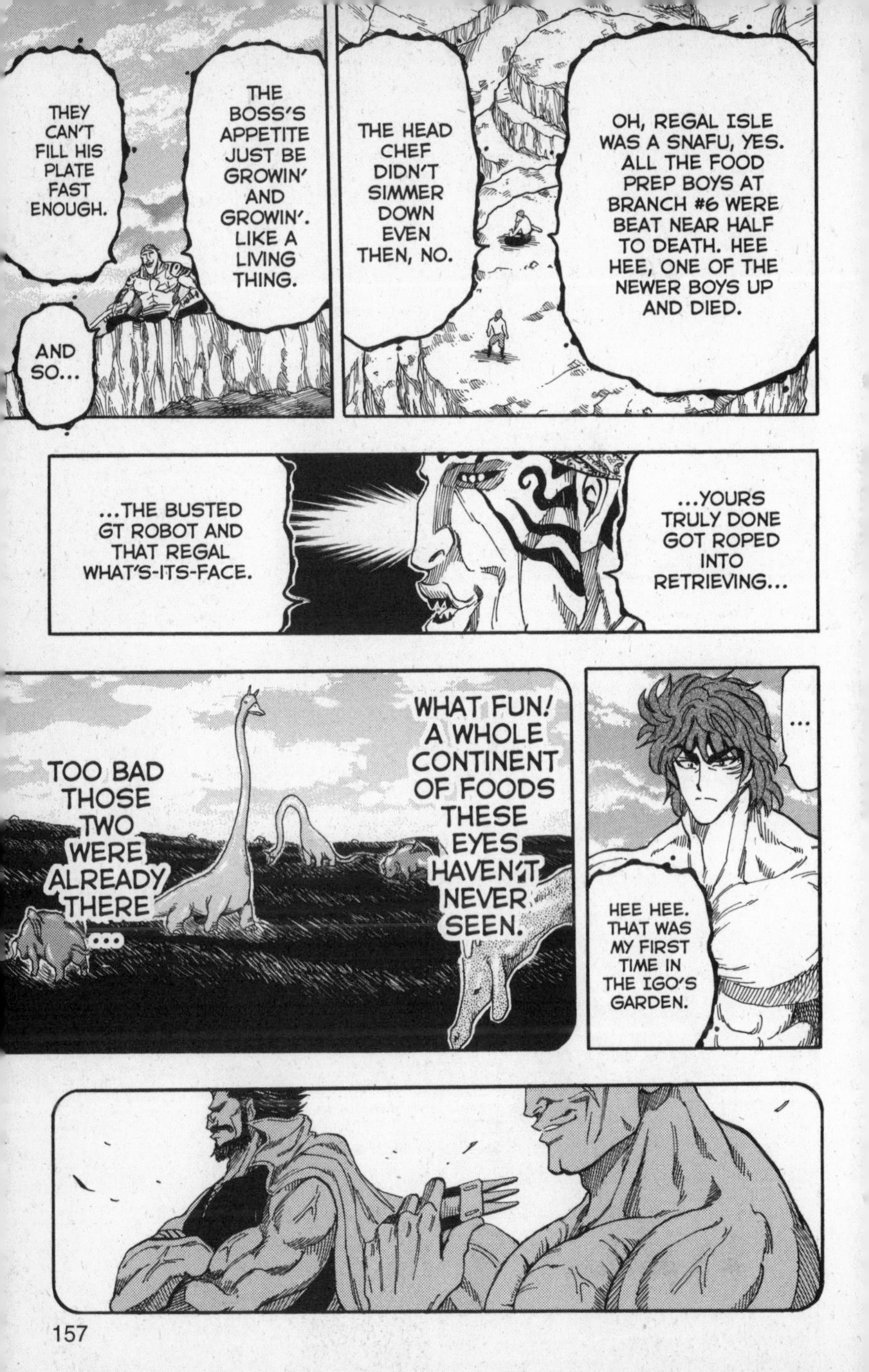
OH, REGAL ISLE WAS A SNAFU, YES. ALL THE FOOD PREP BOYS AT BRANCH #6 WERE BEAT NEAR HALF TO DEATH. HEE HEE, ONE OF THE NEWER BOYS UP AND DIED.
THE HEAD CHEF DIDN'T SIMMER DOWN EVEN THEN, NO.
THE BOSS'S APPETITE JUST BE GROWIN' AND GROWIN'. LIKE A LIVING THING.
THEY CAN'T FILL HIS PLATE FAST ENOUGH.
AND SO...
...YOURS TRULY DONE GOT ROPED INTO RETRIEVING...
...THE BUSTED GT ROBOT AND THAT REGAL WHAT'S-ITS-FACE.
...
HEE HEE. THAT WAS MY FIRST TIME IN THE IGO'S GARDEN.
WHAT FUN! A WHOLE CONTINENT OF FOODS THESE EYES HAVEN'T NEVER SEEN.
TOO BAD THOSE TWO WERE ALREADY THERE...

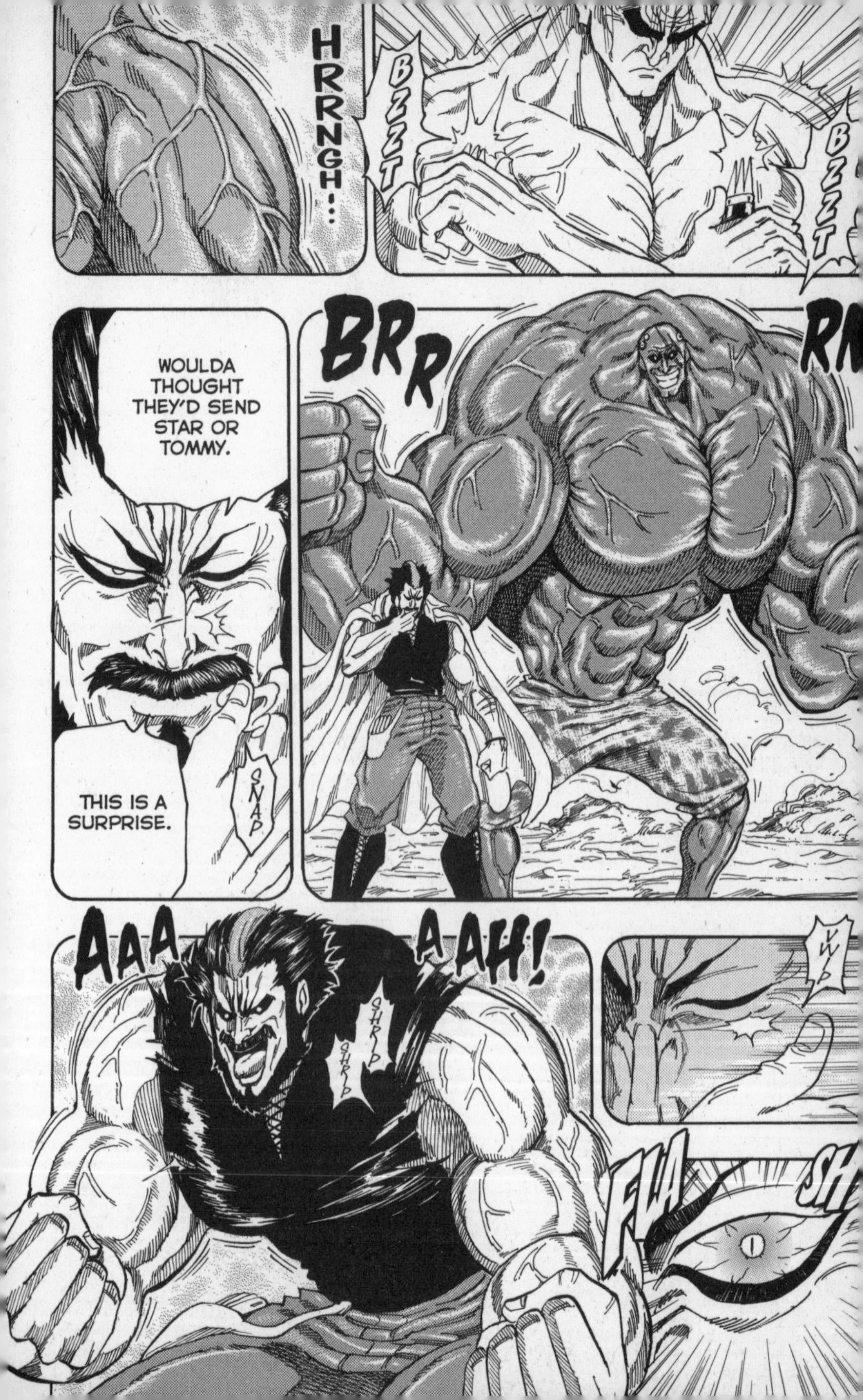
BZZT
BZZT
HRRNGH...
BRR
RN
WOULDA THOUGHT THEY'D SEND STAR OR TOMMY.
SNAP
THIS IS A SURPRISE.
VWIP
FLA
SH
AAA
AAH!
SHRIP
SHRIP

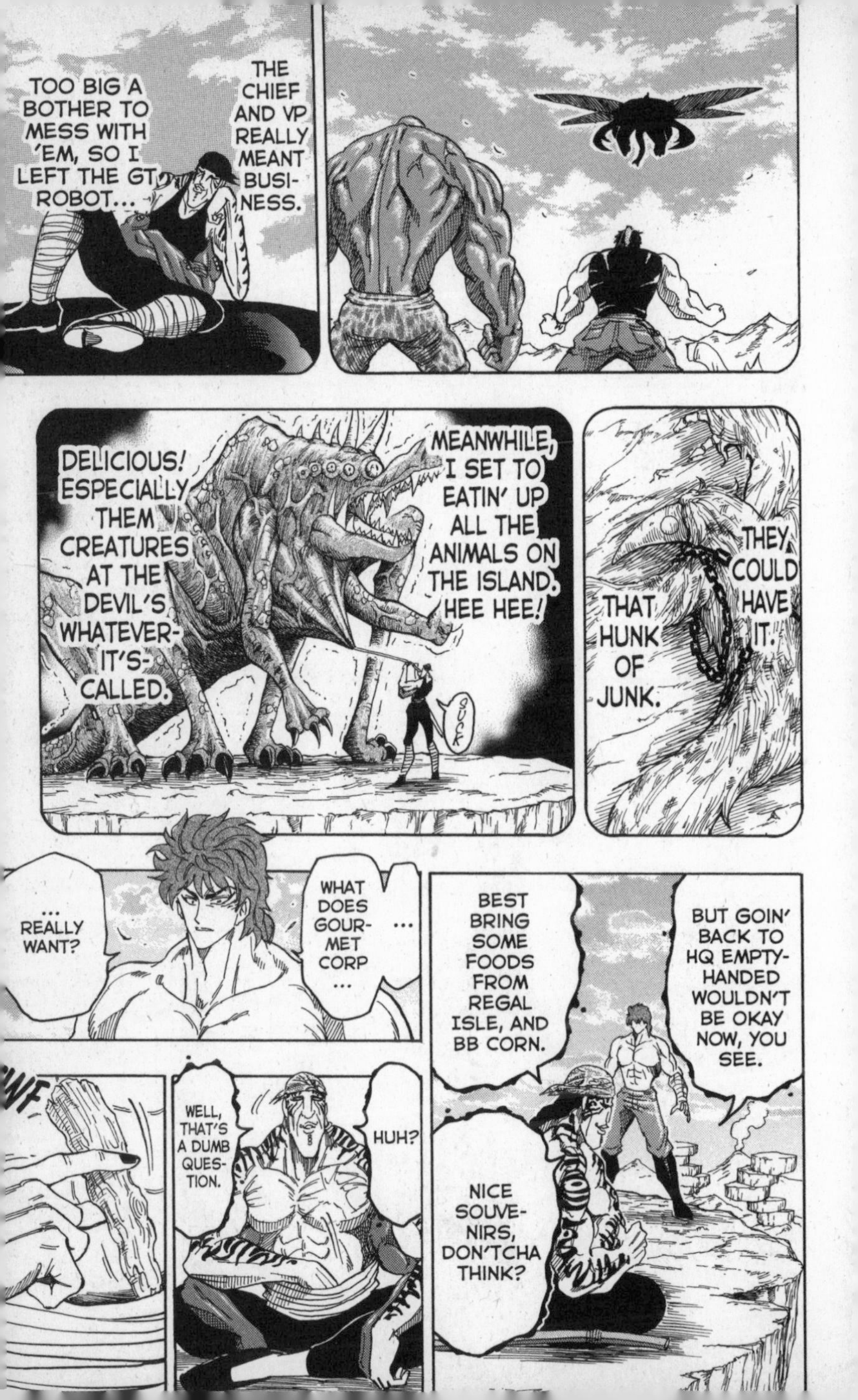
THE CHIEF AND VP REALLY MEANT BUSINESS.
TOO BIG A BOTHER TO MESS WITH 'EM, SO I LEFT THE GT ROBOT...
THEY COULD HAVE IT.
THAT HUNK OF JUNK.
MEANWHILE, I SET TO EATIN' UP ALL THE ANIMALS ON THE ISLAND. HEE HEE!
DELICIOUS! ESPECIALLY THEM CREATURES AT THE DEVIL'S WHATEVER-IT'S-CALLED.
SUCK
BUT GOIN' BACK TO HQ EMPTY-HANDED WOULDN'T BE OKAY NOW, YOU SEE.
BEST BRING SOME FOODS FROM REGAL ISLE, AND BB CORN.
NICE SOUVENIRS, DON'TCHA THINK?
...
WHAT DOES GOURMET CORP ...
... REALLY WANT?
HUH?
WELL, THAT'S A DUMB QUESTION.

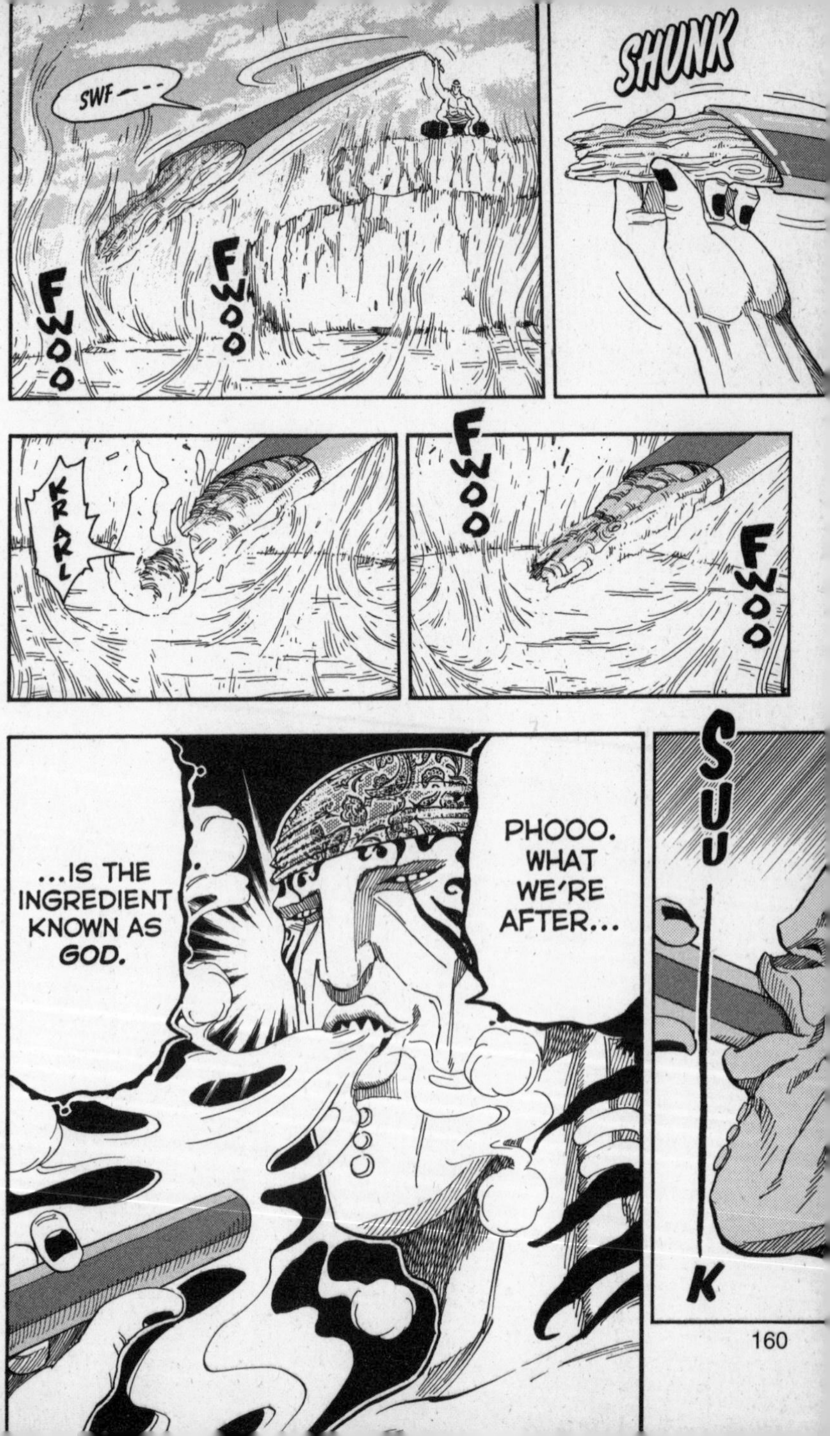
SHUNK
SWF---
FWOO
FWOO
FWOO
FWOO
FWOO
KRARL
SUUUK
PHOOO. WHAT WE'RE AFTER...
...IS THE INGREDIENT KNOWN AS *GOD.*

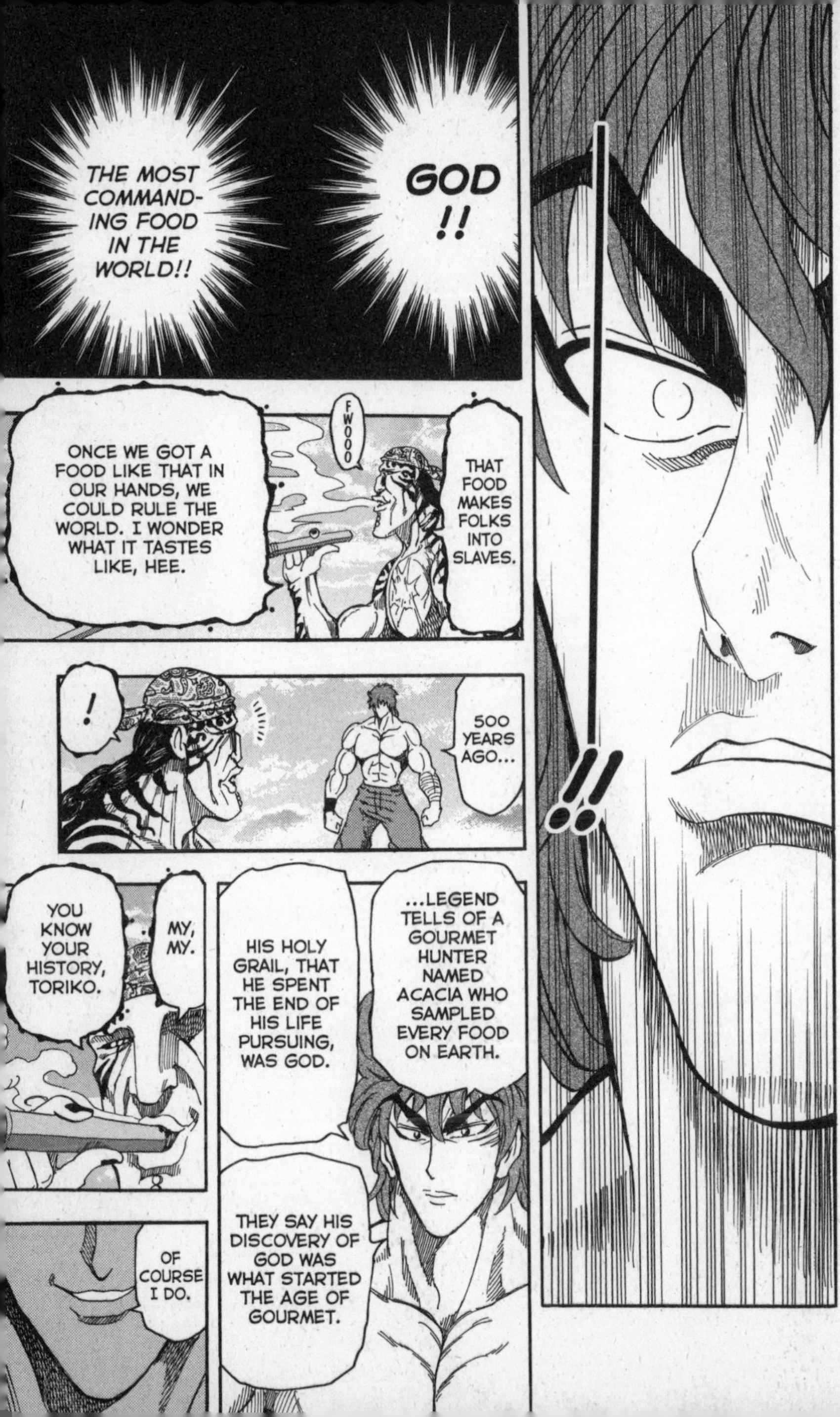
!!
GOD !!
THE MOST COMMANDING FOOD IN THE WORLD!!
THAT FOOD MAKES FOLKS INTO SLAVES.
FWOOO
ONCE WE GOT A FOOD LIKE THAT IN OUR HANDS, WE COULD RULE THE WORLD. I WONDER WHAT IT TASTES LIKE, HEE.
500 YEARS AGO...
!
...LEGEND TELLS OF A GOURMET HUNTER NAMED ACACIA WHO SAMPLED EVERY FOOD ON EARTH.
HIS HOLY GRAIL, THAT HE SPENT THE END OF HIS LIFE PURSUING, WAS GOD.
THEY SAY HIS DISCOVERY OF GOD WAS WHAT STARTED THE AGE OF GOURMET.
MY, MY.
YOU KNOW YOUR HISTORY, TORIKO.
OF COURSE I DO.

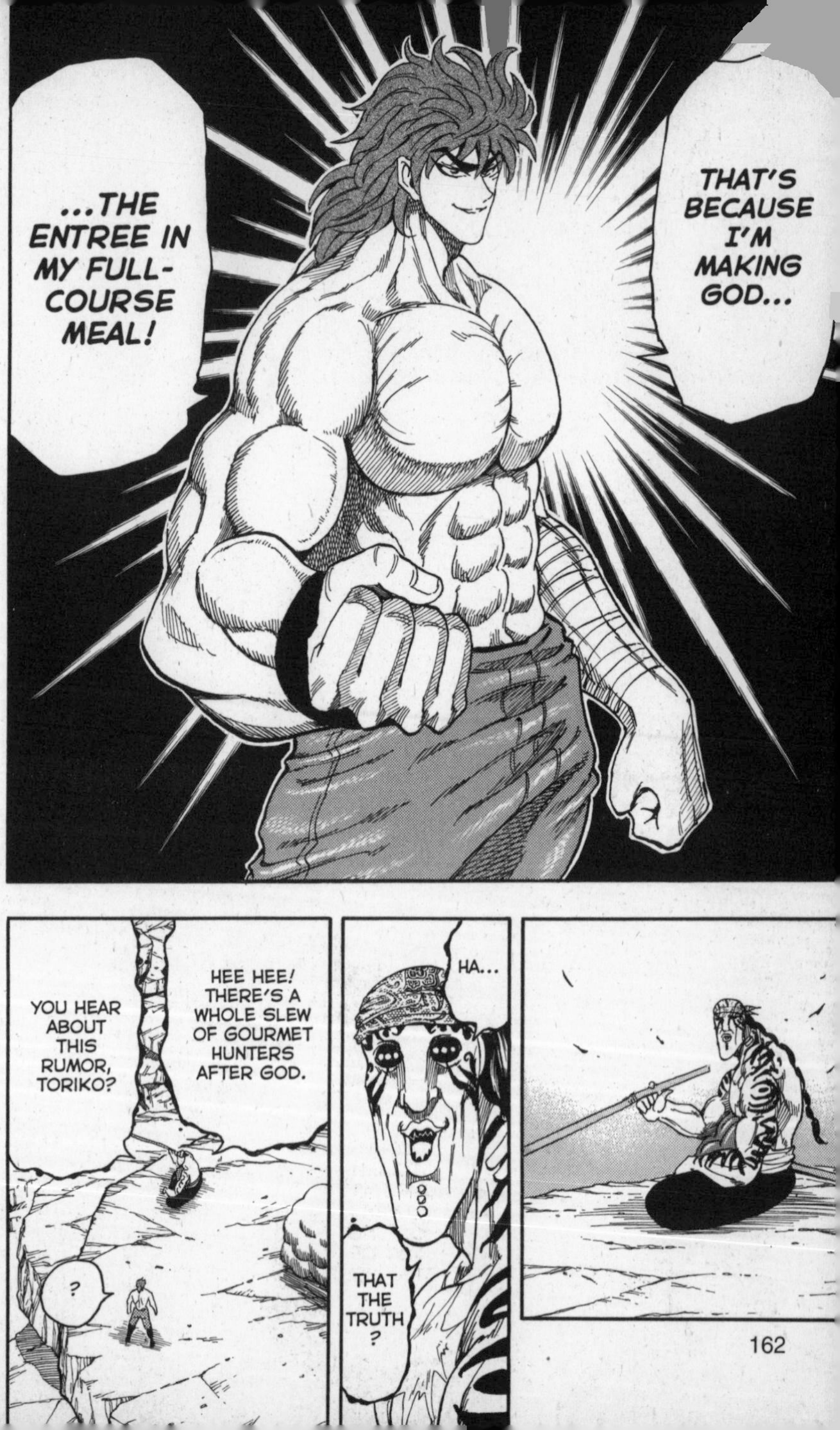
THAT'S BECAUSE I'M MAKING GOD...
...THE ENTREE IN MY FULL-COURSE MEAL!
HA...
THAT THE TRUTH?
HEE HEE! THERE'S A WHOLE SLEW OF GOURMET HUNTERS AFTER GOD.
YOU HEAR ABOUT THIS RUMOR, TORIKO?
?

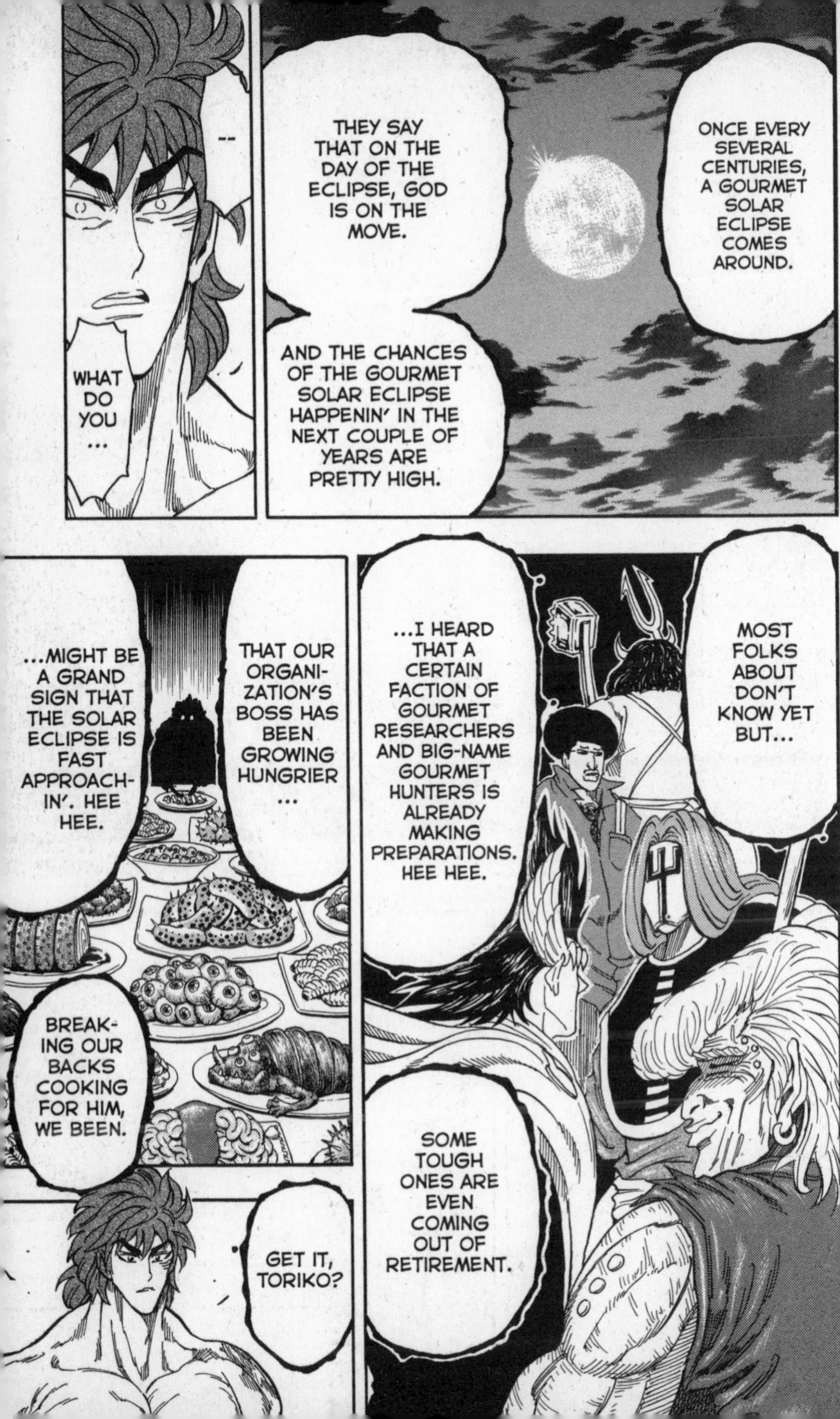
ONCE EVERY SEVERAL CENTURIES, A GOURMET SOLAR ECLIPSE COMES AROUND.
THEY SAY THAT ON THE DAY OF THE ECLIPSE, GOD IS ON THE MOVE.
AND THE CHANCES OF THE GOURMET SOLAR ECLIPSE HAPPENIN' IN THE NEXT COUPLE OF YEARS ARE PRETTY HIGH.
--
WHAT DO YOU ...
MOST FOLKS ABOUT DON'T KNOW YET BUT...
...I HEARD THAT A CERTAIN FACTION OF GOURMET RESEARCHERS AND BIG-NAME GOURMET HUNTERS IS ALREADY MAKING PREPARATIONS. HEE HEE.
SOME TOUGH ONES ARE EVEN COMING OUT OF RETIREMENT.
THAT OUR ORGANIZATION'S BOSS HAS BEEN GROWING HUNGRIER ...
...MIGHT BE A GRAND SIGN THAT THE SOLAR ECLIPSE IS FAST APPROACHIN'. HEE HEE.
BREAKING OUR BACKS COOKING FOR HIM, WE BEEN.
GET IT, TORIKO?

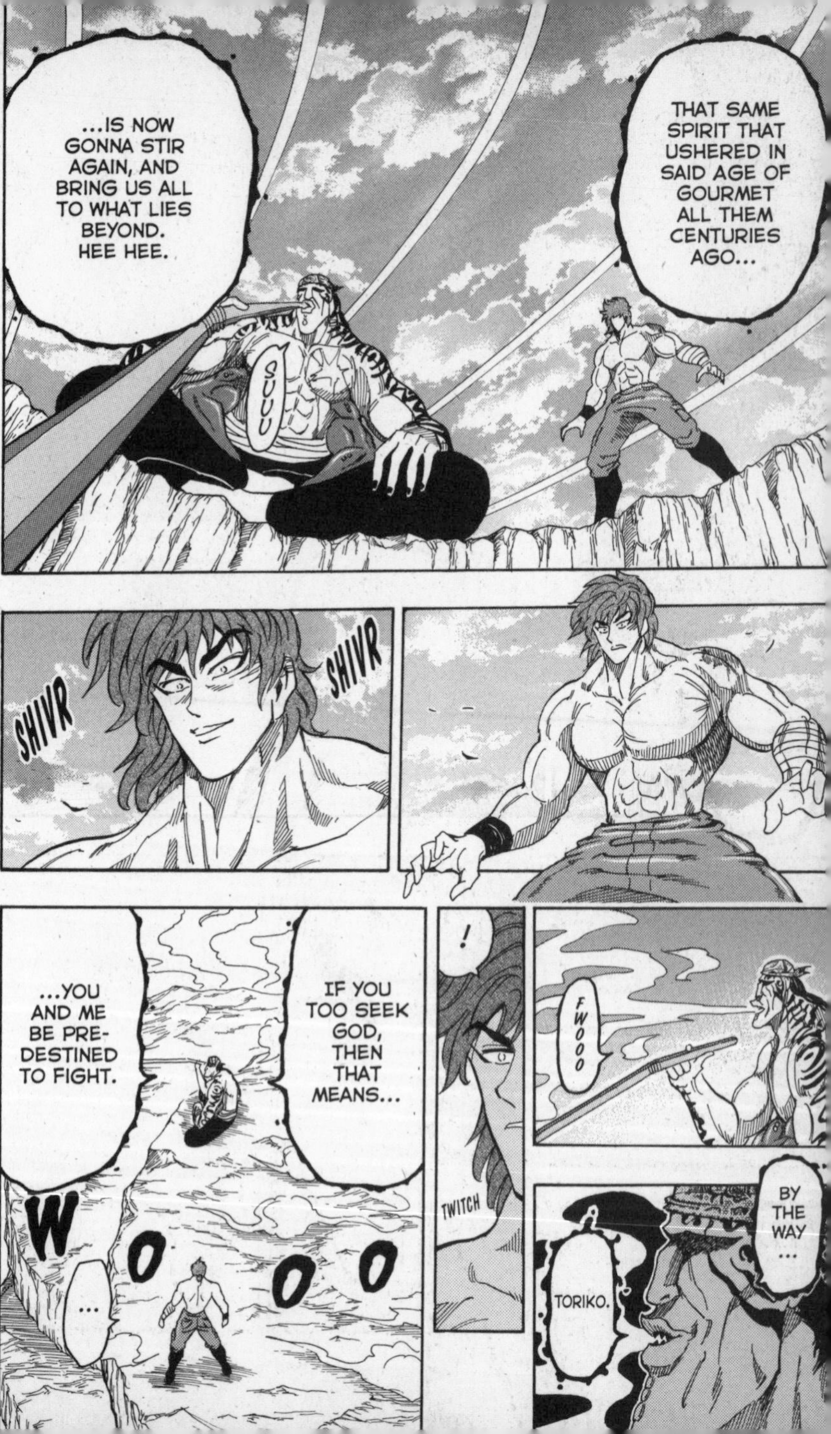
THAT SAME SPIRIT THAT USHERED IN SAID AGE OF GOURMET ALL THEM CENTURIES AGO...
...IS NOW GONNA STIR AGAIN, AND BRING US ALL TO WHAT LIES BEYOND. HEE HEE.
SUUU
SHIVR
SHIVR
FWOOO
BY THE WAY...
TORIKO.
!
TWITCH
IF YOU TOO SEEK GOD, THEN THAT MEANS...
...YOU AND ME BE PRE-DESTINED TO FIGHT.
WOOO
...

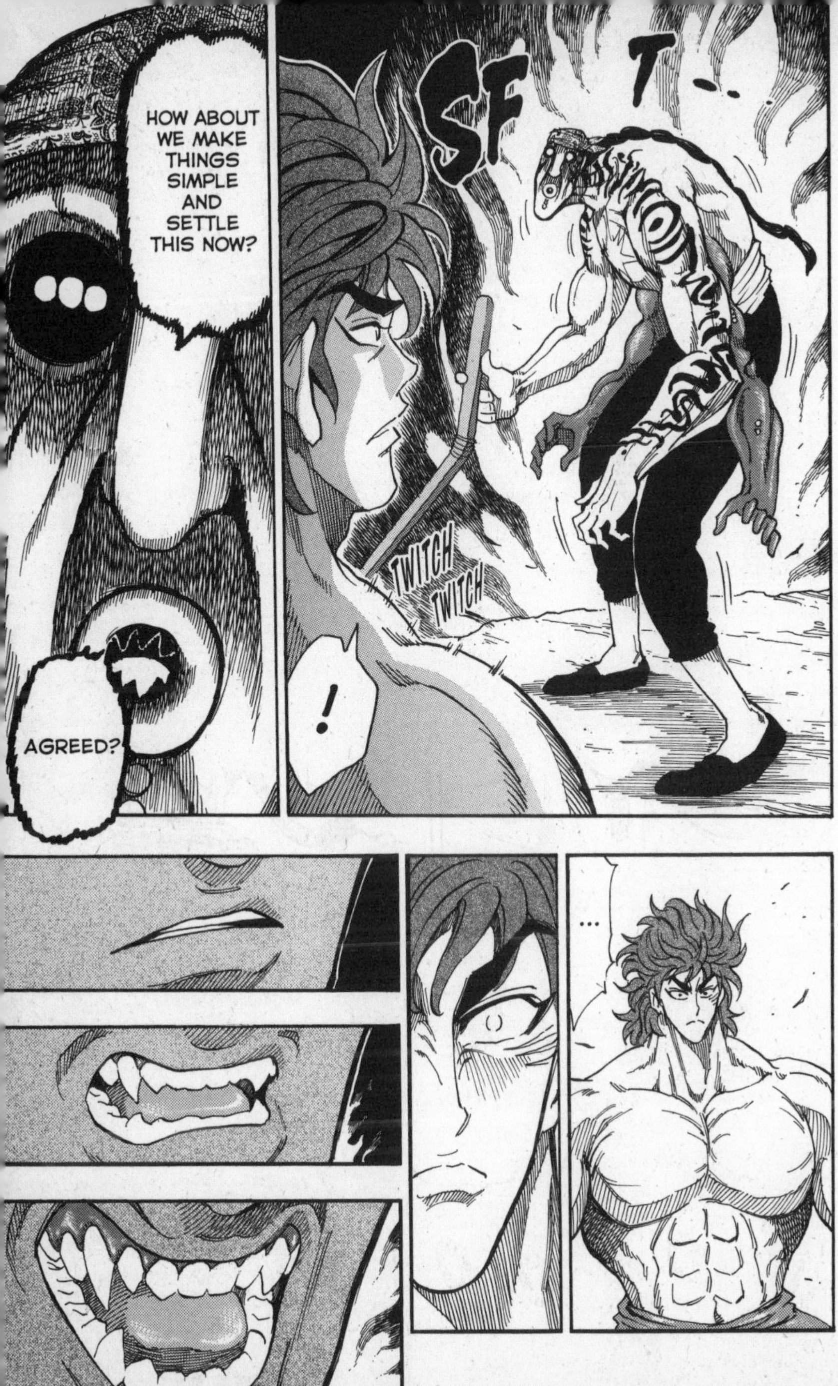
SF
T...
TWITCH
TWITCH
!
HOW ABOUT WE MAKE THINGS SIMPLE AND SETTLE THIS NOW?
AGREED?
...

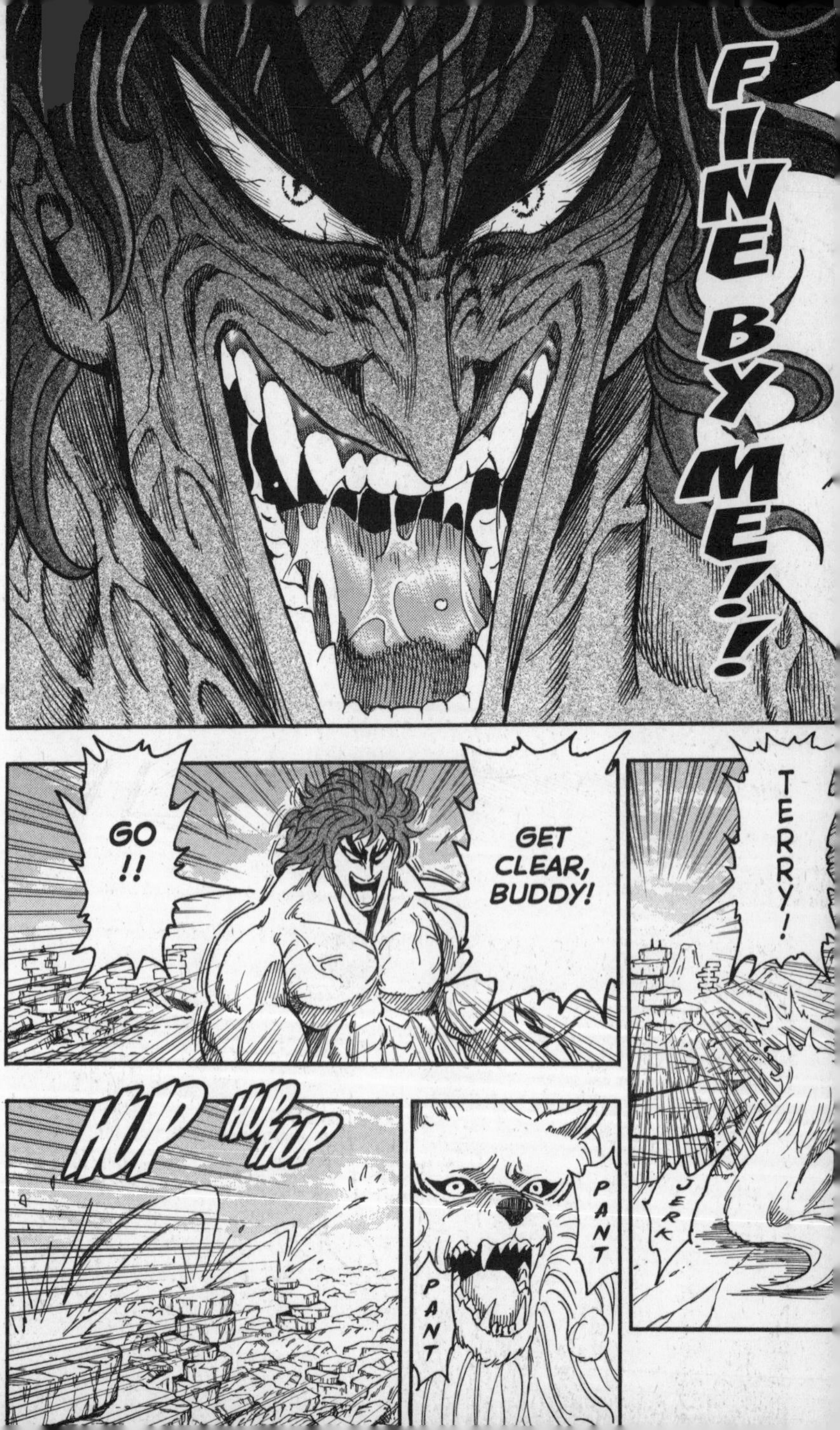
FINE BY ME!!
TERRY!
JERK
GET CLEAR, BUDDY!
GO!!
PANT
PANT
PANT
HUP
HUP HUP

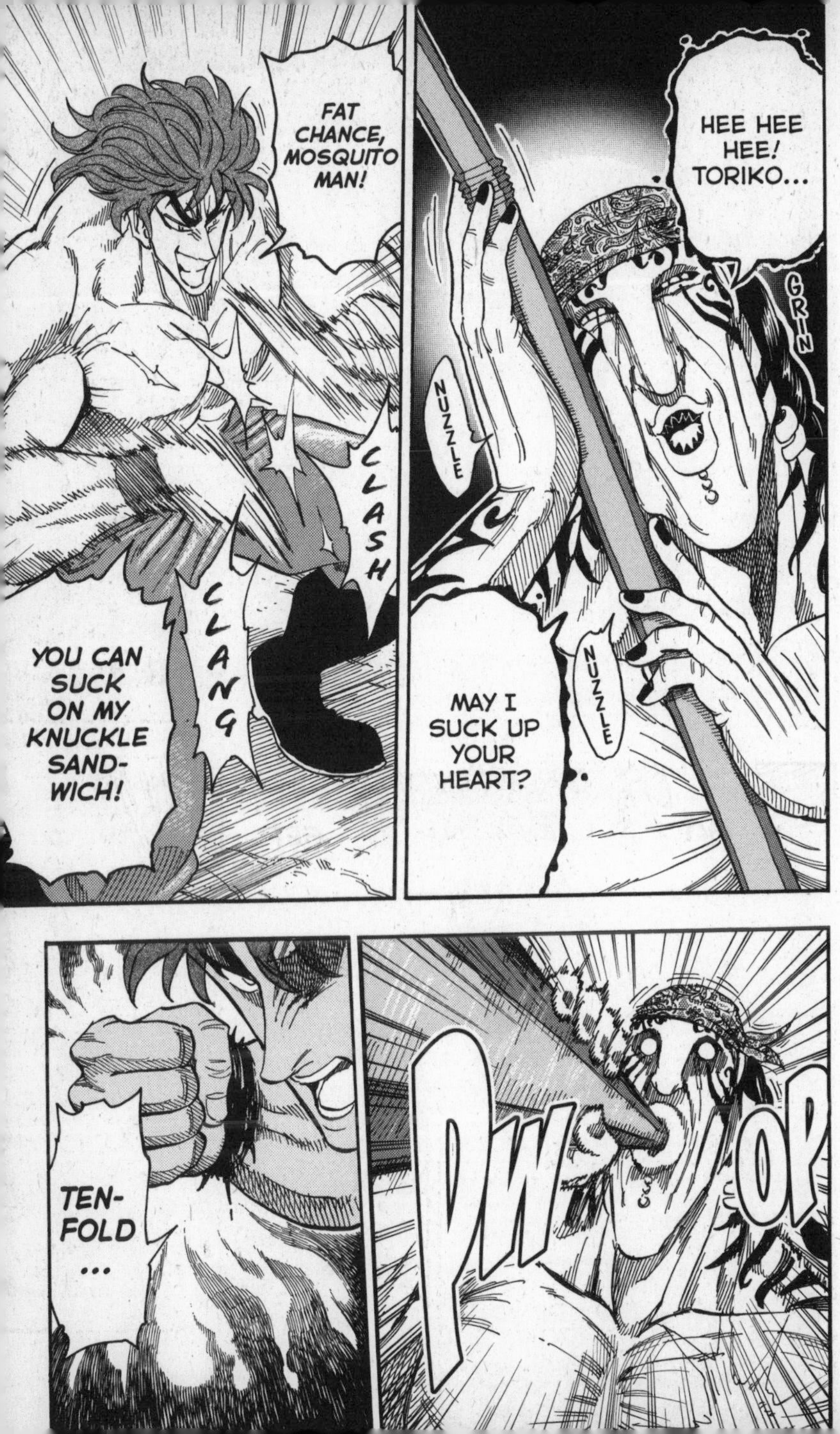
HEE HEE HEE! TORIKO...
GRIN
NUZZLE
NUZZLE
MAY I SUCK UP YOUR HEART?
FAT CHANCE, MOSQUITO MAN!
CLASH
CLANG
YOU CAN SUCK ON MY KNUCKLE SANDWICH!
TEN-FOLD ...

TORIKO

GOURMET CHECKLIST

Vol. 045

COCOA MAYONNAISE
(NATURALLY GROWING FOOD)

CAPTURE LEVEL: LESS THAN 1

HABITAT: WARM, RICH SOILS

LENGTH: --

HEIGHT: 5 METERS (TREE)

WEIGHT: --

PRICE: 1 POD OF 500 G / 2,500 YEN

(IN STORES)

SCALE

THE COCOA MAYO IS A VARIETY OF DECIDUOUS TREE IN THE
LACQUER FAMILY. ITS MATURED FRUITS ARE RICH IN FAT AND
FILLED WITH BITTER COCOA AND ACIDIC MAYONNAISE FLAVORS.
IT'S A POPULAR DRESSING FOR CRISP LETTUCE GREENS, AND
SOME PEOPLE PUT IT ON EVERYTHING!

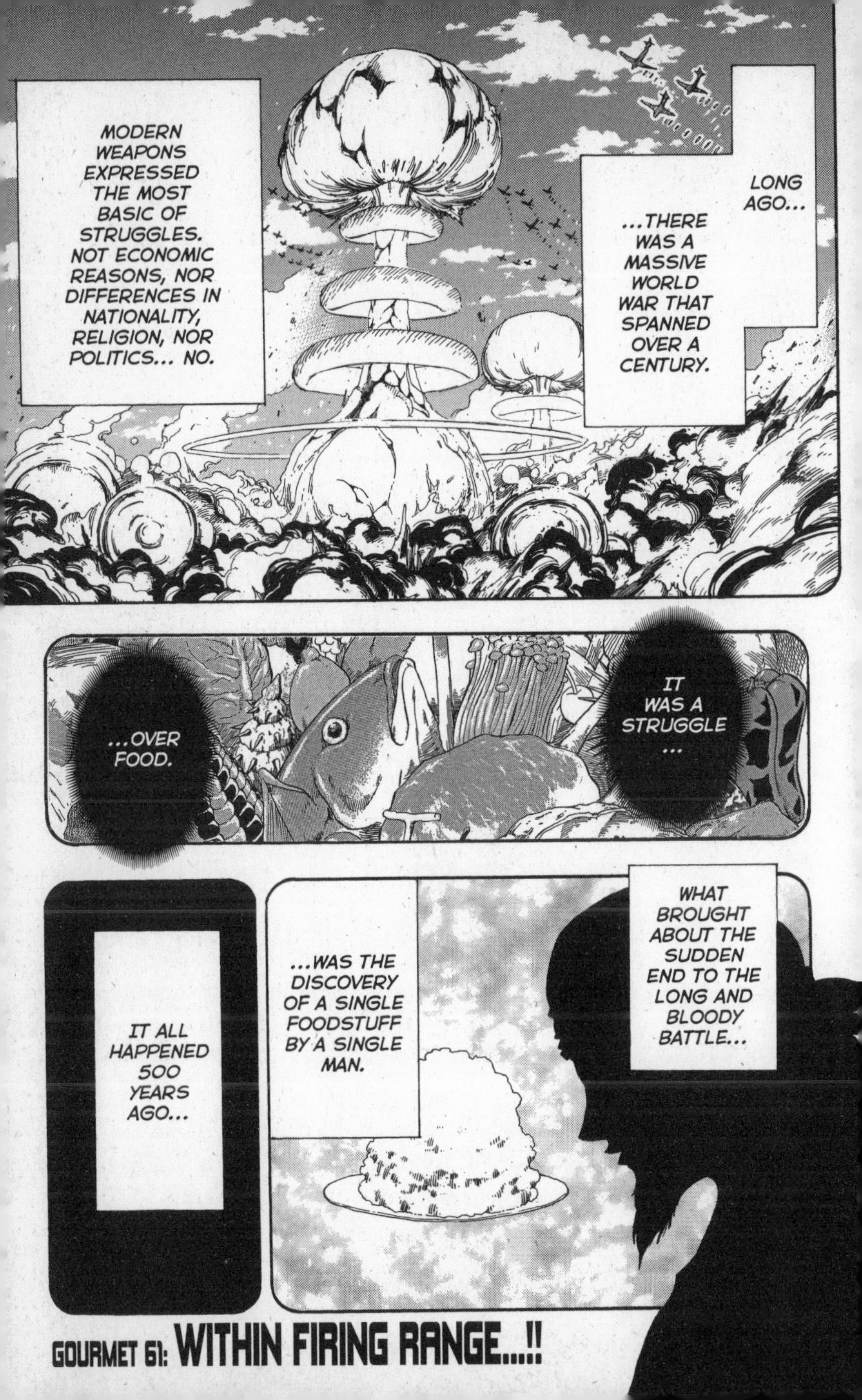
LONG AGO...
...THERE WAS A MASSIVE WORLD WAR THAT SPANNED OVER A CENTURY.
MODERN WEAPONS EXPRESSED THE MOST BASIC OF STRUGGLES. NOT ECONOMIC REASONS, NOR DIFFERENCES IN NATIONALITY, RELIGION, NOR POLITICS... NO.
IT WAS A STRUGGLE...
...OVER FOOD.
WHAT BROUGHT ABOUT THE SUDDEN END TO THE LONG AND BLOODY BATTLE...
...WAS THE DISCOVERY OF A SINGLE FOODSTUFF BY A SINGLE MAN.
IT ALL HAPPENED 500 YEARS AGO...
GOURMET 61: WITHIN FIRING RANGE...!!

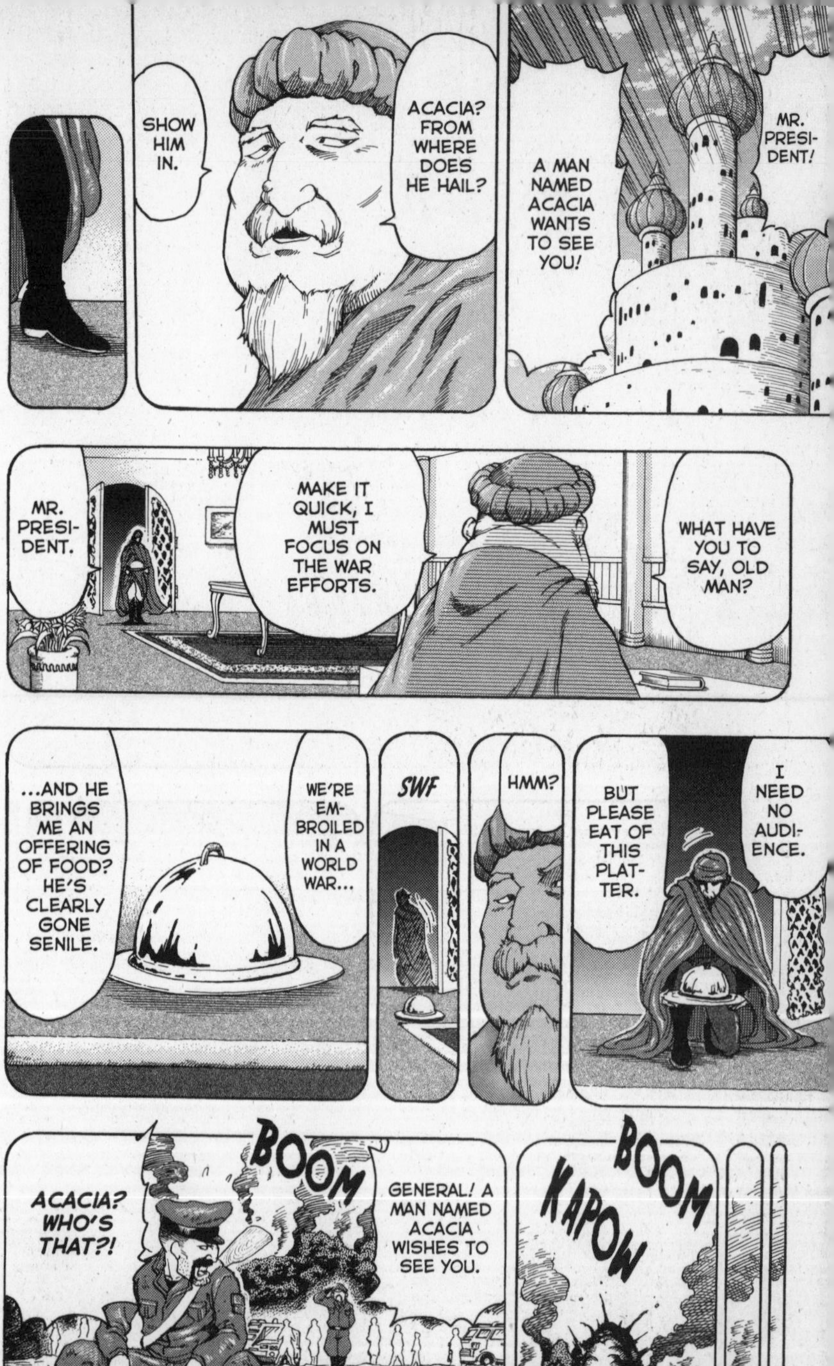
MR. PRESIDENT!
A MAN NAMED ACACIA WANTS TO SEE YOU!
ACACIA? FROM WHERE DOES HE HAIL?
SHOW HIM IN.
WHAT HAVE YOU TO SAY, OLD MAN?
MAKE IT QUICK, I MUST FOCUS ON THE WAR EFFORTS.
MR. PRESIDENT.
I NEED NO AUDIENCE.
BUT PLEASE EAT OF THIS PLATTER.
HMM?
SWF
WE'RE EMBROILED IN A WORLD WAR...
...AND HE BRINGS ME AN OFFERING OF FOOD? HE'S CLEARLY GONE SENILE.
BOOM
KAPOW
BOOM
GENERAL! A MAN NAMED ACACIA WISHES TO SEE YOU.
ACACIA? WHO'S THAT?!

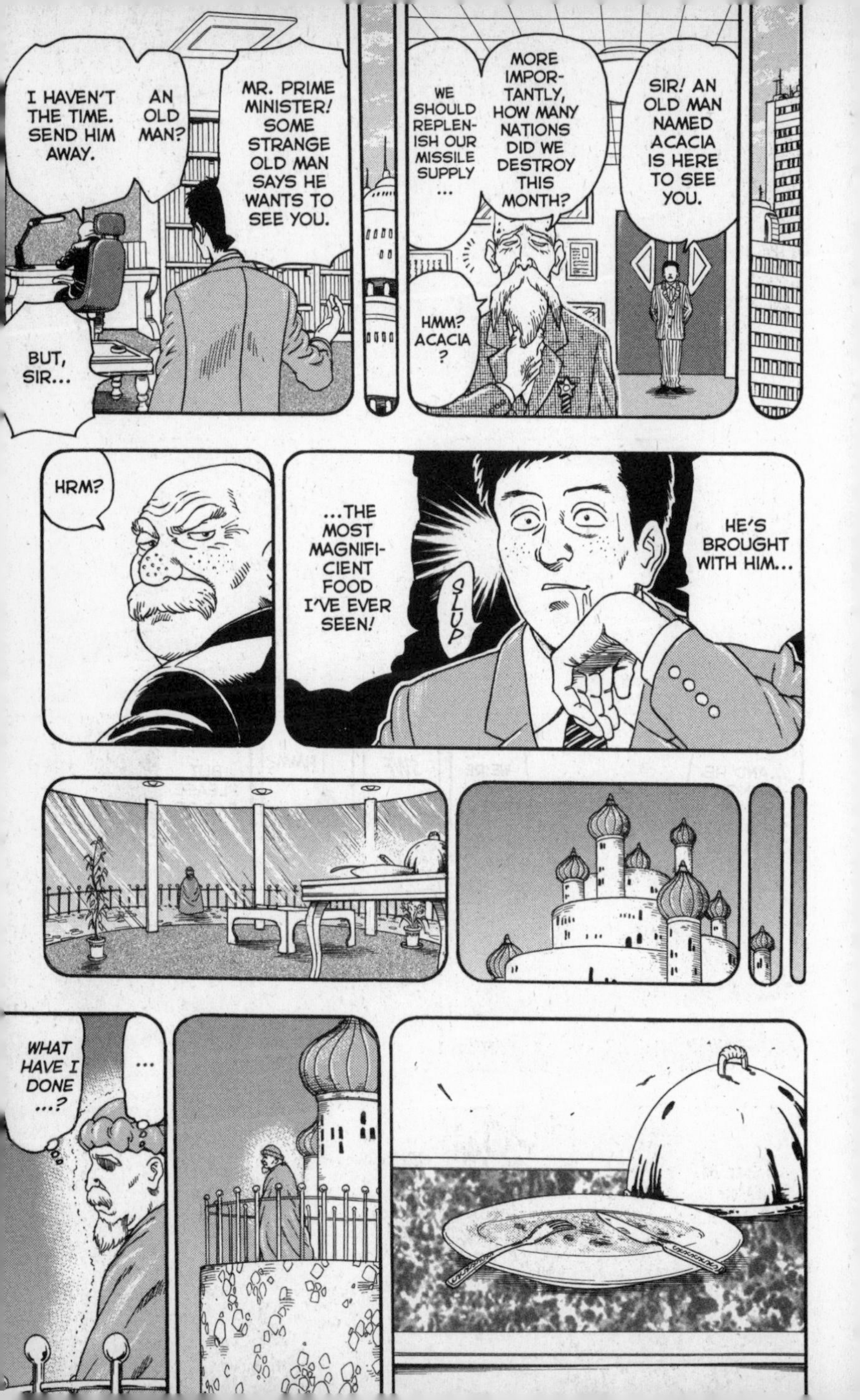
SIR! AN OLD MAN NAMED ACACIA IS HERE TO SEE YOU.
MORE IMPORTANTLY, HOW MANY NATIONS DID WE DESTROY THIS MONTH?
WE SHOULD REPLENISH OUR MISSILE SUPPLY ...
HMM? ACACIA ?
MR. PRIME MINISTER! SOME STRANGE OLD MAN SAYS HE WANTS TO SEE YOU.
AN OLD MAN?
I HAVEN'T THE TIME. SEND HIM AWAY.
BUT, SIR...
HE'S BROUGHT WITH HIM...
...THE MOST MAGNIFICIENT FOOD I'VE EVER SEEN!
SLUP
HRM?
...
WHAT HAVE I DONE ...?

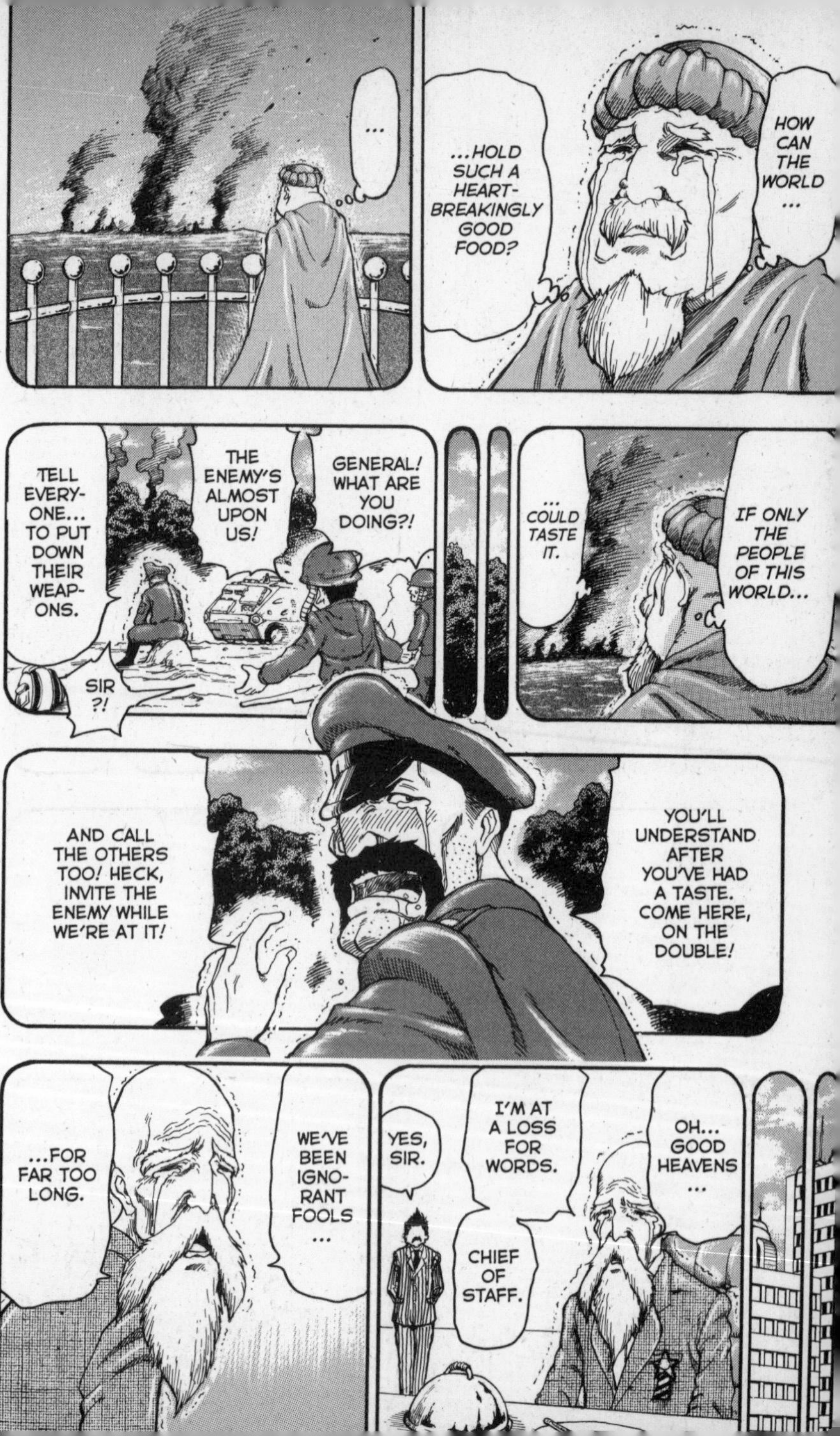
HOW CAN THE WORLD ...
...HOLD SUCH A HEART-BREAKINGLY GOOD FOOD?
...
IF ONLY THE PEOPLE OF THIS WORLD...
... COULD TASTE IT.
GENERAL! WHAT ARE YOU DOING?!
THE ENEMY'S ALMOST UPON US!
TELL EVERYONE... TO PUT DOWN THEIR WEAPONS.
SIR ?!
YOU'LL UNDERSTAND AFTER YOU'VE HAD A TASTE. COME HERE, ON THE DOUBLE!
AND CALL THE OTHERS TOO! HECK, INVITE THE ENEMY WHILE WE'RE AT IT!
OH... GOOD HEAVENS ...
I'M AT A LOSS FOR WORDS.
CHIEF OF STAFF.
YES, SIR.
WE'VE BEEN IGNORANT FOOLS ...
...FOR FAR TOO LONG.

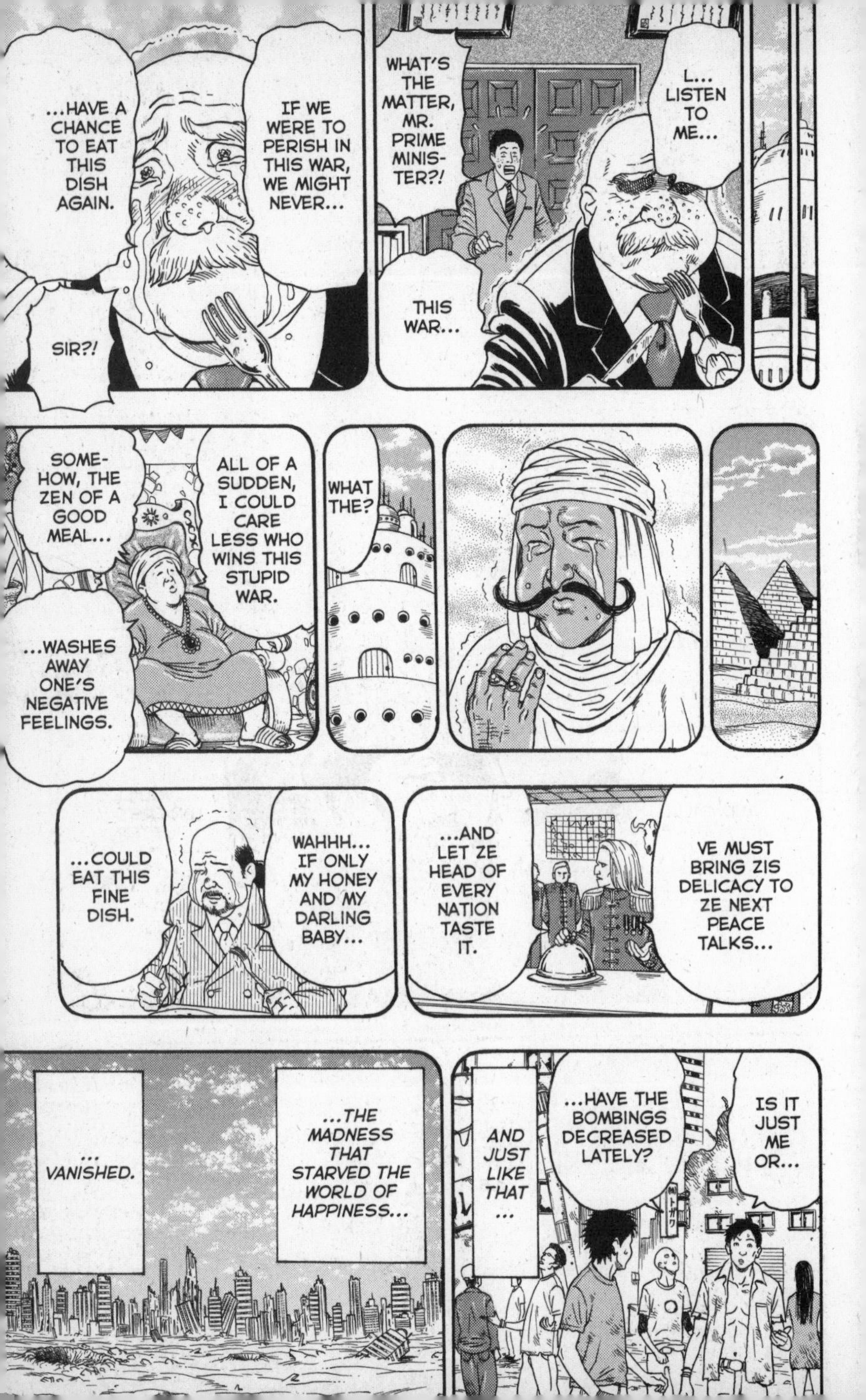
L... LISTEN TO ME...
WHAT'S THE MATTER, MR. PRIME MINISTER?!
THIS WAR...
IF WE WERE TO PERISH IN THIS WAR, WE MIGHT NEVER...
...HAVE A CHANCE TO EAT THIS DISH AGAIN.
SIR?!
WHAT THE?
ALL OF A SUDDEN, I COULD CARE LESS WHO WINS THIS STUPID WAR.
SOME-HOW, THE ZEN OF A GOOD MEAL...
...WASHES AWAY ONE'S NEGATIVE FEELINGS.
VE MUST BRING ZIS DELICACY TO ZE NEXT PEACE TALKS...
...AND LET ZE HEAD OF EVERY NATION TASTE IT.
WAHHH... IF ONLY MY HONEY AND MY DARLING BABY...
...COULD EAT THIS FINE DISH.
IS IT JUST ME OR...
...HAVE THE BOMBINGS DECREASED LATELY?
AND JUST LIKE THAT...
...THE MADNESS THAT STARVED THE WORLD OF HAPPINESS...
...VANISHED.

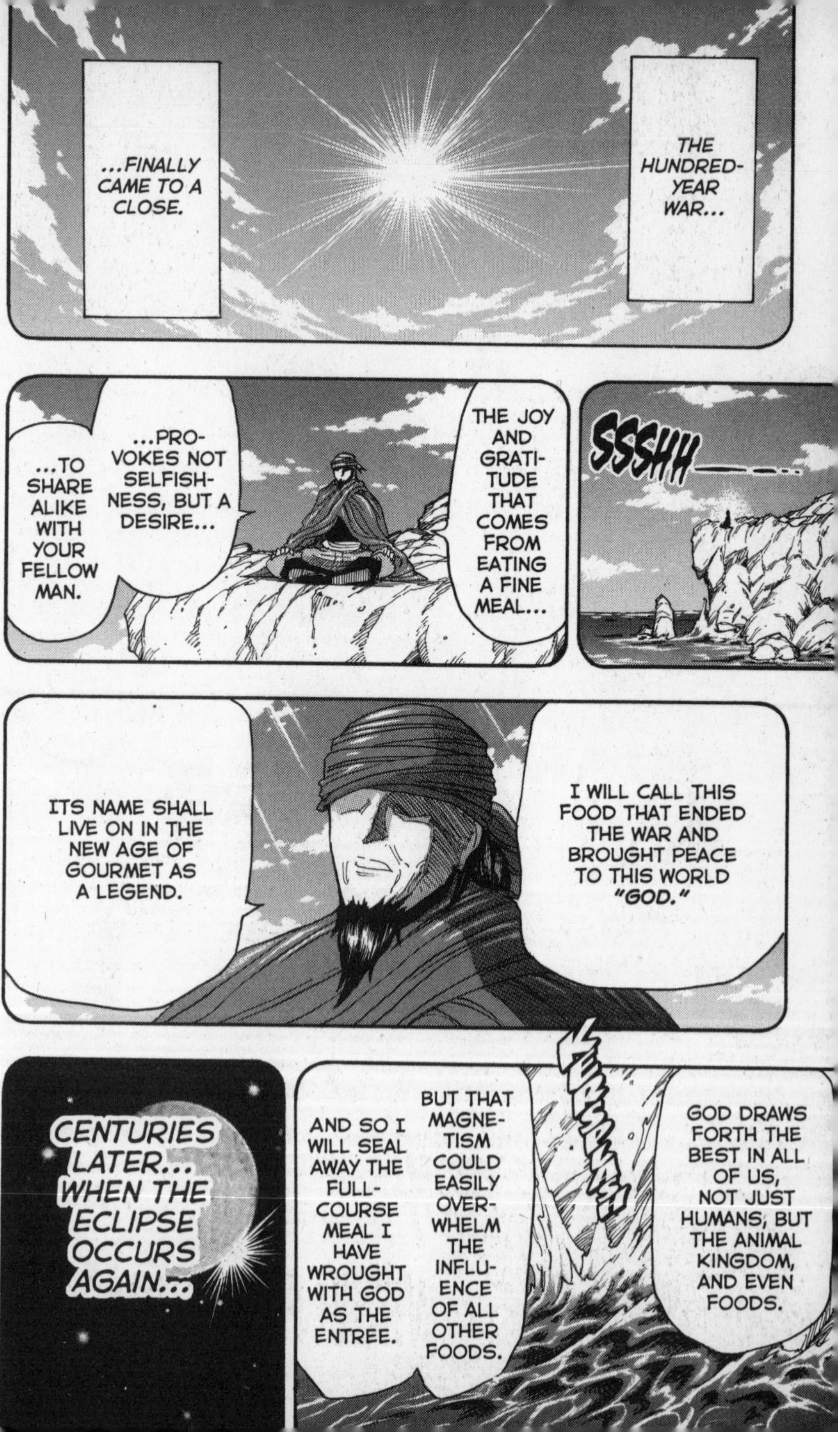
THE HUNDRED-YEAR WAR...
...FINALLY CAME TO A CLOSE.
SSSHH
THE JOY AND GRATITUDE THAT COMES FROM EATING A FINE MEAL...
...PROVOKES NOT SELFISHNESS, BUT A DESIRE...
...TO SHARE ALIKE WITH YOUR FELLOW MAN.
I WILL CALL THIS FOOD THAT ENDED THE WAR AND BROUGHT PEACE TO THIS WORLD "GOD."
ITS NAME SHALL LIVE ON IN THE NEW AGE OF GOURMET AS A LEGEND.
GOD DRAWS FORTH THE BEST IN ALL OF US, NOT JUST HUMANS, BUT THE ANIMAL KINGDOM, AND EVEN FOODS.
BUT THAT MAGNETISM COULD EASILY OVERWHELM THE INFLUENCE OF ALL OTHER FOODS.
AND SO I WILL SEAL AWAY THE FULL-COURSE MEAL I HAVE WROUGHT WITH GOD AS THE ENTREE.
CENTURIES LATER... WHEN THE ECLIPSE OCCURS AGAIN...

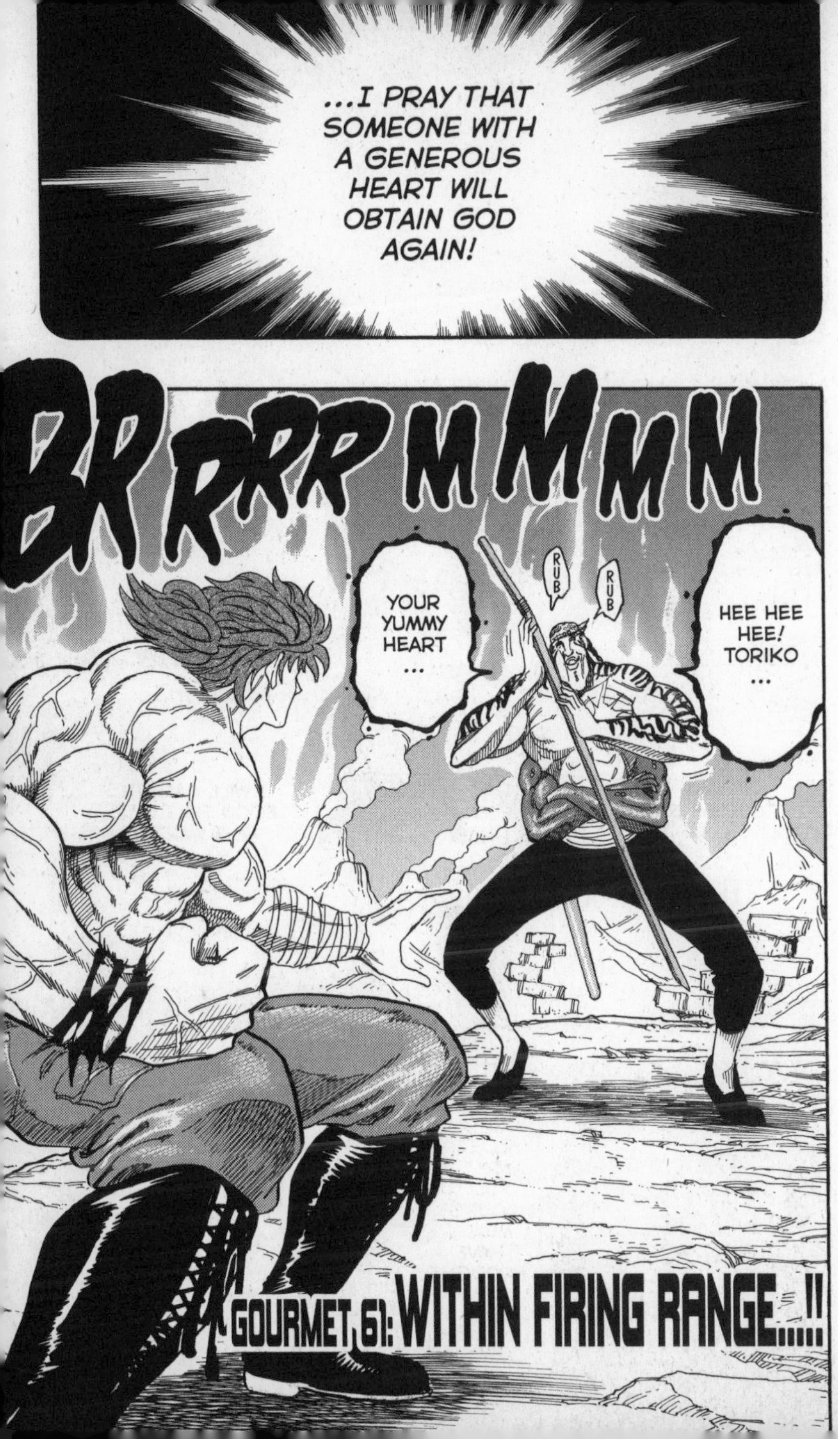
...I PRAY THAT SOMEONE WITH A GENEROUS HEART WILL OBTAIN GOD AGAIN!
BRRRRMMMMM
HEE HEE HEE! TORIKO ...
RUB
RUB
YOUR YUMMY HEART ...
GOURMET 61: WITHIN FIRING RANGE...!!

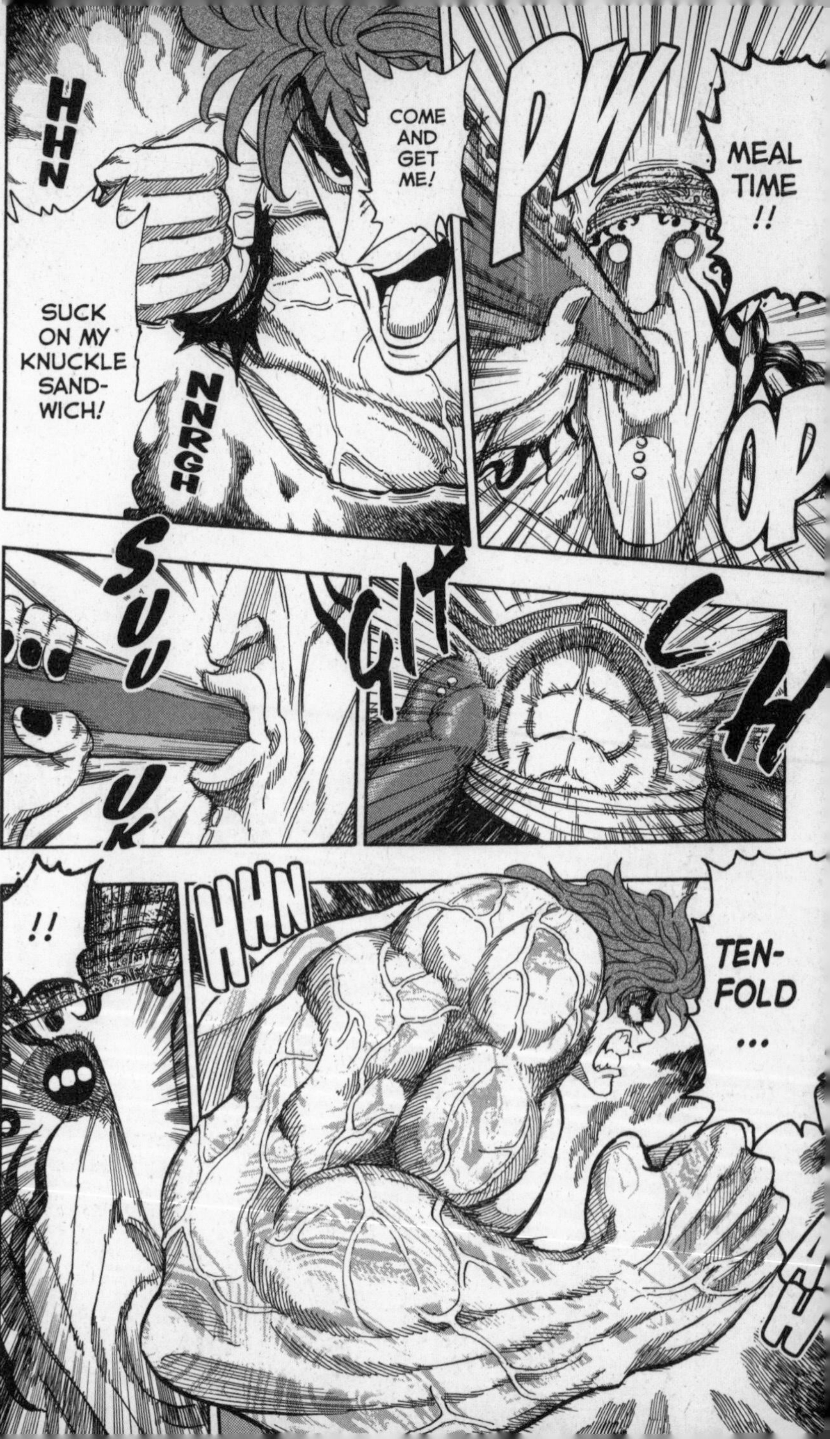
PW
MEAL TIME !!
OP
COME AND GET ME!
HHN
SUCK ON MY KNUCKLE SANDWICH!
NNRGH
CH
GIT
SUUK
TEN-FOLD ...
HHN
!!
AH

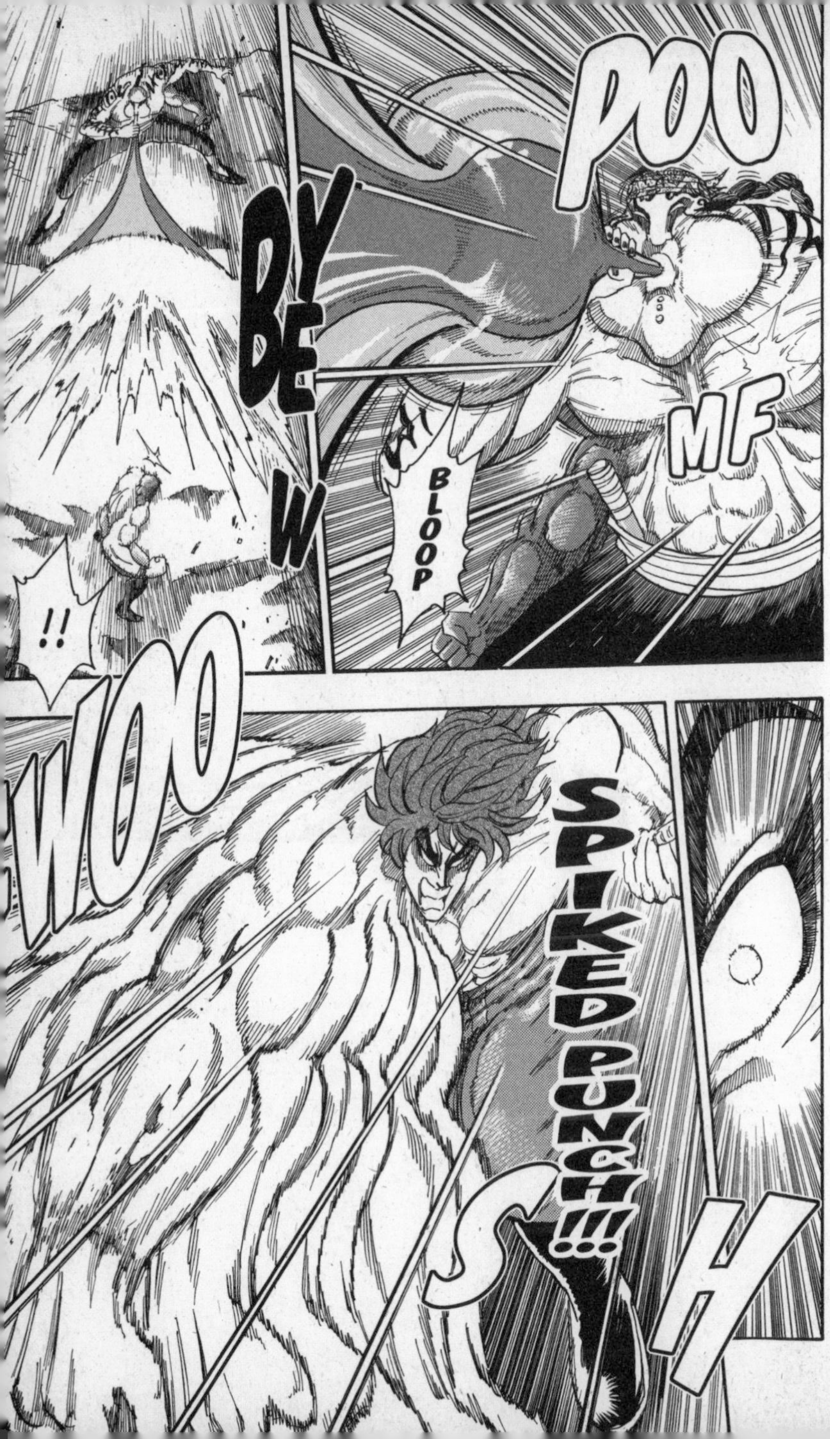
POO
MF
BLOOP
BYEW
!!
WOO
SPIKED PUNCH!!!
SH

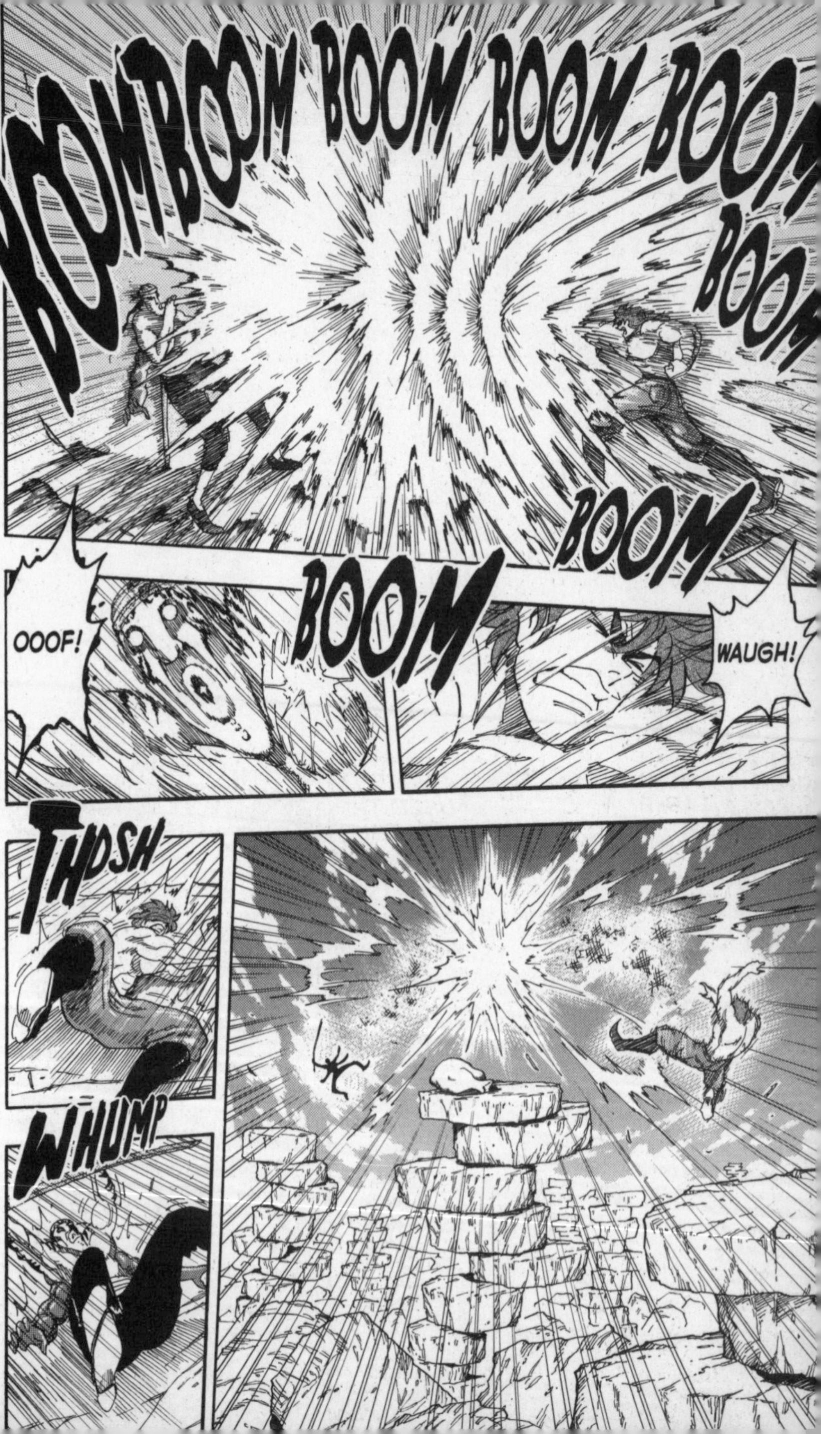
BOOM BOOM BOOM BOOM BOOM
BOOM
BOOM
WAUGH!
BOOM
OOOF!
THOSH
WHUMP

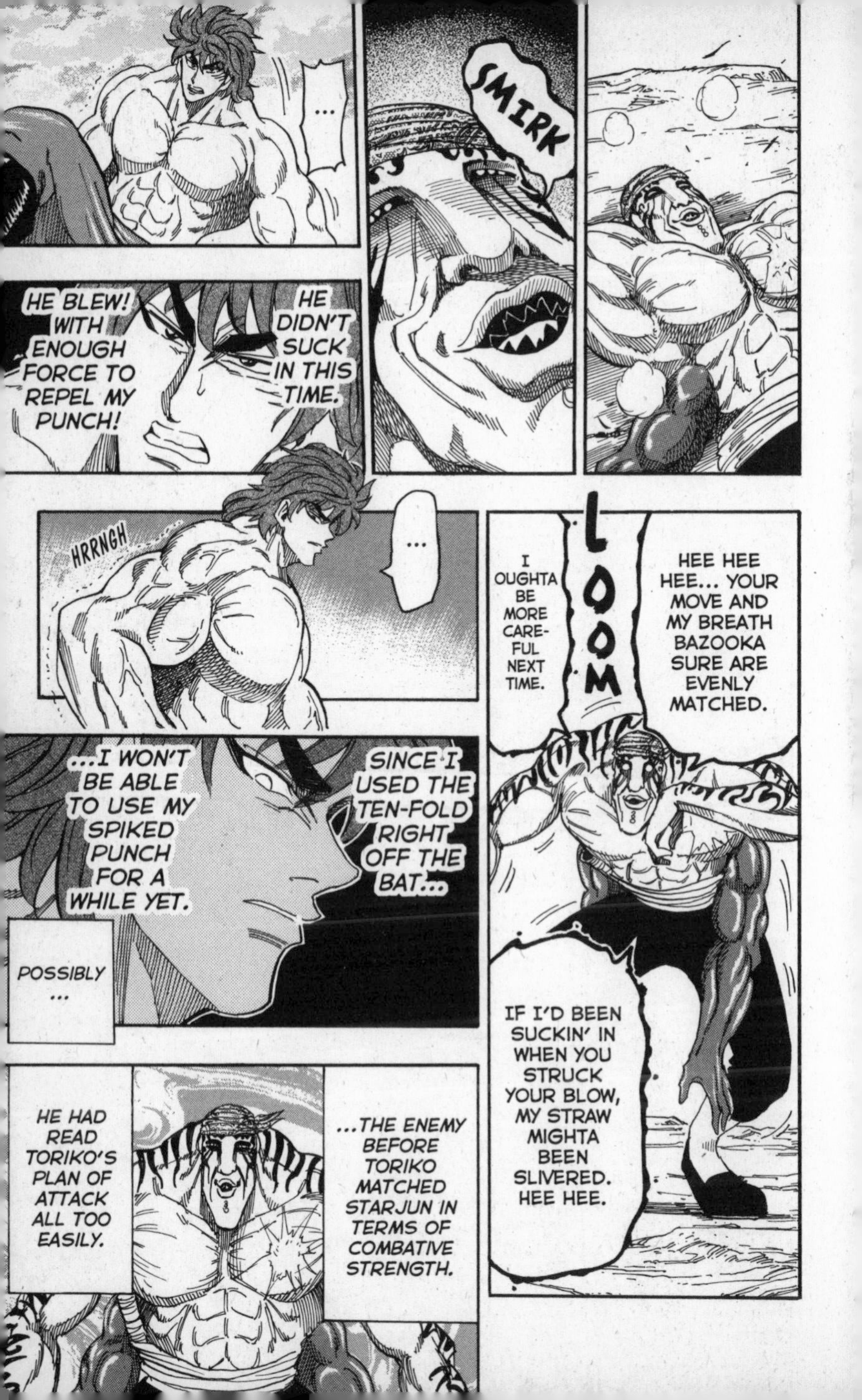
SMIRK
...
HE DIDN'T SUCK IN THIS TIME.
HE BLEW! WITH ENOUGH FORCE TO REPEL MY PUNCH!
HEE HEE HEE... YOUR MOVE AND MY BREATH BAZOOKA SURE ARE EVENLY MATCHED.
LOOM
I OUGHTA BE MORE CARE-FUL NEXT TIME.
IF I'D BEEN SUCKIN' IN WHEN YOU STRUCK YOUR BLOW, MY STRAW MIGHTA BEEN SLIVERED. HEE HEE.
...
HRRNGH
SINCE I USED THE TEN-FOLD RIGHT OFF THE BAT...
...I WON'T BE ABLE TO USE MY SPIKED PUNCH FOR A WHILE YET.
POSSIBLY ...
...THE ENEMY BEFORE TORIKO MATCHED STARJUN IN TERMS OF COMBATIVE STRENGTH.
HE HAD READ TORIKO'S PLAN OF ATTACK ALL TOO EASILY.

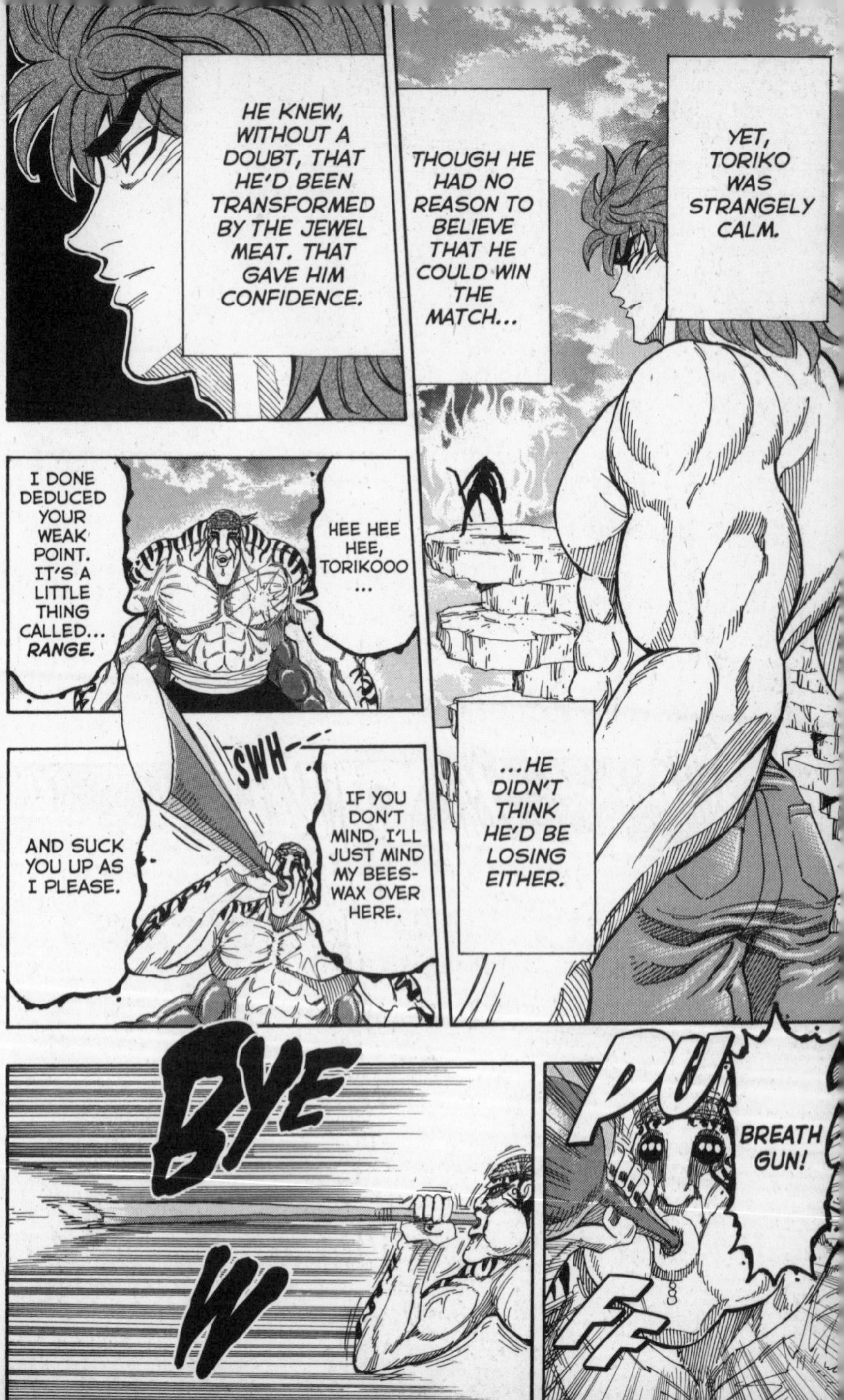
YET, TORIKO WAS STRANGELY CALM.
THOUGH HE HAD NO REASON TO BELIEVE THAT HE COULD WIN THE MATCH...
...HE DIDN'T THINK HE'D BE LOSING EITHER.
HE KNEW, WITHOUT A DOUBT, THAT HE'D BEEN TRANSFORMED BY THE JEWEL MEAT. THAT GAVE HIM CONFIDENCE.
HEE HEE HEE, TORIKOOO ...
I DONE DEDUCED YOUR WEAK POINT. IT'S A LITTLE THING CALLED... *RANGE.*
SWH
IF YOU DON'T MIND, I'LL JUST MIND MY BEES-WAX OVER HERE.
AND SUCK YOU UP AS I PLEASE.
PU
BREATH GUN!
FF
BYE
W

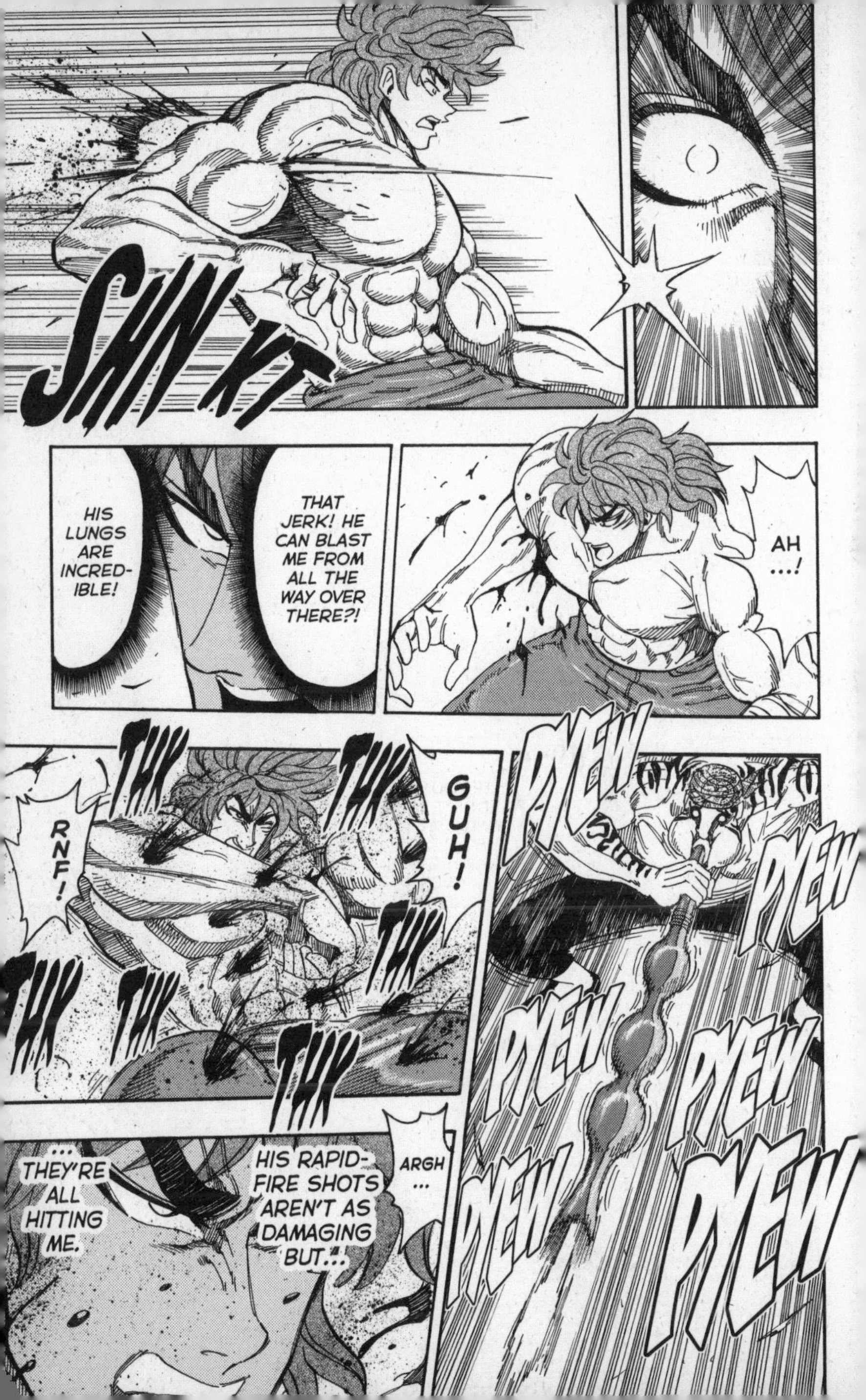
SHN KT
AH ...!
THAT JERK! HE CAN BLAST ME FROM ALL THE WAY OVER THERE?!
HIS LUNGS ARE INCREDIBLE!
PYEW
PYEW
PYEW
PYEW
PYEW
PYEW
THK
THK
GUH!
RNF!
THK
THK
THK
THK
ARGH ...
HIS RAPID-FIRE SHOTS AREN'T AS DAMAGING BUT...
... THEY'RE ALL HITTING ME.

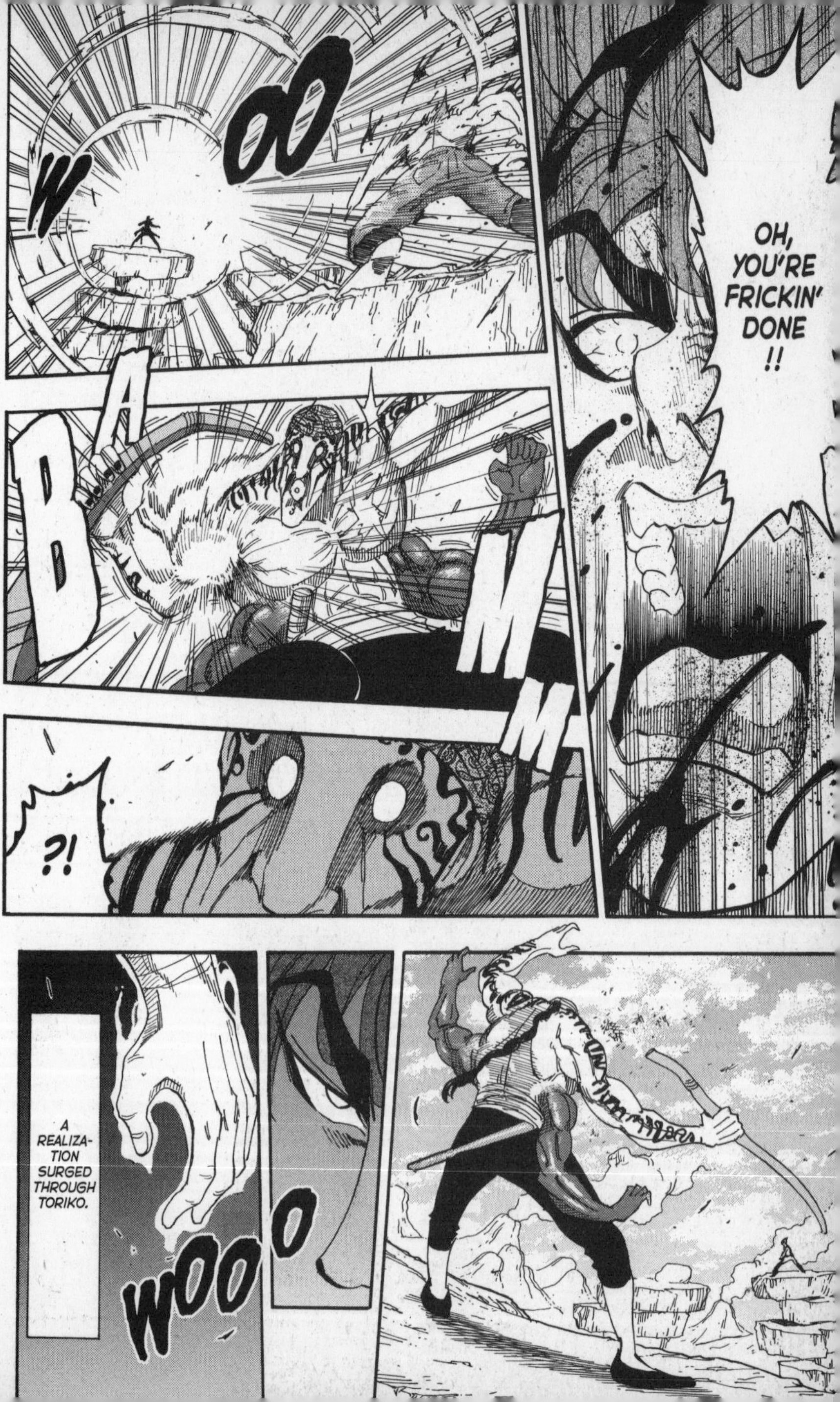
OH, YOU'RE FRICKIN' DONE !!
WOO
BAMM
?!
WOOO
A REALIZATION SURGED THROUGH TORIKO.

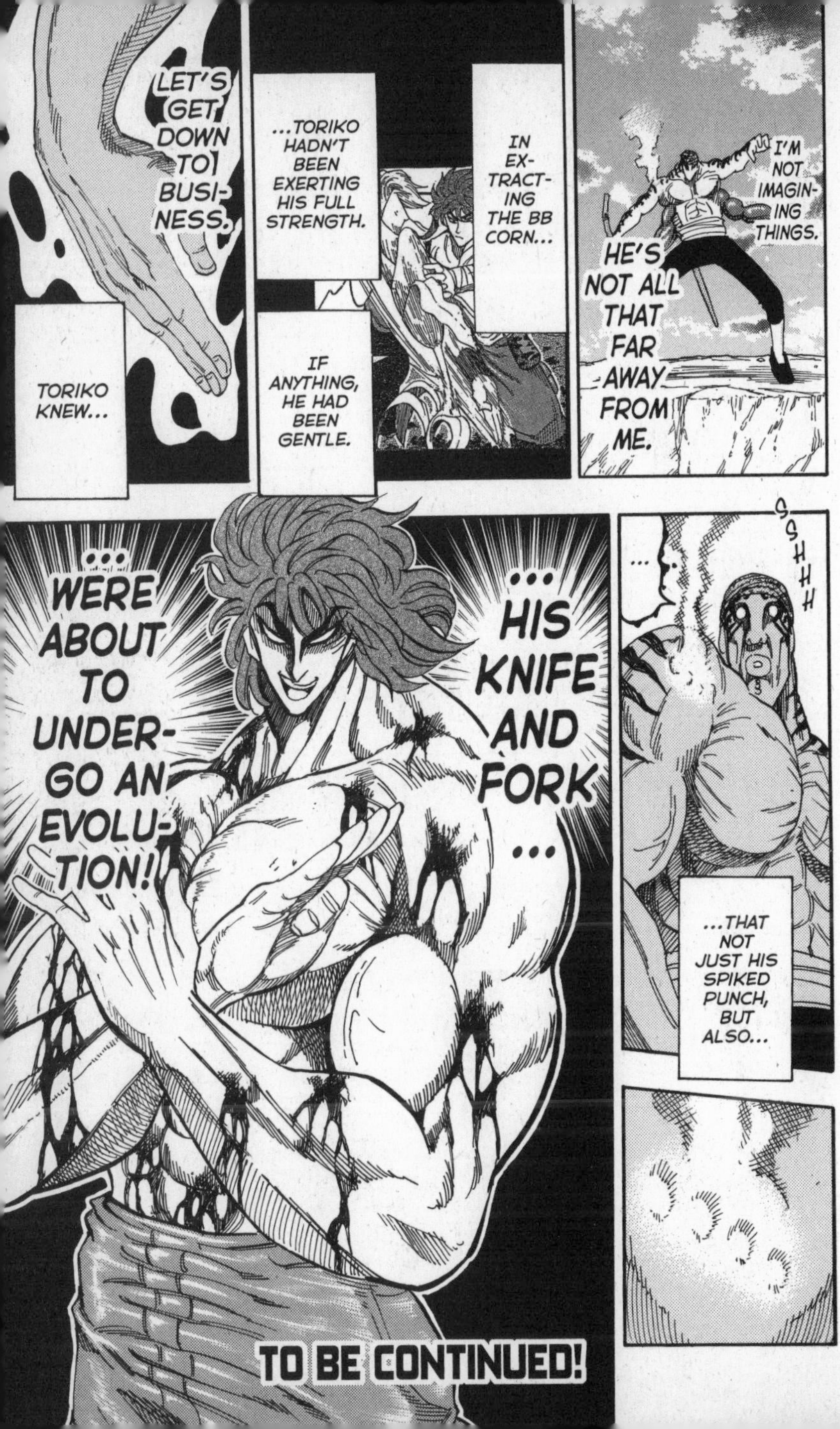
I'M NOT IMAGINING THINGS.
HE'S NOT ALL THAT FAR AWAY FROM ME.
IN EXTRACTING THE BB CORN...
...TORIKO HADN'T BEEN EXERTING HIS FULL STRENGTH.
IF ANYTHING, HE HAD BEEN GENTLE.
LET'S GET DOWN TO BUSINESS.
TORIKO KNEW...
SSHHH
...
...THAT NOT JUST HIS SPIKED PUNCH, BUT ALSO...
...HIS KNIFE AND FORK...
...WERE ABOUT TO UNDERGO AN EVOLUTION!
TO BE CONTINUED!

TORIKO

GOURMET CHECKLIST

Vol. 046

ROCK DRUM

(CRUSTACEAN)

CAPTURE LEVEL: 27

HABITAT: ROCKY SHORES AND MOUNTAINS

LENGTH: --

HEIGHT: 35 METERS

WEIGHT: 50 TONS

PRICE: 1 KG / 20,000 YEN (MEAT), 100 KG / APPR. 6,000,000 YEN (SHELL)

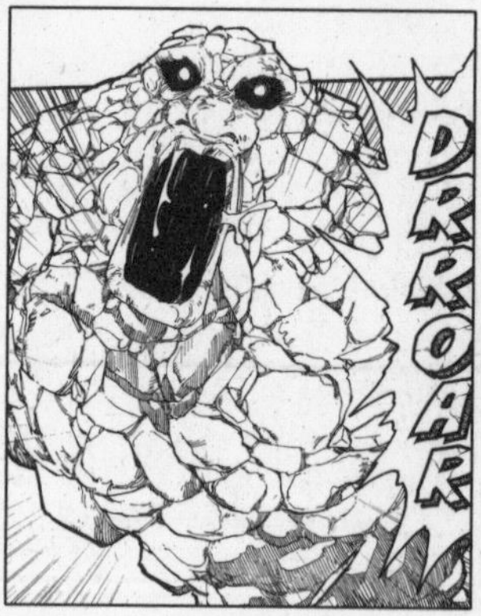
DRROAR

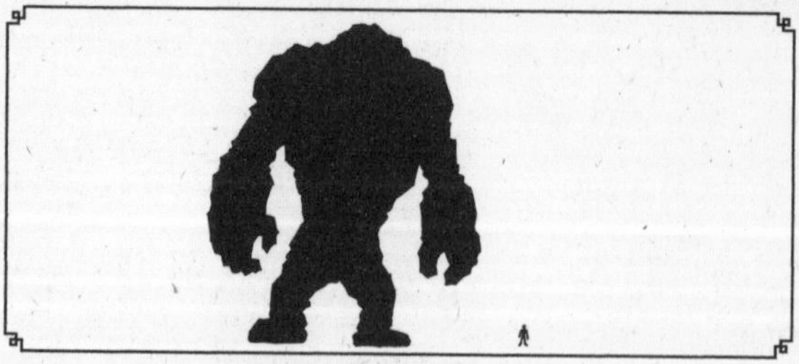

SCALE

THESE GIANT CRUSTACEANS ORIGINALLY INHABITED ROCKY SHORELINES AND CLIFFS, BUT THEIR MASSIVE APPETITE LED THEM TO TREK FURTHER INLAND IN SEARCH OF FOOD. THOUGH ROCK DRUMS CAN BE EATEN, THEY ARE MORE HIGHLY VALUED FOR THE CARBONIC ACID SHELL, TOTED AS THE WORLD'S FIRMEST, FINEST AND MOST FLAWLESS MARBLE. THE SHELL IS TEN TIMES MORE VALUABLE THAN THE HIGH-PROTEIN SKIN AND MEAT THAT IT ADHERES TO. UNFORTUNATELY, GOURMET HUNTERS WHO ARE COMMISSIONED TO HUNT THEM DOWN ARE OFTEN KILLED BY THE SHEER MIGHT AND FORMIDABILITY OF THE ROCK DRUM.

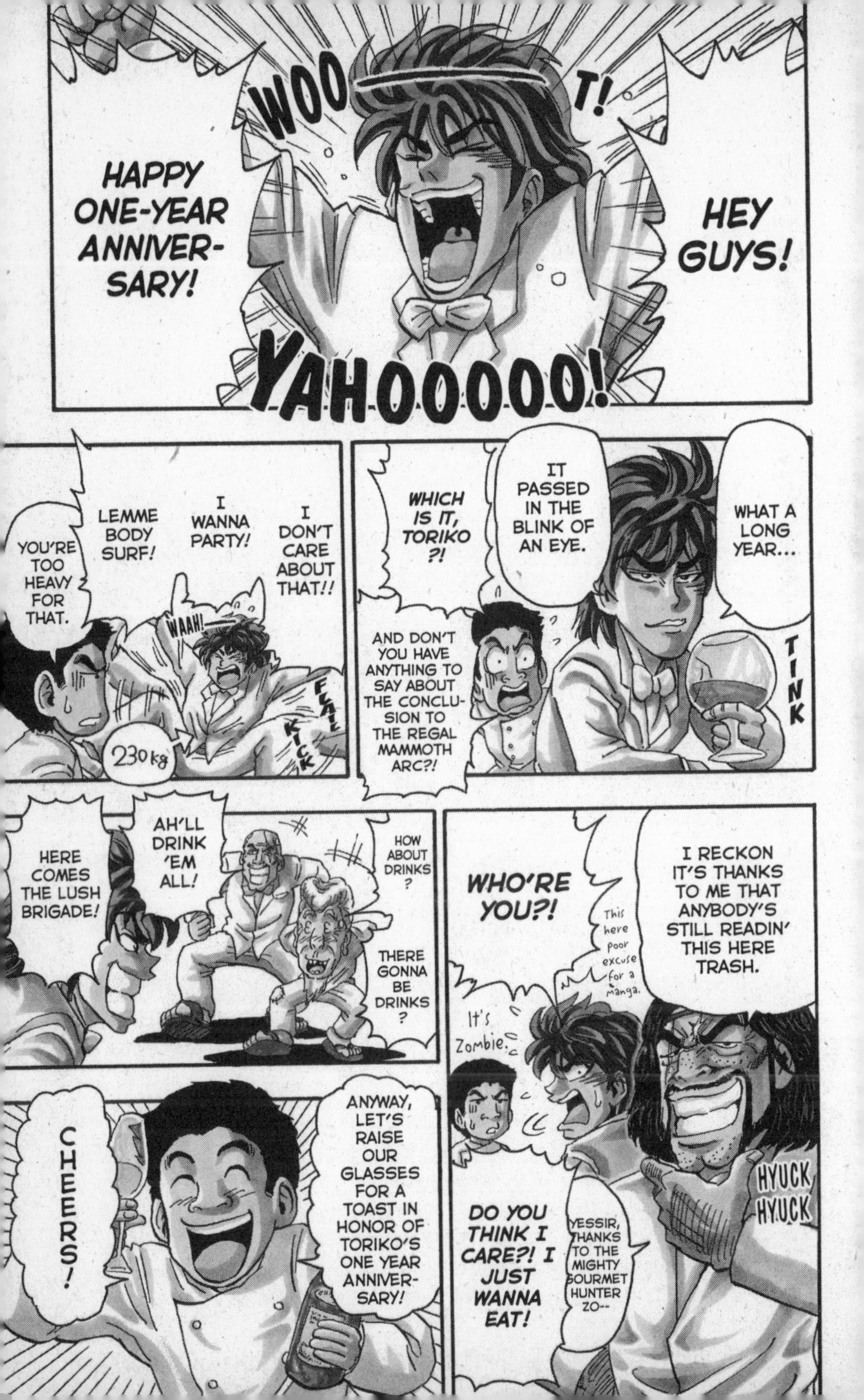
WOO T!
HEY GUYS!
HAPPY ONE-YEAR ANNIVER-SARY!
YAHOOOOO!
WHAT A LONG YEAR...
TINK
IT PASSED IN THE BLINK OF AN EYE.
WHICH IS IT, TORIKO?!
AND DON'T YOU HAVE ANYTHING TO SAY ABOUT THE CONCLU-SION TO THE REGAL MAMMOTH ARC?!
I DON'T CARE ABOUT THAT!!
I WANNA PARTY!
LEMME BODY SURF!
WAAH!
YOU'RE TOO HEAVY FOR THAT.
FLAIL
KICK
230kg
I RECKON IT'S THANKS TO ME THAT ANYBODY'S STILL READIN' THIS HERE TRASH.
WHO'RE YOU?!
This here poor excuse for a manga.
It's Zombie.
HYUCK HYUCK
YESSIR, THANKS TO THE MIGHTY GOURMET HUNTER ZO--
DO YOU THINK I CARE?! I JUST WANNA EAT!
HOW ABOUT DRINKS?
THERE GONNA BE DRINKS?
AH'LL DRINK 'EM ALL!
HERE COMES THE LUSH BRIGADE!
ANYWAY, LET'S RAISE OUR GLASSES FOR A TOAST IN HONOR OF TORIKO'S ONE YEAR ANNIVER-SARY!
CHEERS!

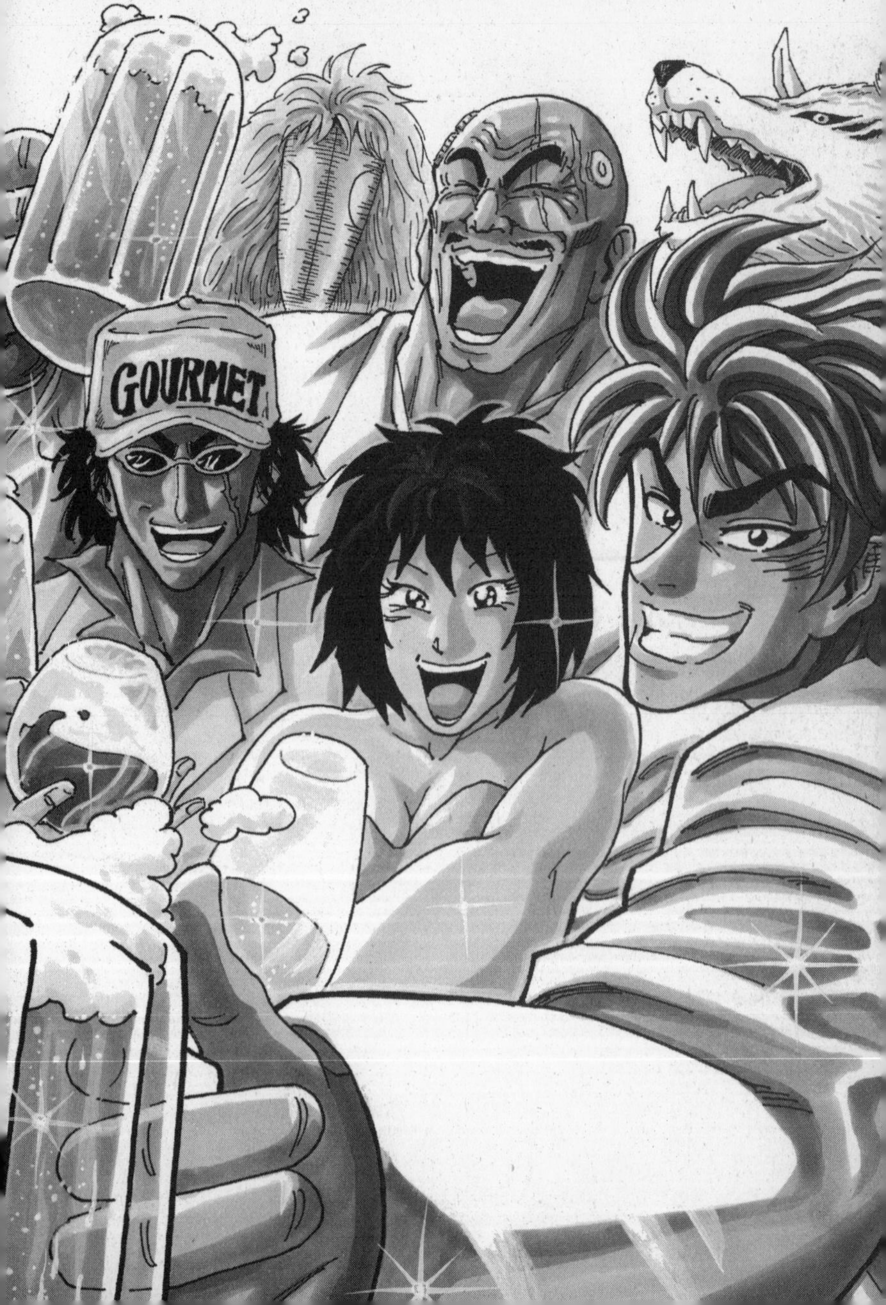
GOURMET

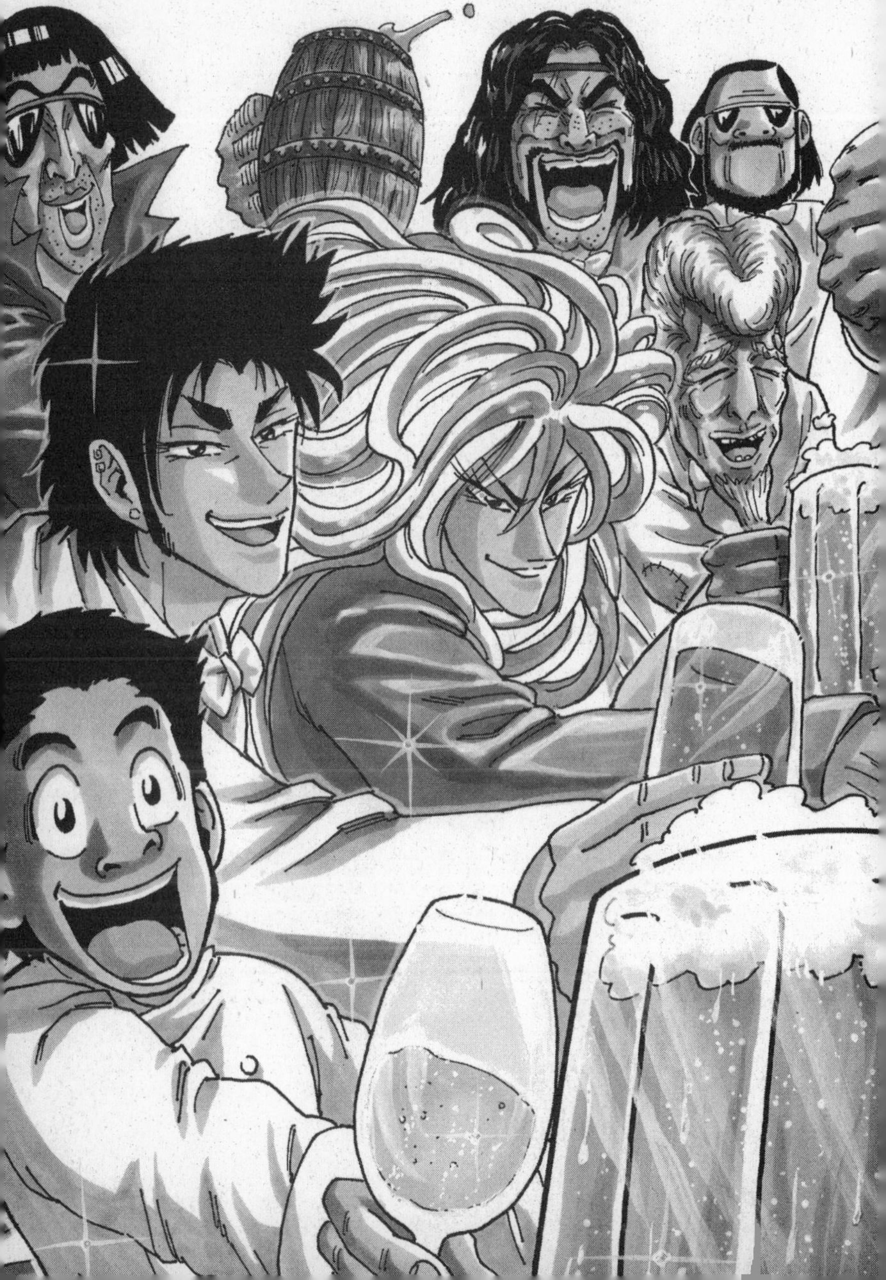

TORIKO

GOURMET CHECKLIST

Vol. 047
CREAM MUSHROOM
(FUNGUS)

CAPTURE LEVEL: 3

HABITAT: HUMID CLIMATES
(REGAL ISLE, BIOTOPE #1,
MUSHROOM WOODS, ETC)

LENGTH: 25 CM

HEIGHT: ---

WEIGHT: 700 G PER STALK

PRICE: 85,000 YEN PER STALK

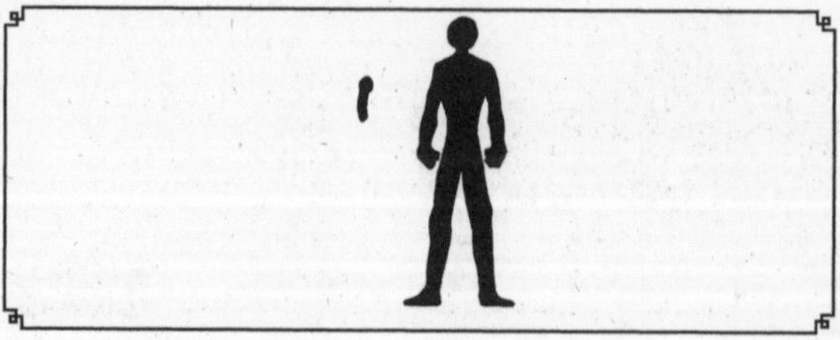

SCALE

NOWHERE ELSE CAN YOU FIND A MUSHROOM THAT COMBINES THE
AROMA OF THE MATSUTAKE MUSHROOM WITH THE SWEET CREAMY
SCENT OF MILK. EVEN RAW, CREAM MUSHROOMS ARE SWEET AND
FLAVORFUL, BUT LIGHTLY ROASTED AND TOPPED WITH SOY SAUCE,
THEY'RE A SNACK TO DIE FOR. THE RECOMMENDED SOY SAUCE IS
THAT OF THE SOY SAUCE HOPPER.

TORIKO

GOURMET CHECKLIST

Vol. 048

SOY SAUCE HOPPER
(INSECT)

CAPTURE LEVEL: 5 (ADULT)

HABITAT: FORESTS AND FIELDS

LENGTH: 5 METERS

HEIGHT: 1.5 METERS

WEIGHT: 400 KG

PRICE: 500 ML / 20,000 YEN

(SOY SAUCE)

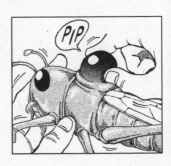

SCALE

THIS INSECT HARBORS A SACK OF GRADE-A QUALITY SOY SAUCE ON ITS BACK. ADULTS CARRY A MORE DISTILLED VARIETY THAN JUVENILES, BUT SEEING AS HOW ADULTS EXCEED FIVE FEET IN LENGTH, IT'S VERY DIFFICULT FOR AN AMATEUR TO CAPTURE ONE. THEIR BIG DEWY GRASSHOPPER EYES MUST MAKE PEOPLE DROP THEIR GUARD, BECAUSE IT'S FAIRLY COMMON FOR CASUAL HUNTERS TO GET KICKED BY THE HOPPER'S ROBUST BACK LEGS. INSTEAD OF GOING AFTER ONE YOURSELF, WE RECOMMEND YOU HIRE A PROFESSIONAL GOURMET HUNTER.

CHARACTER PROFILE

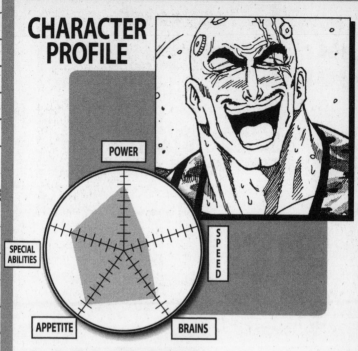

POWER

SPECIAL ABILITIES

SPEED

APPETITE

BRAINS

MANSOM

AGE	55	**BIRTHDAY:**	**AUGUST 8**
BLOOD TYPE	**B**	**SIGN:**	**LEO**
HEIGHT	**205 CM**	**WEIGHT:**	**180 KG**
EYESIGHT	**20/13**	**SHOE SIZE:**	**35 CM**

SPECIAL MOVES/ABILITIES

● Frying Pan Punch, Frying Pan Sandwich

Number three in the IGO's chain of command, he's the IGO's Development Chief and the Gourmet Research Facility Director. He has both superhuman strength and superhuman tolerance for holding his liquor. He's paranoid that people are always calling him handsome, but he's never actually been called that.

COMING NEXT VOLUME

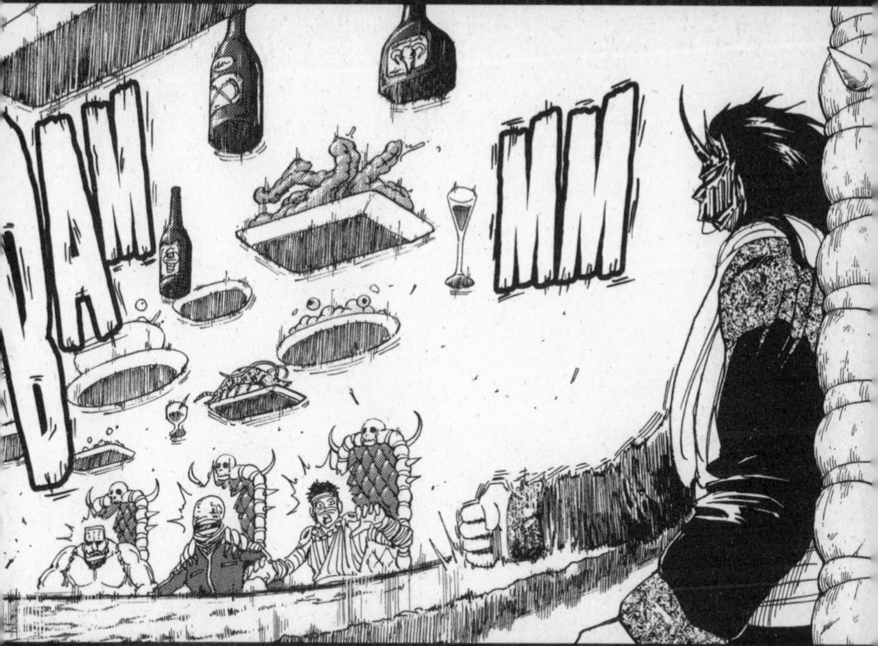

SOUP OF THE CENTURY

Toriko will have to evolve his fighting utensils if he hopes to survive the onslaught of the powerful Grinpatch. And the stakes are raised even higher as Gourmet Corp. sends some of its fiercest members to an icy continent to procure a soup so rare it only appears once in a hundred years.

AVAILABLE MARCH 2012!

CHARACTER PROFILE

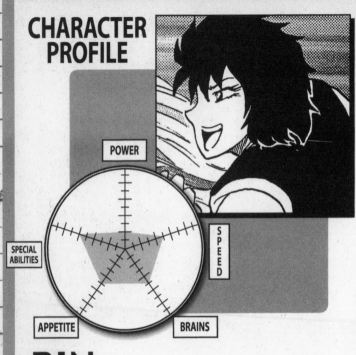

POWER

SPECIAL ABILITIES

SPEED

APPETITE

BRAINS

RIN

AGE 20		**BIRTHDAY:** DEC 20	
BLOOD TYPE O		**SIGN:** SAGITTARIUS	
HEIGHT 168 CM		**WEIGHT:** TOP SECRET	
EYESIGHT 20/13		**SHOE SIZE:** 26 CM	

SPECIAL MOVES/ABILITIES

● **Fragrance Attack, Fragrance Bazooka, etc.**

An animal trainer who works for the IGO. She uses a cornucopia of pheromones to bend animals to her will. But she's still having trouble making the beast of her dreams (Toriko) bend.